Religious Philosophy as
Multidisciplinary Comparative Inquiry

Religious Philosophy as Multidisciplinary Comparative Inquiry

Envisioning a Future for the Philosophy of Religion

Wesley J. Wildman

Published by State University of New York Press, Albany

© 2010 State University of New York

All rights reserved

Printed in the United States of America

No part of this book may be used or reproduced in any manner whatsoever without written permission. No part of this book may be stored in a retrieval system or transmitted in any form or by any means including electronic, electrostatic, magnetic tape, mechanical, photocopying, recording, or otherwise without the prior permission in writing of the publisher.

For information, contact State University of New York Press, Albany, NY
www.sunypress.edu

Production by Kelli W. LeRoux
Marketing by Anne M. Valentine

Library of Congress Cataloging-in-Publication Data

Wildman, Wesley J., 1961–
  Religious philosophy as multidisciplinary comparative inquiry : envisioning a future for the philosophy of religion / Wesley J. Wildman.
      p. cm.
  Includes bibliographical references and index.
  ISBN 978-1-4384-3235-9 (hardcover : alk. paper)
  ISBN 978-1-4384-3236-6 (pbk. : alk. paper)
  1. Religion—Philosophy. I. Title.

BL51.W5865 2010
210—dc22   2009054440

10 9 8 7 6 5 4 3 2 1

For Bob Neville

Contents

Preface	ix
Chapter 1. Religious Philosophy among Kindred Disciplines	1
Religious Philosophy as a Form of Philosophy	1
Religious Philosophy as a Form of Religious Studies	13
Religious Philosophy as a Form of Theology	26
Chapter 2. Tasks, Contexts, and Traditions of Religious Philosophy	35
Tasks of Religious Philosophy	35
Contexts of Religious Philosophy	45
Traditions of Religious Philosophy	50
Chapter 3. Religious Philosophy, Modernity, and Postmodernity	57
The Successes and Failures of Modern Epistemology	57
The Successes and Failures of Postmodern Criticism	63
Beyond Modernity and Postmodernity	72
Postmodernism and Apophasis in Religious Philosophy	79
Chapter 4. Religious Philosophy and Multidisciplinarity	85
The Importance of Multidisciplinarity in Religious Philosophy	86
Case Studies on Multidisciplinarity	95
Incommensurability as Invitation	114
Chapter 5. Religious Philosophy and Comparison	125
What is Comparison?	126
Comparing Approaches to Comparative Philosophy	134
Comparison and Religious Philosophy	156

Chapter 6. A Pragmatic Theory of Inquiry   167
    Problem Solving and Inquiry   168
    The Biological and Sociological Basis of Inquiry   174
    Controversial Features of the Pragmatic Theory of Inquiry   196

Chapter 7. Religious Philosophy and Inquiry   207
    Religious Dimensions of Inquiry   207
    Religious Philosophy and the Demarcation Problem   214
    Case Study: Religious Philosophy, Religion, and Secularism   237

Chapter 8. Traditions in Transformation   247
    The Ontotheological Tradition   248
    The Cosmotheological Tradition   255
    The Physicotheological Tradition   261
    The Psychotheological Tradition   273
    The Axiotheological Tradition   283
    The Mysticotheological Tradition   294
    Status Report   304

Afterword: Religious Philosophy in the Modern University   307
    Summary of the Deconstructive Case in Support
      of Religious Philosophy   308
    Summary of the Constructive Case in Support of
      Religious Philosophy   311
    Religious Philosophy and the Diversity of
      Higher Education   313
    Conclusion   317

Notes   319

Bibliography   337

Index   357

Preface

Is there a future for philosophy of religion? Can the many projects that claim the label "philosophy of religion" be rendered together in such a way that consensus around disciplinary tasks, methods, and boundaries can emerge? More generally, what can philosophy contribute to the study of religion? And what can philosophy, in league with the academic study of religion, contribute to our understanding of human nature, and of the ultimate realities and liberating life ways that religions promote and claim to engage? Can philosophy extend beyond analysis of the historical context and validity of arguments about religious subject matters to offer literary evocations of religious themes, constructive theories of religious objects, and evaluations of the claims religions advance about religious topics?

The answer to these questions may have been straightforward at one time. If so, however, at that time the questions never would have been framed in this way. The phrasing of the questions already expresses the two great problems that haunt traditional philosophy of religion in our time, namely: it suffers from unresolved contradictions about method and scope arising from internal diversity of its activities and fundamental disagreements about human reason, and it is significantly out of step with the academic study of religion. The questions also express the enormous promise of philosophy of religion—namely, that it is creatively flexible in method, subject matter, and disciplinary engagement, especially among the emerging generation of younger philosophers of religion.

This book offers an answer to these questions that addresses these two fundamental problems, justifies the apparent promise of contemporary work in philosophy of religion, and resolutely criticizes the parochial elements in traditional philosophy of religion. The result is a description of a possible future for philosophy of religion, not as a discipline but as a field of multidisciplinary comparative inquiries—a field rooted in a theory of rationality that makes sense of the diversity of activities that people are attempting at the junction of philosophy and religion, and one that fully engages the academic study of religion.

In what follows, I briefly discuss the two fundamental problems facing traditional philosophy of religion. This will help to explain why I construe the challenges facing philosophy of religion in the way I do—that is, in relation to a fight about intellectual and religious parochialism, rather than in relation to battles over legitimacy among the diverse activities claiming the name *philosophy of religion*. This discussion will also explain why I advocate the temporary deployment of a distinctive name for the field of philosophy of religion.

First, then, with regard to disputes over legitimacy of diverse activities within philosophy of religion, I offer the following prefatory remarks. To see that philosophy of religion is not one project and has no unifying method or vision, it is sufficient to consider the largely antithetical projects of prominent philosophers of religion. For instance, the names of William Alston, William Desmond, David Griffin, Jean-Luc Marion, Bernard McGinn, Alister McGrath, Thomas Morris, Robert Neville, D.Z. Phillips, Alvin Plantinga, Joseph Prabhu, Wayne Proudfoot, Arvind Sharma, Donald Wiebe, and Nicholas Wolterstorff correspond to prominent lines of work within philosophy of religion, many of which severely conflict with one another over questions of appropriate tasks and methods. There are plenty of other lines of work as well. I know of no work that evaluates, or even fairly describes, philosophy of religion as it currently exists, as a whole, in all of its diversity. To the extent that a meaningful identity for philosophy of religion involves reconciling such diverse and often mutually allergic projects, its future is dark indeed. Thought of as a discipline, philosophy of religion seems still to be writhing in agony over the loss of a disciplinary identity—a loss due to the breakdown of consensus about method and aims, subject matter and scope.

One way forward in this situation may be to assert the prerogatives of one kind of philosophy of religion over others in order to constrain legitimate activities to the point that they have a unified method and scope befitting the designation *discipline*. I consider this intellectually arbitrary and thus inevitably an ideologically motivated strategy. Practically speaking, moreover, it is counterproductive and results merely in showing other scholars in the academy, who are inevitably burdened with having to assess the value of any particular kind of inquiry such as philosophy of religion, that the philosophers of religion cannot keep their own house in order. The intellectually and strategically superior way has short-term and long-term components.

The short-term component is to furnish a viable social container for the diverse projects at the junction of philosophy and religion, one within which debates over method are decorously confined and courteously conducted. I will argue that these diverse projects are best understood as forms of multidisciplinary comparative inquiry at the junction of philosophy and religious studies. This defines philosophy of religion not as a discipline, with the connotations of well-defined method and scope, but rather as a field of diverse but related inquiries.

The long-term component is to furnish an underlying theory of rationality, whose absence triggers the agonized writhing over the legitimacy of activities within philosophy of religion. This calls for a general theory of rationality, whose application to multidisciplinary comparative inquiry at the junction of philosophy and religious studies explains the diversity that actually arises there. I will furnish the relevant components of such a theory of rationality in this book. This will allow me to argue that the diversity of activities at the junction of philosophy and religious studies is after all a tremendous virtue, makes good sense in relation to this theory of rationality, and assures most philosophers of religion that their diverse projects have a bright future.

This theory of rationality requires, but importantly also permits, philosophers of religion to look more kindly upon mortal enemies in their field. It calls on them to accept the loss of disciplinary identity once forged by relative methodological consensus and to recognize that this consensus actually masked ideological narrowness and religious parochialism, which we should be grateful to leave behind. But not everything goes in this hearty embrace of pluralism in philosophy of religion. The proposed theory of rationality identifies the most profound intellectual defect in traditional philosophy of religion as undiagnosed or obstinate religious bias. Though the theory of rationality explains why such projects exist and also why they are rationally feasible to a limited degree, it also sharply challenges philosophers of religion to confront the problem of bias as vigorously as possible in the name of improving the efficiency of inquiry. The idea of a field of multidisciplinary comparative inquiries at the junction of philosophy and religious studies is thus not merely a practical way of enclosing diverse but related inquiries. It also offers a way to demarcate the most efficient lines of philosophical inquiry from those that are inefficient due to the arbitrary neglect of relevant resources from the academic study of religion.

With this, I come to the second fundamental problem facing traditional philosophy of religion—namely, the tragic-comic phenomenon of philosophy of religion and the academic study of religion having nothing to do with one another. Against this trend, I will argue that the academic study of religion *needs* philosophy, and philosophy *needs* the academic study of religion. Both are better when they work together, and with other disciplines relevant to whatever particular religious subject matter is an object of philosophical inquiry.

Though philosophers such as Hegel and Schleiermacher once played important roles in the founding of the academic study of religion, before social scientists and historians took the lead, relatively few philosophers of religion are luminaries in the academic study of religion any more. Where religious studies textbooks have changed dramatically in the last half century, reflecting the rapid development and diversification of scholarly work in the academic study of religion, most philosophy of religion textbooks remain in the "classic Western questions" mode, perhaps with a conciliatory chapter about the world religions and religious pluralism appended in recognition of changing times. The *Routledge Companion to Philosophy of Religion* is a welcome exception to this dominant and disastrous trend.[1] Where philosophy of religion is most confidently defined, its debates most focused, and its conversations most efficient, its interests tend to be aligned with the institutional and intellectual interests of a particular religious tradition—for example, as in the Society of Christian Philosophers. Correspondingly, where that alignment with a religious community no longer exists, or is regarded as a problem to be overcome, philosophy of religion struggles to identify its tasks, its methods, and its social location.

I suspect that many religious studies faculty in secular university settings are wary of hiring philosophers of religion—whose intellectual work strikes them as parochial or unconsciously in thrall to a particular theological outlook, uncritically assumed to be the proper context for philosophical reflection on religious themes. In effect, such philosophers of religion pay little or no attention to the academic study of religion and proceed as if philosophy and religious studies had nothing to offer one another. The sheer number of such philosophers of religion poses a difficulty for the minority who strive to realize a more integrated, constructive, and mutually critical vision of the relationship between philosophy and the academic study of religion.

Young philosophers of religion, who are well trained in the academic study of religion and who bring that training to their philosophical work, are in an increasingly difficult position. They know how to speak to more narrowly trained philosophers of religion but find the range of conversation topics possible in such circles limited and often rather remote from their primary research interests. They quickly identify like minds in philosophy of religion conferences. When together, many of these young scholars cautiously express feeling like fish out of water if they have a job—and, if they don't have a job, they worry about ever getting a chance to work for a tenured position. They wonder how they should describe themselves: whether they should call themselves comparativists or historians, and whether to stop talking about philosophy of religion in order to avoid being misunderstood as covert theological apologists on behalf of a particular religious tradition. They wonder how they are supposed to communicate their understanding of a fruitful working relationship between philosophy and the academic study of religion to their colleagues and potential employers. They debate the future of their discipline, if indeed it really is still a discipline as such, or ever was one. This, at least, is my experience with the creative young philosophers of religion self-consciously working at the intersection of philosophy and religious studies.

Conferences discussing the viability of philosophy of religion grapple with the same questions. One of the most notable instances was the Twentieth World Congress of Philosophy in 1998, whose fourth volume of proceedings on Philosophies of Religion, Art, and Creativity presents a snapshot of the diverse self-understandings of philosophers of religion at the turn of the twentieth and twenty-first centuries.[2] Another is the year-long series of lectures on the future of the philosophy of religion, hosted by Buddhist philosopher David Eckel and his Institute for Philosophy and Religion during 2007 and 2008 and culminating in a symposium on the topic for younger scholars.[3] It seems clear that there is a rich array of ways to conceive of a fruitful relationship between philosophy and the academic study of religion, and indeed that this may be one of the most exciting areas of intellectual work associated with religious studies. It is equally clear that philosophers of religion, who reject the restrictions associated with serving the interests of a particular religious community or tradition, are struggling to articulate what it is that they are doing, and the ways they seek to transform traditional philosophy of religion in the secular academic context.

Traditional philosophy of religion, functioning as an affiliate of particular religious traditions, will doubtless continue. But the future of philosophy of religion in secular academic settings is as a field of multidisciplinary comparative inquiries. I will argue that this is in fact what is emerging. I shall call this multifaceted venture "religious philosophy" in parallel with the phrase "religious studies"—neither is a religious venture as such, but both take religion to be the object of study. I would rather call the venture "philosophy of religion," and hopefully one day that name will once again be available to define a field of multidisciplinary comparative inquiries. At present, however, a different name is needed in order to articulate a much-needed contrast with the traditional types of philosophy of religion, which are decidedly *not* multidisciplinary comparative inquiry and which operate largely independently of the academic study of religion.

The term *religious philosophy* is helpfully vague. It has been used before here and there, most notably in passing by William James in his *Varieties of Religious Experience*, but no particular usage has taken hold within scholarly circles. Under-determination of the phrase makes it well suited to tolerate the definition "multidisciplinary comparative inquiry"—and certainly better suited to this task than other plausible candidates for naming the full range of philosophic approaches and resources I address here. Terms such as *philosophy of religion* or *philosophical theology* register only aspects of the whole or carry unwanted baggage. These terminological side effects unnecessarily complicate my task.

It would be possible to spill much ink on discussing these terms of art, their historical development and nuances, the subtly different strands of meaning within each, and their proximity to other complex terms such as *theology* and *philosophy*, *religious studies*, and religion. However, since the plan here is to attach a specific meaning to a selected phrase by means of a "strong reading together" of diverse philosophical endeavors, there is little point in laboring over these semantic and historical details. It will be more effective to say what "religious philosophy as multidisciplinary comparative inquiry" means, to show that it makes sense of the associated philosophical practices, and then to argue for the possibility and importance of a field so defined while explaining how allied intellectual activities relate to it. This direct approach also helps to avoid the historical anachronism, to which strong readings are vulnerable when they overreach with claims that the major joints of theory also articulate historical movements. I will not investigate such questions here.

The scope of religious philosophy is broad and its styles are varied, as I have said. In fact, I distinguish (that is, in a certain sense, construct) six relatively distinct traditions of religious philosophy: the onto-theological, cosmo-theological, physico-theological, psycho-theological, axio-theological, and mystic-theological. Each tradition is amenable to a wide range of approaches, including the styles I will discuss under the following designations: phenomenological, comparative, historical, analytical, literary, theoretical, and evaluative. These traditions and styles of religious philosophy arc across the world's religious and philosophical traditions and through the variety of intellectual ventures that human beings undertake.

This *actual diversity* is the primary data set requiring the idea of religious philosophy as a field of multidisciplinary comparative inquiries at the intersection of philosophy and religious studies, drawing on other disciplines as appropriate. The *basic intelligibility* of this idea of religious philosophy derives not from this data set, however, but from the location of religious philosophy within a general theory of rationality. Framed in this way, religious philosophy is a field related to—but much broader than and without some of the difficulties of—traditional philosophy of religion. It has great promise because it takes full advantage of the advent of comparative philosophy and the emergence of novel multidisciplinary approaches to religion that make explicit use of the natural and human sciences. And it operates in league with, rather than independently of, the academic study of religion.

Despite the diversity of inquiries it encloses, the field of religious philosophy has a relatively coherent goal. It aims to generate interpretations of every kind of religious phenomena, from the mundane to the sublime and from individual experiences to social practices, with due attention to social and cultural context, and with concern for the questions of meaning, truth, and value, which properly belong to philosophy. Individual inquiries may reflect only certain aspects of this inclusive goal, but most inquiries are compatible with it. The result is a family resemblance among inquiries in religious philosophy, but with some possibility of articulating this diversity in relation to fundamental human cognitive resources and inquiry practices.

The efforts of religious philosophy are not directed toward the identity interests of any particular religious community and indeed may sometimes confound those interests. Yet religious philosophy can help religious people gain a more sophisticated self-understanding, even as it helps any person gain a deeper understanding of religious beliefs and practices. Religious philosophy also operates contrary to the exclusively objectifying and distancing strategies of inquiry sometimes used within the scientific study of religion, instead concerning itself with the internal self-understandings of religious people as well as with externally measurable features of religious behavior. In all, religious philosophy offers a continuum of inquiries that fully acknowledge the integrity of religion while engaging questions of meaning and truth that are vital for religious people and groups.

Objections to a role for philosophy in the study of religion are prevalent in many higher education contexts at the present time, as evidenced by outspoken critics of any attempt to engage and evaluate religious truth claims, meanings, and values within the academic study of religion. According to this criticism, the emphasis should be on description, comparison, and historical and conceptual analysis, not on evocation, construction, or evaluation. This conflict exists within philosophy of religion as well as religious studies. In my view, the philosophical version of this controversy should be enclosed within the field of religious philosophy rather than the cause for excluding descriptive and analytical work as shallow, or constructive and evaluative work as arrogant. Religious philosophy as I define it does enclose this debate. It comprehends both the narrower descriptive and analytical tasks and the broader constructive and evaluative tasks in a single framework on the pragmatic basis that types of inquiry can never be ruled out in advance of a thorough assessment of their efficiency and effectiveness in actual practice. As the argument of the book unfolds, I will take up criticisms of the very possibility of constructive and evaluative types of inquiry.

It is important to ask how far religious philosophy as a field of multidisciplinary comparative inquiries can go. The Afterword argues that religious philosophy understood as multidisciplinary comparative inquiry has a natural and vital place within the modern university. But this presupposes that the field has genuine intellectual promise. My answer to the question about the prospects of religious philosophy takes shape within the fallibilist, hypothetical, pragmatic theory of rationality presented in this book. In this framework of interpretation, the question is an empirical one that cannot be settled in advance of trying. The multidisciplinary and comparative inquiries of religious philosophy can overcome the difficulties of disciplinary parochialism and covert religious bias, which plague some traditional forms of philosophy of religion. They also open up new lines of research that have been notably underexplored in traditional philosophy of religion. Thus, I conclude that the prospects for religious philosophy are wide open and extremely promising.

While most material in this book is entirely new, some sections derive from research and writings that I have produced while working my way across some of the wide territory of religious philosophy. These earlier writings have been modified, some dramatically, to support the aim of the book. I acknowledge previous publishers in the few cases where older material has survived the reworking process. The existence of this prior work is important. This book is a programmatic methodological reflection, but it is built inductively upon a considerable amount of experience actually doing first-order religious philosophy in the sense of multidisciplinary comparative inquiry. These efforts have sometimes involved wrong turns and bad hypotheses that did not withstand scrutiny. But they have also yielded a consistent and unusually broad point of view on what philosophical inquiry, rightly conceived, can contribute to the academic study of religion.

The diversity in styles and traditions of religious philosophy is such that discussing every type of inquiry that arises at the junction of philosophy and religious studies in detail would be an absurdly large task. This would also wrongly suggest more neatness in philosophical activities across cultures than is actually found there. In practice, local contexts and active traditions of debate bring an exquisitely distinctive character to each act of philosophical reasoning about religious matters. Rather than a systematic approach, therefore, each chapter presents a discussion of religious philosophy from a particular angle; each is an exploratory venture into the vast host of philosophical resources available for studying religion. I intend the combined effect of these chapter-length forays to support my claim that diverse philosophic activities reveal repeating thematic patterns. This is the basis for the construction of distinguishable traditions of religious philosophy and the enumeration of several styles.

The first three chapters locate religious philosophy in various ways. Chapter 1 on "Religious Philosophy among Kindred Disciplines" describes the field of religious philosophy relative to the connections it sustains with allied disciplines, focusing particularly on philosophy, religious studies, and theology. Chapter 2 on "Tasks, Contexts, and Traditions of Religious Philosophy" discusses the way the diverse inquiries of religious philosophy take shape within social contexts and specialized traditions. This chapter describes the seven styles of religious philosophy listed above. Chapter 3 on "Religious Philosophy, Modernity, and Postmodernity" takes up the question of how to conceive religious philosophy in relation to the debates in epistemology, justice, and hermeneutics, which mark the uneasy and somewhat incoherent divide between modernity and postmodernity. Parts of this chapter draw on material used in a Festschrift essay about Wentzel van Huyssteen's reflections on multidisciplinarity and theory in science and religion, though most signs of that original context have gone.[4]

The terms of the phrase *multidisciplinary comparative inquiry* require extended discussion. To that end, Chapter 4 takes up the first term; Chapter 5 discusses the second; and Chapter 6 treats the third, with

Chapter 7 relating inquiry specifically to religious philosophy. Parts of the chapter on comparison draw on earlier work in comparative philosophy, particularly an essay in Robert Neville's Crosscultural Comparative Religious Ideas Project,[5] and an essay entitled "Comparing Religious Ideas: There's Method in the Mob's Madness."[6] The case study in Chapter 7 is related to an essay in the proceedings of a 2002 Goethe Institute conference on Religion in Dialogue with Science, Tradition, and Plural Cultures,[7] subsequently adapted for a lecture tour of Chinese universities organized by Dr. Wang Zhongxin's China Christian Scholars Exchange Program.[8]

Chapter 8 on "Traditions in Transformation" surveys six traditions of religious philosophy across several cultures and indicates the way in which each is in a process of transformation in reaction to deepening crosscultural philosophical knowledge, the potent impact of the sciences, and the tangled threads connecting modernity and postmodernity. The six traditions of religious philosophy discussed in this chapter are not always traditions identified as such by the philosophers who contribute to them. Rather, they are the results of deliberately uniting together similar philosophic activities for the sake of constructing distinctive arcs of inquiry with common features—such as principal focus of attention, fundamental intellectual instinct, distinctive conceptual and linguistic techniques, and chief liabilities. This chapter also endeavors to evaluate the health status and intellectual promise of each tradition in light of the way the constitutive elements of each are undergoing transformation in the contemporary situation.

Finally, the Afterword attempts to reassess the place of religious philosophy, as defined here, within the modern university. These brief remarks answer prevalent skepticism about intellectual shortcomings of tasks related to religious philosophy, recapitulating the book's argument that religious philosophy as multidisciplinary comparative inquiry can rise above these difficulties. I also press the positive case that religious philosophy, understood as multidisciplinary comparative inquiry, has a natural and vital place in modern universities—particularly those that enshrine the morality of open inquiry to which secular universities aspire—because of the indispensability of religious philosophy to the academic study of religion.

The several subsections of each chapter begin with what amounts to an abstract. This is intended both to prepare the reader for the central direction of the argument that follows and to orient readers seeking to locate parts of the book of special interest to them.

Throughout, I have expressed key Sanskrit, Chinese, and Greek words in several different ways on their first major appearance. Reference to Sanskrit words is by means of the International Alphabet of Sanskrit Transliteration (IAST) system. The primary reference to Chinese words is by means of Hanyu Pinyin (漢語拼音 or 汉语拼音) transcription, but I also append the Wade-Giles (威妥瑪拼音 or 韦氏拼音) equivalent, and the traditional and simplified Chinese characters where appropriate (as above). The ancient languages I can read do not include Sanskrit and Chinese, which are the focus of transliteration, transcription, and translation here owing to their classical status (like Greek and Latin) for several ancient traditions of religious philosophy. Nevertheless, recognition of linguistic contexts requires that the religious philosopher at least indicate which word is meant in each case, so as to expose what is said to proper scrutiny by experts.

This illustrates the invidious position of the religious philosopher in relation to matters of crosscultural comparison. Much the same is true with regard to the challenge of multidisciplinary competence. It would be easy to retreat from crosscultural engagement in the face of potential linguistic embarrassment. But the better way is steadily to embrace ignorance, to learn other disciplines and other languages throughout a lifetime, and to be scrupulously honest about the limitations of one's ever-developing philosophical toolkit. This is what inspires a new generation of religious philosophers to exceed contemporary efforts.

If it seems impossible at this stage to imagine true working competence for philosophical purposes across a wealth of disciplines and cultural traditions, it is important to keep in mind that this may not always be so. Indeed, a precious few religious philosophers already exhibit complex multidisciplinary and multilinguistic skill sets. As in all things, we develop these skills when we put our minds to the task. This involves transcending the limitations of traditional training patterns and developing new traditions that envision and support more pertinent modes of research and education. It is partly for the sake of such new educational traditions, and for the students that will be formed within them, that this book is written. And it is principally because of those current and future students that the prospects for religious philosophy remain intriguingly and importantly open.

I am grateful to the excellent staff at the State University of New York Press who guided this book through production: Nancy Ellegate, Kelli Williams-LeRoux, Thomas Goldberg, and Anne Valentine. I am thankful for Derek Michaud's excellent indexing work and for Mark Shan's and John Berthrong's help checking Chinese characters. I am pleased to acknowledge the pervasive influence of my academic colleagues and former students on the arguments of this book—especially Peter Berger, John Berthrong, Frank Clooney, David Eckel, Paula Fredriksen, Steve Katz, Livia Kohn, Tim Knepper, and John Thatamanil.

I have been fortunate to work in an environment—within Boston University and amid other institutions in the Boston area—where the value of multidisciplinary comparative inquiry has been clearly understood. Prior to coming to Boston, I was privileged to work intensively and at length with great thinkers such as Huston Smith, John Searle, Claude Welch, and Van Harvey. But the most serendipitous event of my career was to arrive at Boston University as a pragmatist religious philosopher and theologian, well versed in William James, not really understanding the environment into which I was moving, and subsequently finding that it was so well suited to my pragmatist philosophical sensibilities. Far and away, the most important part of that environment is my colleague and friend Bob Neville.

In our hundreds of conversations, Bob has ushered me into his own fascinating world of thought and opened up to me a creative way of thinking about thinking. He confirmed my frustrations with Jamesian pragmatism and introduced me to the other paleo-pragmatists, as he likes to call them, and particularly to Charles Peirce; this was like discovering my intellectual family. He helped extend my existing education in world religions at the feet of Huston Smith by involving me in the groundbreaking Crosscultural Comparative Religious Ideas Project, which culminated in 2001 with three volumes on which Bob and I worked closely together.[9] He supported my intense interest in multidisciplinary research from the beginning, encouraging me in my efforts to inject life into the unique doctoral program in Science, Philosophy, and Religion within Boston University's Graduate School. Most importantly, he has taken great interest in my ideas and in my life. He has been "Uncle Bob" to my children, who live on the other side of the planet from their relatives, and he has always known just how to support me as a firm and faithful friend through the joys and sorrows of my life. It is to him that I dedicate this book. And he will understand when I say that this dedication is made with immeasurable gratitude and affection, but also with a sense of bemused delight that my life has been so unexpectedly blessed by his presence in it.

Chapter 1

Religious Philosophy among Kindred Disciplines

The field of religious philosophy sustains complex relationships with kindred disciplinary areas—including especially philosophy, religious studies, and theology. Each of these disciplines also confronts religious philosophy, as I define it, with forceful critiques as to its possibility or advisability. I will address such objections in the process of describing how religious philosophy relates to each of these three disciplinary areas.

Religious Philosophy as a Form of Philosophy

Religious philosophy overlaps significantly with philosophy that inquires into the big questions of metaphysics, epistemology, and ethics when those questions touch on religious themes. Big-question philosophy in the contemporary situation faces serious challenges to its possibility and prospects. Nevertheless, three considerations suggest that religious philosophy understood in these terms remains viable, and indeed may possess untapped potential: the overcoming of the modern aberration of epistemic foundationalism, the contemporary emergence of comparative philosophy, and the increasing philosophic usefulness of the natural and social sciences.

Big-Question Philosophy

In one respect, religious philosophy just is inquiry aiming to answer the big philosophical questions of metaphysics, epistemology, and ethics insofar as they possess religious significance. The idea of "religious significance" is difficult to pin down because the interests of religious groups and individuals vary dramatically across cultures and contexts and eras. Yet there is no question that a significant number of philosophical issues are religiously potent in many contexts. Thus, I will move on to consider the more pointed problem, which is identifying the relationship between religious philosophy and "big-question philosophy."

Most philosophers worldwide would accept that ethics, aesthetics, epistemology, and ontology are proper domains for philosophical reflection, even if they do not agree on why they do it or how they should. Consider ontology. At the most basic level, ontology is the branch of philosophy that deals with the "what" and "how" of existence: trees exist in one way, ideas in another, and some ideas refer to things that do not exist at all. Philosophers seek explanatory principles that unite descriptions of what exists into coherent ontological theories of reality. Historically, these principles have included being and relation, space-time and causation, creativity and chaos, *jīva* (soul) and *prakriti* (material nature), *pratītya-samutpāda* (dependent co-arising) and *vijñāna* (consciousness), *qi* (*ch'i* or 氣 or 气; life force) and *de* (*te* or 德; inner power of integrity), *yin* (*yīn* or 陰 or 阴; darker feminine element) and *yang* (*yáng* or 陽 or 阳; lighter masculine element).

Once the domain of ontological principles of explanation is entered, it also has to be allowed that some ontological principles have more explanatory scope than others. For example, *vijñāna* struggles with the physics of brute material interactions described in classical mechanics, while space-time has difficulty comprehending the emotionally textured quality of intense aesthetic experiences. Thus, comprehensive ontological models of reality typically require several explanatory principles and nested layers of explanation, which show how the principles fit together coherently. Principles familiar from the natural sciences—quantifiable aspects of reality (for example, what we call force, mass, and acceleration) and the equations expressing relations between them (for example, $F = ma$)—operate at the more determinate level of this nested network of explanations. At more encompassing levels, we might see vaguer explanatory principles such as matter or causation, consciousness or *pratītya-samutpāda*.

There seems to be no principled way of blocking questions about the ultimate integrating explanatory principles, those that unite everything that is into the most comprehensive and coherent interpretation. This is how the big philosophical questions of ontology yield ideas of God and creation in the West, Brahman and *saṃsāra* (cycle of lives) and *śūnyatā* (ultimate emptiness) in South Asia, and *Dao* (*Dào* or *Tao* or 道; ultimate way), *Tian* (*Tiān* or *T'ien* or 天; heaven), and *Shang Di* (*Shàng Dì* or *Shang Ti* or 上帝; ultimate emperor or supreme God) in East Asia—in each case understood as ultimate explanatory principles for ontology. Of course, these are not necessarily religious ideas in this context; they are principles for the ontological interpretation of reality. And the semantic content of these words might be quite different, even indigestibly different, than that of the same words in religious contexts. But there is no question that there has been two-way traffic between the ideas inspiring and structuring religion and the ideas prominent in philosophical explanations of reality.

In much the same way, ethical questions about the good, aesthetic questions about the beautiful, and epistemological questions about the truth and human reason also yield principles that invite controlled speculation about ultimate explanations. Philosophers use such explanatory principles to find a properly weighted place for every human understanding and experience, and for every aspect of reality, within the widest possible domain of reflective equilibrium. At the most basic level, this is why religious philosophy is closely related to philosophy.

The Place of Inquiry

In historical and crosscultural perspective, the achievements of big-question philosophy are plentiful, diverse, and difficult to harmonize. Thus, they may strike the onlooker as hypothetical exercises in constructive modeling, with contextual factors explaining both why some models prove more plausible than others in particular settings, and why models take on distinctive features that make consistency with competitor models problematic. Before concluding that big-question philosophy operates in a slippery world of relativistic delusions, however, let us take seriously the possibility that hypothetical exercises in constructive modeling could be a form of inquiry.

We might construe such exercises as follows. Explanatory principles function as the hypothetical core of our explanatory model, which we then develop in rich detail to take account of the host of relevant considerations. This process of development involves both elaboration into new areas and correction of existing ideas, where resources for correction exist. The more adequate, applicable, beautiful, coherent, consistent, and fruitful the result, the more entitled we are to believe that the hypothetical explanatory model might refer truly to the world in which we live and move and have our being, and thus the more likely we are to respect it and to use it in other applications (such as moral reasoning or political philosophy). Some forms of correction are obvious, as when an explanation simply can't account for some feature of reality, perhaps because it predicts events that do not occur. We see this with explanations of scientific inquiry that don't match the way scientific practice actually operates. Other forms are subtle, as when we compare competing explanatory models and conclude that one is superior to another in important respects such as coherence or elegance. If some hypotheses are able to subsume or eliminate others, and if other corrective resources are sufficiently plentiful, then we have reason to think that this sort of hypothetical philosophical inquiry might be capable of advance. The promise of advance gives such inquiries special value beyond the basic value that properly belongs to the careful systematic or poetic or narrative elaboration of explanatory hypotheses.

It is no small thing to assert that philosophy (in any specialization) is a species of inquiry, as I do here of big-question philosophy and also of religious philosophy. The word *inquiry* suggests solving a problem through an organized, rational procedure that yields an answer to the problem, an answer that purports to be true, along with reasons for believing the answer that are thoroughly tested within a community of experts. The ideal of truth-seeking is built into the idea of inquiry—even when inquiry is the fallibilist, hypothetical procedure I conceive it to be, and even when confidence about truth-finding is low. Unfortunately, truth-seeking has become so controversial in contemporary Western philosophy that direct assertions of the value of rational truth-seeking have become uncommon. It is a more visible ideal for inquiry in the sciences or in history but even there the philosophy of science and historiography have disclosed that truth seeking, which once seemed to be a straightforward and commonsense task, is more like stepping gingerly through an epistemological minefield.

The loss of confidence in truth-seeking inquiry is a step-child of big-question philosophy itself. As creative constructions, the best of the big-question explanatory hypotheses are intellectually impressive, culturally influential, and the objects of sustained study by generation after generation of philosophers. Unfortunately, however, some of these creative philosophers were so certain of their constructive models that they made definitive claims on behalf of those models—claims that some of their contemporaries and most of their successors deemed overblown. Certainty of this sort entails unreasonably aggressive claims for the ability of human reason to plumb with confidence the ontological, moral, aesthetic, and epistemological depths of reality.

With the very idea of big-question philosophy under suspicion, historical and crosscultural awareness delivered a killing blow by disclosing the parochial character of most claims to philosophic certainty. Ignorance of important alternative theories appears to have played a large role in inflating philosophic confidence, and criteria for judging the adequacy of philosophical constructions were often indebted to insufficiently scrutinized local plausibility structures. In this way, the idea of truth-seeking inquiry fell into disrepute right along with confidence in the powers of human reason and certainty about the creative models of reality that constructive philosophers produced. It has been an unfortunate era for philosophers with aspirations to inquire into the big questions of life, and doubly unfortunate for those who seek to engage religious themes in the process.

Whether, as I claim, a fallibilist, hypothetical mode of inquiry can be separated from overblown claims to truth and then made both intelligible and feasible as a vehicle for philosophical inquiry into religious topics, remains to be seen. For now, it is enough to note that religious philosophy is in the same predicament as big-question philosophy. To rescue one from its predicament is very likely to rehabilitate the other as well.

Competing Philosophic Ideals

In some philosophic styles, ideals of analysis (such as clarity and logical consistency) have supplanted the ideals of truth-seeking and problem-solving that guide inquiry. This is understandable because the modest ideals of analysis work relatively well even in the context of intractable disagreement among philosophic theories. But such modest analytical ideals also limit the scope of topics available for philosophical analysis because clarity and logical consistency typically demand determinateness of ideas, which is easiest to achieve when the scope of interpretation is narrow and tightly controlled. Big-question philosophy's quest for integrated, large-scale interpretations of phenomena requires vague ideas—that is, ideas that are capable of mutually inconsistent specification—in order to link different levels and types of phenomena under unifying explanations. There is logic to vagueness but it applies mostly at the semantic level of concepts rather than at the level of syllogistic analysis. Thus, big-question philosophy cannot live on analysis alone.

In some other philosophic styles, the ideals of consciousness-raising critique and deconstruction of unexamined prejudices have the ascendancy. Such scrutiny is invaluable as a component of philosophical inquiry because it aids in the efficient correction of tentative hypotheses. These styles of philosophical work typically are allergic to big-question philosophy, however, because large-scale constructive interpretations necessarily make numerous assumptions to stabilize modeling efforts within the dynamic process of hypothesis and correction. This renders the large-scale interpretations of big-question philosophy relatively unattractive to critically minded deconstructionists; they sense too many unsteady assumptions for the constructive effort to be worthwhile. Yet critical deconstructive philosophy routinely leaves a trail of breadcrumb hints about big-question philosophic matters, treasured insights that fascinated readers pick up as they follow along behind. While there is a place for constructive hinting even in critical philosophy, this covert way of entering philosophic insights into discussion can also protect them from public scrutiny and evaluation. This forgoes the need for justification, the opportunity for improvement, the risk of failure, and the taking of responsibility for philosophic influence. Achieving those virtues requires inquiry, no matter how daunting the task of inquiry may appear.

In yet other philosophic styles, the primary task is historical reconstruction and comparison of important philosophers' great ideas. Like analysis and deconstruction, historical work is crucial for expressing and refining hypotheses in big-question philosophical inquiries. But historical interpretation and big-question philosophical interpretation are quite different tasks requiring quite different skills, and they are subject to quite different norms for excellence. Philosophers uncomfortable with first-order philosophic interpretation sometimes confine themselves to historical studies, rightly more confident about their methodology. But historical work in philosophy sometimes seems in thrall to a rarely discussed conviction—namely, that we dare not directly debate the theories we study with our own theories of similar scales, because (presumably) we know better than the giants we study what human reason can accomplish. The irony here is too often lost in the noise of contemporary philosophic activity.

In still other philosophic styles, the aim is poetic expression, perhaps as a form of appreciation or testimony. The ideals in this case are existential potency, richness of descriptive texture, and conformation of the mode of expression to the nature of the thing expressed. Antimetaphysical philosophy often resorts to poetic expression, which is sometimes called "theopoetics" in the context of religious philosophy. There is a great weariness in posturing at having a firm metaphysical grasp on an intractable subject matter. Poetic appreciation can offer sorely needed relief from this weariness. Moreover, the indirectness of poetic testimony applies the balm of humility to the nausea of futile grasping after explanatory power, and conforms philosophic speech to the ungraspable, uncontrollable contours of its profound subject matter. In fact, such theopoetics is an essential component of elaborating hypotheses within a process of inquiry. Theopoetics is also theopoiesis—it conjures that of which it speaks—so there is danger in it that demands the same scrutiny that we would apply to any other kind of philosophic speech about big questions. Humility in the form of eschewing philosophic control through processes of inquiry can easily mask control exercised over imaginations through unchecked poetic rhetoric.

Some philosophers persist in practicing the philosophy of big questions—metaphysics, ontology, theology, and the foundations of ethics and aesthetics. Few of these philosophers do so systematically; in fact, systematic philosophies have been rare in the last century. Unfortunately, mainstream philosophers in many contexts tend to marginalize such adventurous thinkers, confident that their vigilance protects the discipline from an unseemly variety of philosophic enthusiasm. So it seems, at any rate. Yet the philosophy of big questions persists nonetheless. And in the hypothetical, fallibilist form I am commending, it persists in a morally pleasing way—simultaneously fearlessly adventurous and humbly aware of its inescapable limitations.

This hypothetical fallibilist approach to big-question philosophy also registers the virtues of other philosophic styles as proper to the various phases of its work. The ideals of poetics belong both to the art of elaborating hypotheses and to the governing epistemic posture of fallibilism. The ideals of historical work appear in the contextualizing of hypothetical models in vast traditions of religious philosophy and in the sensitive contextual interpretation of ideas. The ideals of criticism and deconstruction play roles in the testing of hypotheses against their practical consequences, in the cross-checking of hypotheses against one another, and in the fallibilist attitude to any and every explanatory hypothesis. The ideals of analysis are present throughout the process of inquiry, guiding the elaboration, testing, and refinement of hypothetical explanatory models toward optimal clarity and consistency. These ideals are reconfigured when they appear in big-question philosophic inquiries, to be sure. But the religious philosopher interested in multidisciplinary comparative inquiry will not hesitate to interpret narrower forms of philosophic activity as *stylistic contractions*. And they will argue that such contracted styles of philosophic activity are governed by ideals that are *abstracted* from the context of their proper application in inquiry. Inquiry, after all, is the fundamental biological and social manifestation of human rationality, as this book will argue in some detail.

Arguments Against the Possibility of Big-Question Philosophy

Philosophy has special virtues when it is pursued as logical analysis, as deconstruction, as history of ideas, and as poetics. These virtues mean that there can be no objection to the restrained exercise of rationality in these forms. Moreover, the results of these types of philosophical activity confirm their usefulness. But neither this pattern of usefulness, nor the appealing epistemological asceticism that often drives these forms of philosophy, entails the impossibility or even the inadvisability of more adventurous forms of philosophic inquiry into the big questions of life. Establishing such a negative result soundly would require an argument that necessarily operates in the same domain of big questions that it attempts to restrict.

People have offered such arguments, of course—notably Immanuel Kant and A.J. Ayer—but critics have been quick to point out the territorial irony. In Kant's case, the problem was the vastly unanalyzed premise of the perspective (the transcendental "I") from which his adumbration of the boundaries on human rational capacities was credible. In Ayer's case, it was the self-referential character of any criterion for the meaningfulness of statements; bold universal policing dictums typically undermine themselves. Indeed, Kant and Ayer themselves were troubled by these features of their philosophic programs.

Each failure of in-principle arguments against adventurous forms of constructive philosophic inquiry underlines the hypothetical character of such restrictions. The arguments relevant to evaluating hypotheses about the capacities of human reason struggle to achieve the decisiveness often intended for them. Such arguments can, however, exert cumulative pressure for or against particular hypotheses. The most potent instance of cumulative argumentative pressure is an interpretation of the history of big-question philosophy as a contradictory tangle of ideas—an argument that would be made against the rich and ancient literary heritages of Western, South Asian, and East Asian philosophic traditions alike. According to this skeptical cumulative critique, each of the major debates is intractable and the collective effort is futile.

The sharpest form of this argument is Kant's attempt in the transcendental dialectic of the *Critique of Pure Reason* to show that contradictions result when reason extends beyond its domain of proper operation to questions of psychology, metaphysics, and theology: "the antinomy of pure reason will exhibit to us the transcendental principles of a pure rational cosmology. But it will not do so in order to show this science to be valid and to adopt it.... [T]his pretended science can be exhibited only in its bedazzling but false illusoriness, as an idea which can never be reconciled with appearances."[1] Calling this the antinomy of pure reason, Kant presents strong arguments in favor of opposite metaphysical claims, drawing the conclusion that such metaphysical topics are beyond the reach of pure reason altogether. For him, arguing endlessly over such metaphysical themes is the sort of illusory trap into which human reason falls instinctively.

Kant's offering of parallel arguments on behalf of opposite conclusions marks the Enlightenment rebirth of comparative philosophy, though on behalf of a decidedly negative conclusion about whether such comparison can further constructive philosophic inquiry. He points out that, "it is only for transcendental philosophy that this sceptical method is essential" because it is only there that "false assertions can be concealed and rendered invisible." The root of the problem is that these inquiries concern "transcendental assertions which lay claim to what is beyond the field of all possible experiences.... [T]hey are so constituted that what is erroneous in them can never be detected by means of any experience."[2]

Time and new perspectives have shown that Kant's reasoning is not decisive, and on three levels. At the strategic level, Kant's approach is not effective in a fallibilist epistemological framework. Only the foundationalist for whom nothing less than certainty will do could feel convinced that the dueling arguments of the four antinomies, if sound, decisively dispose of the sorts of reasoning involved. The fallibilist engaged in the hypothetical form of inquiry I describe here will see only the lack of corrective resources needed to advance inquiry at that point, and will not incautiously generalize this negative result as Kant did.

At the logical level, Kant's presentation of the antimonies abstracts these arguments from the context of the large-scale modeling efforts that produce them, yet these contexts are highly relevant for assessing argumentative force. For example, the first antinomy argues that the world has a beginning and is spatially limited, and also that the world has no beginning and is spatially unlimited. But the meanings of the key terms are only stabilized in the context of the wider theoretical ventures in which such arguments appear, such as the worldviews of Augustine (354–430 CE) and Aristotle (Ἀριστοτέλης; 384–322 BCE), respectively. Kant's abstracting move disguises this semantic dependence. When this problem is corrected, the antinomy seems more innocent. Suppose Augustine's and Aristotle's worldviews are large-scale explanatory hypotheses of the sort used in big-question philosophy. Suppose further that Augustine's worldview entails X (world is finite-in-age-and-spatial-extent) while Aristotle's worldview entails not-X. If we have no empirical basis for preferring X over not-X, then we have no leverage on the decision between Augustine and Aristotle *in that respect*. But X and not-X arise in a context of ideas that may allow other resources to impact the choice between them by making one entire worldview more plausible than the other. Neglecting the semantic and logical implications of theory dependence produces fallacies of equivocation in philosophy as in any other theoretical endeavor.

Finally, at the content level, Kant was overconfident about what could and what could not be exposed to experience. In relation to the first antinomy again, imaginative physical cosmologists are finding ways to test the claims that the universe has a finite age and that it is spatially finite—note that, despite Kant, conceptual reconsideration forced spatial (size) and temporal (age) limitation into separate possibilities. Neither of the two opposed arguments in the first antinomy is as compelling as Kant claimed, and the question may eventually be decidable, if not based on direct observation then indirectly and probabilistically within the framework of quantum cosmologies. In either case, what Kant thought was an irresolvable dispute may prove to be tractable and thus relevant for choosing between the hypothetical explanations of big-question philosophy.

How does this softening of the antinomy of pure reason affect Kant's severe dichotomy between the noumenal and phenomenal realms? Kant thought he had showed that it is disastrous to apply reason beyond the domain of its allegedly proper application, and traced many philosophic errors to a lack of the required discipline among philosophers. The antinomy of pure reason was a crucial factor in his judgment about what reason could and could not achieve, and where it could and could not be applied successfully. But Kant never entertained the possibility of hypothetical philosophical inquiry in a fallibilist epistemological framework. To formulate a fallible philosophical hypothesis about something in Kant's off-limits noumenal realm cannot be ruled out a priori. It may well prove to be futile, in the sense that resources to correct the hypothesis and thereby warrant belief in it cannot be located. But, what for Kant was a strict rule is for the proponent of hypothetical inquiry in a fallibilist epistemological framework merely a suggestion for how to expend philosophic energy most efficiently. And whether or not the suggestion is a wise one is ultimately transformed into an empirical question. Thus, the opening for big-question philosophy remains, even in the presence of crosscultural and historical pluralism of reasoned philosophic opinion.

The Prospects of Big-Question Philosophy

The specter of apparently intractable disagreement within big-question philosophy does not establish its impossibility or futility any more than Kant's and Ayer's and others' policing pronouncements did. By the same token, as just noted, merely to defeat in-principle arguments against the philosophy of big questions is not to establish its possibility, and yields few insights into the best method for conducting it. In fact, the task of big-question philosophy appears to be extremely difficult, at best. Yet our impression of its prospects may change with time. Three important considerations collectively suggest that now is the wrong time to abandon it, or the religious philosophy that has so much in common with it.

First, the kind of epistemic foundationalism that has prevailed in most modern Western philosophy has now mostly collapsed. (I take up this theme in Chapter 3.) Its artless insistence on certainty in the foundations of knowledge proved unsuitable even for mathematics and natural sciences, and it was a particularly inapt standard for big-question philosophy. The early American pragmatists Charles Peirce and John Dewey deliberately rejected epistemic foundationalism and worked hypothetically within a fallibilist epistemological framework across the whole range of philosophical questions, including the big questions of metaphysics and morality and religion. The nonfoundationalist approach caught on more widely in the last half of the twentieth century, especially after W.V.O. Quine's famous 1951 article, "Two Dogmas of Empiricism." The response to this essay accomplished for Anglo-American analytic and language-oriented philosophy what the early pragmatists had achieved earlier in the century. (I take up the theme of inquiry in Chapter 6.)

The surrendering of foundationalist aspirations is a boon to big-question philosophical inquiry. Hypothetical, fallibilist modes of inquiry accommodate big-question philosophy in a way that foundationalist modes of inquiry could not because of the difference in expectations about how confident the philosopher needs to be about an interpretative hypothesis. The nonfoundationalist approach helpfully invites the philosopher to explore philosophical territory in order to locate resources for correcting hypotheses, rather than forcing the philosopher to be confident that sufficient resources exist before inquiry even begins. Some big-question inquiries may prove futile, but we can't easily determine where these dead ends are without trying. Despite the importance of nonfoundationalism for big-question philosophy, however, it is important to note that all streams of nonfoundationalist philosophy—including those within American pragmatic philosophy, Anglo-American analytic philosophy, and Continental postmodern philosophy—have currents that resist discussion of metaphysics and theology as well as currents that support it. But this resistance is not due to epistemological policing of the Kantian or logical positivist sort.

Second, increasingly detailed and integrated knowledge in the natural, social, and cognitive sciences is also changing the prospects for big-question philosophy, even as it challenges prevailing approaches to less controversial domains of philosophical reflection. For example, it no longer makes much sense to study epistemology in isolation from the cognitive sciences, or ethics separately from evolutionary theory. The contemporary scientific picture of the natural and social worlds is not seamless, but rather an elegant, semi-consistent patchwork of piece-wise robust theories. Yet it is far more richly connected to physical nature—as measured by both predictive accuracy and explanatory richness—than all past understandings of the natural world. Its impact on philosophy in all areas is correspondingly more important than ever.

The emerging scientific view of the world has serious weaknesses in its handling of aspects of reality that lie beyond the reach of the physical sciences, especially consciousness and value. It is important to guard against such limitations lest we fall prey to what Alfred North Whitehead termed the fallacy of misplaced concreteness, whereby (in this case) we foolishly treat as real or important only that which we can conveniently study with the natural sciences. This is the bet of scientism, and it is ultimately a losing proposition. Even with these difficulties, however, the emerging scientific picture of the natural world and of human beings holds great promise for big-question philosophy. (I take up the theme of multidisciplinarity in Chapter 4.)

Third, our era has witnessed the birth of comparative philosophy, in which big-question philosophy takes on a crosscultural aspect. In systematically comparing answers to big philosophical questions, the possibility exists for inference-to-best-explanation arguments where formerly there were only unconvincing attempts at direct deduction of answers. The direct-inference approach is exemplified by cosmological arguments for the existence of God, where some feature of the world (say, its contingency) is supposed to entail the existence of God (in this case, as a necessary being). But comparative philosophy effortlessly establishes that quite a few metaphysical options are compatible with the apparent contingency of the world, and the existence of a necessary being is merely one of them. In fact, the world's religions and philosophies furnish a long series of examples of the same problem with direct-inference arguments in big-question philosophy. The inferences typically run more soundly in the other direction, from metaphysical and theological hypotheses to their conditions. This is the domain of inference-to-best-explanation argumentation. (Chapter 5 takes up the theme of the role of comparison in inquiry.)

The comparative philosophical approach could have been imagined prior to our era, and sometimes was partially explored. I mentioned above Kant's adventures in comparative philosophy, and there are medieval and ancient examples also—with particularly impressive examples in the debate traditions of South Asia. But a full-blown approach to comparative philosophy was never feasible before recent decades because the scholarly interchange over world philosophy was usually unsophisticated. The prospects for, and the very nature of, big-question philosophy are materially different due to the development of comparative philosophy.

These are three reasons to hold out hope in our time for what I have been calling big-question philosophy. They correspond to the three defining words of the term *religious philosophy* as I use it here: *multidisciplinary comparative inquiry*. For any of this to work, however, inquiry needs to be understood as the nonfoundationalist, fallibilist, venture described above (and in detail in Chapter 6). Religious philosophy may not always be identical with big-question philosophy. But the considerations about the possibility and prospects of one typically apply to the other.

Religious Philosophy as a Form of Religious Studies

Religious philosophy and the academic study of religion share the goal of understanding religion. In this sense, religious philosophy is a part of religious studies. Religious studies rightly seeks objective scholarship—partly for its own sake, and partly to overcome a history of bias as it gradually distinguished itself from its theological and often Christian roots. While some forms of theology and philosophy of religion are incompatible with this criterion of objectivity and fair treatment of religions, religious philosophy as multidisciplinary comparative inquiry exemplifies it.

The Goals of Religious Studies

In the previous section, we saw that the word *philosophy* lacks consensus definition in the Western context. Much the same is true of South Asian philosophy, where the aftermath of colonial influence has produced a deep divide between traditional Indian philosophy and British analytical philosophy. In both contexts, it is not uncommon to see hostility toward or condescending dismissal of some philosophical practices by proponents of others. This drives home the social character of the contemporary Western and South Asian philosophical enterprises. They have a common structure of insiders and outsiders, renegades and conformists, warriors and workers. Each sub-tradition has characteristic practices, legitimacy relative to segments of the history of philosophy and slices of contemporary life, and rationalizations for its behavior toward other parts. The variations in style of inquiry come with tradition-borne criteria for what counts as admissible work and what is truly excellent. Education of young philosophers instills and activates these criteria, thereby perpetuating them and the traditions that bear them.

Like *philosophy*, the phrase *religious studies* lacks clear definition. This is partly due to infamous battles over how to construct an adequate definition of religion, which must contend with the unwieldy cluster of phenomena under investigation. But it also reflects controversies among those who study religion comparable in magnitude to the turf wars of philosophers. The inherently multidisciplinary character of religious studies helps here, however. Religious studies scholars typically identify themselves professionally as sociologists or anthropologists, historians or philosophers, with a specialty in one or another aspect of religion—an historical era or a geographic region, for example. Most expect to work alongside people with quite different types of expertise, and they are accustomed to making use of insights from other disciplines that operate according to methods quite different than those of their chief specialization.

This drives home the fundamental goal of religious studies: it is to understand religion as such—not merely what any one given discipline can comprehend of religion, but religion as a whole, in all its intricate variations and manifestations. This goal is supported by the cultivation of specific virtues in religious studies. These include paying close attention to the details of religious phenomena, avoiding abstractions that can distort the intricacy of religious practices and ideas, taking proper account of social and historical context in interpreting religious texts and artifacts, and prizing objectivity of description so as to win both agreement from qualified experts and, where appropriate, recognition from adherents. The training of religious studies scholars includes scrupulous attention to these virtues as well as evaluation of skills in the central discipline for each student.

Flowing out of this fundamental intellectual goal is a little discussed but pervasive practical goal: to inform people about religion so as to increase mutual understanding and global security, and to guide diplomacy and political policy decisions. Religion has always had a politically and socially explosive character and wars driven by religion have been common in human history as a result. Political tensions and cultural misunderstandings are frequently exacerbated by ignorance of the points of view of those involved, and those points of view almost always have a religious dimension. Ignorance of religion is as dangerous as religious extremism, and equally infuriating to those negatively affected by it. The academic study of religion has a crucial role to play in alleviating the problem of ignorance, just as religions themselves must tackle the problem of extremist violence.

Religious philosophy is fully *compatible* with these fundamental and practical goals of religious studies. Moreover, many aspects of religious philosophy are *indispensable* for achieving these goals. This is the twofold basis of my assertion that religious philosophy is a vital part of the academic study of religion.

First, regarding indispensability, despite appearing to be a stronger claim than mere compatibility, the indispensability of religious philosophy is easier to demonstrate because it only needs to be established for some styles of religious philosophy rather than all styles. The argument is straightforward. To understand religion obviously involves understanding what religious people think and believe. Indeed, religious ideas are a conceptually crucial and socially potent part of religion. Like other aspects of religion, however, religious ideas are extremely complex and intricate, as are the sacred texts that inspire many of them and the traditions of debate that nurture and refine them. Thus, several domains of scholarly expertise are vital for constructing a satisfying understanding of religious ideas: expertise in the interpretation of sacred texts, expertise in the commentarial traditions that arc out of those texts, expertise in the systematizations of belief that prove so influential for stabilizing religious identity, and expertise in the crucial conceptual debates that often influence the course of a religion's development. Religious philosophers are the experts in several of these domains, so they play an essential role in understanding religious ideas, and thus are indispensable for achieving the goals of religious studies.

Second, regarding compatibility, subsequent chapters will discuss the tasks of religious philosophy in more detail, and I will take up the question of the compatibility of these tasks with the academic study of religion again in the Afterword. At one level, the question of compatibility is answered easily: religious philosophers are obviously concerned with understanding religion and conveying a sound understanding of religious beliefs to those they teach and influence. That would seem to settle the matter. Yet complications arise because not all styles of religious philosophy focus merely on understanding religious ideas and beliefs, in the mode of history of ideas. Some aim to mount inquiries into first-order religious topics. That is, while all religious philosophers study the truth claims of religions and religious believers, some religious philosophers also seek to evaluate those claims from as many points of view as possible. For example, all religious philosophers ask what religious people have believed about ultimate reality and seek careful accounts of those beliefs—a formidably complex task. But some religious philosophers go further to ask what the most compelling idea of ultimate reality is, whether it is possible to prove the existence of a divine being, and how one might reconcile apparently contradictory ideas of ultimacy. Such questions still dominate textbooks in philosophy of religion. While these are philosophical questions of the first importance, it is not obvious that these questions are compatible with the goals of religious studies, if construed narrowly.

Wariness in Religious Studies Toward Philosophy

The disciplinary battles within religious studies that are most important for understanding the place of religious philosophy have concerned fairness and objectivity. There is no obvious reason why religion's well-earned reputation for nurturing true believers and myopic convictions should pass on to scholars the infection of biased judgment. After all, religious studies is not an inherently religious activity, any more than religious philosophy is, despite the unfortunate suggestion of the adjective. But definitions of religion, along with the descriptions, analyses, interpretations, and evaluations they inspire, have historically displayed palpable bias. This was especially true in the early years of religious studies, prior to the founding of religious studies departments in the United States and Europe in the late 1960s. In earlier works, a pattern of bias in favor of or specifically hostile to Christianity, which just happened to be the religious affiliation of most early religious studies scholars, is plain to see. Standard examples are early interpretations of Hinduism as fundamentally polytheistic; the unreflective dismissal of tribal religions as primitive; the promotion of Christianity as the "one true" religion above its "incomplete" or "distorted" or even "evil" rivals; and the framing of religion as mere superstition within a philosophy of history that posits humanity moving away from superstition and toward science, and thus away from religion toward atheistic or naturalistic humanism.

Even though more recent work has mitigated these early problems to a significant extent, a legacy of suspicion remains. This legacy takes the forms of wariness about the historic role of Christianity within religious studies, censoring the promotion either of religion in general or of any particular religious perspective in the teaching and study of religion, caution about philosophical modes of religious studies that evaluate religious truth claims, and rejection of theological modes of religious studies that seek to do intellectual work on behalf of particular religious institutions and traditions. Numerous works express or respond to such suspicion—though in a host of differently modulated ways, sometimes historically and sometimes programmatically framed, and often in connection with arguments for the place of religious or theological studies in the university.[3]

Unsurprisingly, therefore, religion scholars tend to stress modes of inquiry that explicitly target objectivity and have built-in safeguards for detecting and correcting bias. Thus, historical, phenomenological, philological, sociological, and anthropological approaches to religious studies are ascendant. Comparative approaches, once important for unifying religious studies as a field, are currently in decline due to the increasingly specialized character of work within religious studies. This development endangers the identity of the multidisciplinary venture of religious studies, resulting in members of a department having rather too little in common, and potentially triggering the dissolution of religion departments, returning specialists to their native university departments. Meanwhile, philosophical and theological approaches are under a cloud within the academic study of religion because of a widespread perception that they lack the requisite objectivity.

Indeed, suspicion of philosophy and theology as components of the study of religion has been so strong in recent years that the number of employment opportunities in U.S. colleges and universities devoted to philosophy of religion has been in marked decline (judging both from positions advertised and from numerous discussions about individual departmental histories).[4] The proportion of such positions relative to religious studies positions as a whole also is also declining, as departments sometimes replace retiring philosophy of religion professors with appointments in other areas of the ever widening field of religious studies. This partly reflects a need for rebalancing teaching expertise as religious studies generates more specialties. But I suspect that the shift also reflects lingering concerns about the lack of objectivity and ideological neutrality in philosophical and theological studies of religion.

I am not sure what the evidence is for this purported distinctive lack of objectivity in philosophical and theological approaches to religion. There seems to be the potential for bias throughout the social sciences and humanities, to various degrees—and even in the natural sciences, judging from numerous episodes in the history of biology and physics.[5] This potential for bias is typically managed though procedures that help willing experts detect and correct it. The widespread perception of bias in philosophical and theological approaches to religion probably reflects a belief that such procedures do not or perhaps cannot exist in those cases, as compared with the cases of historical and sociological approaches. The perceived solution, oddly, is not to insist on unbiased philosophy of religion and theology, which would be fitting, but rather to limit or eliminate philosophical and theological approaches within religious studies. Evidently, something else is afoot.

The concern about objectivity in the philosophical and theological study of religion is twofold. On the one hand, it expresses a strategic preference for defining religious studies in league with history and the human sciences rather than with the humanities, thereby simultaneously consolidating an intelligible place for religious studies in the academy and disentangling the academic study of religion from its theological and often Christian roots. On the other hand, it reflects a belief that sufficient resources for diagnosing and correcting biased interpretations of religious phenomena do not exist in philosophy and theology. I will take up the former, more strategic concern in the next section, and defer discussion of the latter, more philosophical concern until the subsequent section.

The Changing Identity of Religious Studies

In general terms, as difficult as the changing academic job market is for newly minted PhDs in philosophy of religion, these transformations in religious studies strike me as a well-intentioned effort to correct mistakes of the past, in the name of a richer and more accurate understanding of religion. Yet there is something unduly defensive about the current attitude of religious studies toward the historic role of Christianity in founding and nurturing the discipline.

The motivation of early Enlightenment scholars of religion such as Friedrich Schleiermacher and Georg Hegel may have included justifying Christianity's superiority in relation to other world religions. But they and other Enlightenment thinkers also sought to understand unfamiliar religions, which in their time was vastly more difficult than it is in ours. There is plenty of room for more pride of ownership of the Enlightenment Christian pioneers of religious studies. It is in the early nineteenth century that we see the most sustained and determined efforts to give birth to the objective study of religion, under challenging circumstances, through a long period of gestation within the womb of Christian theology reaching back into the medieval theology of Thomas Aquinas (c. 1225–1274) and earlier. After a difficult post-Enlightenment delivery lasting more than a century, this vast effort finally bore fruit with the field-defining works of Max Müller, Max Weber, Emile Durkheim, and William James.

The new-born discipline of religious studies transformed many aspects of Christian thought, provoking a sharp divide between Christian theologians who privilege Christianity and Christian theologians who do not. Some among the first group explicitly depreciate other religions, while others ignore religious studies and focus on nurturing Christian identity and self-understanding while maintaining abstract courtesy toward other religious traditions. Most in the second group take for granted the value and importance of non-Christian religions and insist on allowing this assumption to affect their interpretations of the meaning of Christianity. The same theological split is now evident in analogous forms of theological activity within religious traditions other than Christianity.

Meanwhile, the academic study of religion went its own way. Having left behind humble origins in the womb of Christian faith—nurtured by missionaries and curious philosophers and theologians—it allied itself with existing ventures in philosophy, in history, and in the human sciences. Its distinctive practice was comparison of religious ideas and practices, with comparison understood as serving a variety of intellectual and practical purposes. The theological interpretation of religious pluralism was gradually confined to strictly theological contexts, and the focus on the Bible gradually broadened to all sacred literatures of the world's religions.

The unfolding transformation had several stages. First, the American Academy of Religion changed its name and character in precisely this way. Founded in 1909 as the Association of Biblical Instructors, and renamed in 1922 to the National Association of Biblical Instructors, it originally had a distinctively Christian profile. In 1964 it adopted its current name in an attempt to lessen or eliminate the Christian-Jewish emphasis expressed in the word *biblical*. Most of the over fourteen hundred undergraduate religion departments in the United States were founded in the 1960s and 1970s, and quite a few of these were in state schools where a premium was placed on nonpartisan approaches to religious studies. Certain key exemplar departments of religion began before this period, and some key societies and journals did also, including notably the Society for the Scientific Study of Religion (founded in 1949) and its *Journal for the Scientific Study of Religion* (founded in 1962). These initiatives spurred the professionalization of religious studies. Thus, if the founding intellectual transformation occurred at the beginning of the twentieth century, the professionalization transformation came several decades later, in the 1960s and 1970s.

Second, if we mark 1972 as the midpoint in this burst of professionalization within religious studies, graduate statistics from the American Academy of Religion reveal an interesting trend. In the three decades from 1972 through 2002, 1.1 million research doctorates were granted in the United States, with about 165,000 of those in the humanities, and 13,216 in religious studies, theology, or religious education. The interesting trend is the relative proportion of religious studies doctorates. The 6,805 doctorates in religious studies were awarded most heavily toward the end of this three-decade period—eventually overtaking the 6,411 doctorates in theology and religious education, which outpaced religious studies at the beginning of this period. The academic study of religion has come into its own as a scholarly field, staking out territory in distinction from the confessional and institutional interests of Christianity and other religious traditions, and finding a home within the contemporary Western university.

A third notable period of transformation occurred with the new millennium and is still underway, and this makes it difficult to assess. The general character of this transformation is consolidation, though sometimes in rather exclusionary ways. It has three components. One is the decision of the American Academy of Religion no longer to hold its annual meeting jointly with the Society of Biblical Literature, which took effect for the first time in 2008. This was a highly controversial and deeply hurtful parting of the ways, for some, and a long-overdue divorce of an unhappy marriage for others. It reaffirms the intention of the leaders of the academic study of religion in North

America to dissociate their field from the special interests of specific religious communities. A second component is the increasing stress on scientific aspects of the study of religion. This is most evident in the central role of the social sciences but also in the growing role of the psychological and cognitive sciences, and even evolutionary theory, in framing interpretations of the origins and functions of religion.

The final component of the consolidation transformation, and the most important for my immediate concerns, is the loosening of the traditional ties between religious studies and the humanities. This is manifest in the hiring realities and changes in religion departments discussed above, whereby philosophy of religion has a shrinking profile within religious studies. It is also manifest in the shift away from literary and artistic approaches to religion, presumably because they suggest a degree of engagement with first-order religious topics that strays too far from the emerging identity of religious studies. The only traditionally humanities discipline left with an unquestioned role in religious studies is history, so long as it is conducted on the terms of secular history departments. The historical disciplines are far and away the most empirically driven of the humanities, to the point that some prefer to designate these disciplines "historical sciences" so as to avoid taint from the humanities.

Thus, the consolidation transformation appears to involve solidifying an identity for the academic study of religion around the model of the human sciences, with the historical sciences playing an indispensable role. This leaves the formerly crucial task of comparing religious ideas and practices in an odd position, because it has only a slender natural affiliation with the social sciences, and because it runs counter to the professional ideal of area expertise, which dominates the social sciences. It also raises a sharp question about the compatibility of the humanities with the academic study of religion. This compatibility question is particularly pointed in relation to some aspects of religious philosophy.[6]

There has been and still is fractiousness surrounding this three-staged transformation in the social and academic location of religious studies—that is, its founding, professionalization, and consolidation as a social science. In and through the disagreements, the academic study of religion has succeeded in consolidating its academic profile through an alliance with the social sciences and through freeing itself from older partnerships with the humanities. It is a success story, then, from the point of view of overcoming parochial beginnings and adopting standards of objectivity, which are crucial for the social usefulness of education in religious studies. That success ought to be sufficient reason to claim the family heritage with pride, rather than shame-facedly trying to rewrite history by neglecting the actual origins of the discipline within medieval and early modern philosophy and Christian theology. The complicated birth of religious studies testifies as much to the sound instincts and hard work of early theologically motivated scholars of religion seeking to take seriously unfamiliar religious traditions, as to the need for religious studies to strike out on its own and claim space for itself to grow outside the direct influence of Christianity and Christian theology.

There is a danger that the success of religious studies contains the seeds of its own undoing as a multidisciplinary academic field. To the extent that it is exclusively a matter of historical or social-science research, why maintain a religion department at all? Why not absorb religious studies back into the disciplines that it is so intent on resembling? This is a nontrivial problem. The growing scarcity of serious comparativists and the decentralization of the humanities within religious studies has robbed many departments of a feasible core identity. When departmental members identify more strongly with a home discipline such as sociology or anthropology or history than with religious studies as such, the basis for a department becomes questionable. This is the price of exchanging the original vision of religious studies—as a truly multidisciplinary venture embracing the humanities and the social sciences—for the coveted credibility of modeling the field after the social sciences and history alone.

Objectivity and Neutrality in Religious Studies

I have identified two reasons for the concern within religious studies about objectivity in the philosophical and theological study of religion. As just discussed, the first is a belief that the social sciences and history provide a better model for objectivity and fairness than the humanities. The second directly concerns the problems with objectivity in religious philosophy, and is the topic of this section.

Philosophical and theological modes of thought must now contend with a widespread assumption within religious studies that they are inevitably biased and unworthy of a place within the scholarly study of religion. This problem is akin to the rejection of big-question philosophy by many other styles of Western philosophy, but in the religious studies context the suspicion is exacerbated by the history of bias recounted above and the struggle for objectivity that it provoked. Yet there seems to be no intrinsic reason why philosophic inquiry cannot be religiously unbiased at least to the same degree that any other sort of inquiry in religious studies is. If we are to use the hermeneutics of suspicion for policing the scholarly study of religion, we should do so evenhandedly, applying it to social-science and historical approaches as well as to philosophical approaches.

Every mode of religious studies has succumbed to bias in various ways, from phenomenological descriptions to early translations of sacred texts, and from historical analyses to the prodigious analytical and comparative efforts of the sociology and anthropology of religion. If these approaches can build in means of detecting and correcting bias, why should philosophical and theological modes of thought be unable to do the same? They have the longest history with religious studies, and it is their inquiries that gave birth to the discipline. Do they not have the credentials to sponsor unbiased inquiry? Of course, there must be a refusal within religious studies of forms of philosophy and theology that do not prize the ideal of objectivity and fairness. But this criterion should be applied universally rather than serve as rationalization for continuing to neglect the unexamined assumption that philosophical and theological modes of thought are necessarily biased in favor of one tradition or another.

This is a larger question than can be answered here. Other chapters will help support my claim that objectivity and fairness in inquiry are virtues that religious philosophy—*when conceived as multidisciplinary comparative inquiry*—can rightly claim for itself. For now, I focus on the unreflective nature, and indeed the injustice, of this charge against religious philosophy.

It is ironic that religious studies is stressing the virtues of objectivity and neutrality in the very same period when so many other intellectuals are not only attacking the possibility of objectivity and neutrality but also questioning whether we should even regard them as virtues, instead of, say, self-deceptive evasions of responsibility. To be fair, philosophers are playing the leading role in this hermeneutical attack on these sacred cows of academia, so perhaps religious studies scholars should dismiss their efforts as merely trying to argue that "everyone else is as bad as we philosophers know ourselves to be." But there is more to it than this.

The principal question for religious studies is how to move around within the ideologically complex landscape of religion without succumbing to bias for or against particular ideas or practices that appall or disgust or excite or convince us. Suppose we read the Upaniṣads, and we are swept away with the mind-bending claim that *Ātman* is Brahman. This sort of thing happens all the time in religious studies; it is partly the existentially gripping subject matter that draws people into these fields in the first place, regardless of their religious orientations. Does this powerful emotional reaction to a new encounter with an ancient idea mean that we are not worthy to be called scholars of religion? What if that reaction causes us to change our personal religious beliefs and our family's religious practices? Are we then not fit to carry the sandals of our more prosaic, rigidly self-disciplined, or emotionally ascetic academic colleagues, who never feel a flutter of first-order enthusiasm for anything they study? And what if we are so disgusted by the religious aspects of so-called female genital mutilation that we start spending money and time on efforts to ban the practice throughout the world? Does that reaction condemn us to the minor leagues of the academic study of religion while colleagues not easily moved to action play in the majors?

Emmanuel Lévinas devoted his life to disclosing the gentle but radical moral claim that the Other exerts upon us.[7] In his framework, with which I have great sympathy, if the face-to-face encounter with an unfamiliar person does not produce reactions of the sort described above, then it is likely that we are neither living authentically nor operating as a scholar with true wisdom. If objectivity and neutrality have to mean lack of involvement—keeping phenomena at an existentially safe distance, or moral impotence—then they certainly do seem unworthy of being called "virtues." Rather, in this case, objectivity and neutrality would be forms of self-destruction in that they deny the primal moral responsibility of human beings. By contrast, in the spirit of Lévinas, objectivity can only mean seeing things as they really are—value-laden and interested from beginning to end—and adjusting one's life appropriately to this reality, which necessarily means giving oneself over to an uncomfortable but ultimately rewarding encounter with the Other. This is a much more complicated existential and intellectual project than the abstracted objectivity lauded in superficial battles over allegedly tainted scholarship in religious studies.

It is doubtful whether religious studies can afford to take on board so nuanced and challenging a notion of objectivity at this time. Individual scholars can and do, of course. For the sake of its disciplinary identity, however, religious studies remains for now in the posture of making sure people don't get it confused with anything that would destroy its credibility in the academic world. For that purpose, the rhetorical device of invoking simplistic ideals of objectivity and neutrality continues to be useful, despite lacking conceptual depth.

One way this rhetoric is useful seems quite clear. Religious studies can invoke the simplified ideals of objectivity and neutrality to rule out of bounds intellectual activity that is primarily in service of the interests of a particular religious tradition. Let's call this the

Loyalty Criterion for the sake of identification. The college teacher who starts proselytizing in the classroom on behalf of a particular meditation method or way of salvation or sacred text is insufficiently objective and neutral to fulfill the requirements of a religious studies teacher in the contemporary, often highly secularized, academic context. The scholar who stipulates the meaning of God in terms of one particular religious sub-tradition's perspective—without apology or explanation, and while remaining ignorant of, or defiant toward, a religious world full of alternative conceptions of deity—is likewise insufficiently objective and neutral to fulfill the requirements of a religious studies scholar in the contemporary academic context. The historian who reads the arc of history unselfconsciously in terms of the supernatural cosmology of his or her own religious tradition violates the Loyalty Criterion. Proselytizing and biased stipulation of the meanings of key terms are perfectly acceptable in an appropriate religious subculture, even as academic practices. But they are incompatible with, and actually disloyal to, the ideals of religious studies in the contemporary academy.

The real difficulty arises not with such black-and-white violations of the Loyalty Criterion's simple ideals of objectivity and neutrality, but with the numerous gray-area situations. For example, when a university hosts a divinity school that provides seminary training for professional religious leadership, what posture should religious studies specialists take toward colleagues in such educational contexts? If personal religious convictions do not necessarily prevent objectivity and neutrality as a scholar and teacher, then why should institutional obligations to a particular religious tradition cause a problem? If institutional obligations to work on behalf of a religious tradition do not impair objectivity or neutrality, then what of the Loyalty Criterion?

Perhaps what matters most are not personal feelings, religious commitments, or institutional locations, but the style of work and the virtues prized within it. Such a nuanced interpretation of the Loyalty Criterion may be fairer but it is more difficult to implement than criteria based on external features such as social and institutional location. This places religious studies in a difficult position, torn between unattractively simplistic ideals of objectivity and neutrality, on the one hand, and the difficult-to-implement but highly desirable ideals of fairness and perceptiveness, on the other hand.

Objectivity, Neutrality, and Religious Philosophy

I contend that relatively unbiased and ideologically neutral forms of philosophical and theological reflection are possible. These ideals can only ever be approximated, due to the limitations of human self-awareness and the realities of existential passion and social context. But what I am calling religious philosophy, understood as multidisciplinary comparative inquiry, takes the ideals of objectivity and neutrality seriously by establishing procedures of correction that can detect and overcome intellectual defects of bias and ideological distortion. This will hopefully become increasingly clear in subsequent chapters.

Theology is complicated because, unlike religious philosophy, it can also be an institutional activity of concrete religious traditions, serving their needs to form identity and educate believers. But not all theology is the property of a Jewish, Christian, Muslim, Hindu, Buddhist, or Daoist religious community. Some theology has no home apart from the academic setting that hosts the community of theologians that pursue it. Likewise, philosophy of religion as it is currently practiced is also sometimes a religious activity pursued on behalf of a a philosopher's personal religious faith, an intellectual extension or expression of religious institutional interests. But not all philosophy of religion has this character. Religious philosophy, as I describe it, encompasses multidisciplinary forms of theological and philosophical reflection on religion that prize impartial analysis and refuse institutional religious bias.

Of course, every kind of inquiry has institutional support and social contexts. Religious philosophy's institutional home is the modern academy, which is an extraordinarily useful, albeit complex, cultural creation. It is ambiguous, like all human institutions, and far too easily believes its own press both about objectivity and about the unquestionable value of its efforts. Yet its attempt to foster simultaneously valuable and objective scholarship in all fields of human endeavor is important and honorable. Without this nurturing environment, religious philosophy would be the work of rare and marginalized thinkers, if it could be pursued meaningfully at all. Within the institutional framework of the modern academy, however, religious philosophy has shown great promise, despite its tension with forms of theology and philosophy of religion that are indebted to specific religious traditions.

Religious Philosophy as a Form of Theology

The most adventurous forms of religious philosophy intend to inquire into ultimacy, in the double sense of matters that are ultimately religiously important and of ultimate reality itself. This places religious philosophy in close proximity to theology, understood not as an intellectual activity legitimating the

practices and beliefs of a particular religious institution but as inquiry into topics of ultimate importance to religious people and traditions. Religious philosophy as theological in this particular sense invites critiques from religious traditions as to its possibility or advisability. The success of tradition-based, confessional forms of theology depends largely on satisfying concrete institutional needs, such as articulating local beliefs in a persuasive way for intellectually curious believers. These criteria for success are complex but relatively easy to meet—so easy that intellectual success can virtually be guaranteed. By contrast, religious philosophy in its most theological modes must take seriously the possibility of failure if its scrupulous approach to ultimacy proves ineffective.

The Meaning and Tasks of Theology

When Moses sought the face of God, so the story goes, God told him to take cover for his own safety and then showed Moses merely his back through a cleft in a rock. When Job sought understanding of unjust suffering, he was blasted with a complaint-silencing vision of divine power. When Arjuna sought a vision of Krishna, he was terrified and amazed and begged for release from the pain and severity of that intensely clear spiritual awareness. The *Dao De Jing* launches off with what appears to be a claim on behalf of the impossibility of naming the *Dao*. In tradition after tradition, religious mystics testify to the impossibility of comprehending ultimacy. Some refuse even to speak of it. The sacred texts of the world's traditions uniformly decline to affirm that human beings ever have comprehensive understanding of, or significant control over, ultimate paths of liberation and ultimate realities. So what makes religious philosophers so eager to discover and articulate ultimacy?

Religious philosophers are motivated by the same drives that motivate all outrageous achievements, from climbing a mountain to carving a face from solid rock: fascination, curiosity, longing for connection, and the desires to overcome fear, to praise beauty, to express the self, and to assert power. It is important not to isolate intellectual pursuits too far from bodily, political, and artistic endeavors, at least as far as motivations are concerned. This would mask biological and social common ground, the awareness of which greatly helps to situate the most theological of religious philosophic inquiries, to figure out how to proceed with them, and to estimate their prospects.

It seems that theological pursuits, for want of a clearer designation, are an instinctive part of human life. They are indulged whenever cultural conditions are stable enough to permit stories and speculations about the wider cosmological and spiritual context of worldly human joys and sorrows. Judging from ancient cave art, they appear to be present in the most ancient traces of human civilization.[8] They are certainly present in the earliest literary traces of human civilization. Most people, even the most practical and prosaic among us, wonder about ultimate matters. Most religious institutions use theology to tidy up beliefs, define identity, and legitimate social practices, whether or not they use the word *theology* to name what they do.

We definitely need a word for all this activity. In fact, the word *theology* has been catching on, jumping from tradition to tradition, as religious thinkers seek names for what they have been doing all along anyway. So now we have Jewish, Christian, Muslim, and Hindu theology. Even nontheistic forms of Buddhism and Daoism and Confucianism, in need of a name like every other religious tradition, sometimes speak of their traditions' intellectual work as "theology."[9] Some say we need to check the "theological impulse." Others say we should indulge it. Everyone affirms the near ubiquity of theology in religion, to the point that rare instances of its absence in religious sub-traditions are noteworthy and puzzling.

The alliance of theology with the institutional interests of religious traditions has made it difficult for religious philosophers to claim the word *theology*. Religious philosophy has no difficulty recognizing the value and legitimacy of theological work allied closely with religious traditions and institutions, even though it cannot accept the limitations on inquiry into ultimate matters that prevail in such forms of theology. Yet religious philosophers, too, need a word for thinking carefully about ultimacy. Can *theology* serve? Common understandings of theology, when allied with the institutional interests of religious traditions, are intellectual testimony or textual exegesis or systematic statements of doctrine. By contrast, religious philosophy conceives of this thinking as multidisciplinary comparative inquiry into ultimate matters. This conceptual difference is as significant as the corresponding difference in the practitioner's social location and obligations.

Perhaps, then, *philosophical theology* serves better than *theology* to suggest what the most theological edge of religious philosophy does and how it does it. Philosophical theology has many associations with religious traditions, especially in Catholic Christian circles, yet it does suggest a contrast with institutionally oriented theology, which might well be called "confessional theology" by contrast, to express its orientation to traditional religious confessions. This would leave the word *theology* in the vague position that it probably needs to occupy if it is to serve as a general designation for the human instinct to reflect on ultimate matters.

This brief meditation on names confirms that no usage is ideal. I shall refer to the theologically more aggressive aspirations of religious philosophy as "philosophical theology" when I need to contrast it with confessional theology, which self-consciously serves the interests of religious institutions. Even there, however, religious philosophy's approach to philosophical theology is as multidisciplinary comparative inquiry, an approach that would not be universally, or even widely, accepted among philosophical theologians. When speaking compactly, I will continue to say that religious philosophy has theological interests and aspects, hopefully without obscuring awareness of both continuity with, and difference from, other forms of theological activity.

Theological Critiques of Religious Philosophy

The tradition of philosophical theology within religious philosophy is as ancient and venerable as philosophical thinking itself. It has always remained partially independent of religious traditions, though rarely completely distinct. The resulting overlap and interchange between philosophical theology within religious philosophy and confessional theology has often been mutually fruitful but it has also provoked mutual hostility. If religious philosophy has sometimes dismissed confessional theology as placing institutional loyalty ahead of the ideals of open inquiry, confessional theology has charged religious philosophy with gross naïveté about what is possible in theological inquiry and has warned religious philosophers about the spiritual impudence of attempting to gain an intellectual grasp on ultimacy unsheltered by the wisdom of traditional confessional theological traditions. As the image of Moses behind the rock suggests, confessional theologians say, we must be careful when we seek God's face. While philosophical theology is only one aspect of religious philosophy, as I have defined these terms, it is an important part. The deep challenges to its feasibility or advisability from within religious and theological traditions deserve a response. These challenges are at least as compelling and difficult to handle as the philosophical critiques of metaphysics and the religious-studies critiques of bias that I discussed above. The main critiques are three.

First, it is imprudent to make ultimacy an object of inquiry, at the best of times, and thoroughly impertinent when philosophical theologians take it upon themselves to compare and theorize about ultimacy, as if their very being were not deeply entangled in the reality they seek to grasp. To make the point concrete using personal symbols for ultimacy, to begin theological reflection at all is to count on the grace and good humor of God.

Second, philosophical theology tends to presuppose the rational accessibility of its object, yet this is contrary to common sense. Ultimacy must somehow first give itself over to scrutiny or it would not be ultimate. To neglect or mask this condition of all theological reflection is self-deceptive and intellectually shallow. Philosophical theologians need to become more sharply aware of the epistemic presumptions of their work, which is to recognize what confessional theologians in theistic traditions have long called "divine revelation."

Third, the basic social fact of theological reflection is that it is borne within vast living traditions teeming with discussion and debate. This is recognized clearly in confessional modes of theology and ignored most often in philosophical theology, where the supporting traditions are thinly dispersed and fragmented by comparison. This critique is an important reminder that philosophical theology is in some way parasitic upon the vast streams of tradition that frame religious experience and guide thinking about ultimacy in each new generation of human beings. These streams of wisdom and practice are the raw material from which theological ideas spring and against which their implications are sometimes tested. The tradition-borne character of theological reflection is an extremely useful fact for theology conceived as inquiry, because vast traditions serve to stabilize hypotheses about ultimacy over many centuries, thereby promoting testing against changing cultural conditions and shifting metaphysical tastes. Yet philosophical theology often neglects or marginalizes the complicated, messy world of religion in search of a pure land of philosophical ideas about ultimacy. This is both futile and self-deceptive.

Perhaps the sharpest practical conclusion from confessional theology's threefold critique of religious philosophy's theological aspirations is simply that the prospects of the latter are uncertain in a more-or-less spectacular way. Philosophical theology in the sense of multidisciplinary comparative inquiry simply may not get very far. Confessional theology cannot rule out the possibility of philosophical theology in this sense any more than antimetaphysical arguments can. But confessional theology certainly gives no reason to believe that philosophical theology within religious philosophy is likely to be highly successful. The emphases on multidisciplinarity and comparison involve resources that confessional theology typically ignores. But philosophical theology also refuses the authoritative constraints of revelation and tradition that have made confessional theology so productive (and also sometimes destructive) over the centuries. The question of how effective we can make philosophical theology, as a species of religious philosophy, is an empirical one. The elements of comparison and multidisciplinarity are relatively new in the history of philosophical theology, so I think that the question of its prospects is quite open.

Distinguishing Confessional Theology and Religious Philosophy

In addition to this practical concern, the threefold critique originating from confessional theology raises a spiritual challenge to the theological aspirations of religious philosophy. Few who take ultimate matters with intellectual seriousness are likely to remain insensitive to the spiritual and moral dimensions of inquiry aimed at ultimate matters. All forms of theology, including both confessional theology and philosophical theology, involve the inquirer existentially in the subject matter. This circularity is unavoidable because spiritually attentive people are more or less ultimately concerned about ultimate matters. Any intellectual work tries to allow for biases and special interests of inquirers, but there is something odd about trying to abstract from spiritual interests in ultimate matters. To abstract from such interests may well distort the object of inquiry more than if the driving motivations and existential entanglements were fully recognized and embraced.

This is an ancient problem within theology, with analogues in the study of literature and the arts. Sometimes, the circular self-involvement of theological reflection is embraced directly, as when Augustine pens his autobiographical theological study *Confessions*, or Anselm (c. 1033–1109) writes his famous *Proslogion* in the form of a prayerful address to God. Both of these works are profound acts of philosophical theology as well as ventures in spiritual engagement with the object of inquiry. It is a mistake for philosophical theologians to neglect or deny the fact that inquiry into ultimate matters is inherently and ineluctably a spiritual activity.

In grappling with this problem, twentieth-century German-American Christian theologian-philosopher Paul Tillich defined the "theological circle" as that domain of intellectual reflection on ultimate concern in which one accepts one's existential involvement in the subject matter and treats this entanglement seriously within the inquiry itself. By contrast, philosophical reflection on ultimate matters abstracts from this involvement, and thus takes place outside the theological circle. Tillich used this distinction to define theology in relation to philosophy, insofar as they are both concerned with ultimate matters, allowing that the same person might do both activities at different times.[10] While this is a perceptive and intelligent definition, theological inquiry is rarely neat in this way. In practice, theologians experiment with abstracting from their existential involvement in their subject matter to various degrees, with making a virtue of it in a variety of ways, with dialectically registering and challenging such involvement, and so on. All of this is generally theological and all of it can serve the interests either of religious institutions or of philosophical inquiry into ultimate matters. Tillich's famous distinction is insensitive to these practical struggles with the self-referring quality of theological work. The same is true of most such sharp distinctions.

It is truer to reality to distinguish confessional from philosophical theology in terms of social contexts, purposes, and resources, allowing that there is a wide variety of emphases. When theology stresses the social location of religious institutions, the purpose of maintaining or reforming religious identity on behalf of such institutions, and the authoritative resources of sacred texts and traditions—it tends toward the confessional. When theology's social location is chiefly the intellectual and literary history of religions, when its purpose is inquiry into ultimacy, and when its resources are description, comparison, analysis, and multidisciplinary theory building—and when it refuses to treat the sacred texts and traditions of any particular religion as decisively authoritative—it tends toward the philosophical (in the sense defended here).

The complex overlaps are fascinating and show that crisp distinctions in this area are suspect. In fact, there appears to be mutual dependence between these two emphases within theological work. Western philosophy has usually refused to recognize divine revelation in sacred religious texts as an authoritative source of knowledge about ultimate matters, yet it has allowed Western religions to exercise pervasive influence over the conception of ultimacy that dominates Western philosophical theology. Likewise, Christian, Jewish, and Muslim confessional theology would be inconceivable without the conceptually rich and historically influential world of Western philosophy.

In the context of South Asian philosophy, the epistemological debates of *pramāṇa* theory explicitly raised the issue of whether to admit the authority of sacred texts. Should the authority of the Vedas or parts of the Vedas be accepted as one of the *pramāṇa* (epistemologically relevant factors) in theological work? Roughly, to answer yes to this question was to be a member of an orthodox philosophical school. To answer no, as a member of Buddhist, Jain, and the materialist Cārvāka schools would, was to be unorthodox. This neat distinction helped people to know where they stood and facilitated scholarly debates over the value of sacred texts for guiding beliefs about ultimate matters. In practice, however, things were not so neat. As in parallel Western debates, sophisticated hermeneutical approaches to the Vedas and emphasis on the more philosophical Vedic material of the Upaniṣads allowed orthodox schools (such as Vedānta) to develop highly abstract philosophical treatments of religious topics that seem almost indistinguishable from similar discussions within the unorthodox schools of Buddhist philosophy in respect to the role of authority in theological inquiry. Moreover, wherever there is debate, there is mutual dependence.

Picturing religious philosophy as inquiry helps to understand these overlaps and mutual dependencies. In the most general terms, inquiry is about solving problems and satisfying curiosity. This can be an extremely intensive activity when the topic is complicated, so the efficiency of inquiry becomes important. The most efficient method of inquiry appears to be creatively and intelligently formulating hypotheses and then subjecting those hypotheses to relentless scrutiny and testing, aimed at refining hypotheses and coordinating them into consistent theories that express a richly satisfying understanding of the topic. (See Chapter 6 for more on this.) From where does religious philosophy, as a species of multidisciplinary comparative inquiry, get its starting hypotheses? Historically, the answer to this question is that religious traditions furnished hypotheses about ultimate questions. This is not surprising because the religious traditions encode accumulated wisdom about ultimate matters.

For its part, from where does confessional theology get its metaphysical frameworks and its philosophical cosmologies? From philosophical processes of theologizing that produced them through centuries of painstaking effort. This, too, is unsurprising; it only makes sense to take advantage of polished theories, accommodating them to the special interests of religious institutions. South Asian theologians drew on the cosmology and metaphysics of key philosophers such as Śaṅkara (788–820 CE) and Nāgārjuna (c. 150–250 CE), and East Asian philosophers capitalized on the cosmology and metaphysics of early philosophical interpreters of the Chinese Classics. Early Jewish and Christian theologians did this with Plato (Πλάτων; 428/427–348/347 BCE), and both Plotinus (Πλωτῖνος; c. 204–270 CE) and Aristotle furnished vital theoretical guidance for medieval theologians, Jewish, Christian, and Muslim alike.

Philosophical theology within religious philosophy is thus deeply entangled historically with the confessional theological activities of religious institutions. For the most part, this has been a mutually beneficial entanglement. Nevertheless, the approaches are distinguishable. The theological aspirations of religious philosophy take the form of multidisciplinary comparative inquiry and acknowledge neither the decisive authority for inquiry of sacred religious texts and traditions, nor the specific interests of religious institutions in the outcomes of such inquiry.

Chapter 2

Tasks, Contexts, and Traditions of Religious Philosophy

Chapter 1 located religious philosophy among the disciplinary areas of philosophy, religious studies, and theology, and addressed objections to religious philosophy arising from those three domains. This chapter deals with the character of religious philosophy more directly. I first discuss the tasks of religious philosophy, then some of the contextual, social, and intellectual factors that influence it, and finally, the subtraditions that give shape to its internal debates.

Tasks of Religious Philosophy

Religious philosophy involves investigation (in the sense of multidisciplinary comparative inquiry) into every kind and degree of religious phenomena. The breadth of religious philosophy derives from the diverse topics it covers (from ideas to practices, from metaphysics to ethics, and from the concrete to the generic), from the diverse styles of its inquiries (phenomenological, comparative, historical, analytical, literary, theoretical, and evaluative), and from the diverse disciplines in relation to which these inquiries unfold (natural sciences, social sciences, humanities, and professional crafts such as law, medicine, and politics).

Breadth of Phenomena

The family-resemblance character of religious phenomena implies that the best definitions of religion are lists of criteria for detecting the religious. Some of the criteria on such lists tend toward the universal in the sense that they apply to one or another aspect of almost every tradition that experts want to call religious, though certainly not every aspect of every religious tradition. That is, they are close to being necessary conditions even if nowhere near sufficient for identifying the religious. Universal or almost universal criteria tend to derive from structural universals across cultures that correspond to recurring problems that human beings absolutely must solve if they are to thrive (for example, finding food, identifying kin groups, reproducing). These problem-solving structures appear sometimes to have been encoded in adaptive traits through the evolutionary process. Though the details of evolutionary psychology are still emerging, this framework helps to explain the presence of some recurring features of religious beliefs and practices.

Other criteria on definition lists are not even close to universal. That is, so far from being sufficient conditions for identifying the religious, they are not even close to necessary conditions. Partial criteria such as "existence of ancestor veneration" make no sense at all in application to some religious traditions but seem crucial for understanding what is important in others. The collective presence of several or "enough" partial criteria indicates a religious phenomena or tradition. That leaves plenty of room for flexibility in application of the designation *religious*.

Criteria for detecting the religious are typically vague because they carry quite different meanings in various contexts. I mean vagueness here in the technical sense of "capable of mutually inconsistent specification": religious studies experts specify universal criteria in mutually contradictory ways in the various contexts of application. For example, "God" is sometimes a supernatural temporal being and other times a nonsupernatural entity, a nontemporal being, or something beyond being. This sort of inconsistency of specification does not make vague criteria useless. On the contrary, it seems to be the only way to do justice to the intricate distinctiveness of each religious practice or idea while still drawing attention to similarities across traditions and sub-traditions.

Obviously, there is plenty of room for dispute with regard to weighting criteria for identifying the religious as well as their relevance to borderline phenomena that some experts might judge to be religious. There are also disputes over whether any criteria are truly universal, which criteria are close to universal and which are partial, and why criteria are nearly universal when they are. In fact, nothing about defining religion is undisputed, not even the issue of whether the activities of definition and identification are worth the trouble or morally justifiable.

What are these universal or partial features of religion? Consider the following list of examples, which could be much longer.[1] I appreciate the broad (though probably not universal) applicability of these criteria. I also appreciate their sensitivity to the social, psychological, intellectual, and spiritual purposes or functions served by practices and beliefs. The religious involves:

- a way to relate every aspect of life to something ultimate and fundamental, in terms of ideas, values, and practices

- an answer to concerns about death and immortality, including the ultimate origins, fate, and meaning of human life and all of reality

- a means of bonding human beings tightly together through obligation, responsibility, and ritual, in order to stabilize social life and realize relational ideals such as peace, pleasure, power, or prosperity

- a solution to the problem of human evil and a means of healing, liberation, social transformation, and personal self-cultivation

- a source of orienting narratives by which we discern our place in a cosmological framework and gather the courage to make moral decisions

These criteria are ways of thinking, answers to questions, means of social cohesion, solutions to problems, and sources of narratives. They refer explicitly and implicitly to ideas and beliefs, narratives and texts, practices and rituals, convictions and longings. They presume the meaningfulness and possibility of something ultimate and fundamental, of the fate and meaning of human life, of evil and happiness, of spiritual discernment and life problems, of cosmological frameworks and moral visions. They stress the value of obligation and responsibility, of healing and liberation, of social stability and transformation, of personal self-cultivation and courageous moral decisions. *Religious philosophy deals with all of these aspects of religion.* This is one way to measure the scope of religious philosophy.

Styles of Inquiry

Another way to measure the scope of religious philosophy is to consider the styles of inquiry relevant to understanding such diverse aspects of religion. Of course, human beings narrate sacred stories, which focus devotion in life-changing ways. We can compose religious music, which brings insight to the religiously sensitive. Even simple actions can express understanding of religious matters. My interest here, however, is specifically in gaining understanding through inquiry, and it is solely this interest rather than neglect or depreciation of alternative ways of creating religious understanding that explains the limitation of focus in what follows. At least the following styles of religious-philosophical inquiry are relevant:

- Phenomenological: When religious philosophy turns its attention to religious phenomena (for example, mystical experience), careful description that strives for objectivity—in the sense of registering what is important about the phenomena at the right places in the description of it—is the starting point for inquiry.

- Comparative: When religious philosophy organizes resources from multiple religious traditions simultaneously (for example, compiling religious ideas of ultimate realities), it must work comparatively—tracking similarities and differences, and being alert to and taking responsibility for the categories guiding comparison.

- Historical: When religious philosophy needs to trace the development of an idea across eras and its causal connections across traditions (for example, the idea of fate), it must work historically—drawing attention to episodes of change, periods of continuity, and patterns of influence in relation to particular contexts and pressures.

- Analytical: When religious philosophy seeks to identify the important features of a religious idea or argument (for example, arguments for the existence of a divine being), it must work analytically—drawing out key concepts, logical moves, and implications.

- Literary: When religious philosophy seeks to indicate rather than theorize about what makes a religious phenomenon important (for example, the futility of resisting finitude and death), it must embrace the freedom and grace of literary testimony—portraying significance in ways that capture the imagination, produce insight, and nurture understanding nontheoretically.

- Theoretical: When religious philosophy seeks a comprehensive understanding of an aspect of religion (for example, religious art), it must construct multidisciplinary philosophical theories that cover the relevant phenomena, meaningfully connect to neighboring phenomena (for example, in the way that art connects to cognitive-emotional capacities for aesthetic appreciation), and strive for coherence and elegance.

- Evaluative: When religious philosophy seeks to evaluate answers to the big questions of religion (for example, the meaning of life), it must assemble competing constructive theories pertinent to the big question and try to detect the superior candidate(s) through arguments about both the premises of competitor theories and criteria used to claim theoretical superiority.

In the first three of these styles, religious philosophy overlaps with phenomenology of religion, comparative religion, and history of religion, respectively. In the last four cases, religious philosophy exhibits a complex array of overlaps with philosophy, theology, and literature. What distinguishes religious philosophy's approach to a religious phenomenon from allied approaches with shared territory?

Overlaps and Distinctiveness

Consider the first three styles of religious-philosophical inquiry. How do phenomenology of religion's descriptions of priestly garments, comparative religion's approach to the use of food in religious rituals, or history of religion's reconstructions of the historical Buddha differ from the approach of religious philosophy to the same topics? Phenomenological description, comparative organization, and historical work collectively and often collaboratively stabilize a concept of the phenomenon in question, making it available in its rich variations and profound dimensions for further philosophical reflection. After that, analytical, literary, theoretical, and evaluative styles of religious philosophy make and defend claims about what is significant about the phenomenon.

While phenomenology of religion aspires to describe in a value-neutral way, religious philosophy asks the very natural "so what" questions about neutral descriptions of religious phenomena, seeking to interpret what is important for religion about them. Similarly, while comparative religion organizes the data of religious practices and ideas based on similarities and differences, religious philosophy asks about the significance of the categories expressed in the underlying judgments of similarity and difference for understanding religion and the world in which religion comes to be. Again, history of religions tracks development of religious ideas and practices and patterns of influence among them, offering interpretations of the contextual factors relevant to formation, change, and continuity. Religious philosophy goes further to ask once again about the significance of such historical interpretations for a broader understanding of religion and reality.

If the distinction between phenomenology of religion, comparative religion, and history of religion on the one hand, and religious philosophy on the other, really is this sharp, then the list above of seven styles of religious philosophy seems to beg for the exclusion of its first three items. But religious philosophy does not merely borrow phenomenological, comparative, and historical results from other parts of religious studies, after which it gets down to its native business. Rather, the intention to discover what is important and true and valuable in a religious phenomenon conditions phenomenological, comparative, and historical work from the outset. This is why the list must include phenomenological, comparative, and historical styles of inquiry.

For instance, religious philosophy directs phenomenological description to some features of a religious phenomenon rather than others, based on the focus of inquiry. It is important to correct for the resulting limitations in descriptive efforts. But it is even more important to recognize that this sort of focusing of attention is ubiquitous in phenomenological work, and that this is so in practice even if Edmund Husserl was correct in theory that absolute objectivity can be achieved in a finite time through disciplined application of his phenomenological method (and I suspect he was overly optimistic about that). The objective aspirations of religious philosophy do not eliminate the focusing of descriptive attention but rather seek clearly to acknowledge it and to incorporate procedures for noticing when it has biasing side effects. Much the same can be said of religious philosophy's relation to comparative religion and the history of religion.

Now consider the latter four styles of religious philosophy. Some of these seem more obviously philosophical but the question about overlapping territories also applies here. How does a theological presentation of divine reality or a literary portrayal of joy in simple acts of kindness differ from the approach that religious philosophy would take to the same topics? The answer to this question depends on the details of each style of religious philosophy, and I will consider each in turn.

First, the analytical style of religious philosophy uses the same set of tools and approaches as philosophical analysis generally. The difference is primarily the subject matter. Of course, particular subject matters may require new tools and new sensitivities. For example, it would be useless for religious philosophy's understanding of a mystical text if the analyst approached the topic treating paradoxical statements as silly mistakes on the part of the author of the mystical text. Moreover, the speech acts in a mystical text require special analysis, forcing the religious philosopher to extend in various ways the speech act theory extant in Western philosophical analysis. Nevertheless, the intention of religious philosophy in the style of analysis is the same as in all philosophical analysis: to clarify understanding of a subject matter through identifying structures and patterns, conceptual meanings and logical relations.

Second, the literary style of religious philosophy eschews analysis and theory for the sake of fidelity of description, clarity of testimony, and force of influence. In this mode of inquiry, religious philosophy can be almost indistinguishable from religious literature of other kinds. Yet the aim of inquiry—widening and deepening the understanding of a religious subject matter—defines the rhetorical interests of religious philosophy in the literary mode. The aim is not merely literary fun or vivid description or savage critique; inquiry is part of the point. In particular, literary approaches are crucial for elaborating the hypotheses that play central roles for any process of inquiry within religious philosophy. This is a significant literary limitation and a burden for the religious philosopher. Within the scope of an inquiring literary intention, however, religious philosophy in the literary style is pleasantly tangled with many other kinds of religious philosophy. Some of the most sublime works of religious philosophy have been in the literary style, including the part of the *Mahābhārata* we call the *Bhagavad-gītā*, the famous little *Dhammapada*, most of the Chinese Classics, and many parts of the Qur'an and the Bible. One cannot rationally set out to write a religious classic, of course, but this array of examples demonstrates the reason why religious philosophy in a literary style has been and continues to be important.

Third, the theoretical style of religious philosophy is similar to theory building in every sphere of human knowledge. The point of a theory is to systematize understanding of a subject matter by constructing an intellectual model of it that registers as many aspects of the subject matter as possible and represents them in the model so as to make clear the importance they actually have in the subject matter. Alfred North Whitehead's criteria for success in theory construction apply to the task regardless of the topic: consistency (logical clarity), coherence (systematic integrity), applicability (comprehensive relevance), and adequacy (registering importance correctly).[2] While Whitehead referred adequacy chiefly to empirical accuracy, in my usage it is a cluster of classes of criteria. Within it, there are aesthetic criteria (virtues of comprehensiveness, style, beauty, elegance, economy, and the like), pragmatic criteria (used to evaluate practical consequences), dialectical criteria (expressing how to detect advantages within a process of systematic comparison), and criteria of judgment (pertaining to the balance in which all other criteria for adequacy are held).

This elaboration of Whitehead's criteria illustrates the complexity of all theory-building ventures—and especially in religious philosophy, within which more of these criteria are pertinent than in biochemical theories of protein assembly or economic theories of supply and demand or psychological theories of moral development in children. Of course, we bring diverse disciplinary perspectives to the task of building theories, and communication across disciplines is not easy. For example, a side effect of disciplinary specialization is that linguistic theories of human language development and neurological theories of the same subject have often been developed in isolation from one another. Ideally, religious philosophy's search for the best theory of religious language pays close attention to every disciplinary perspective on the same topic. But its interests include doing justice to language use in particular religious contexts, and this makes its theory-building effort distinctive even though it overlaps with and draws significantly from other disciplinary perspectives.

Fourth, the evaluative style of religious philosophy derives from the fact that there are many competing theories about almost every religious phenomenon. This pluralism of theories calls for evaluation, where possible. It is common to evaluate competing theories in the natural sciences, the social sciences, and the humanities. In religious philosophy, however, the number of serious competitor theories is often rather large and the best way to evaluate them can be difficult to discern. Whether evaluation is even worth the effort is sometimes also quite unclear.

This activity of religious philosophy overlaps most fully with some implementations of philosophical theology, with which it shares the burden of working philosophically on theological materials. Religious philosophy's demand for multidisciplinary comparative inquiry, however, distinguishes it from many kinds of philosophical theology. One might think of religious philosophy in the evaluative style as a rarely encountered subspecies of philosophical theology, but this probably brings more confusion than illumination due to the diverse extant understandings of philosophical theology.

The use of "evaluative" to describe this style of religious philosophy suggests an overlap with dogmatic theology, in which the truth about life's big questions is pronounced for the sake of clarifying historic identity, focusing living authority, and enhancing self-understanding within a religious tradition. This is an unfortunate resonance. *Evaluation refers not to dogmatic stipulation but to concern with arguments for and against competing theories.* Dogmatic theology, so understood, is one important kind of theological task but it is not a part of religious philosophy. Religious philosophy is concerned exclusively with inquiry, even at the cost of foregoing resources that make dogmatic theology a more tractable form of intellectual work—resources such as belief in authoritative revelation recorded in sacred texts or vested in religious authorities and traditions. In refusing such sources, religious philosophy in the evaluative style may make its task impossibly difficult, but so be it. If religious philosophy cannot discover the best theory of a religious subject matter using the resources to which it limits itself—resources available to any inquiring mind regardless of religious affiliation or interest, and requiring only long training to develop the appropriate sensitivities and competencies—then it must return a null result.

For example, there are many theories of ultimate reality, including several within each major religious tradition. Where dogmatic theology's only obligation is to articulate one of these rationally and persuasively for a religious community to claim as its own, religious philosophy's evaluative task is to consider all of them across religious traditions and sub-traditions—comparing them, discovering or creating categories that make dialectical exchange between them possible, arguing over their premises, deciding whether judgments of superiority are possible, and exposing to scrutiny the criteria that guide such judgments.

The latter four styles of religious philosophy do overlap with other intellectual ventures but they remain distinctive tasks. These four styles of religious philosophy are also clearly distinguishable among themselves. In fact, this point requires further reflection.

Passivity and Audaciousness

Once the phenomenological, comparative, and historical moments of religious philosophy have stabilized a concept of a religious subject matter for inquiry, the latter four tasks of religious philosophy make their contributions, potentially all of them in complementary ways. On the scale of intellectual novelty, in the sense of producing new knowledge rather than redescribing knowledge we already have in hand, the analytical style is the most passive and the evaluative style the most audacious—with the literary and theoretical styles somewhere in between. The contrast between the analytical and evaluative styles is particularly interesting in this respect. These correspond to more and less scrupulously ascetic modes of inquiry in religious philosophy. Analysis aims to talk perceptively about religious topics, including possibly the big questions of religion, while evaluative approaches venture answers to those big questions. The analytical approach is often reduced to hinting as its way of showing the religious significance of the subject matter under scrutiny. The evaluative approach shares the problems of big-question philosophy discussed in Chapter 1.

Consider an example. Having traced the idea of "religious genius" through history and across traditions, and having described important instances of the idea with great precision and sensitivity, a religious philosopher seeks to say as clearly as possible what religious genius is, what are its causes and influences, why it is accompanied by a broad range of cultural and religious interpretations, and what leads to those interpretations rather than others. This can be done in minimalist fashion in the mode of analysis. Once that is done, however, the religious philosopher has a choice to end inquiry with clear-headed analytical observations on these issues or to press further.

One option (the literary style) is to present, and test the coherence of, insights into the religious significance of religious genius in an engaging and illuminating literary style—perhaps in the form of a meditation, a series of insightful reflections, or a story about religious genius. Another option (the theoretical style) is to build a multidisciplinary theory of religious genius—drawing on cognitive science, developmental psychology, the sociology of authority, the epidemiology of representations, mimesis theory, and historical exemplars. Yet another option (the evaluative style) is to consider all theories of religious genius at once, placing them alongside one another for the sake of comparison and debate, in which the premises of each are exposed to scrutiny and the criteria for theoretical superiority are clearly visible for all to see and dispute, and then if possible arguing for the best interpretation of religious genius.

In any one of these ways of moving beyond analysis, religious philosophy asks about the significance of religious genius so analyzed for big questions of religion such as salvation, liberation, social transformation, and even the character of ultimacy. The literary style insightfully articulates a hypothesis; the theoretical style elaborates that hypothesis in great detail in relation to allied disciplines and data; and the evaluative style decides between those theories, where possible. There is no difficulty holding these styles together, nor is there any problem with keeping even the most audacious styles of religious philosophy in meaningful interaction with the more cautious exertions of phenomenological, historical, and comparative work. Where problems arise, it is normally due to transient local community stipulations about what counts as legitimate intellectual work—for example, when historians or conceptual analysts refuse to countenance constructive theory building or evaluation of theories—not to any intrinsic contradictions among the styles of religious philosophy.

I argued earlier that there can be no principled objection to audacious attempts to evaluate theories about religious subject matters, and gave reasons why we should look with renewed favor upon the prospects of religious philosophy as multidisciplinary comparative inquiry. Those arguments apply here in that they limit attempts to block the more intellectually aggressive (literary, theoretical, evaluative) forms of inquiry within religious philosophy. As before, however, much creative and determined work has to be done in each case in order to make any progress at all. It is a large undertaking to ask about the ultimate meaning and value of anything, whether it is religious genius or ultimacy itself. So there is no guarantee of success at the outset, as there can be for the more constrained task of analysis, and also for the expository and proclamatory task of dogmatic theology.

Contexts of Religious Philosophy

Each of the seven styles of religious philosophy—phenomenological, comparative, historical, analytical, literary, theoretical, and evaluative—takes shape under the influence of distinctive conceptual frameworks and socio-historical circumstances. Within any given style of religious philosophy, no single conceptual framework appears to have a decisive advantage over the others in all contexts of inquiry. But certain specialized tasks within religious philosophy are better suited to some conceptual frameworks than others. The role of context in determining framework superiority suggests that the various conceptual frameworks have developed in the presence of distinguishable interests and purposes. These interests and corresponding contexts and frameworks of inquiry remain perpetually relevant within religious philosophy. Rather than being defeaters of human reason, interests and contexts and frameworks function as power sources for conducting rational inquiry in all fields, including religious philosophy.

The Role of Contexts

Foundationalist approaches to religious knowledge have been and remain committed to such perfection of confidence that those who accept such an approach to inquiry should feel no shadow of doubt as to the truth of its deliverances. The most efficient way to create doubt in the mind of a philosopher confident in a putatively indubitable theoretical model is to present a similarly convincing alternative theoretical model of the same subject matter. This draws attention to the fact that the philosopher's heretofore favored model silently draws power from unnoticed contextual features in the form of socio-historical conditions or conceptual frameworks that confer indubitability where none may be warranted. Acknowledging these contextual features of our theoretical modeling efforts throws the relativizing cat among the foundationalist pigeons, and threatens to make truth subject to one or all of the various cages in which philosophers operate: culture, socio-historical context, and conceptual framework.

This is an old, old story by now and one of the reasons that foundationalist epistemology has been abandoned by many philosophers as a vain ideal, to be replaced by one or another form of fallibilism. This story is also one of the pressures driving philosophy toward historical or logical analysis, which can accommodate the contextual features of human inquiry, and away from the grander ventures (what I am calling big-question philosophical questions) that dominate the philosophical classics. This shift in the focus of philosophical effort is understandable. No intellectual enjoys being exposed as an enthusiastic fool, giving unconditional assent to theories that turn out to profit from silent premises, whose credibility competitor theories effortlessly challenge.

I suspect that the move to contract the scope of philosophy is more needlessly ascetic than appealingly modest, and betrays a hankering for the good old days of foundationalist excitement. Back then, arguments were *real arguments* and their premises were *real premises*; philosophical reasoning held the promise of *discovery* and philosophical debate was *purposeful*. But now many philosophers believe that these simple intellectual joys were illusory and, embarrassed at their discipline's slowness to notice this and because of their own disappointment about it, most have sworn not to indulge in the grander forms of philosophical adventure. Instead, they embrace the dubious virtue of self-regulation, confining themselves to analysis and critique befitting the contextual features of human reasoning, and not venturing big-question theories that might prove mistaken.

But what precisely is wrong with philosophical mistakes? Only the philosopher who hankers after foundationalist comforts can be uninspired by the obvious fact that discovering mistakes can help to improve philosophical theories. There is plenty of scope for excitement in big-question philosophy when philosophical theories are formulated hypothetically and explicitly seek correction. Correction is the very lifeblood of the body of fallibilist intellectual inquiry in a world that is not now and never was compatible with foundationalist pretensions.

In such an approach, inquiry's need for correction utterly changes the philosophical attitude to the contextual features of human reasoning. The foundationalist is disappointed by contextual factors and framework dependence in philosophical theory-building efforts, whereas the nonfoundationalist prizes those as sources of correction, which fuel rational advance. The nonfoundationalist fears not uncertainty or mistakes, but depletion of corrective resources, followed by the degeneration of inquiry into authority mongering. It may seem a long way off but the nonfoundationalist philosopher can imagine a world where cultural interaction and historical understanding have enriched to the point that it is difficult to find a philosophic other capable of powering criticism and improvement of philosophical theories. To the nonfoundationalist, that is a chilling vision presaging the final defeat of human efforts to bend the powers of reason toward acts of philosophical inquiry. For now, though, there is plenty of work to do and ample excitement in the doing of it. And the key to the excitement is the very same contextual character of human reasoning that triggers grief-stricken and needlessly ascetic self-denial in the incompletely reconstructed postfoundationalist philosopher.

This, I contend, defines the properly rational attitude to the roles that social contexts, historical locations, and conceptual frameworks play in philosophical inquiry. Nothing about this attitude settles the question of whether philosophical inquiries can get anywhere in the face of the stiff challenges that such contextual considerations pose. That is a matter for rational effort to settle through careful reasoning and social engineering, and it is much too early to draw definitive conclusions. But this does reframe the contextual features of human reason as welcome and needed, and that is a promising shift in perspective.

Contexts and the Styles of Religious Philosophy

In relation to the seven styles of religious philosophy, conceptual frameworks are obviously important. Phenomenological religious philosophy proceeds quite differently depending on guiding assumptions about accurate and fair description. Comparative religious philosophy presumes a theory of comparison, which is an enormously complex and controverted question. Religious philosophy in the historical mode operates within a maze of historiographical questions that may or may not have been settled in fully consistent ways. There is a variety of strategies for analysis, from logical formalization to conceptual clarification. Literary forms of religious philosophy have embraced a range of styles, from fiction to meditation, and from dialogue to autobiography, each with distinctive virtues and limitations. Theory building is pervasively affected by emphases on particular helper-disciplines and ruling criteria for theoretical adequacy. And of course evaluation, if it finally proves intractable, may be defeated by the role of contextual factors in making religious practices and ideas impossible to consider in a common evaluative framework.

Social and historical contexts are also crucial in all seven styles of religious philosophy. To illustrate, I briefly discuss an example from religious philosophy. Mystical experience has been philosophically important for many centuries in all literary cultures, even before William James' *Varieties of Religious Experience* catalyzed greater attention to the subject among philosophers and psychologists. Longstanding philosophical questions in this field of study include the following: whether the cognitions associated with mystical experiences yield reliable information about the worlds of nature and religious realities, whether the diverse types of mystical experiences can be interpreted together in a single theory, whether the significance of mystical experiences is expressible, whether the transformative potency of mystical experiences can be controlled and cultivated, and whether religious experiences are the same or different in various cultural and historical settings.

Most of these controversial issues have enjoyed a period of ascendancy in the Western philosophical study of mystical experiences, and this reflects the way that the distinctive interests of those working in the field shift with time. Reigning interests also vary with the cultural and religious environment: questions of techniques for cultivating mystical experiences and for systematizing mystical cognitions have dominated South Asian philosophical studies while epistemological questions have dominated Western philosophical studies.

The question of whether mystical experiences are the same or different in varied cultural, religious, and conceptual frameworks is particularly illuminating. A fascinating debate has been underway for a couple of decades in the Western philosophical literature on mystical experience that reflects contrasting approaches to the phenomenological and comparative styles of religious philosophy. On the one hand, proponents of the perennial philosophy and its variants and derivatives, such as Robert Forman and Huston Smith, have argued that scrupulous phenomenological description of mystical experiences—spanning diverse cultures, religions, eras, and conceptual frameworks—can and does disclose a shared core experience, which Forman calls the "pure consciousness event."[3] On the other hand, Steven Katz, Wayne Proudfoot, and other so-called "constructivists" have argued in relativized Kantian fashion that conceiving and speaking about all experience occurs relative to a conceptual framework and that there is no way to penetrate behind these frameworks to assess whether the categories used in phenomenological description and comparison refer to the same things.[4]

There is quite a bit at stake here for philosophical inquiry. W.T. Stace argued that exhibiting a common core for mystical experiences is a necessary condition for any claim that the cognitive content of religious experiences can be trusted (note: a necessary, not a sufficient condition).[5] Most on both sides of this debate agree with Stace. Forman thinks that this necessary condition can be met and that much more can be done through phenomenology and comparison of mystical experiences, enough to deliver reliable knowledge of religious realities. Katz thinks that the necessary condition cannot be met and so rates the cognitive dimensions of mystical experience as poor sources of knowledge, even though the fact of mystical experience remains an indispensable component in assessing the cultural and historic importance of religion.

With the stakes so high, it is important to grasp the reason for the disagreement. The difference turns out *not* to be about whether a relativized Kantian framework analysis of conceiving and speaking is required; Forman can allow this. Rather, Forman thinks that phenomenology can establish identity of culturally diverse mystical experiences through a kind of knowledge that Katz, Proudfoot, and other constructivists do not allow. Forman calls it "knowledge by identity" and treats it as a kind of nonsensory, nonintentional, reflective immediacy that is irreducible to either side of William James' distinction between "knowledge by acquaintance" and "knowledge-about." Forman thinks that this third sort of knowledge involves an immediacy of direct contact with consciousness that escapes the limitations of the cognitive framework that constructivists use to argue against the possibility of phenomenological detection of similarity across culturally and historically diverse mystical experiences.[6]

Chasing the fight back one further level, Forman relies on a mystical interpretation of consciousness to support his claims on behalf of knowledge by identity, whereas Katz relies on the ordinary physicalist account of consciousness that dominates the neurosciences. As a result, the underlying worldviews are quite different. Forman's is compatible with a monism of consciousness (among other possibilities) and allergic to physicalism; more or less the opposite applies to Katz. The corresponding motivations for engaging the debate differ—with Forman trying to make known the potential for human self-understanding through mysticism and Katz trying to urge what he sees as commonsense resistance to philosophical enthusiasm and behavioral excesses. Finally, the social environments of the two philosophers also differ: they go to different conferences, enjoy socializing with different kinds of people, read different books, and travel to different places. One social context supports a conceptual framework within which it makes sense to look for crosscultural commonality of mystical experiences, while the other supports a conceptual framework within which it makes sense to limit the study of mystical experiences to its psychological and historical effects.

At this point in the diagnosis, some would conclude that there is no way to press any further; we simply need to pick a side or else avoid the debate entirely. Such interpreters would see this dispute as evidence for their claim that many debates in religious philosophy are intractable, and thus for the futility of inquiry aimed at resolving them. But it is also possible to see the context-based disagreement as offering precisely the sort of tension needed to refine hypotheses about the cause and significance of mystical experience. If functional imaging studies of the brain or neurological lesion studies eventually permit correlations to be established with categories used in phenomenological description and comparison, there might emerge a stable set of comparative phenomenological categories that would make the problem tractable in a way that it is not at present. None of that will be simple. But the contextual features of the disagreement between the pure-experience and constructivist views will help rather than hinder multidisciplinary comparative inquiry, when its time comes.

Traditions of Religious Philosophy

Religious philosophy historically has relied on a variety of distinguishable conceptual frameworks for structure and guidance. Most of these conceptual frameworks have developed into substantial traditions of debate in their own right, often

with parallels across cultures. All such traditions improve the prospects for advancing debate in religious philosophy by stabilizing specialized terminology for carefully refined concepts and by encoding the enabling wisdom of past experience in the constraints of traditional philosophic practice. These conceptual frameworks have special fields of application and are not universally useful. Moreover, they have produced insights that are not completely consistent, from which it follows that religious philosophers should proceed carefully in order to avoid misjudging the strength of philosophical arguments.

Marshalling Corrective Resources in Traditions

Religious philosophy, especially in the theoretical and evaluative styles, often produces bold and controversial argumentation, because it aims to detect the most accurate and profound theories about ultimate religious matters without the aid of information purportedly contained in religious traditions of revelation. Many philosophers believe such matters lie beyond the reach of human reason altogether, as I have noted, but a nonfoundationalist, fallibilist approach gives wide latitude for philosophical experimentation, even on the most profound theological questions. The pertinent question is not the a priori possibility of such reflection, which cannot be known in advance, but rather the fruitfulness of the venture as it unfolds. Conjectures about a priori possibility may well contribute to judgments about whether investments of time and resources are worthwhile, as university administrators would be quick to point out. But actual fruitfulness is philosophically more important.

Fruitfulness depends on the degree to which inquiry can be organized in such a way that with time philosophical hypotheses about religious matters can be improved through finding and activating sources of correction. If insufficient sources of correction exist, then the venture of evaluative religious philosophy will be largely speculative and thus chiefly of aesthetic and practical value—much like literature, though with a different kind of rooting in the varied worlds of human experience. If sources of correction do exist, and inquiry can be organized to take advantage of them, then the evaluative style of religious philosophy may also yield knowledge—knowledge, that is, in the sense of strongly warranted belief, which is what knowledge means in fallibilist, hypothetical interpretations of human reason.

This question about the existence of sources of correction sufficient to power such inquiries is a profound one. It can only be answered through trial and error, and provisional answers can only be trusted to the degree that there exist sound reasons to be confident in the organization of inquiry. After all, as the move from medieval natural philosophy to modern science showed, improving the social organization of inquiry may permit thinkers to gain access to sources of correction that lie unnoticed for centuries. (I return to the theme of the social organization of inquiries within religious philosophy in later chapters.) Thus, the question about sources of correction appears to be an ontological and epistemological one at first, but in fact also includes a large component of human imagination and social engineering.

This is the fundamental reason why religious philosophy gradually and reflexively developed distinguishable traditions of discourse and debate. It is within the constraints of such traditions that thinkers have the best chance of organizing inquiries that can take advantage of whatever sources of correction may exist. How does that work?

First, traditions of religious philosophy develop specialized discourses whose relatively precise and efficient terminology facilitates more and better work with less effort.

For example, there is a formidable array of technical distinctions and terminology used within South Asian philosophical traditions to describe various states of consciousness that are discernible by waking, dreaming, and meditating human beings. This discussion is initially almost impenetrable to Western philosophers, because it seems plagued by speculative distinctions that lack any basis in human experience. But a tradition of South Asian philosophers has cultivated through long effort both the phenomenological astuteness and the practical experience needed to stabilize such distinctions and terminology. When considered independently of its admittedly questionable interpretative metaphysical frameworks, this technical apparatus is extremely useful for the phenomenologist of consciousness and the philosopher alike. It permits a degree of discussion and observation that would be impossible otherwise, and in fact is routinely experienced as impossible by Western religious philosophers. By the same token, the post-Enlightenment suspicion of metaphysics has furnished a wealth of distinctions and arguments that are taken for granted in Western religious philosophy and would benefit South Asian philosophers attempting to give a plausible metaphysical account of the various levels and types of human consciousness.

Second, traditions of religious philosophy accumulate a great deal of wisdom and encode it in practices and working assumptions, which function as tested guides for subsequent inquiries in religious philosophy. This helps philosophers both to avoid needless errors already encountered by others in past efforts and also to focus attention efficiently on the most promising lines of investigation.

For example, the tradition of Catholic religious philosophy is relatively well defined in respect of its boundaries, the crossing of which is said to lead to no good. At its best, this is not an arbitrary imposition of authority for the sake of controlling troublemakers who might hurt the faithful through their cavalier arrogance, but rather the encoding of the memory of past disasters into guidelines that can protect the Catholic philosopher and enhance his or her contributions to the tradition. At its worst, it is something monstrous, and I will return to the problems of authoritarianism and rigidity presently. But in fact the history of Catholic philosophy suggests that those guidelines must be working to some degree. Despite its diversity, this tradition is more unified and focused than any other tradition of religious philosophy squarely rooted in a living branch of Christianity. Moreover, it is highly creative in most periods of Catholic history, including the present time. By contrast, the varieties of religious philosophy that took their rise from Protestant Christianity have gone in every imaginable direction, splintering into seemingly incommensurable sub-traditions, undermining each other, and often destroying the conditions for stable traditions that activate assets for inquiry. Creativity and innovation is extreme, but the work is too often repetitive and superficial for the want of traditional guidance.

Third, traditions of religious philosophy allow multiple experts to cooperate on the same problem, building on each other's results. Cooperation is one of the keys to effectiveness for all social tasks, of course, and probably the main adaptive evolutionary effect of the social capacities of human beings. In traditions of inquiry, cooperation allows groups of experts to undertake much larger, much longer, and far more complex inquiries than could ever be possible for a single philosopher working alone. This is most obvious in the natural and human sciences, but it is also true for traditions of religious philosophy.

For example, the question of the role of religion and ultimacy in a good society is a vast project with rich histories in East Asian, South Asian, and West Asian cultural arcs of religious philosophy. Though cooperation across cultural boundaries has been rare until recently, within each cultural tradition cooperation has been extensive. The large problem has been broken down into numerous sub-problems, which eventually spawned most of the various disciplines in the human sciences, with a fair degree of interdisciplinary cooperation even in the contemporary world's balkanized university contexts.

Fourth, traditions of religious philosophy promote agility in inquiry through group excitement about a recent trend that rapidly catalyzes attention and effort on the emerging problem area.

A recent example is the sudden shift within religious philosophy in the last two or three decades toward so-called "postmodernity." There is something trendy about this, which is attractive in itself to some philosophers. But the trend originated in the power of the fundamental insights of postmodernity—its compelling criticism of epistemic foundationalism and uncritical reification in God-talk, and its attractively modest way of looking for insights in the interstices of the language games and life worlds of human beings. The shift of attention within religious philosophy was almost effortless. It brought with it philosophical versions of the silliness that plagues all trendy phenomena but it also deeply and rapidly transformed the profile of energy expenditure within religious philosophy, which is the mark of agility in tradition.

Fifth, traditions of religious philosophy introduce a degree of conservatism in inquiry, which resists the hasty abandonment of a promising idea when it comes upon hard times, and promotes problem-solving strategies designed to protect the idea if at all possible.

For example, the religiously potent idea of mind-body dualism, which lies behind most South Asian theories of transmigration and most Western theories of immortality, has fallen on hard times. In the West, it always had an uneasy relationship with the idea of necessarily embodied souls, with its concomitant expectation of resurrection rather than immortality of the soul. In the South Asian context, Buddhism directly challenged the realistic Brahmanic ontology of the *jīva* (soul) with its *anātman* (no substantival self) doctrine, which completely changed the meaning of reincarnation. In both contexts, proponents of mind-body dualism had to learn to articulate their outlook in relation to competing and antagonistic ontologies, and interest in mind-body dualism has survived.

With the advent of modern medicine, the neurosciences, and an evolutionary account of mental abilities of animals and human beings, mind-body dualism faces another stiff challenge. These new theoretical frameworks seem to demand a physicalist account of soul, and enough philosophers take physicalism for granted that it is difficult even to get a hearing for mind-body dualism. Yet some religious philosophers fight back. Their philosophical-religious traditions' varied commitments to mind-body dualism draw their attention to the fallacies and casual oversights of physicalist accounts of soul. This in turn leads them to reexamine mind-body dualism for hidden virtues, and then to reconstruct it in a more plausible way relative to recent scientific discoveries. This is more or less what lies behind the dipolar ontologies of William James's radical empiricism and Alfred North Whitehead's process cosmology, and a variety of forms of panpsychism.[7] It also lies behind retrievals of classic Cartesian correlational mind-body dualisms, which persist within various branches of consciousness studies, the neurosciences, and a few corners of contemporary philosophy of mind.[8] The conservatism of tradition keeps potentially useful hypotheses alive and empowers them to swim against the dominant currents of religious philosophy.

The Stodginess of Philosophical Traditions

Traditions of any sort, including those within religious philosophy, can also become slaves to their own compact efficiency, after which they can fail to make needed adjustments. Or they can fall prey to corruption of the very social power needed to maintain structure and function within the tradition, after which they blindly stamp out criticism and innovation.

Some traditions of religious philosophy have done better in this regard than others. For example, the twentieth century saw an ideological battle within philosophy departments in many parts of the world played out over the careers of young philosophers and students of philosophy. In Western contexts, the battle was between Anglo-American analytical approaches and continental phenomenological and postmodern approaches. In the South Asian context, it was between the philosophical inheritance of British colonial power and traditional Indian philosophy. In the Chinese context, it was the Leninist and Maoist versions of the European creation of Marxist philosophy against traditional Confucian and Daoist philosophy. At this point, the energy powering this ugly philosophical infighting seems dissipated in the West—with a few pockets of hostility remaining, mostly among older philosophers who can't forget and forgive past wrongs. South and East Asian contexts remain complicated in this regard, partly because reclaiming local philosophical wisdom is entangled with the difficult task of coming to terms with the deeply ambiguous influence of colonial power, which embraces both the assets of modernity and the deficits of a temporary loss of cultural autonomy.

Another problem amply evident in traditions of religious philosophy is the awkward fact that the positive results and the most prized values of different traditions of inquiry do not always harmonize. At the level of philosophic style, literary forms of religious philosophy typically rate the renegade, convention-disrupting insight above the highly regulated and systematic insight so prized in theoretical forms of religious philosophy. At the level of content, numerous inquiries within religious philosophy have been subject to multiple approaches borne up by different philosophical traditions, and these inquiries have famously produced diametrically opposed results.

For example, the tradition of religious philosophy associated with the hypothesis of classical Christian theism continues to defend a substantivist, personalist conception of God as an omnipotent, omniscient, omnipresent, infinite, intentional, aware, and active divine being. Meanwhile, postmodern religious philosophy tends to refuse this conception of God as anthropomorphic, morally dubious, in thrall to mythology, and covertly biased in favor of the perceived needs of living religious traditions. There are extremely intelligent people on both sides with rather a lot in common, yet they routinely dismiss one another's perspectives without thorough consideration. This situation stands as a stern warning to religious philosophers to make sure they peer out of their local tradition-caves from time to time in order to avoid intellectually embarrassing parochialism. This is also why religious philosophy must be a comparative venture as well as an interdisciplinary form of philosophical inquiry.

Chapter 3

Religious Philosophy, Modernity, and Postmodernity

Having called attention to the theme several times in previous chapters, it is important now to consider in more detail how religious philosophy relates to debates about modernity and postmodernity within Western intellectual life. This involves discussing the rise and demise of epistemological foundationalism and what is involved in conceiving religious philosophy in hypothetical, fallibilist terms. It also requires addressing two clusters of issues: one about generality, abstraction, and universality; and the other about truth, reality, and empirical fidelity. Finally, it involves addressing the positive impact of postmodern thought on contemporary religious philosophy.

The Successes and Failures of Modern Epistemology

Epistemic foundationalism in modern Western philosophy was a creative attempt to increase confidence in the findings of human reason and to eliminate the oppressive influence of arbitrary authority. In context, it was largely successful, despite the fact that its pretensions to certainty were overblown. Contemporary religious philosophers can learn a lot from it even as they criticize it. Modernity produced both the foundationalist epistemological project and its criticism. The shortcomings of foundationalist epistemology were recognized as soon as the foundationalist philosophical project was invented, and modern philosophy already includes a steady stream of nonfoundationalist, holist, fallibilist, biosocial theories of knowledge. Various contemporary forms of postfoundationalist epistemology address the need to move beyond the limitations

of foundationalist epistemology, while avoiding the relativistic chaos of refusing all standards for knowledge.

Modernity

Early modernity and especially the Enlightenment marked an exciting period in the perennial Western philosophical search for an understanding of rationality. It is too easy, however correct, to attack this excitement for naïve hubris. Indeed, many cheap philosophical points have been scored in just this way in recent years. But it is important also to notice the reasons modern philosophers believed it had become possible for them to advance beyond medieval philosophy's view of rationality as artful judgment within an overarching theological framework that rooted human reason in the Logos structure of divinely created reality.

Confidence is always desirable for creatures prone to worry—people with the capacity to imagine alternative scenarios and who constantly confront conflicting opinions on issues that profoundly affect happiness and safety. But the maximal confidence of certainty was not the overriding goal in the Middle Ages that it was to become in the seventeenth century. In the medieval Western context, the pervasive assumptions about human rationality were that even its most confident product was dependent on divine creation (which established harmony between human thought and the knowable world) and subject to divine revelation (which established knowledge of the otherwise unknowable world and trumped speculation about this world).

Ideally, reason harmonizes perfectly with revelation. How was this harmony conceived? In principle, human reason can range broadly across many questions and subjects, yet not with equal confidence or competence. When reason is strongest, producing agreement among experts, revealed truth is happily in perfect harmony. When reason struggles to produce consensus, revelation lights the way with its dispute-resolving power. In theological matters, particularly, the speculative exercise of human rationality was always a kind of incursion into territory where revelation had the final word, through the divinely established authority of the Christian church.

This was a sensible and practical arrangement. It defined basic rules for understanding how human rational activity both connected and failed to connect with the created world. For example, mathematicians could produce proofs in geometry, thus disclosing the basic Logos structure of reality, which always lay beneath the surface of ordinary reality just waiting for reason to discover it. But theologians could only prove the existence of God; they could not deduce from nature or reason unaided by revelation much of importance about the divine nature. This arrangement also provided basic rules for supporting reasonably clear distinctions among social institutions and activities. For example, human rationality could not penetrate politics and economics to any great degree so it needed to defer to, and operate within, the divinely ordained social arrangements of Christendom, with its class hierarchies and significant merging of political and religious authority.

Early modern science and the mathematics that facilitated it appeared to change the rules about the proper domains of operation of human reason. René Descartes famously dreamed of a metaphysics that would extend the (supposedly) apodictic certainty of mathematics to the knowledge of natural, human, and divine realities. The new possibility of such certain knowledge may still depend on God, in some remotely ultimate sense, but proximately reason could operate sure-footedly in domains that, until this time, had been subject to the confusions of endless speculation and intractable disagreement. The key was to find in physics, psychology, and metaphysics the correlates of the axioms of mathematics.

Descartes believed that axiomatic "clear and distinct ideas" could be discovered through a kind of disciplined meditative process that attempted to doubt everything. When in this process the corrosive powers of doubt fail, the metaphysician will have discovered an idea that possesses the same gleaming certainty that Euclid's axioms of geometry inspired in the mathematician of that time. Once the metaphysician assembled enough clear and distinct ideas, these ideas could function as axioms in a deductive system of knowledge that reaches far beyond mathematics to account for human reason itself, for the existence and goodness of God, and for the reality of a world outside the human mind. Indeed, this was the purpose of Descartes' *Meditations* and, in his judgment and in the judgment of many others, its achievement.

Modern Epistemology in Context

This introspective approach to metaphysics was incredibly compelling at the time and only a stubborn refusal to appreciate contextual factors in philosophy would harp on its shortcomings. It would turn out that identifying clear and distinct ideas was much more difficult than Descartes suspected, that the logical import of axioms for metaphysical systems was unremittingly vague, and that even the mathematical-axiomatic model for the whole enterprise was fatally flawed. Yet modernity's epistemological infatuation with certainty, with foundationalism, and with the universal relevance of decontextualized philosophical argumentation was born in this grand adventure.

Of course, these epistemological virtues (or vices) were not new in themselves. It was the infatuation with them and the optimistic faith in their capacity to bring valuable knowledge that was new. This infatuation lasted a long time and, in many ways, persists even today—which is to say, even after the rediscovery of rationality as an act of judgment that expresses a particular perspective and inherent interests, that has political and economic contexts and effects, and that helps human beings dynamically adjust to a complex natural and social environment. In fact, it was surely in part the political promise of loosening the authoritarian grip of religious institutions that made strong claims for reason's autonomy so compelling, even among profoundly religious philosophers.

The overthrow of medieval assumptions about rationality was a civilization-transforming event. It was entangled with the birth of nation-states and partially managed economies, the birth of new social institutions that brought widespread education and made participatory democracy thinkable, the birth of modern science with its technological fruits, and the birth of modern medicine with its astonishing efficacy. There are several hallowed iconic stories of this change whose repetition serves to legitimate it: Galileo's run-in with the Church allegedly over the organization of the solar system, Newton's apple and the invention of the theory of gravity, and the key axiom of Descartes' metaphysics, "I think therefore I am." Each icon is an historical caricature, of course, but even this testifies to the importance both of the change and of our struggle to understand it.

The change is impressive. Whatever causes or enables or makes use of this transformation will have the cultural prestige in modern societies that was reserved for the Church in medieval Christendom. The most prominent recipient of the prestigious mantle of cultural authority is modern science, and especially the natural sciences, which epitomize the rational in modernity. Science is a cooperative venture that produces theories capable of winning unprecedented crosscultural agreement, that seeks out its mistakes and corrects its theories as needed, that makes exciting discoveries about the natural and human worlds, that inspires life-changing technological marvels from electricity to blood transfusions, and that effectively resists the arbitrary imposition of political and religious authority.

It turns out, of course, that philosophers and scientists alike overreached in their claims for modern science. We have discovered through the philosophy of science and through experience that theory choice in the sciences is a prodigiously complex social process with uncertain rational standing, that the boundaries between science and other rational enterprises are quite blurred, and that the technological products of science are sometimes pernicious. Yet none of that completely overturns the significance of modernity for understanding rationality.

Modernity has delivered on its claims for rationality in science, and in a host of other areas, in a stunning way. We should pay attention to its lessons. Modernity teaches us that medieval philosophy greatly underestimated the power of human reason and seriously overestimated the power of religious authority to trump it in the name of divine revelation. Modernity teaches us that carefully delimited inquiries capable of winning crosscultural agreement are possible—though apparently only in some domains, and to that extent there is great value in seeking general formulations of our theories about nature and human beings, including crosscultural and transhistorical formulations. Modernity teaches us that, despite our foundational and universal aspirations, even the best theories—in science as in other forms of inquiry—are always subject to revision, and we must seek out their own flaws in a ceaseless quest for refinement. Modernity teaches us that we are wise to be suspicious of the arbitrary imposition of religious and political authority and that nothing can extinguish the simple candle of truth no matter how violent the attack.

In the final analysis, modernity did not completely overthrow the insights of the Middle Ages into human nature and rationality, though it introduced many new insights that challenge certain medieval assumptions about human nature. In our own thinking about human reason, we do well to interpret the novel lessons of modernity, just summarized, as creative modifications of the robust medieval insight—that rationality is an act of judgment expressing particular perspectives and inherent interests, manifesting political and economic contexts and effects, and facilitating dynamic adjustment to complex natural and social environments.

Rediscovering Postfoundationalism

One of the categories often used to diagnose the failures of modern epistemology is epistemic foundationalism: supposedly, modernism affirms it and critics of modern epistemology reject it. What we need, supposedly, is a third epistemological path that rejects both the futile modern quest for certain foundations and the equally self-defeating refusal of foundational theorizing. A number of religious philosophers have proposed epistemologies answering this description and commended them to other religious philosophers. For example, Wentzel van Huyssteen articulates a postfoundationalist epistemology, and Nancey Murphy a holist epistemology. Both aim to provide relief from a fruitless flight between unsatisfactory alternatives.[1]

Van Huyssteen argues that modernist foundationalism mistakenly supposes that certainty, objectivity, and universality are the marks of rationality, after which many sorts of religious philosophy and theology appear to be thoroughly irrational activities. Meanwhile, extreme forms of antifoundationalism are skeptical of every universal claim, including criteria for distinguishing better from worse in any domain of rational activity, after which many forms of religious philosophy and theology are cast into the outer darkness of utter relativism. Between these two extremes lies a third option, according to van Huyssteen: postfoundationalism. His postfoundationalist account of rationality is sensitive to the terrible way certainty, objectivity, and universality can function as powerful clubs to suppress unwanted and politically awkward viewpoints, particularly those of socially and economically oppressed portions of humanity, whose very survival requires challenging the status quo. It also shares modernism's interest in taking account of the success of the natural sciences. Yet it does this without supposing rationality is either a matter of epistemically certain universality or a self-deceptive struggle against the strangulation of unlimited relativism.

Murphy argues that modern philosophy has doomed religious philosophy to futility because of its unsatisfactory approach to knowledge, language, and causation. The resulting distress and despair bifurcates Western religions into liberal and conservative camps, which busy themselves with fighting each other rather than questioning the mistaken inherited assumptions that they share. She suggests that postmodern insights into holism in knowledge, language, and causation offer a way beyond this impasse. Murphy uses "postmodernism" in a much narrower way than most authors, referring primarily to holism as against foundationalism, especially in epistemology. In fact, Murphy's postmodernism is more or less the same as van Huyssteen's postfoundationalism; van Huyssteen allows "postmodernism" a far broader semantic range to reflect its usage in a wide range of literature.

It is easy to appreciate the resolution of a futile debate. And van Huyssteen and Murphy make good suggestions that religious philosophers should consider seriously. But they remain strangely silent about the very important fact that nonfoundationalism was an early modern discovery. In fact, almost as soon as it was conceived, foundationalism was recognized as a tempting but impossible dream by a steady stream of thoughtful philosophers. The early modern philosopher David Hume was already a postfoundationalist in something like van Huyssteen's sense—rejecting the possibility or value of definite foundations for human knowledge, speaking freely of habits of association and interpretation and judgment, and situating human rationality in a biological, historical, cultural framework. The late nineteenth-century American pragmatists Charles Peirce and John Dewey were self-consciously holist in their epistemologies in something like Murphy's sense—expounding a biological, historical, and cultural framework for understanding rationality that incorporated evolutionary theory, affirmed the fallible and hypothetical character of all theorizing, and prized correction of hypotheses in processes of inquiry.

This stream of nonfoundationalist philosophers was inspired by sound ancient and medieval wisdom about human rationality, in relation to which modernist enthusiasm for certainty always seemed, well, enthusiastic. In the final analysis, just as van Huyssteen's postfoundationalism and Murphy's holism are restatements of long-established responses to modernist pretensions, so reading the modern-postmodern debate in terms of epistemic foundationalism does not reach deeply enough into the disagreement. With that, then, I turn to a discussion of postmodern criticism and its implications for understanding human nature and reason.

The Successes and Failures of Postmodern Criticism

Ideologically sensitive critical interpretation within modern Western philosophy was a creative attempt to correct the context blindness of intellectual analysis of ideas and their social importance, and thereby to diagnose and rise above the oppressive influence of authorities exhibiting distorted visions of, or no genuine interest in, human well-being. In context, it was largely successful, despite the fact that its suspicion of ideology was insufficiently discriminating. Contemporary religious philosophers can learn a lot from it, even as they criticize it. Modern Western powers made use of colonial expansion and cultural imperialism to advance their own interests but modernity also produced the potent critiques of such practices that still inspire postmodern criticism. For religious philosophers to achieve a balanced view of human reason, they need to overcome the shame that haunts postmodernity without any

evasion of the fact that religious ideas are cultural artifacts with powerful political and cultural side effects.

Postmodernity

Like nonfoundationalist epistemology, ideological criticism in the peculiarly intense and far-reaching form we know was a modern invention, and can and should be traced to the beginning of modern philosophy.[2] Indeed, the political elements in the motivation of early modern philosophers such as René Descartes and John Locke already expressed deep criticisms of ideology in the politics and cultural practices of their day, every bit as much as the more obvious criticisms of Voltaire. Anything that affects one's personal safety, country of residence, and means of income is a central focus of attention, for philosophers just as for any other person. The critical ideas that made early modern philosophers into political targets and forced them to relocate or align themselves with influential protectors caused trouble because they drew into open discussion ideologies that ruling elites prefer to keep hidden. Criticism surfaces ideological interests and provokes resistance. In many ways, this is the deepest political story of modernity, and thus the reason why using the name *postmodernity* to describe the locus of ideological criticism conveys a misleading caricature of the actual ideological life of modernity.

As the modern period unfolded, Western philosophy developed a multifaceted capacity for criticism—criticism of its own efforts at conceptual modeling and analysis, of principles guiding political and social organization, and of cultural products from science and technology that have since transformed the world. The largest single factor in the flourishing of ideological criticism and self-criticism was historical consciousness. By this, I mean the sharpening awareness of the commonsense intuition that ideas and values, people and societies, have historical and social contexts. In time, this intuition strengthened to the point that it became a persistent and pervasive feature of intellectual life—both the cause for celebration of intricate particularity of phenomena and the drive for digging beneath the pretensions of authority to manifest the contextual structures that actually make authority work in particular forms of social organization.

I call the basic form of historical consciousness a "commonsense" intuition because we rely on it all the time in our assessments of people and their motivations. We know people have contexts, and we train ourselves to recognize them in order both to take advantage of them and to protect ourselves from those who would take advantage of us. We routinely allow for people's backgrounds when we make decisions about how critical to be of their behavior and beliefs. Each of us derives both shame and pleasure from reflecting on the way we ourselves became the particular person that we are, forging an identity from the raw materials available in biology, social context, and life circumstances. When we encounter unfamiliar cultures and places, languages and races—and even when we become aware of something alien and impenetrable within someone we may know quite well—we call on contextual features of reality to explain how this otherness could feel so strange to us.

Notwithstanding some casual rhetoric to the contrary, the fact that historical consciousness is the sort of thing that can "arise" like an awakening giant, and thereafter massively influence philosophy and politics and society, is *certainly not due* to a sudden "emergence" of these commonsense intuitions about particularity and context. Everything we know historically and biologically indicates that the cognitive capability for awareness of context is a culturally universal feature of our species and has been present from the very beginning—indeed, primates display many of the same cognitive characteristics, which allow them to assess the motivations and interests of other individuals. Rather, the importance of historical consciousness for the birth of modern criticism arises from awareness of the power that hidden ideas possess *when they are encoded in social discourse and political relationships*.

For example, people narrate their own submission to authority, courtesy of stories told to them by others—by parents who want their children to fit in and be happy, and by ruling elites whose aspirations for social welfare as well as for personal power are well served by this dynamic. These stories often involve timeless interpretations of the origins of extant social practices and traditions, cosmological-religious frameworks that rationalize the status quo, and object lessons in the way that heeding threats and promises is good for you whereas noncompliance leads to chaos, misery, and untimely death. Historical consciousness unmasks this reflexive power dynamic simply by offering an alternative narration of the rise and fall of ruling elites—one in which ambition and greed play as large a role as compassion and good intentions, one that is neither timeless nor religiously and cosmologically rooted, and one that can be intelligently resisted both for personal gain and for the greater good. Historical consciousness draws its power, in other words, from telling a story that is compelling enough to compete for plausibility in people's imaginations with the received stories that social orders rely on for their stability and desirability.

Nothing is more subversive of a conventional story than a plausible retelling that makes all of the apparent facts line up differently than we learned. We see this in criminal court cases all the time, and it is routinely exploited in the formulas for television dramas about crime and justice. Historical story telling in its academic form adds the endearing quality that it postures at indifference to the effects of its narratives. After all, historians are committed to seeking out the truth in a scholarly haven, protected from political interference by a noble institution that prizes academic freedom.

The origins of so-called postmodern criticism lie in historical consciousness that manifests ideology by narrating it. Such narration lures into the open typically hidden but powerfully operative habits of mind, after which we can see them for what they are, and hopefully rationally decide what to do with them. This is fascinating and exciting and liberating all at once. But unmasking functional ideologies can also be profoundly disabling for individuals and societies alike. It can overwhelm people with awareness and responsibilities that they might rather were the problems of bold leaders willing to make momentous decisions on behalf of others. The French Revolution infamously drove home not only the dependence of elites on functional ideologies but also the value of ideological opacity for keeping everyone calm and avoiding the horror of social chaos. But some people have little to lose by provoking chaos because they have so little invested in the status quo, and thus ideological criticism naturally becomes the ally and leading tool of revolutionaries.

In its most familiar postmodern form, ideological criticism is not the intellectual engine of political revolutions so much as the tool of intellectuals who seek to unmask power transactions within cultural discourse, often on behalf of those whose identity and hopes have been written out of conventional identity narratives. So Camille Paglia retold the history of human sexuality in such a way as to make social conventions about sex seem no longer rooted in timeless natural law but rather arbitrary cultural constructions, which serve the interests of a homogenized majority insecure about the strange and varied sexual impulses that suffuse their lives.[3] Michel Foucault did something similar for insanity, the accumulation of knowledge, medical care, sexuality, prisons, and other topics, both ordinary and taboo.[4]

Postmodern or late-modern philosophers have taken this task of unmasking, or manifestation, in a more theoretical direction. After all, if ideology is so obviously dangerous, then it is vital to understand how it arises and functions, and thereby how to control it. Philosophers from Paul Ricoeur to Jacques Derrida and from Hans-Georg Gadamer to Jürgen Habermas have trained their critical and analytical powers on all forms of communication and interpretation, from writing and speech to advertising and media, theorizing about ideology in the process. In this way, discourse rather than politics became the native territory for ideological analysis.[5] Unsurprisingly, these philosophers discovered for the domain of discourse exactly what historians, political theorists, and cultural analysts discovered for ideology in social contexts—namely, that power is an intrinsic aspect of all facets of human life and that interpretation is always marked by interests.

This, it must be said, is not surprising. In fact, it is completely continuous with our everyday experience of people's motivations and interactions. Power and interestedness suffuse human relationships. Hidden motives and unconscious desires pervade acts of communication. We don't need Sigmund Freud to tell us this and we don't require Jacques Derrida's analyses of ideological discourse to make us aware of it either. What we all need help with is coming to terms with the *consequences* of these facts of human life, particularly after we become aware of how completely they penetrate all of our discourse and relationships. To know that human interactions are perpetually power laden and that interpretation is inevitably interested does not necessarily help us manage the problems for justice and human welfare that result. In particular, to regulate the effects of ideology and to take responsibility for its inevitability in human discourse and politics, we need to understand how ideological discourse arises and how it functions.

This is where thinkers from Freud and before to Derrida and beyond have proved so important for postmodern philosophy. They have shown us how we use ideas and even philosophy itself to mask the presence of powerful ideas, which remain undiagnosed but still operative beneath the surface—with their influence now buttressed by the very philosophical superstructure that might have been bent to its detection and criticism. This was an alarming discovery for intellectuals. It represents the historian not only as an innocent storyteller who narrates the truth regardless of its disruptive effects, but also as complicit in the protection of ideologies about which he or she may be completely unaware. Later historians will point out our historical blind spots. In the meantime, historians are left anxious because even their best work is deeply entangled in the ideological piloting and controlling of human social orders.

It is in this way that postmodern thinkers developed an extreme allergy to the more systematic forms of narration such as those evident in history and philosophy, political theory and theology. The more systematic the narration, the more powerful the ideas articulated in the narratives. This alarming species of late-modern awareness paralyzes theory-building ventures of all kinds and commends in their place an indirect kind of discourse. This type of discourse eschews systematic organization of thinking in favor of the theoretically unenforced insight that flits through consciousness without any distorting buttressing from theory. The literary styles arising thereby promise to be extremely valuable. Presumably, such literature will allow us to diagnose the presence of ideology in any theoretical venture without having to get our own hands dirty with the power of narratives and theories to structure imaginations.

Postmodern Criticism in Context

Despite these impressive gains in awareness and understanding, philosophical analysts of ideology in politics and discourse have been one-sided in several ways.

First, they ask the impossible and insist on the undesirable. The indirect play of postmodern philosophical thinking and writing, whether in application to religion or politics or any other topic, is far and away the most ascetic form of philosophy ever attempted. Hedged about with restrictions on what can be said and how it is to be said, this is a more ritualized form of discourse than the religious world of liturgy, and its priests strive for a purity of consciousness that even most religious ascetics recognize as essentially futile and self-deceptive. I will return to this issue in the next section, diagnosing the problem in terms of shame. For now, I note simply that this quest for purity of mind, innocence of motive, and cleanliness of hands is a deeply moving gesture toward our flawed human condition, in which we are fated to entangle ourselves in the unjust side effects of even our best intentions. Therefore, it is to be admired rather than mocked. But hopefully one does not have to become such a priestly savant oneself in order to think authentically and usefully toward the ends of goodness and beauty and truth.

Second, the postmodern philosophical analysts of ideology have tended to imbue ideology with a fundamentally negative valence. This is partly an inheritance of Marxist thought, but it produces a situation where ideology is something only one's political enemies have, and not the sort of thing one would willingly claim for oneself. The subsequent realization that all discourse is ideological makes this negative valence fundamentally disabling. In fact, ideology in the sense of a conceptual representation and rationalization of political practices is as useful as it is dangerous. And ideology in the sense of improperly diagnosed biases of interpretation or incompletely recognized power transactions in discourse is likewise a matter of useful efficiency as much as a threat to justice and honesty. We cannot expect ourselves to understand everything about our motivations and impulses; we could not get anything done if we had to be perfectly self-aware first. We have to manage what we don't recognize in ourselves through social mechanisms of education and correction. In the meantime, the coded frameworks of interpretation and meaning that we call ideologies are invaluable in helping us engage our social worlds constructively. Without partially hidden frameworks for orienting ourselves to the endless complexities of social life and politics, we have only painful exposure to the harsh light of more self-awareness than we can tolerate, producing paralysis and impotence. Thus, we need both partially submerged frameworks for social orientation and efficient mechanisms for correcting those frameworks when they produce undesirable or unjust effects.

Third, the postmodern philosophical analysts of ideology have tended to operate at too large a distance from the natural sciences, particularly neglecting evolutionary biology. This derives partly from a deeply ingrained suspicion of science as the ultimate master narrative—give it an opening in the conversation and it will take over completely, vitiating the claim of highly particular perspectives for a seat at the table of debate. But, if this very real danger can be managed—and surely it can—then it seems self-defeating to neglect the obviously useful resources offered by a biological account of human knowledge and social relationships. Even at the beginning of the nineteenth century, William James had showed that biological considerations are at least as useful as analytical psychological considerations in explaining human behavior, from the formation of habits to the structures of perception and cognition. Cutting biology out of the explanatory picture makes unintelligible both the structurally universal features of human cultures and the universality of ideological processes and interestedness in interpretation. This in turn leads to overestimating the degree of arbitrariness and irrationality in ideologically loaded social and interpersonal transactions, underestimating the degree to which power transactions penetrate every kind and level of discourse, and missing relevant strategies for management—strategies that become easier to identify in the presence of a biological framework of interpretation.

Fourth, the postmodern philosophical critics of ideology have represented their intellectual achievements as opposed to modernity.

This is probably true in a few relevant respects—and truest of all in respect to intensity of awareness about the pervasiveness and inescapability of ideology in politics and discourse. But mostly this sharp contrast perpetuates a deeply distorted reading of modern politics and philosophy. The result is a caricature of modernity as a vastly influential but ultimately morally corrupt and intellectually contrived master narrative about human individuality, technological control over nature, certainty, democracy, and capitalism. By narrating this as a disaster, postmodern cultural critics inevitably distance themselves from the sources of their own thought in modern philosophy and politics, and disguise the fact that ideological criticism was a modern creation every bit as much as nonfoundationalism in epistemology was.

Overcoming Shame

Postmodernity, and even the disagreement between modernity and postmodernity, is haunted by shame—over colonialism, over paternalism, over expansionist political and economic ideologies, over the ill-effects of consumption and consumerism, over the ecological and social disasters of technology, and over the ongoing failure to transform the world into the disease-free and hunger-free Shangri-La that the modern West pictured. There is plenty of guilt mixed in there; after all, there is no shortage of reasons for guilt about modern Western behavior. But shame pertains to one's deepest identity rather than to wrong behavior, and it is identity-related shame rather than guilt that drives the postmodern determination to live up to its critical and self-critical aspirations.

Unfortunately, as ordinary people well understand, being haunted by shame inhibits creative self-assertion. In postmodern philosophy, something similar obtains: it is easier to criticize and self-criticize, to mock savagely and to play ironically, than to take responsibility for the building, sustaining, and conceptual interpretation of civilization-sized projects. Every act of philosophical self-assertion, if not thoroughly self-critical, reeks of negative associations with the thinly rationalized ideologies of hated predecessor philosophies. The power of postmodern philosophy and critical theory to raise consciousness is second to none. But its power to produce large-scale, existentially orienting, and intellectually satisfying conceptual interpretations of the world we inhabit is sorely limited. That was modern philosophy's strong point, and the source of many ideological disasters, so it is no wonder creative and systematic theoretical interpretation has been arrested in postmodern philosophy. It is shame at work.

The haunting of shame will end—but not when we get our philosophy of human rationality straight, not when the Western world pays reparations for its colonialist adventures in slavery and exploitation, not when religion either goes away or reclaims its former control over human societies, not when the Western world finally imparts its life-transforming wisdom to the rest of the world, and certainly not when the Western world humbly withdraws into its own territory and leaves the rest of the world alone. Rather, the haunting will end when we listen to the non-Western world closely enough to realize not only that we have a lot to learn from other cultures but also that we actually strongly disagree with an enormous amount of what non-Western people do and believe—from worldviews to religion, from medical treatments to child-rearing practices, from politics to economics.

Shame abates in this case when the West notices its particularity, overcomes its embarrassment (as if it must hide the fact that most Western people actually prefer living the way they do), becomes comfortable with being what it is and can be, takes uncommon responsibility for its beliefs and practices, and articulates that respectfully in relation to real knowledge of the Other with which it remains in perpetual, mutually enriching dialogue.

Shame is a powerful force in Western consciousness at the present time, particularly among the well-informed intelligentsia. Liberalism in politics has lost its way because it is shame ridden and does not know how to assert itself without multiplying its sins. Conservatism in politics is dangerous because it is in denial about being ashamed and asserts itself with populist bluster as if there were never much to feel guilty about in the first place. Even philosophical debates in epistemology can be haunted by shame, to the point that we might understate the intellectual weaknesses of a postmodern perspective, lest we find ourselves attacking our own conscience. There is a lot to be ashamed about, to be sure. But we overlook at our peril postmodernity's double role as the raiser of consciousness about past Western sins and also as the conveyor of paralyzing, even if well-earned, guilt and shame.

I think postmodernity is deeply mistaken, in its own shame-ridden way, about the possibility and value of generality in theory building, despite the insight of its critiques. It is all too easy to emphasize the postmodern critique of modernity's grandiose self-assessment, while overlooking the real achievements of modernity in substantiating its claims for universal and transcultural aspects of human rationality through scientific and other forms of organized intellectual inquiry. Likewise, it is easy to oppose extreme postmodernists whose universal relativism is already self-defeating, and then meekly overlook the deep error of mainstream postmodern rejection of generality and theory. That is every bit as large an error and every bit as morally disastrous as the modern overconfidence in generality. which neglects fidelity to details and contexts. Religious philosophers should attack postmodernity at its very shame-ridden heart, just as most of them accept its attack on the ignorant enthusiasm that haunts the house of much modern epistemology and politics.

Beyond Modernity and Postmodernity

The fight between modernity and postmodernity is fundamentally not about foundationalism, which was both invented and criticized by modern philosophers; nor about colonialist expansionism and cultural imperialism, which were both used and attacked in the modern period. Rather, it is a multifaceted dispute over generality and justice, exacerbated by shame about the grand intellectual and moral mistakes of modernity. Religious philosophers need to move beyond the one-sided and artificially opposed insights of modernity and postmodernity while preserving the meaning and value of inquiry within religious philosophy. This requires finding a wise balance between the affirmation and the critique of generality, abstraction, and universality, and reinterpreting the morality of assertion in terms of the morality of correction. These goals are best served by a theory of fallibilist rationality, in which the clear affirmation of hypotheses connects truth and reality to socially borne processes of hypothetical inquiry that prize every kind of correction.

Critiquing and Affirming Generality

The disagreement between modernity and postmodernity has been the object of a thousand characterizations, most of them fascinating, including van Huyssteen's and Murphy's sensitive offerings from the camp of religious philosophy, mentioned above. In relation to the corner of this civilizational battle that concerns the *epistemology of religious philosophy*, I consider it a multifaceted fight over generality and justice, driven by awareness of cultural and religious pluralism, on the one hand, and the need for security and identity, on the other. To be secure and to know oneself and one's people is, in part, to understand the world around us as far as possible in a particular way—namely, through theoretical interpretations of natural and social reality that take in as much as possible while faithfully accounting for variations and differences. But this is all very complex and something simpler is often more immediately useful.

In practice, the quest for security and identity demands a memorable narrative interpretation of reality that minimizes complexities for the sake of maximizing orienting and action-supporting power. The awareness of cultural and religious pluralism confronts this need with another need: to register details of difference and disagreement faithfully, refusing to ignore complexities. Every time theory building aims for generality, it risks delivering on the need for security and identity at the cost of fidelity to details. Whenever theory building aims to do justice to the details of variation, the chances of a satisfying general interpretation are greatly reduced. The modern epistemological project, whether foundationalist or nonfoundationalist in character, stresses the possibility and value of generality in theory building. The postmodern criticism project is primarily a watchdog enterprise, pointing out in the name of justice and honesty the failures of the quest for general theories, and especially their disastrous moral and social ramifications. Both can be brilliant. And both can be sanctimonious.

"Generalizations are empirically flat footed, low energy, center-confirming, periphery delegitimating, abuses of power." I shall call this the Generality Critique. If the Generality Critique is correct, then it is a victim of its own acuity. The self-referential deconstruction of generalized critiques of generalization is the first reason why intellectuals perpetually suspicious of generalization have to move carefully.

I once attended a meeting of the Pacific Coast Theological Society in which a memorable exchange occurred. Someone made a remark about the need for balance between generalizations and details in historical work and noted historian John Dillenberger quietly replied, "Details are everything in history!" The remark had sufficient weight to close off that phase of the discussion. In context, Dillenberger was pushing back against a perceived rush to generalization, and so the comment was warranted. As a matter of fact, however, while historical scholarship is nothing without attentiveness to details, it is also useless unless it contains generalizations that create understanding of patterns, trends, forces, movements, and styles—and also their failures and exceptions. To rush to pattern recognition is to commit Hegel's error in his *Philosophy of History* all over again, whereby details are coerced into the rational pattern, with the more recalcitrant among them simply neglected or deliberately read out of the historical interpretation.[6] But to stay only with details is to produce a meaningless list of events, a kind of senseless recording of what happened. Evidently, the person to whom Dillenberger responded was formally correct: good historical work does indeed balance generalizations and details.

Some people affirming the Generality Critique unconditionally may be taking an extreme point of view for the sake of some larger political purpose. But the danger with this is that rhetoric opposed to generality cannot come clean about its own biases and agendas; generality in the form of systematic analysis is required to diagnose them. Others affirming the Generality Critique do so more moderately because they simultaneously make the Generality Affirmation, which asserts, "Generalizations are inevitable for human thought and life and thus are valuable when they are formulated artfully and subjected to perpetual criticism." We might appreciate the moral and political agendas of extremists who blindly critique the very generality they rely on for their moral analyses, but most of us prefer the artfulness of the moderates who accept the risk of generalization because of its inevitability and thus seek to generalize skillfully.

Fallibilist Generality in Ceaseless Correction

Unapologetic embrace of generality in a characteristically fallibilist form is not present in many contemporary religious philosophers. In van Huyssteen's case, for example, after approving Calvin Schrag's pragmatic and praxis-oriented approach to rationality,[7] he states that the significance of this is (a) "the complete impossibility to think of rationality in abstract, highly theoretical terms" because (b) "rationality is present and operative in and through the dynamics of our words and deeds, and it is alive and well in our discourses and action."[8] I think this is misleading, if not inconsistent. I am happy to grant (b), as the early pragmatists did, and as van Huyssteen does. But neither this nor Schrag's version of pragmatism entails (a). Whether it is possible to think of rationality in abstract, highly theoretical terms must be an empirical matter, on van Huyssteen's own account. Indeed, whether abstract generalizations and highly theoretical constructions are ever possible must be an empirical matter: we have to try and see.

A deeply puzzling feature of van Huyssteen's approach to rationality is his simultaneous embrace of fallibilism in inquiry and yet definitive rejection of abstract generality, high theory, comprehensiveness, and universality. I consider this to prejudge a crucial issue about human rationality and the world in which it arises and seek to discern van Huyssteen's reasons for preemptively settling on his position. As far as I can see, van Huyssteen's reasons extend only as far as the "(b) entails (a)" move related above, which I think is flawed. Van Huyssteen might be correct about (a), and the associated impossibility of abstract generality, high theory, comprehensiveness, and universality. But if he is correct, it is not because it follows from (b) or similar premises. Moreover, I would say that van Huyssteen's own theory of rationality challenges the impossibility expressed in (a): his theory is a coordinated, systematic series of abstract and highly theoretical generalizations, comprehensive in scope and universal in intent. Merely noticing the biological, historical, and cultural embedding of all human rationality does nothing to interfere either with the possibility of such discourse or (evidently) with its appearance in van Huyssteen's own writings.

A more consistent conjunction of the Generality Critique and the Generality Affirmation does not reject abstract generalization or high theory from the outset, as if somehow we just knew what was possible with human rationality in advance of any experience. Rather, alert to the moral and political and intellectual dangers of generalization but also intrigued by the common features in rationality across cultures and eras, we should embrace epistemological fallibilism and then venture both to advance and to correct hypotheses about the rational structures of reality. When we do this, we find that we can generalize in some domains of reality more successfully than in others.

For example, generalizing about human nature at the level of emotional dynamics and psychological formation is extremely hazardous, while it is more straightforward at the level of the basic glucose-ATP biochemical energy mechanism, which all human beings share in common with most living beings. Generalizing about the right place to put rocks in a garden is not likely to win consensus, no matter how strong the enclosing aesthetic tradition, whereas generalizing about the physical theories that explain why rocks stay put when laid in a garden is an adventure in inquiry that has won impressive consensus. Generalizing about moral values across cultures and eras has been notoriously ineffective, and yet more recent anthropological work has discovered some very basic and widespread moral intuitions and evolutionary psychology has speculated about a partial basis for them.

Abstractions, generalizations, theories, and systems are not ruled out by a nonfoundationalist epistemology, whether van Huyssteen's or Murphy's or the early pragmatists. (Note that I do not join van Huyssteen in using "postfoundationalist" because, as I mentioned above, foundationalism and nonfoundationalism were entangled throughout modern Western philosophy; *post* is misleading in application to foundationalism.) Nonfoundationalism problematizes these ideas and rightly warns their purveyors about lurking moral and political dangers. But the detractors of abstractions, generalizations, theories, and systems also have to face the difficulty that they can't know what is possible and impossible, in advance, in a theory of rationality or on any other topic.

Nonfoundationalist epistemology, or in my terminology a pragmatic theory of inquiry (see Chapter 6), is more than merely a set of warnings. It is a bracing invitation to allow curiosity full rein and to formulate hypotheses freely and test them as carefully as the realities of social organization and individual ingenuity permit. It overturns the skeptical rule mongering of philosophers from Kant to Comte to Ayer and situates in the proper context the grave concerns about generality in thinkers from Derrida to Foucault to Lyotard. We can no more halt hypotheses about universal features of reality in this new epistemological world than we can ignore warnings about ideological bias lurking in our abstract theoretical constructions. Can we produce any useful general theories? I think we are entitled to answer this question in the affirmative, even if it means citing as evidence van Huyssteen's abstract, highly theoretical theory of rationality, which paradoxically dismisses "abstract, highly theoretical" discourse about human reason as impossible.

To put this another way, we do well to distinguish between the morality of assertion and the morality of correction. On the one hand, there is something deeply moving about the postmodern philosopher's hesitation to assert a theory, even when he or she actually has one in mind and really wants to think in public about it. This is the ascetic element of self-restraint in postmodern intellectual work mentioned earlier. But these theories are inevitably encoded within critical postmodern forays, where they turn out to be relatively immune to correction. Thus, the shame-driven suppression of theory actually recapitulates the very ideological encoding of theory to which postmodern criticism so vociferously objects. On the other hand, not to struggle emotionally over the morality of assertion suggests an unattractive insensitivity to the misery of others and to the role of ideological blindness in rationalizing it, even and especially in philosophy. So philosophers need to fight among themselves over whether and how to assert their theories, their perspectives, themselves. Yet they improve their situation not one whit if paralyzing shame causes them to eschew assertion or to sublimate it within criticism in a pitiful pretense at being theory free.

The ideologically fairsighted solution to this problem is to liberate ourselves for self-assertion by taking criticism more seriously. If the worst thing we can do is to submerge theory in criticism where it is immune to review, and if we cannot think or interpret without the generalizations of theory, then let us cautiously assert theories in such a way that they are already explicitly framed to seek out and profit from correction. The morality of correction is liberating because it untangles assertion from the paralysis of shame and most deeply shows that the lessons of postmodern criticism have been absorbed. If we can't avoid theory and if we can't afford to hide our dependence on it, then we had better get it out into the open where it can be discussed, debated, corrected, and improved.

The philosopher who has absorbed the lessons of postmodernity and resolved to interpret the morality of assertion through the morality of correction experiences a freedom to assert that is breathtaking after the tortured self-accusations of postmodern criticism. It can also be irritating or outrageous to those who feel that the shame-clothed altar of criticism is violated by the vigorous assertion of theories explicitly organized to engage all relevant sources of correction. Like priests with their backs to the world and their faces to the altar, the postmodern protectors of shame need to turn around, face the people, and exchange their sackcloth of shame for robes of celebration. The dangers of assertion, of generality and theory, meet their match in, and only in, a tireless devotion to self-criticism and the search for correction.

Truth, Reality, and Empirical Fidelity

Fallibilist, hypothetical theories of inquiry promote a freedom of investigation that makes foundationalists feel queasy for lack of anything solid to stand on and postmodern skeptics indignant because of the provisional embrace of abstract generality and high theory. But such theories of inquiry are far from unconstrained. Inquiries only produce warranted belief if their hypotheses can be corrected. Problem recognition, hypothesis formation, and theory correction are enormously complex phenomena and require social settings, traditions that stabilize shared values, embodied research techniques, and cultural resources to create the leisure and materials for inquiry. With all of this social and psychological fabric in place, however, there is still no guarantee that even a single hypothesis in a single inquiry is capable of correction sufficient to produce consensus among qualified experts. Just as we cannot rule out in advance the possibility of abstract, general theories of anything, so we cannot take for granted that the hypothetical process of theory building will find the traction needed to decide that one hypothesis is better than another.

In some inquiries, we never do seem to gain the traction required. Yet, in others, strangely enough, we do: hypotheses in such domains produce consensus decisions about their adequacy because they can be corrected relatively quickly. Some inquiries encounter the corrective "feedback" as a booming voice that exercises a decisive and rapid influence on inquiry, whereas in others inquirers hear only a whisper or nothing at all, after which broad consensus is not possible without arbitrariness or coercion. Any serious test of the hypothesis that I can plunge my head through a metal girder using brute force alone will produce serious injury along with decisive results and probably universal consensus that my hypothesis needs modification. Perhaps I first need to meditate, for instance, or eat something special, or at least pray for extraordinary powers before trying again, assuming a successful convalescence. But there is no question that something caused all of the qualified observers to conclude that my hypothesis was false and to modify accordingly whatever dangerous process of inquiry led to this incident.

I shall call the idea of correctability a "feedback potential" to stress its reflexive operation, to register the possibility of its varying in strength, and to suggest that clever forms of social organization might succeed in gaining feedback resources to aid inquiry that formerly were unavailable. This feedback potential is necessary to make sense of truth and reality in science and religious philosophy alike, indeed in all forms of rational inquiry. It invites and requires metaphysical articulation. The idea of correctability is amply present in the early pragmatists and it played a key role in their answers to the essentially metaphysical question, "Why does reason work?" They had a deficient understanding of the social requirements and implications of inquiry but they recognized that variation in this mysterious feedback potential accounts for why some inquiries are more effective than others.

Any pragmatic argument for realism turns on the fact that a feedback potential corrects some of our hypotheses with enough force to create consensus among qualified experts in the process of carrying out extended, tradition-borne, socially contextualized inquiries. For the pragmatist, in fact, this is the very meaning of reality: *reality is the whence of correctability in rational inquiry*. This way of thinking recovers the Pythagorean recognition of happy consonance between the Logos of human reason and the Logos of reality, but in a decidedly more tentative way. The mystery of correctability may be the pragmatist's basis for speaking of a shared public reality but the feedback potential's variations in strength make reality seem (pragmatically) fuzzy. This is nowhere truer than in religious philosophy but there are elements of this even in fundamental physics, or wherever the feedback potential is weak or nonexistent or awaiting activation through the ingenious rearrangement of social resources for inquiry.

It is this variability in the experienced strength of the feedback potential that finally and fundamentally explains different disciplinary styles. In fact, for pragmatic theories of inquiry, science is defined not in the first instance as the study of particular subject matters using particular methods but by conformation of inquiry to the strongest regions of the feedback potential. Science is that correlation of social organization and topics of inquiry optimized to produce consensus based on clear and strong correctability. This, in turn, helps to nail down what we think of as physical reality in ontology and functional naturalism in methodology.

In other words, the pragmatic theory of inquiry recognizes the dependence of inquiry upon this feedback potential and makes it the central metaphysical hypothesis in any theory of rationality. After being centralized in this way, the feedback-potential hypothesis serves as the fundamental explanation of disciplinary demarcation—from different forms of social organization to different ways of producing consensus, and from different topics to different methods. This is a metaphysical hypothesis connecting truth and reality, on the one hand, to the function of norms in embodied practices and traditions of inquiry, on the other.

It follows that there is an answer to the question of why rationality works. But it is an answer that cannot be articulated without venturing metaphysical hypotheses capable of connecting reality to experience and truth to consensus—hypotheses on the order of the feedback-potential hypotheses that I have described. Some contemporary religious philosophers seem singularly unwilling to entertain such hypotheses. The absence of *truth* in the index of van Huyssteen's *The Shaping of Rationality* is a symbol of this pervasive unwillingness. Similarly, Murphy hesitates to accept correspondence criteria in belief formation, focusing on coherence criteria. But I have argued that we should attack postmodernity's preemptive policing of possibilities as urgently as we attack the naïve epistemological enthusiasm of modernity. In other words, we should more completely move beyond the limitations of both, which is simultaneously to recover the insights of each, always present as shadowy reflections within its opposite.

Postmodernism and Apophasis in Religious Philosophy

The constructive contribution of postmodernity to religious philosophy is the recovery of apophatic instincts in a relevant

contemporary form. Contemporary religious philosophy should gratefully accept this reminder.

The Deeper Influence of Postmodernity

I have suggested that a fallibilist form of hypothetical reasoning humbly and creatively seeking correction by all possible means is the best way to recover and articulate what was most viable in modernity's fondness for generalized and comprehensive theory building. This is of great importance for religious philosophy because it holds open the possibility of constructive theoretical approaches to religious topics at a time when there is a lot of skepticism about theory in all things religious—with attendant questions about the viability of religious philosophy itself, at least in the theoretical and evaluative styles. This approach leaves quite open in principle the question of how good such theoretical efforts can be. That question is to be answered within traditions of inquiry devoted to pursuing issues of philosophical importance in the study of religion. Similarly, I have argued that the fallibilist, hypothetical approach described here registers postmodernity's critical attitude to the abuse of power and the hubris associated with theoretical ventures in human inquiry. I pointed out that this postmodern correction to modernity's enthusiastic excesses was born within modernity itself and has coexisted alongside modern epistemic foundationalism. In this respect, therefore, postmodernity picks up on and amplifies a modern theme when it criticizes epistemic foundationalism.

Yet the influence of postmodern thought on contemporary religious philosophy is broader than this. In the area of religious thought, postmodernity takes a stand against claims to adequacy made by intellectuals on behalf of conceptual portrayals of religious realities. In this respect, postmodernity is not a reaction against modernity but rather a retrieval of the much older insights of apophatic mystical theology. Traditions of apophatic mystical theology have flourished within all of the major religions, including in the West, particularly prior to the flowering of modernity. It is fair to say that these traditions of wisdom badly needed to be retrieved after several centuries of modern breast-thumping confidence in the powers of human reason. This contribution of postmodernity to religious philosophy stands relatively independently of its epistemological warnings about the political and intellectual dangers of ideology-laden generality and theorizing. And this is also a distinctly positive, constructive, and truth-intending contribution rather than merely a critical watchdog effort.

A significant amount of postmodern philosophy, especially and classically in continental Europe but lately also in the English-speaking world, has theological overtones. The word "God" is rarely spoken, of course, because God is dead or irrelevant or unspeakable. But the cavernous hole resulting from this silence rings every small noise with theological echoes. The message is clear and consistent: the most religiously significant aspects of reality are not expressed in propositional speech but rather are conjured indirectly—as that which is manifest in and in spite of human decisions and behavior, as that which appears in the shortcomings and breakdowns of human reason, and as that which peeks through the interstices and unseen corners of human social organization.

This viewpoint is not necessarily amenable to the intricate analysis of religious doctrines, to the systematic organization of theological theories, or to the unreflective implementation of doctrines in the religious beliefs and practices of ordinary people. But it can be a potently theological posture, even in the absence of traditional linguistic markers of theology (such as "God," at least in Western religions). This theological potency derives from a kind of testimony to what is manifest in reality, yet constantly escapes fully adequate characterization, and is routinely subject to human attempts at control and exploitation.

It is strange to see theology appearing within postmodern philosophy, which would typically describe itself more readily as antitheological than as theological. It is moving to see postmodern philosophers who are sensitive to the theological overtones of their work struggle to name it in a way that avoids misunderstanding. Controversial Algerian-Jewish-French philosopher and literary critic Jacques Derrida is such a thinker. He began by blurring the boundaries between philosophy and literary criticism in his deconstruction of the definitiveness of authorship and meaning, of interpretation and truth. Without abandoning these beginnings, he ended up as a kind of Talmudic theologian, whose deconstruction gradually became testimony to something that transcends criticism and demands that we recognize it. He was content to be called an atheist, and he was by the ordinary standards of religion. But he refused to say straightforwardly that he was an atheist because of his growing awareness of that to which his deconstructive analyses indirectly and inevitably testified.

To the prophetically minded moral theologian, to the evangelically minded death-of-God theologian, and to the apophatically minded mystical theologian alike, the development of Derrida's thought, and indeed this feature of postmodern philosophy generally, is deeply reassuring. It invites recognition of a simple fact: namely, that life demands interpretation in theological terms, whether these terms are those of familiar intellectual traditions of the major religions, those of mystical traditions that try to gesture toward the inherently unspeakable, or those of prophetic social movements trying to name what has been suppressed or neglected.

Apophatic Postmodern Religious Philosophy

Among apophatic approaches, the distinctively postmodern emphasis on human life and thought is relatively unusual. In the modern period, the apophatic instinct was often present in romantic poets and nature mystics for whom the natural world was the wellspring of spiritual insight, and nature was sighted relatively rarely in religious philosophy as such. The evolutionary vision of nature—with its savage predation, heartless extinction, incredible fecundity, and endless forms most beautiful—combined with rapidly increasing scientific understanding of and technological control over nature to rob the natural world of some of the thrill of mystery that had so appealed to nature romantics.

Meanwhile, the last century of modern technology, modern medicine, and modern managed economies was also the century of devastating world wars, genocides in many parts of the world including Europe, the worsening of avoidable poverty and disease, the exploitation of poor nations by wealthy colonial powers and multinational corporations, the development of weapons with which human beings can destroy the ecospheric conditions for their lives, and the emergence of ideological and religious extremists willing to obtain and use such weapons. The twentieth century truly was a time of epic human self-assertion. This is what drove postmodern thought to meditate on human power, its achievements and possibilities, its irrationalities and side effects, its cruelties and blind spots, its future and fate. These trends in human behavior are only strengthening and the need for philosophical scrutiny is only increasing.

The close study of actual nature has deconstructed the gleaming pictures on which natural theology traditionally relied to leverage knowledge of an active and benevolent deity. In the same way, close study of the human condition has made manifest the maze of constructions with which human beings make sense of their existence and has also deconstructed claims to their definitive legitimacy. The arbitrariness of the human construction of meaning is not a bad thing in itself, of course; we have to live and make sense of our lives. But the self-deceptive fiction that these constructions are somehow given, or otherwise definitive, is dangerous under certain circumstances. It is a kind of obliviousness, at best, and it invites, legitimates, and masks abuse of power, at worst.

The question for religious philosophy lying within the deconstructive manifestation of human self-interest and violence in networks of cultural meanings is Derrida's question: along the way, do we encounter something unquestionable, something that pushes back by questioning us? As soon as we aim to conceive this hypothetical something as a divine being, postmodern philosophy resolutely answers that no such locus of coherent transcendental consciousness and intention is encountered. This answer expresses an empirical claim, I think, and it is a convincing claim at that level. To the extent that human meaning making can ever serve as evidence for or against the existence of a determinate-entity deity, the intelligibility and focus we would look for does not seem present, which is not to say that it cannot still be believed.

The more plausible explanatory scenario is the weaving of human dreams beneath the vastness of the cosmic sky and above the terrifying depths of possibility, a weaving not governed or regulated by anything except complex human desires and the measured and unmeasured exercise of power. This godless world is not without an abysmal ground, however—or a Creative Dao, a God Beyond All Gods, or a One Beyond Comprehension. The name of God still testifies to this fact, and to the reality it hints at, so long as that name is wrested away from the religious legitimators of cultural meaning making. In fact, it cannot finally be wrested away. Like the mystical theologians before them in all traditions of positive religion, however, postmodern religious philosophers can testify to this deepest of theological truths, even if they remain on the underside of the traditions they address.

Whether or not the reasoning is sound, there is no question that the trajectory of postmodern thought within religious philosophy is decisively against the idea of God as a determinate entity that can be conceptualized more or less adequately. With Derrida, it also affirms the name of God as a pointer to something unconditioned that we seem to encounter in our experience of reality. Yet it insists with those strange theologians on the underside of large religious traditions that the fate of the religious philosopher who intends to speak of this unconditioned is apophasis. This does not mean utter silence, for apophasis is a complex form of indirect speech. Nor does it mean unintelligibility, for apophasis involves intelligible trajectories of artful speech. But it does mean that creative trajectories of intelligible theological speech finally yield to silence and that the deepest theological truth is conjured in the echoes left behind after the collapse of words, and not finally expressed in their utterance.

Chapter 4

Religious Philosophy and Multidisciplinarity

The phrase *multidisciplinary comparative inquiry* defines the meaning of religious philosophy as it is articulated here. The next three chapters examine each of the key words of this phrase. This chapter considers multidisciplinarity; Chapter 5 deals with comparison; and Chapter 6 fleshes out the theory of inquiry, which has been sketched to that point.

Since multidisciplinarity is not commonly associated with existing efforts in religious philosophy, I first present an argument that it should be. This will involve showing that it is vital for the adequacy of many inquiries into religious topics that philosophers might undertake. In fact, I will argue that the degree of abstraction needed to formulate *mono*disciplinary inquiries in religious philosophy is typically so high that it distorts the subject matter under investigation. I illustrate this argument in two case studies. One, on the existence of God, shows the necessity of multiple disciplinary perspectives in an inquiry that often has been conducted within the realm of conceptual analysis alone. The other, on food in religion, shows that multiple disciplinary perspectives are sometimes surprisingly useful and yield deep insights even on topics that typically have not been treated by religious philosophers.

This chapter also takes up an objection to multidisciplinarity—namely, that multidisciplinary research is impossible because disciplinary discourses are incommensurable. I answer this objection by diagnosing disciplinary differences in terms of the social dimensions of the theory of inquiry, which is slowly emerging through the chapters of this book. This frames incommensurability not as an unavoidable fact of distinctive languages or concepts but rather as an often tractable challenge facing inquiring communities. In other words, experts in apparently incommensurable disciplines can often learn to communicate if the will exists to bend the inherent flexibility of specialized discourse communities to the task.

The Importance of Multidisciplinarity in Religious Philosophy

Religion is prodigiously complex, so multiple disciplinary perspectives will have natural roles to play within any sophisticated inquiry. Studying any aspect of religion—an idea, a specific practice, a recurring theme—typically requires a degree of intelligent abstraction to isolate the most salient features and to make the inquiry tractable. Some inquiries may be able to restrict themselves in such a way that a single discipline (such as logical analysis) is the only relevant perspective, but the degree of abstraction required to achieve monodisciplinary focus is extremely high, often producing intolerable distortion of the subject matter. Usually, multiple disciplines are required both to register the complexity of the theme under discussion and to guide intelligent abstraction toward the most salient features for study. Thus, there should be no preset limit on disciplines allowed to contribute to inquiries in religious philosophy; creative openness in the search for relevance and corrective resources is the optimal approach.

Multidisciplinarity in Context

There is evidence from all scientific and literary cultures of a struggle to balance specialized knowledge and integrated knowledge. Specialized knowledge requires tremendous attention to detail and an intense investment of time and energy, which precludes gaining such expertise in a large number of domains of knowledge. Integrated knowledge requires an encyclopedic appreciation of specialized knowledge domains, which can serve as a framework for the artful cultivation of wisdom suitable both for harmonizing knowledge and action and for solving large problems. Tension between the two types of expertise arises partly because of natural economies of time and energy and partly because temperamental differences push intellectuals toward varied kinds of excellence.

Two great exemplars of integrated knowledge are Confucius and Plato, and they have served as inspirations for Eastern and Western cultural streams. Many before and since them have prized a practical harmony of knowledge and action that builds character and wisdom, thereby giving birth to cultural ideals such as the "Confucian scholar official" of East Asia and the "Renaissance man" of the West. There are countless exemplars of specialized knowledge, and their number increases as knowledge specializations multiply. This has given rise to ideals of intensive expertise, such as "scholar's scholar" and "genius scientist"—as well as to common caricatures of these ideals, such as "egghead" and "mad scientist."

The balancing act between integration and specialization has become increasingly problematic. At this point, to simplify a complex academic trend especially in the Western world, eggheads are taken seriously while Renaissance people are dilettantes, because is it widely assumed that nobody can possess the requisite encyclopedic knowledge, let alone harmonize it in coherent and practical ways. In earlier periods, the relative weight of approval and disapproval has been roughly opposite to this. For example, Galileo Galilei ran into difficulty with the natural philosophers of his day because he was prepared to forego furnishing a comprehensive analysis of the causes of motion, which could compete with their Aristotelian theory, and instead confined himself to a mathematical description of motion. To medieval natural philosophy, Galileo's sort of disciplinary specialization represented the abandonment of prized principles of integrative understanding, and indeed, for all its other virtues, it was exactly that.

The idea of multidisciplinarity has to be understood against this background of sometimes harmonizing and sometimes conflicting ideals of specialization and integration. Multidisciplinarity strikes a compromise between the two sets of ideals. It grants the specialist's instinct that encyclopedic knowledge is impossible to gain in the modern world and, even if in hand, too complex and multivocal to integrate. It also concedes the integrationist's point that many important problems cannot be resolved or even comprehended within specialized disciplinary frameworks. It then proceeds with *problem-oriented research*. This involves identifying an important problem and drawing on the insights of multiple specialized disciplines as needed to gain a solid understanding of the problem and to strive for a solution—practical or theoretical as the subject matter demands.

The recent history of multidisciplinarity is joined at the hip with the history of academic disciplines. Burgeoning knowledge spawned numerous disciplinary specializations through the nineteenth century, defining the modern university as well as transforming the education of children in many parts of the world. Traditional Western and

Eastern integrationist ideals became increasingly impractical, even by the lights of their most ardent proponents. Yet these same ideals also seemed increasingly vital to avoid the disaster of balkanized knowledge and a world of specialized experts, who were essentially culturally ignorant and socially ineffective.

Unsurprisingly, a host of attempts were made through the modern period to fight back against the pernicious side effects of disciplinary specialization even while prizing the knowledge gained within specialized inquiries. These range from innovative educational approaches for young children that prize integration and creativity, such as Montessori schools, to the reorganization of university departments to promote cooperation across specialties. Other results include the founding of new problem-oriented "interdisciplines" such as women's studies, religious studies, political economy, and bioinformatics.

The literature devoted to multidisciplinarity recounts the history of attempts to preserve the integrationist ideal in the face of a flood of specialized knowledge, furnishes a philosophical rationale for multidisciplinary problem-oriented research, and offers strategic advice to educational administrators.[1] This literature has generated a host of hybrid terms such as *crossdisciplinarity*, *hyperdisciplinarity*, *interdisciplinarity*, *multidisciplinarity*, *nondisciplinarity*, and *transdisciplinarity*. These terms supposedly express fine distinctions among different methodological approaches to problem-oriented research, relative to the methodological constraints imposed by the subject matter and by the cooperating disciplines. While such names can be useful in particular contexts, particularly for raising consciousness about methodological subtleties, they are of limited value philosophically. Situating problem-oriented research within a general theory of inquiry yields deeper insights into the possibilities and meanings of such research.[2]

Complexity and Abstraction in Religious Philosophy

The process of stabilizing the identity of an interdiscipline such as religious studies is well worth discussion as an illustration of the difficulties and opportunities of multidisciplinary work. Such a discussion naturally belongs in a chapter on multidisciplinarity. I made some remarks on this subject in Chapter 1. My interest here is more specifically in the way problem-oriented research takes shape within religious philosophy. Our understanding of this topic owes a great deal to what we have learned about religion from its academic study in the last century but the focus on philosophical inquiry takes us in another direction.

Human life flows in a mostly unproblematic stream of bodily processes, habitual thoughts and actions, energy and information exchanges with our environment, and social interactions with other beings. This flow has ever-changing emotional coloring and physical texture, and the overwhelming majority of this flow is beyond our conscious awareness—indeed, this needs to be the case in order for the prodigious complexity of human life to be manageable. Conscious attention dances across this flow much as a spotlight flashes over a landscape, illuminating one part of it and then moving on. It is because we have the ability to focus attention within the flow of experience that we can sense problems as determinate aspects of the flow of experience rather than mere discomforts lacking specific features. It is because we can sustain that focus through changing circumstances, with the aid first of language and subsequently of writing and tradition, that we can imagine solving complex problems.

The way problems emerge from the flow of experience is so complex yet so reflexive that it lies on the distant borderlands of understanding, where even the most attentive philosophers struggle to describe and analyze it. Problem emergence is wholly automatic in some respects, and yet it is also subject to the entire range of physical, personal, cultural, and contextual conditioning factors. This conditioning gives problem emergence emotional, intellectual, and social significance, while the almost wholly automatic character of problem emergence places conditioning factors beyond convenient regulation and often even beyond recognition, making its side effects even more potent.

At the heart of the way problems emerge from the flow of experience resides the abstracting power of conscious attention. Cognitive scientists have isolated more than one kind of attention, and it is important not to reduce attention to just one of its variations, such as focus in the visual field. Yet visual metaphors remain helpful. To notice something is akin to arresting the sweep of a spotlight over the landscape of experience, training it somewhere particular. It is the *focusing* of attention that makes the object of attention into a determinate something.

The power of attention to create determinate things, in the sense of abstracting them from a continuous complex flow of experience, is a foundational insight of phenomenology in all traditions. In the context of Buddhist philosophy, this potency is what underlies the emergence of the concept of self, followed immediately by attachment to self and the attendant suffering. Some Buddhist meditation practices are supposed to penetrate through the conscious structures of thing-abstracting to the experiential flow beneath. This perspective and the related meditation techniques are already evident in the Buddha's traditional teachings and have been a staple of Buddhist philosophy ever since.[3] In Western philosophy, Immanuel Kant compellingly diagnosed the role of human cognition in constituting the world of experience as an intelligible system of determinate particulars.[4] Subsequently, Edmund Husserl presupposed this abstracting move in his interpretation of how anything is a thing for human experience.[5] William James came to a similar conclusion operating in the domain of empirical psychology, with a deeply embodied notion of consciousness.[6]

On all of these accounts, we discriminate more than we discover, and we constitute at least as much as we encounter. The existence of public behaviors, shared to some extent, shows that our various experiential flows are compatible to a degree and in key respects sufficient for the construction of social worlds and for the prosecution of empirically oriented inquiries such as those of the natural and human sciences. Yet, in other respects, our embodied cognitive faculties play around within the flow of consciousness in highly distinctive ways—and with apparent spontaneity that suggests the playing around may have produced quite different outcomes. It is particularly through focusing on the contingency of abstraction from experience—of thing making and world construction—that modern philosophy and psychology arrived at the importance of interest and power in explaining the particularities of our play (that is, our sensations, perceptions, actions, and interpretations). This insight has had definitive significance for postmodern thought, as we saw in the previous chapter. The *reasons* attention pauses where it does determine the respects in which the object of attention is problematic or interesting and may also express the operation of assumptions by which we and others unconsciously or deliberately exercise power. That is, objects of attention show up with determinate features according to our interests.

For example, at the most basic level of sensation, the flow of experience can be disrupted by pain—in the sense that the specific discomfort becomes the focus of attention, usually in respect of how to stop it. If marketers are successful, we immediately associate attention to pain (in respect of how to stop it) with a specific pain-relieving product. In the aesthetic domain, the flow of experience might suddenly intensify so as to draw our attention to something exquisitely beautiful—which strikes us as curious or wonderful or surprising, or challenges us to photograph or paint or understand it. As we stretch ourselves to do so, we will inevitably draw on existing resources and techniques of expression, accepting or resisting them according to the ways they help or hinder our aspiration. In our social worlds, certain people show up within the flow of our experience as abstracted kinds and, thus, loaded with affiliated judgments and interests. Such abstractions can be politically potent when widely shared among people with power or privilege; they can also be extremely useful in a more or less practical way when it comes to seeking help or asking directions or locating a plumber to repair a leaking pipe.

As attention slices through the flow of experience to conjure determinate objects and classes of objects, which we engage in specific ways, it selects some features, leaving other possible features unthematized in the background. Interested attention thus creates objects by *abstracting* features and relations from the experiential environment, which seems endlessly dense with interpretative possibilities. Without the abstraction of attention, there are no problems, and there is no problem solving, because nothing ever shows up for us as determinate and tractable. As Martin Heidegger said in his way, and Charles Peirce in his, the biological rootedness of human life and consciousness is the indispensable frame for any theory of interpretation.[7] In any such hermeneutics, the power to abstract is both the enabling condition for any interpretation and a constant problem to be overcome in inquiry aimed at refining interpretation.

Abstraction in academic pursuits such as religious philosophy is no different from the ordinary abstraction sketched above. It operates in the very same way, both as the enabling condition of interpretation and a perpetual problem to be overcome through inquiry. Something about religion grabs our attention and, in the case of religious philosophers, the exciting struggle is typically to understand it in relation to everything else we take as relatively more settled knowledge. We are guided in the first instance by the way this something shows up for us: the features that stand out rather than those that merge unnoticed into the background, and the aspects that the patterns of our experience cause us to notice where others would see something different. We then formulate a problem that expresses a thoughtfully deepened version of our instinctive reaction to the way this subject matter stands out for us.

As we communicate with others, either in person or by means of scholarly literature, we quickly understand that there are features we did not immediately notice but now judge to be importantly relevant to the problem at hand. We refine our statement of the problem accordingly. Especially important in this refinement process is the role of the academic disciplines, which have something to say about the subject matter, typically from very different angles. A logical puzzle embedded in religious behaviors can pop out to a philosopher that might not be noticed by other equally perceptive thinkers, whereas the philosopher might not be prepared to notice the relevance of social conditioning or state of mind in analyzing the same subject matter. The subject matter determines the relevant disciplines in some basic sense. In practice, however, the religious philosopher needs considerable experience and convenient access to good advisors in order to discern which parts of which disciplines might be relevant to the subject matter. So it is the religious philosopher, as conditioned by formative experience and social context, who selects the disciplines that determine the emergent shape of the problem and that subsequently play roles in the unfolding inquiry.

The endlessly subtle ways in which a religious phenomenon links up with other features of experience cannot possibly all be registered in the problem—certainly not at the outset of a process of inquiry but also not at its end point. There is too much interpretative density to be compressed into the narration of a problem's conceptual structure, no matter how sophisticated the corresponding process of inquiry. Thus, at any and every stage of its emergence and refinement, the religious philosopher's problem selectively connects hypothetical lines of interpretation to some features of experience rather than others. This is abstraction. It is inevitable. Without abstraction, the interpretative density of phenomena would prevent the emergence of the problem. Yet with abstraction there comes attachment to hypothetical formulations of the problem. This attachment is crucial for powering inquiry, because inquiry requires a degree of personal determination and social organization that only strong attachment can produce. Just as abstraction inevitably biases perception, however, so attachment makes correcting for those biases a challenging problem for inquiry.

The art of inquiry, therefore, consists first in intelligent abstraction of a problem and second in managing attachment to the form of the problem so as to promote necessary refinements. Multidisciplinarity is a key resource in both cases, though not the only relevant resource. Some objects cast grossly distorted shadows when the light source and screen are placed just so. While potentially amusing and useful, such shadows may not produce the sought-after type of understanding of the object abstracted in the shadowy image on the screen. Intelligent abstraction is analogous to arranging the light source and screen so as to produce the sought-after understanding of the projected object. Managing attachment is analogous to *realizing* that one perspective on the object in question may mislead as much as it promotes understanding and then being *willing* to work the angles. The angles are produced within the subspecialties of a discipline, and several disciplines quickly multiply the number of angles available. The ability to abstract intelligently improves as integrated encyclopedic experience builds, as do the twin capacities to recognize limitations of perspective and to use disciplinary perspectives to gain better understanding.

Creatively Open Multidisciplinarity and Styles of Religious Philosophy

This analysis of the roles of varied disciplines in guiding abstraction and managing complexity immediately implies an important conclusion: there is no natural way to define rules governing what disciplines should play roles within religious philosophy. The creatively open approach to multidisciplinary inquiry I am endorsing is far from random chaos, however. The requirements to guide abstraction and manage complexity are quite restrictive but not of disciplines as such; rather, they restrict the way available disciplines contribute to inquiries in religious philosophy.

The various styles of religious philosophy might appear to require or invite limitations on disciplinary contributions to inquiries concerning religious phenomena. There is some truth to this, but the issue is complex so I pause here briefly to discuss the seven styles of religious philosophy in relation to the ideal of creatively open multidisciplinarity.

The phenomenological style of religious philosophy has a certain claim to independence from other disciplines, at least when the task of phenomenological description is conceived as attentiveness to phenomena—maximally unconditioned by preconceived ideas, including especially those preconceptions that academic disciplines set in place. On the one hand, this attitude to description can yield surprising insights that resist prevailing assumptions about phenomena long established within particular academic disciplines. It was freeing scholarly perception from doctrinally focused philosophy of religion that enabled religious studies scholars to detect the (now obvious) fact that religion, after all, is not solely or even centrally about beliefs and ideas. Rather, in religion, beliefs share the stage with practices, individual cognitive interests with group management interests, and so on. On the other hand, familiarity with the insights of a wide range of disciplines can also efficiently disrupt the hegemony of one or two disciplines over a subject matter within religious studies. This was the case in the decentralization of beliefs and ideas within religious studies just described. We will also see this below in the case study about food. Even in phenomenology, therefore, there can be no objection in principle either to allowing phenomenologists to free themselves from extant disciplinary frameworks or to encouraging them to absorb relevant disciplinary insights wherever they arise.

The historical and analytical styles of religious philosophy are interesting cases because they appear to be defined in large part by the practices and assumptions of single disciplines—history and logical analysis, respectively. But appearances are misleading in both cases. Just as historical work generally has profited enormously from paying attention to allied human sciences such as psychology and anthropology, so the historical style of inquiry within religious philosophy cannot isolate a pure form of historical practice from entanglements with disciplines that disclose patterns and forces within human affairs. Logical analysis of religious arguments often enough presumes the purity of its mission, as if the philosopher need never consider anything other than the formal validity of arguments, which arise around religious ideas. As the case study on the existence of God shows, and as should be perfectly obvious on other grounds, however, the formalizing of arguments necessary to make them ready for logical analysis is hazardous interpretative work. Logical analysis is especially prone to mistakes when the philosopher maintains the pretense that the meaning of often symbolically deployed concepts is in every case perfectly obvious and clear. A wide array of disciplines stands ready to aid the philosopher likely to err in this way.

The remaining four styles of religious philosophy are more or less obviously creatively open with regard to multidisciplinarity. Comparative work routinely requires drawing on every imaginable disciplinary insight to coordinate religious phenomena across the chasms of culture and era, to stabilize and correct the categories that are used in such coordination efforts, and to interpret the significance of the similarities and differences than then arise. Literary creations in religious philosophy are the original exemplars of intellectually creative openness. And the theoretical and evaluative styles of religious philosophy heavily depend on relevant disciplinary insights wherever they may arise to guide theory formation and refinement, as well as to fuel comparative analysis and assessment.

There can never be any objection in principle to the attempt to pursue an inquiry into some religious phenomenon under the purview and aided by the practices solely of one academic discipline. Energy permitting, there is no harm in trying and then seeing what happens. Difficulties arise, however, when such an attempt is not seen for what it is, and the inevitable abstractions are thereafter codified into the intellectual practices of a group, perhaps buttressed by enthusiastic identity politics and hostility to competitor outlooks. In hypothesizing the impossibility of truly natural limitations on the disciplines that may contribute valuable insights and methods to inquiry, religious philosophy as I articulate it here rules out not the monodisciplinary experiment but only attachment to the prerogatives and exclusive dependence on the practices of any one single discipline.

Case Studies on Multidisciplinarity

An abbreviated case study on the existence of God in Christian and Hindu thought illustrates the necessity of a multidisciplinary approach in a philosophical inquiry, which typically has not taken one, in either the Western or South Asian contexts. A second abbreviated case study on food in religion, a topic rarely broached by philosophers, compactly illustrates the surprising usefulness of multidisciplinary approaches in religious philosophy. Rather than an overbearing obligation, taking account of multiple disciplinary perspectives is an exciting aspect of religious philosophy. It opens up worlds of understanding that remain closed to the monodisciplinary inquirer, and adds depth and subtlety to interpretation of topics that often have not been a part of the religious philosopher's repertoire.

The Indispensability of Multidisciplinarity: On the Existence of God

The previous section's statement of the role of multidisciplinarity in managing the abstraction necessary for formulating problems for inquiry is quite general. The analysis holds for every domain of experience and every type of inquiry. Here I focus on a single problem so as to illustrate concretely the need for multidisciplinarity in religious philosophy. For this purpose, we can do no better than examining one of the classic themes in traditional philosophy of religion—namely, arguments for the existence of God.

The analysis of abstraction above argued that the way a problem emerges from the undifferentiated flow of experience is crucial for understanding what counts as a solution and what issues get elided or go unnoticed. These considerations in turn dictate what roles multiple disciplinary perspectives can play. How does the problem of the existence of God emerge for the religious philosopher? There is not one answer to this question—and that helpfully shows that contextual abstraction is at work in each case. Here I consider two medieval cases—one from the West and one from South Asia—and one contemporary Western example. The processes of abstraction in these three cases are fascinatingly different. This in turn provokes the question about what religious philosophers today can do to minimize unintentional parochialism. As we will see, an important part of the answer is multidisciplinarity.

Among Western philosophers, one of the most explicit accounts of the emergence of the problem of God's existence is that of Saint Anselm (1033/4–1109) in his *Proslogion*. He begins the argument by imagining a fool who says there is no God. Despite this opening gambit, neither apologetic nor evangelical interests appear to spark the problem for Anselm. Rather, before relating the proof, he describes a strange kind of internal cognitive dissonance. He seems mesmerized by the strength of his faith in God's reality yet puzzled by the fact that he is unable to furnish a rational proof for the existence of God that matches the strength of his preexisting faith. His quest to love God wholeheartedly drives him to seek such a rational proof not for the sake of bolstering faith but really to explain it to himself. Or so the *Proslogion* frames the matter.[8] This is *fides quaerens intellectum* (faith seeking understanding). Much the same was true many centuries earlier for Saint Augustine, who formulated this way of describing theological argumentation about God.

No doubt in part because of the intense mystical experiences to which Anselm apparently was prone, the way the problem presents itself to him is the existence of "something than which nothing greater can be thought."[9] Nothing more prosaic than this sort of formula could do justice to his experience of God as stretching comprehension to the limit. Indeed, Anselm goes on to argue that God is "something greater than can be thought"[10] and to interpret the "inaccessible light" in which God dwells to be this very impossibility of human understanding.[11] This takes him far from the reach of empirical considerations of evidence and probability and leads him to look internally, to the conceptual structure of the key phrase and to the experience of thinking it for oneself, which is what his proof spells out in detail.[12] He was familiar with arguments for God's existence based on features of the world from his knowledge of Augustine's writings, and yet the problem does not appear to him in these terms. Even in his *Monologion*, which is more like a reflective soliloquy than the *Proslogion's* prayerful address to God, Anselm's arguments for God's existence are geared not to observable features of the world but to ontological questions of dependence and variations in intensity of being.[13]

Anselm's proof is deceptively complex, and it is worthwhile noting in passing that it is not logically identical with simpler versions of the so-called ontological argument that are loosely associated with his name. He is captivated by the power of words and concepts to link with reality. This is how he can feel deeply persuaded by the *Prologion's* argument for God's existence. He is satisfied to show that properly understanding a special phrase ("something than which nothing greater can be thought") means to understand that this something must also exist. The knowledge that this concept exists in the mind bootstraps into knowledge that the object referred to by the phrase exists in reality. He seems oblivious to the possibility that existence is not the sort of perfection that can be made subject to considerations of more and less greatness, which is the standard objection seen in later philosophers, including Immanuel Kant. But this is no mere oversight; in Anselm's Platonic conceptual framework, being is indeed subject to variations in intensity and, thus, can be more and less great, just as his argument supposes.

The *Monologion's* ontological argument is logically quite different but equally revealing about the contextual features guiding the way Anselm abstracts the problem of God's existence. In this case, Anselm is fascinated by ontological dependence of things of the world on something else, something other. He divides the question of how to interpret this dependence in several parts. (1) He rules out the possibility that something can come from nothing as obviously incoherent. (2) He rules out the possibility that all things come from one another in a closed system of interdependence as incoherent on the grounds that relations must inhere in substances and cannot be self-subsisting. (3) He reduces the possibility that all things come from something else to two cases. (3a) Either they derive from multiple things that are individually self-subsisting, which he rules out by arguing that they must share the one "power to exist through oneself," which is after all one thing; or (3b) they derive from one thing, which he accepts, thinking of this one thing as God. It is striking to see that Anselm effortlessly captures here (1) varieties of nihilism, (2) the Buddhist doctrine of dependent co-arising (*pratītya-samutpāda*), and (3a) the ontological pluralism widespread in Chinese philosophy. Equally, it is unsurprising that he could not give these positions their argumentative due, as he was doubtless unfamiliar with any philosopher or philosophical literature that defends them.

For Anselm, therefore, the emergence of the problem of the existence of God seems strongly conditioned by his Platonic philosophical heritage, his personal mystical experiences, the emphasis of his monastic community on a life of prayer, and his unrelenting quest for rational arguments that would round out his passionate faith with profound understanding. We must allow that Anselm's arguments were penetrating analyses of the question of God's existence, which covered more alternative possibilities than others at the time could imagine, and this shows the power of the abstract formulation of his problem. Despite this, and without anachronistically imputing any failure of intelligence or avoidable narrowness of perspective to Anselm, it is still possible with the benefit of hindsight to detect a parochial quality in both arguments. And this shows the dangers of abstraction in this case, dangers that subsequent philosophers were quick to point out.

For us to rehearse in our time either of Anselm's arguments for the existence of God without modification would properly invite the charge of parochialism. While remaining inspired by his basic insights, we would need to reach beyond Anselm's formulation of the problem and toward a different kind of abstraction, one that takes full account of the relevant disciplinary perspectives that we have at our disposal. The *Monologion* argument would be completely recast if a few disciplinary specialties of South Asian and East Asian philosophical traditions were allowed to contribute. Once attention to those world philosophical traditions had placed alternative theories of ontological dependence on the table, the question of assessing the superior view would arise, just as it did for Anselm, though this time with the benefit of substantial literatures and robust arguments on all sides of the question. The test for which theory of dependence was the most satisfactory could no longer be settled by appealing to what an imagined local audience finds obvious, which is the way Anselm settled it. Rather, the key criterion would be which theory of dependence makes the best sense of the vast patchwork of knowledge of the world that we have from the sciences. The question may or may not be answerable in these terms, but it certainly is a better question, and multidisciplinarity sensitivities are the key to making it a better question.[14]

Articulating the *Proslogion* argument in our time demands a patient debate over the question of whether being can vary in intensity and the connected question of whether being can be a property of a thing. Especially important disciplines in this regard would be the natural sciences. Their explanatory success through the last half millennium does not depend on the idea of variations in intensity of being and has, thus, rendered that idea questionable or perhaps superfluous. Reasserting a theory of variations in intensity of being would require a major initiative in philosophical cosmology, which integrates the natural sciences into a full-throated philosophical interpretation of every domain of existence. There is some potential in such a project because the natural sciences are infamously tone deaf to the music of values, and some might argue that the way to repair this lack is to reintroduce the idea of variations in intensity of being that correspond to degrees of emergent complexity.[15]

Furthermore, the *Proslogion's* dependence on the idea of "existing in the understanding" would need to be rethought. This idea in Anselm's thought world draws on an understanding of knowledge that is no longer as robust and integrated as it seemed to him; cognitive science and psychology now interpret human understanding very differently. Thus, it cannot possibly be sufficient to evaluate Anselm's argument in the *Proslogion* by means of logical analysis alone. Almost everything of intellectual interest lies in the philosophical assumptions and contextual factors that induced him to abstract the problem of God's existence in the particular way he did. Insights from multiple disciplines can intervene to disclose the lurking assumptions and the elided questions.

Anselm's arguments are among the most purely ontological ways of abstracting the problem of God's existence from the flow of human experience and, thus, are least vulnerable to shifting disciplinary perspectives. Yet, even in these cases, it has been possible to detect ways in which multidisciplinary sensitivities would limit the downside of abstraction, while properly complicating the arguments themselves. It is a vast failure of contemporary philosophy of religion that it has not come to terms with this challenge and continues to treat the *Proslogion* argument chiefly in theological or logical terms.[16] While these efforts have value within their disciplinary domains, they easily fall prey to the criticism of disciplinary parochialism. The value of multidisciplinarity for overcoming theoretical parochialism and for making arguments properly sensitive to the all of the considerations appropriate to their soundness is no mere bonus or optional accessory, therefore, but a requirement of any fair evaluation of Anselm's arguments and necessary for any attempt to resuscitate them plausibly in a contemporary philosophical context. This conclusion applies equally well to other contemporary arguments for the existence of God, whether or not they are revoicing arguments of the past.

A century before Anselm, Hindu philosophy displays a flurry of systematic attention to the problem of the existence of God. Less is known about the social context for these writings, by comparison with Anselm's, but the texts themselves offer hints about how their authors expected them to be received. One of the influential factors in Hindu philosophical arguments for the existence of God was pressure from the growing Buddhist movement and particularly its strengthening rejection of the idea of God as an existent entity.[17] Other schools of Indian philosophy were almost equally opposed to the idea of God as an existing being, and their debates with Hindu theists also helped to inspire the systematic discussions that appear in the tenth and eleventh centuries.

For example, Mīmāṃsā philosophers tended to be atheistic. They regarded devotional connections to imagined deities as superstitious and confused and committed themselves to studying the Vedas for information about how to operate the technology of religious ritual for the sake of desirable ends. Mīmāṃsā philosophers were confident in the causal intricacies that link the human execution of Vedic ritual with specific worldly effects, but their confidence is to be explained not by belief in a divine being, who ordains and regulates and acts, but rather simply to facts of life within a karmic universe. Systematic arguments for the existence of God in this period appear to have been inspired at least as much by the Mīmāṃsā viewpoint as by Buddhist atheism or the atheism either of the Cārvāka school or of some Sāṃkhya philosophers.

Thus spurred into action, Hindu theists of this period tried to support traditional faith by formulating arguments for the existence of a supreme being who is Lord of all—Īśvara. The most celebrated early works of this period on the Hindu side are those of Udayana, a late tenth- and early eleventh-century philosopher. He is most remembered for synthesizing two existing streams of logical thought (Nyāya and Vaiśeṣika) into one coherent framework, which later was dubbed Navya Nyāya, or the New Nyāya school. His *Ātmatattvaviveka* (also known as *Bāuddhadhikāra*) explicitly battles with Buddhist atheism, while his other main work, *Kusumāñjali*, contains the most compact statement of his proofs for the existence of Īśvara.[18] Neither these two works, nor any others of Udayana, appear to be directed to Buddhists, however—not even the *Ātmatattvaviveka*. Moreover, no Buddhist philosophers are known to have responded in detail to Udayana's arguments. Udayana's primary audience in the *Kusumāñjali* was probably his Nyāya students, for whom the book would have served a double role as a debate manual and as an uplifting theological inquiry—though he is not known to have had any students, he surely must have had many. Udayana may have expected Mīmāṃsā and Buddhist philosophers to overhear the arguments for the existence of God, but it appears to be chiefly a document for insiders.

The proofs in the *Kusumāñjali* number nine, and a tenth was added by subsequent philosophers in Udayana's Nyāya school.[19] Few if any of the ten proofs would have been compelling to Mīmāṃsā or Buddhist philosophers. Udayana appears to be much more concerned to shore up the faith of his readers in a personal God. Thus, Udayana appears to have an explicitly apologetic rather than an evangelical purpose in the *Kusumāñjali*. For their part, Buddhists and Mīmāṃsākas would have rejected key premises that need to be shared in order for Udayana to engage them. For example, three arguments in one way or another presuppose the divine authority of the Vedas, whereas Buddhists reject Vedic authority and Mīmāṃsākas interpret that authority very differently. Six further arguments turn on dependence of the world of our experience on a personal divine being: there must be an absolute cause behind all effects that is all-knowing and not itself caused; there must be a wise organizer behind all patterns and groupings within nature; there must be an ontological basis for all contingent beings; there must be a source of the universe that lies beyond the universe; there must be an omniscient knower behind all knowledge; and there must be an omniscient perceiver or contemplator behind everything that cannot be perceived or contemplated by human beings. But, in each case, Buddhists would invoke the doctrine of dependent co-arising to reject the dependence premise of the argument.

The tenth argument—that the morally just quality of karma and reincarnation cannot be secured without an outside entity to dispense the fruits of actions fairly—might have succeeded in engaging Buddhists. But the Buddhist no-self doctrine (*anātman*) famously clouds the moral intelligibility of karma and reincarnation because of its rejection of a soul (*jīva*) that traverses multiple lives, so the question of divine administration of this moral system really is a secondary issue within the Buddhist camp. This tenth argument would probably have been more effective against Mīmāṃsā philosophers, who share one of the premises of the argument—the karmic interconnectedness of reality—and dispute the conclusion that only a God could ensure that outcomes are completely just. But this argument would reduce to a dispute over the problem of suffering, and in particular whether karmic administration of reality guarantees perfect fairness. Where Mīmāṃsā philosophers tended to put their faith in the karmic system and the mechanistic technologies of ritual, Nyāya theists such as Udayana thought that something more was needed: namely, Īśvara.

Despite these scattered hints that some of the arguments might engage atheists, the apologetic force of Udayana's arguments is far more prominent. His introduction to the proofs underlines this. There, he makes clear that everyone (including Buddhists, Cārvākas, and Mīmāṃsākas) worships Īśvara under one of numerous descriptions (he lists fifteen), so the question of Īśvara's existence is really settled before the argument even gets started. While this would have irritated Buddhists, Cārvākas, and Mīmāṃsākas, it is just the sort of rhetorical move that appeals to insiders who appreciate knowing that their philosophical and religious enemies are overlooking an enormous inconsistency in their own atheistic positions. In fact, Udayana goes much further than this and characterizes his philosophical inquiry into God's existence as a kind of worship, at least when it follows after hearing the sacred scriptures read. This rhetorical move, much as in Anselm's *fides quaerens intellectum* approach, reinforces faith rather than calling it into question. After all, existence proofs might induce doubt even if they are deemed sound by those who appreciate them, and this possibility is arguably minimized in these kinds of approaches.

Someone trying to reassert Udayana's arguments a millennium later, which is to say now, may or may not be motivated by the desire to shore up Hindu faith in a personal deity while attacking Buddhist and Hindu atheism.[20] But they would be doomed to parochialism if they simply repeated Udayana's proofs. Paying close attention to other disciplinary insights would be necessary to escape this problem. For example, critical historical and literary analysis interferes with any straightforward attribution of unquestionable authority to the Vedas, and particularly with the proofs that require the premise that Īśvara composed the sentences of the Vedas personally. Similarly, as with Anselm's *Monologion* proof, Udayana's ontological dependence premises need to be evaluated not merely against context-specific intuitions about the ways of nature but also against a patient synthetic philosophical interpretation of the whole of nature—a philosophical cosmology. Without the natural sciences to help stabilize such large-scale speculative philosophical efforts, philosophical cosmology is of little value for evaluating anything.

Contemporary philosophers of religion typically furnish rather different answers than those of Anselm or Udayana to the question of how the problem of God's existence arises. Yet the contextual factors conditioning the way the problem is abstracted are just as illuminating for locating elements of the problem that are elided or overlooked and just as useful for detecting the necessity of taking account of multiple disciplinary perspectives.

For example—and this is not atypical—Richard Swinburne in *The Coherence of Theism* explains that he has both apologetic and evangelical interests. That is, he says the problem of the coherence of theism arises for believers (he speaks only of Christian theistic believers) when they consider the conceptual tensions among the sentences they use to describe God, and also when they consider the same issue in the minds of those they are obliged to convert.[21] In *The Existence of God*, Swinburne expresses compassionate solidarity with the everyday believer who worries about whether God (answering to a rough description assumed to be coherent) really exists. He also explicitly addresses himself to the skeptical critiques of David Hume and Immanuel Kant, setting out to show that reasonable confidence in God's existence can be rationally established in the probabilistic terms of confirmation theory.[22] He further acknowledges that few philosophers of religion accept the possibility of deductive proofs for God's existence, so he concentrates his efforts on an inductive proof that combines the force of several reinforcing a posteriori (experience-based) arguments.[23]

Given the way the problem of the existence of God arises for him, it is not surprising that Swinburne is interested primarily in registering features of the problem that address the apologetic and evangelical interests of a particular community of believers, and to do so in a way that is philosophically precise according to the high standards set by Hume, Kant, and those influenced by their thinking about the possibility of demonstrating the existence of God. This is unquestionably valuable as a goal, and Swinburne's skill in pulling it off is why he is so highly regarded as a philosopher of religion. But this way of abstracting the problem of God's existence marginalizes other crucial questions. Other disciplinary perspectives need to play roles in order to frame a more philosophically satisfying version of Swinburne's problem—a version that still uses his strategy of seeking an inductive proof that combines the force of several reinforcing a posteriori arguments.

Swinburne's idea of God is crucial for assessing the extent of disciplinary parochialism present in his framing of the problem of God's existence. He lays out the theistic hypothesis in four dense pages, of which the highlights are as follows.

> There exists now, and always has existed and will exist, God, a spirit, that is, a non-embodied person who is omnipresent... He knows about goings-on everywhere without being dependent for that knowledge on anything, and can control by basic actions all states of affairs everywhere... God is creator of all things... God is at each moment of the world's history responsible for its operation... God is perfectly free... God is omnipotent in the sense (roughly) that he can do whatever it is logically

possible that he do. He is omniscient, at any rate in the sense that he knows at any time whatever it is logically possible that he know at that time ... God possesses these properties described in some sense necessarily, and he is in some sense a necessary being.[24]

Swinburne acknowledges that there are other ideas of God—in particular, he addresses divine eternity as "outside of time" rather than his preferred interpretation of "existence without beginning or end." He rejects views with an atemporal or supra-temporal aspect to God's eternity, even when they also seem to allow a temporal aspect to God's life (as in Augustine and Thomas Aquinas). Swinburne argues that the reasons for affirming an element of timelessness in God's nature are weak, but this argument is not convincing and displays a lack of deep sympathy for the theological intuitions of Christian theologians in the era of creedal formation, especially Augustine. Swinburne is more persuasive in demonstrating that timelessness is deeply incoherent with God's personal characteristics, particularly God's knowledge, intentions, and powers to act.[25] But then he opts for the latter, more anthropomorphic alternative—dispensing with the alternative, atemporal model of divinity, once again showing a lack of concern for the considerations that constrained early Christian theologians away from highly anthropomorphic formulations of the divine nature. Giving a larger place to the discipline of Christian theology in framing his argument might not have induced Swinburne to choose a different God hypothesis, but it certainly would have forced him to engage profound theological arguments against his view of God as a temporal being, as well as to take better account of the classical viewpoint that the atemporal and temporal aspects of the divine nature can and must be held together.

Unfortunately, Swinburne does not explore ideas of God beyond such simple variations on the idea of God he wishes to defend, nor does he broach nontheistic ultimate religious explanations for reality such as those of most forms of Buddhism, many parts of Chinese religions, some aspects of Indian religions, and some versions of religious naturalism. Of course, he is free to select whatever hypothesis he wants, so there is no problem with a narrow evaluation of alternatives at this level. This narrowness, however, becomes deeply problematic when constructing a cumulative inductive case for the existence of a God answering to the description in Swinburne's hypothesis. At that level, the failure to take account of other hypotheses invalidates the calculation of probabilities that are essential to Swinburne's confirmation-theory approach.[26] Both kinds of "calculations"—in fact, they are qualitative estimates—require knowledge of alternative hypotheses of similar scales. Knowledge from disciplines in other traditions of philosophy would have made all the difference here.[27]

Finally, Swinburne's estimation of the prior probability of his God hypothesis reflects a lack of influence from disciplines such as cognitive psychology and evolutionary biology. He explicitly assumes that "no *a posteriori* arguments other than those which I discuss, have any significant force."[28] But the argument that evolutionary conditioning and cognitive reflexes bias people to believe in Gods of a relatively highly anthropomorphic sort, such as that of Swinburne's God-hypothesis, is relevant. It is not a defeater of Swinburne's hypothesis, which some writers on evolutionary psychology and religion sometimes casually assume, but it has significant force and cannot be ignored without invalidating probability estimates. It is important to keep in mind that some of these arguments and the associated evidence from experimental psychology were already well understood long before the late 1970s when Swinburne wrote *The Existence of God*. Of course, the evidence base has become far more robust since that time.

This brief analysis of the process of problem abstraction in Swinburne repeats the lessons learned from pondering what would be involved in updating Anselm's and Udayana's arguments for the existence of God. On the problem of the existence of God, which is possibly the most central problem of traditional philosophy of religion, insights from multiple disciples are not merely useful accessories. They are essential in order to become aware of elements of the problem that are elided in a particular context for abstraction, and also to frame the substance of the argument in properly complex ways. But the benefits of multidisciplinarity go far beyond these forms of watchdog utility. Multidisciplinarity also opens up vast stretches of philosophical territory, which are relatively unexplored in traditional philosophy of religion, with surprising and exciting results, as we will see in what follows.

The Surprising Usefulness of Multidisciplinarity: Food and Religion

Philosophers eat food much more than they talk about it. Occasionally there are publications and conferences on the philosophy of food or the philosophy of wine.[29] But on the question of food in religion, the silence from philosophers is impressive. Anthropologists and ritual theorists, sociologists and psychologists, theologians and ecologists have a lot to say about food in religion.[30] So why are philosophers silent? There surely are questions of meaning and morality to be asked and analyzed and answered here—questions that belong in the domain of religious philosophy, understood in a properly broad way. Without a multidisciplinary approach, however, a philosophical inquiry into food in religion never gets started; indeed, food may never suggest itself as interesting material for philosophical consumption.

So how would a philosophical approach to food in religion proceed if it were to take advantage of the resources of other disciplines? I suggest the following, perhaps surprising, hypothesis. *The relation between human beings and food can serve as a template for an exceptionally refined philosophical interpretation of human nature, including its religious aspects.* Because of the vast variety and intricacy of human relations with food, the resulting philosophical interpretation is unusually comprehensive and sensitive to aspects of both religion and human life that other philosophical-theological anthropologies tend to overlook.

Obviously, it is not possible to develop such a philosophical-theological anthropology here.[31] But the aim of this abbreviated case study is to show how multidisciplinary approaches in religious philosophy can be surprisingly useful, and that requires only a sketch of the moves that a philosopher interested in such a philosophical-theological anthropology might make. In what follows, this sketch takes the form of several philosophical insights related to food and religion that take their rise from multiple disciplinary perspectives on the subject and suggest how the central thesis might unfold in a longer project.

Each of the topic designations below consists of three words. The first reflects the most direct connection to food; the second refers to the way this aspect of food takes on emotional or cultural significance; and the third expresses the connection to the theme of the self. The significance of food for an understanding of the human condition in its religious aspects arises jointly in relation to all three levels of description. There is a kind of artistic arbitrariness in the naming of these themes, but each is nonetheless substantive for a philosophical interpretation of food and religion.

Dependence, finitude, and self-protection: Our dependence on food for survival is one of the most straightforward exhibitions of human finitude, and indeed of every life form's finitude. Because food resources are usually limited, the struggle to access and control them runs very deep in nature and is a basic priority within the cognitive systems of all organisms having capacities for knowledge, memory, and the acquiring of skills. While self-protective instincts are often diagnosed as moral defects among human beings, this line of analysis shows that at their core they are a necessary condition for the emergence and sustenance of complex forms of life and, therefore, of moral and cultural achievements of every kind.

Cooperation, belonging, and self-love: Game theoretic models of cooperation in food gathering and defense suggest that cooperation offers impressive evolutionary advantages and, for this reason, caused cognitive and emotional dispositions toward social cooperation to become adaptive traits in hominid populations. Human beings are thus built to belong to groups and to deal cooperatively with food in those groups. This involves developing the cognitive means to solve problems such as freeloaders who take advantage of group benefits (a strong young man eating bananas) without themselves contributing anything significant (climbing a dangerous tree to gather bananas). One of the side effects of these problems is a tendency toward the performance of costly signals such as expensive food rituals or exorbitant acts of hunting bravery, which establish reputation and set a standard of group membership. Because of this evolutionary heritage, the sharing of food is loaded with in-group versus out-group significance, evaluations of worthiness, and expressions of loyalty and deference within hierarchical social structures. It is in such social contexts that children learn to identify themselves as this and not that, as ours and not theirs, as beloved by these and regarded with suspicion by those. Every act of group eating recapitulates these formative events by which human beings learn the art of self-love in a group context.

Hunting, power, and self-assertion: While some food gathering involves reaping and gathering, omnivores only hit the protein jackpot if they are willing to hunt and kill. Humans need protein because we cannot synthesize all of the necessary amino acids and must digest and metabolize some to survive. While we have learned how to get protein from plants such as beans, early humans had to hunt other animals to survive. This job naturally went to the testosterone-infused males of the species, whose hormonal makeup made them less worried about danger and whose role in reproduction made them more dispensable in child rearing. The dance between hormones and behavior is writ large in hunting, particularly when killing must be accomplished with spear and club rather than bullet and rifle sight. The rush of excitement involved in cooperating to trap an animal and in leaping to brave acts of violence on behalf of the group is utterly intoxicating and brings enormous social prestige and expanded reproductive opportunities. These are the primal experiences of self-assertion among male humans, and the drive to perform such feats persists even as it is transmuted into alien cultural settings. Women assert themselves with greater social nuance but similar skill and fierceness, particularly in relation to their maternal investment in offspring and the fabulously complex competitive aspects of securing resources to support children. In their various ways, the food securing process requires human beings to assert themselves over their environments, over the plants and animals in those environments, over each other, and over the mana of life and death. Food manifests these primal meanings of power and self-assertion.

Gathering, patience, and self-realization: The carbohydrate fuel needs of human metabolism are met chiefly by gathering rather than hunting. This means enormous amounts of walking for women and the elderly, often carrying babies and tired toddlers or monitoring and guarding children as they run around playing. It also involves transmitting wisdom about plants to the next generation so as to make the complex and dangerous plant environment intelligible and tractable for human consumption. Just as hunters need to combine training in existing methods with the invention of new techniques, so gatherers must educate but also innovate through testing new food sources and preparation methods. The routine of movement and gathering requires prodigious patience, particularly when resources are scarce, as they are guaranteed to be from time to time and from place to place. In lean times, the energy required to gather can easily exceed that provided by what is gathered. These are the biological roots of the kind of self-realization that emphasizes attentiveness and observation, and that makes the environment come alive as navigable and consumable and ready-to-hand for the purpose of human self-cultivation.

Sharing, community, and self-giving: Sharing, even with strangers, is easy when resources are plentiful. Community boundaries expand in times of abundance, with relatively less concern about freeloaders and less anxiety about the performance of costly signals to authenticate group membership. But the strange feature of human community is that food sharing persists even in lean times. In apes, food sharing amid scarce resources is highly circumscribed and guided by the boundaries of community identity, but it persists, along with other forms of altruistic behavior. Game theoretic models can make sense of such acts of sharing to some degree, though the most exorbitant acts of generosity among humans and other animals, including self-sacrifice for non-kin, are difficult to interpret. They may be expressions of impulses freed from the family- and community-focused regulation, which typically constrains them. Regardless of the evolutionary back story, this behavioral possibility for human beings, born in food sharing, expands into a moral universe of virtues in which self-giving beyond the limits of community and convention can become a worthy end in itself.

Agriculture, regulation, and self-containment: Sophisticated awareness of the environment nurtured in gathering practices can eventually yield the technologies of cultivation and environmental control that we call agriculture. The production of food, working with the rhythm of seasons and vagaries of weather, was revolutionary for human life. By means of it, the natural environment was transformed from a navigable and partly nutritious maze of uncertainty into a regulated process that could be significantly predicted and controlled. There were dramatic changes in the rules about the control of food resources and the meaning of social prestige. Differentiation of food production effort necessitated trade of goods to ensure survival. Culture became rooted to places as well as practices, and home meant particular landscapes as well as particular people. People could design their own destinies to some degree because a patch of fertile land gave them a basis for self-containment, from which they could reach out through numerous cultural and economic transactions to others, or not, as they chose. Human individuals became more differentiated because of this self-containment in localized food production practices. This new form of the self-other dialectic in human life unleashed a host of previously unknown corporate cultural possibilities, such as complex civilizations.

Health, medicine, and self-healing: While hunters bravely and prestigiously provided protein, gathering technologies did more than bring in carbohydrate fuels. They also steadily isolated correlations between the consumption of food and human health. The degree of knowledge and innovation involved in gathering far exceeds that of hunting because the interactions between ingested substances and human health are monumentally complex—hidden causes and side effects call for long processes of trial and error to identify stable correlations. The result is the codification of transmissible knowledge in traditions of health. These include wisdom about the nutritional and medicinal properties of ingestible foodstuffs and topical balms and pastes. These wisdom traditions allowed human beings to regard themselves with ever-increasing intensity as repairable through self-healing. They established ideals of health and well-being and corresponding technologies of healing to preserve and recover those ideals. Human ill health at all levels, from depression to disease, was transformed from an expression of the fickle whims of fate to a problem that wisdom traditions could sometimes solve.

Savoring, sensuality, and self-awareness: Eating is not merely ingestion. The food environment first becomes tractable under the impact of sensory responses to what we ingest. Pleasant flavors tell us about what is safe and good to eat, and without properly adapted tastes, the environment would remain a chaotic ramble of chance interactions with foods. We are particularly drawn to the textures that mark the presence of lipids and the sweetness that signals some types of carbohydrates. But on the foundation of these basic taste-based survival capacities develops a cultural industry of savoring. This marks the transformation of the food environment from nutritious mother to sensuous lover and simultaneously alters our self-perception on a similarly dramatic scale. We become aware of individual differences in food preferences and allergies, at the most basic level. We encounter ourselves as hungry not merely for nutrition but also for sensual experiences of eating. Our memories of glorious food draw us back to food again and again as a source of pleasure. Sensual encounters with food awaken us to a world of valuational particulars, of personal tastes powered not by obligation or need but by simple preference. This is the root of a peculiar kind of sensual self-awareness. It is deeply linked to sexual behavior and cultural practices, but our encounters with food are an essential component in the emergence of sensuous self-awareness.

Energy, culture, and self-expression: So much of nature is concerned with the sequestering and transformation of energy through consuming food. While food is relevant to structural integrity through lipid reuse and to functional capacity through protein, its provision of energy through carbohydrates is its most obvious function. When we don't eat, we notice the loss of energy first, and only extended malnutrition manifests the result of ingesting insufficient protein and lipid. Plentiful food means plentiful energy, which enables activity in excess of that related to simple survival. Then there is fun-filled play, creative uses of intelligence, the satisfying of curiosity through inquiry, the building of traditions of knowledge, and the crafting of social habits far more intricate than those needed for basic cooperation and defense. In short, there is culture. Plentiful food permits intelligent social beings to perform amazing cultural displays of energy sequestering and transformation. The energy from stored grains is crushed into portable breads, which drive up cities and economies. The energy from fruits and vegetables moves muscles to erect monuments and to scale mountains. There is little survival value to any of this. This is self-expression in a world of almost unlimited possibilities, and food energy is an immovable necessary condition for it.

Parties, celebration, and self-transcendence: When there is enough of it, food is for fun as well as for survival and nutrition. Humans celebrate over food above all. Food unleashes so many aspects of experience, as described above, that it is the ideal focus for celebratory activities. We indulge our sensual fantasies with party food; we explore complicated social possibilities in strange rituals of approach and avoidance, which frequently involve party food; we dance with exhilaration and then rest from dancing while drinking and eating party food; and we lose ourselves in altered states of consciousness with party food and drink in hand. Ecstasy is jointly rooted in sex and food, but ecstasy has different properties in each case. The sublime tastes and textures and mind-altering properties of food and drink produce socially potent forms of ecstasy, which sex typically cannot—just as sex produces intensity of ecstasy, which food typically cannot, regardless of how socially elaborated its ingestion. In both cases, however, we learn the art of self-transcendence, of finding self through losing track of the habits of self-regulation, to which we normally subject it. Food is a doorway to self-transcendence.

Entheogens, shamanism, and self-exploration: Some kinds of food and drink have such special mind-altering properties that they offer opportunities for spiritual self-exploration unavailable to most people in any other way. Some people have psychiatric conditions, which offer similarly oblique access to hidden possibilities of self-awareness through psychotic states. Some learn to channel such states in socially useful forms, such as shamanic journeying for the sake of securing healing resources. But most people can reliably gain access to the weirder possibilities latent within human consciousness by means of the mind-altering food substances we call entheogens. Of course, people vary in the degree to which they are affected by ingestion of hallucinogenic mushrooms or laboratory-produced chemicals, but almost everyone is affected to some degree. The effects are typically so pronounced, in fact, that there are social prohibitions against most forms of mind-altering foods for fear that the basic biological effects will swamp ordinary reasonableness. But the taboo-breaking quality of such experiences only enhances their potential for self-exploration in the minds of those who recognize the entheogenic doorway and venture through it.

Digestion, excretion, and self-alienation: Nothing shows more clearly our symbiotic balance with the world of bacteria than digestion and excretion. Evolution is often taught in such a way as to disguise this point, but the microbial world was where the lion's share of adaptation occurred, producing simple organisms with virtually all of the biochemical processes needed to make functional multicellular organisms and eventually sensate and intelligent life. Microbial evolution also occupied the large majority of the four billion years of earth's evolutionary timeline. Bacteria lie at the root of every food chain and every large organism in a kind of negotiated settlement between the fortuitously enabling and the mindlessly destructive properties of the microbe-dominated environment. Thanks to mitochondria, bacterial symbiogenesis lies at the root of the energy-processing capabilities of all cells. That is what makes glucose work so efficiently as fuel energy and why we have livers with the energy-sequestering power to transform glucose into fats and back again. Bacteria are also crucial for digestion of food and for the absorption of digestion's waste products back into the earth in productive ways. Human beings have strange relations with fecal matter. Young children in toilet training often regard their poop as part of themselves and experience simple forms of confusion and even grief when it is changed from something they live with quite comfortably to something they are supposed to eliminate. They are taught not to play with it or touch it—for good reason, because it has passed back into the realm of bacteria and, thus claimed, is no longer safe for us. Cities are built on vast piles of excrement and hide from it through ingenious plumbing arrangements, which implement wise rules about how to keep ourselves safe from those parts of the aggressive world of microbes to which we are not adapted for harmonization. Whether it is in toilet training or waste management, in taboos or aversions, we specifically and deliberately alienate ourselves from the fecal products of food digestion. We can psychologize this self-alienation to our heart's content, and indeed we must do so as the psychological significance of our relations with food and excrement are profound. But the driving force behind all of this is the dark and barely understood rapprochement between bodies and the bacterial ocean, which first yields, then suffuses and surrounds, and ultimately receives those bodies.

Diversity, luxury, and self-denial: With agriculture, the differentiation of food passes from environmental circumstance to economic design. The ultimate result is prodigious diversity of edible plants and animals, combined in the most amazing ways to create a luxurious wealth of sensory possibilities. The first thing human beings in complex economies do with this unaccountable evolutionary privilege is to forget whence it comes. Contemporary humans in developed cultures are typically thoroughly alienated from the agricultural sources of food, from food-production processes, and from mechanisms of food distribution. We consume honey without much thought for the hive of bees that produced it. Meat eaters consume animal flesh with only the vaguest conception of how it arrives at their table. Even the civilizational miracle of bread, from grain production and processing to the making and moving of loaves, is rarely appreciated. As Karl Marx so forcefully pointed out, this is a dangerous form of alienation that masks the dependent character of human life. In the end, it is not merely willful denial of dependence; it is also self-denial that supports a bizarre posture of refusing to acknowledge being the sort of creatures that in fact we are. This food-based self-denial yields quickly to the denial of death and thence to a host of cultural and civilizational disasters.

Scarcity, survival, and self-loss: Civilization sometimes falls apart—through economic depression, natural disasters, ecological catastrophe, or the ravages of war. At those times, we are more an open book to ourselves than usual. The typically hidden impulses and anxieties over the food and drink necessary for survival come to the fore, where they cannot be suppressed and prove difficult to regulate. At those times, we move in mass migration hordes, hoping for help from those who are better off. Or we hunker down in simple desperation, devoting most of each day to searching for food in an eerie recapitulation of the daily grind of our gatherer ancestors. We become attenuated under such circumstances—thinned out and stretched, as the flush of self-expression built upon plenty yields to the blank stares of the hungry. We lose ourselves, at least as fortunate cultural circumstances gave us to understand who we were. Our existential state begins to resemble the liminality of our bodily existence, as we float on the edge of reabsorption into the vast bacterial ocean. There is nothing redemptive about this kind of self-loss. It is simply a waste of complex beauty.

Ubiquity, ecology, and self-destruction: It is ironic that the least obvious characteristic of food is its ubiquity. Virtually everything is food for something, and the way our bodies equip us to diagnose our environment as nutritious is quite different from the way other animals and plants do this. It all fits together in a vast and incessant digestive redirection of energy and resources. An ecology is not an organism but a mind-bogglingly complex and flexible synthesis of energy relationships, a superorganism. It is in this sense that it is a living thing. But ecologies are not infinitely flexible. As desertification shows, human agriculture is capable of destroying rich ecologies and leaving in their place relatively less fecund and more desperate ecological settings. We are capable of polluting rivers and ground water to the point that we sicken ourselves and other animals. Indeed, almost every aspect of the ecological footprint of our species is related to the production and consumption of food, from deforestation to the destruction of fisheries. The ubiquity of food is such that our perishing will not be the end of life on earth; everything that survives us will keep feeding, oblivious to our departure. But our peculiar relationship to food lies at the root of ecological self-destruction, and we cannot address one problem without facing the other.

Nonfood, ritual, and self-cultivation: Finally, it is precisely the sheer boundlessness and variety of food that makes possible the ritual transformation of it into nonfood. The milk poured over the statue's feet is ostensibly wasted, and yet something is achieved in the *puja* ritual among communities of Hindus using milk that could not be achieved using anything nonedible. This symbolic marking of food as nonfood expresses a peculiar recognition of everything that food is for us and leverages practices of spiritual self-cultivation. The Eucharistic meal among Christians transforms bread and wine, basic staples of food and drink, into memorial elements for the searing of the mind with burning narratives. The simple Shabbat prayer every Friday evening centers a Jewish family on food in a way that cultivates loyalty and belonging and memory. The disciplined refusal to eat during daylight hours during Ramadan is for Muslims a relentless reminder of their dependence on Allah, with hunger and the viscerally felt dependence on food being the proximate trigger for memory. It is no wonder that religious ritual is so richly knitted into the world of food.

These perspectives on food jointly constitute merely a starting point for interpreting the human condition, as I have said. But this should be enough to show how fruitful a multidisciplinary appreciation of food can be for religious philosophy, and in ways that correct many deficiencies in approaches to the human condition pursued within traditional philosophy of religion. Multidisciplinarity makes all the difference.

Incommensurability as Invitation

Incommensurability defeats multidisciplinarity and also comparison, translation, crosscultural understanding, and even dialogue—so it is said. But strict incommensurability is an abstraction from the fact of communication difficulties, an abstraction that presupposes a mistakenly static view of the human condition and human cultures. In fact, the dynamism of human beings and their social projects allows them to create communication and understanding where once there was little or none. Moreover, a theory of inquiry properly tuned to the biological and social realities of human life can facilitate the

interpretation of disciplines as having crucial cognitive structures in common even when their styles and subject matters are extremely diverse. This is the deepest explanation for why incommensurability does not defeat multidisciplinarity so much as invite inquiring communities to regard incommensurability as a practical problem that can be engaged and, with the right will and skill, mitigated.

The Challenge of Incommensurability

Multidisciplinary approaches are clearly important for making inquiries properly complex and for managing side effects of the abstraction associated with problem emergence. Yet a few contemporary philosophers argue that some disciplines and even some intradisciplinary projects cannot be brought into conversation with each other because they lack a common language or a shared conceptual framework. This same claim of incommensurability can be applied to the linguistic and conceptual gaps between cultures and between eras, and even to the very idea of comparison itself. While it is obvious that communication in all of these situations is frequently difficult, the incommensurability thesis goes further, arguing that genuine communication is impossible and that the difficulties cannot be overcome.

The incommensurability thesis has a complex history, with a few strands reaching back into the far past of many major philosophical traditions. In the form that is of concern here, it is essentially a child of twentieth-century Western philosophy. The timing is ironic. This was the century of biology, and especially of evolutionary biology, in which we discovered that human beings have more in common at the basic levels of bodily function and cognitive structure than was ever suspected previously. This would appear to furnish a basis for confidence that the familiar communication difficulties between disciplines and even across cultures should be tractable. Yet the impression of cultural and interdisciplinary difference, to the point of incommensurability, blossomed in the same period. A deep suspicion of science is evident in much of the rhetoric surrounding the incommensurability thesis, which suggests that support of the incommensurability thesis may function culturally as a preemptive attack on a looming scientific hegemony. Even if fears of bland scientific dominance are overblown, the incommensurability thesis resists reductionism and honors particularities in a way that is culturally useful and politically important. These virtues say a lot about the motivation for propounding incommensurability in the first place, and even more about the reasons for insisting on it in the face of increasing biological evidence for commonality among human beings across cultures.

There are at least four major roots of the incommensurability thesis, all from the second half of the twentieth century. One is Ludwig Wittgenstein's reflections on language use, which were important subsequently for a host of intellectuals from philosophers to literary critics, and from anthropologists to historians.[32] Wittgenstein argued that language always operates in a social context and that we make meaning not because language refers to objects but because language works to help us get things done. Wittgenstein distanced himself from the functionalist suggestions of this view but the loosening of ties between words and objects effectively binds the meaning-making power of language to the language games that arise within specific forms of life rather than to an objective world that all language users refer to in common. While Wittgenstein himself assumed that language games interpenetrate and mutate, some philosophers developed a view of language games more as hard-edged marbles that neither overlap nor change—or rather as boundaryless practices, which coexist without sufficient cognitive traction for translation and communication across language games. Within religious philosophy, a fierce advocate of incommensurability and nontranslatability in roughly this sense was Dewi Z. Phillips.[33] A less extreme approach is that of George Lindbeck, who interpreted religious doctrines neither primarily as objective truth claims nor primarily as symbolic expressions of religious feeling but rather as the rules for language games that arise within distinctively religious forms of life.[34] Whether in Phillips' dramatic or Lindbeck's moderate version, the incommensurability thesis, as it derives from Wittgenstein, rests on the lack of a clear way to relate the terms of different language games. This is immediately relevant to incommensurability between disciplines, which can be understood as language games arising within particular forms of life.

A second root of the incommensurability thesis is the philosophical and literary study of acts of interpretation, or hermeneutics. One of the important contributions of hermeneutics is its patient exhibition of the potential chasm between an author's intention and a reader's interpretation. This explains our experience of the way that many texts seem loosed from the mooring of the author's intended meanings, or artifacts from their maker's design intentions, so as to give rise to multiple, irreducibly conflicting interpretations. Hans-Georg Gadamer's image of interpretation as the fusion of horizons—the horizon of a text and the horizon of an interpreter—expresses not only the creative possibilities for interpretation but also the fundamental indeterminacy of meaning in the abstract; interpretation is a creative contextual act that makes meanings.[35] In the context of multidisciplinarity, individual disciplines can be thought of as multiple horizons to be integrated with that of the interpreter for the sake of forwarding an inquiry. The density of meanings in the individual disciplinary perspectives, the arbitrariness of the process of problem abstraction, and the creativity of the act of fusion make reliable multidisciplinary ventures seem utterly fanciful. In this case, the incommensurability thesis arises from the very richness of the interpretative act—and, thus, from the lack of any standard by which to regulate or synthesize interpretative insights from multiple disciplines.

A third root of the incommensurability thesis was the philosophical reaction against structuralist strategies for the analysis of human language and cultural artifacts such as literary texts or historical traditions. Beginning in linguistics and subsequently reaching into disciplines from anthropology to literary criticism, structuralism asserted the value of typological structures as analytical rubrics for guiding interpretation. The basis of this claim is that such structures reflect deeply rooted universal psychological features of human beings—or at least local habits of practice within particular human societies deriving ultimately from shared biology and commonalities in the environments that condition in intelligible ways the variations of psychological development and cultural expression.[36] There is ample evidence to support some structuralist contentions, and indeed, the evidence is increasing with deeper knowledge of evolutionary psychology. Nonetheless, structuralism's hermeneutical optimism fractured under the weight of the irreducibility of historical contingencies and individual intricacies as factors in explanations of texts and traditions, of mind sets and worldviews, and of interpretation and meaning making. The particularity of an object of interpretation, its difference or otherness, unmasks the abstraction inevitably involved in structuralist modes of interpretation.[37] In this case, the incommensurability thesis arises as a kind of testimony to the irreducibility of particularity and the impossibility of comprehensively understanding others. This affects multidisciplinarity because of the intricate particularity of disciplinary discourses, and the way that this distinctiveness is inevitably effaced in taking results out of context and applying them to the quite different context of the problem that drives a multidisciplinary inquiry.

Finally, a fourth root of the incommensurability thesis was in the philosophy of science, where incommensurability was a key aspect of an important hypothesis about competition between scientific research programs. The driving realization in this case was that prominent early rational formulations of scientific advance—such as the empiricist account of science as inductive generalization from observations, or the view of naïve falsification that emphasizes the falsifiability of scientific generalizations rather than the means of their creation—bore little resemblance to the historical description of the social practices that nurture and advance scientific theories. This produced highly skeptical interpretations, such as that of Paul Feyerabend who argued that science has no distinctive rational method and owes its cultural prestige solely to the usefulness of its products.[38] It also produced more moderate responses, such as Thomas Kuhn's account of relatively rational normal science occasionally interrupted by periods of revolutionary theory change, for which no fully rational account can be given.[39] The field of science and technology studies has amplified this analysis, perpetuating a contrarian view about the claims to objectivity and rationality—claims dominating at least the public reception of science, if not the imaginations of scientists themselves.[40] Both Feyerabend and Kuhn used the word *incommensurability* during the 1950s to describe the logical relationship between competing scientific research programs. Both referred to a lack of a common standard, which enables a scientist advocating one research program to express in a familiar conceptual scheme and a familiar web of social practices the conceptual elements and social dimensions of another scientist's research program. It is from this usage in the philosophy of science that the word appears to have gained wide distribution in numerous intellectual contexts. The application to disciplinary incommensurability, as well as to more distant issues such as cultural incommensurability, derives fundamentally from the assumption that disciplines and cultures are like scientific research programs in respect of the role that active conceptual schemes and social practices play in preventing effective translation.

In light of these four root sources for the idea of incommensurability, it is evident that the incommensurability thesis is not a single, well-defined proposition. Its versions vary in strength and differ in the domain of application. Thus, its implications for multidisciplinarity and comparison, and ultimately for religious philosophy, depend on the details of the incommensurability claim in a given instance. Recognizing the need for specificity, if only for the sake of argument, I identify the heart of the incommensurability thesis to be the following threefold claim about conceptual schemes: (1) Conceptual schemes are inextricably embedded in practices and assumptions of worldly realities (theories, disciplines, languages, cultures). (2) Conceptual schemes are incommensurable when all attempts to take the measure of one family of ideas or one web of practices in the terms of another necessarily distort what is interpreted to such a degree that co-measuring is rightly deemed a pernicious waste of time. (3) Conceptual schemes are often incommensurable in this sense. If all three parts of this claim are upheld, then much co-measuring (such as translation and comparison) is in fact a creative fiction masquerading as communication and, thus, can easily place an implicit, distorting exercise of power beyond the reach of effective criticism.

To indicate the particularity of this statement of the incommensurability thesis, consider some alternatives. One stronger version links incommensurability with an ontologically loaded form of conceptual relativism, whereby *reality itself differs across conceptual schemes*. But we need to set aside this relativist form of the incommensurability thesis on the grounds that it is incoherent. Suppose incommensurability requires that reality vary across conceptual schemes. The obvious lack of any way to discern that reality is different for two such conceptual schemes entails that there can also be no way to decide if the conceptual schemes in question are in fact incommensurable. Therefore, no situation can be devised in which incommensurability, so understood, can be known to be rightly applied.[41]

Another stronger version of the incommensurability thesis asserts that it is *always meaningless to co-measure (for example, compare or translate) across conceptual schemes*. The problem here is that this statement seems false on its face. There is meaning in translations and reexpressions even when there is also inaccuracy and distortion.

A weaker version of the incommensurability thesis simply *asserts well established facts such as framework-dependent meanings, theory-laden data, and convention-relative values*, without drawing any final epistemological or ontological or moral conclusions. But such a modest descriptive approach fails to disclose what is most deeply problematic about the idea of incommensurability.

The above statement of the incommensurability thesis puts the nub of the problem in an optimally sharp form. It avoids overstatement that voids definitions tying incommensurability to conceptual relativism or meaninglessness of translation. It fully acknowledges the difficulties that plague communication across different traditions, disciplines, cultures, eras, conceptual frameworks, and languages. And it identifies the fundamental problem of incommensurability as a moral one—namely, that the distortion inevitable in co-measuring is unfair, socially dangerous, and intellectually disingenuous. I think that these moral defects are what most bother people about cavalier approaches to communication difficulties and generalized interpretations of complex phenomena. Moreover, it is essentially for moral reasons that some welcome incommensurability as a strategic means to protect the beautiful intricacy of cultural details and disciplinary perspectives—details that tend to be elided whenever co-measuring is indulged.

Incommensurability and the Dynamic Sociality of Inquiry

To frame incommensurability as a moral problem is both to acknowledge its severity and to intimate a solution. As a moral problem, incommensurability is a matter of degree rather than an insurmountable block to communication. While there may be no way to avoid the moral quandaries entirely, if there are techniques for managing communication difficulties, then it should be possible to mitigate the associated moral problems.

The reason incommensurability is taken to be an insurmountable difficulty is partly because the exaggerated but implausible interpretations of it discussed above—especially conceptual relativism—are fairly widespread, and partly because people seeking to protect precious particularities from the careless caricatures of gross generalizations have a strategic interest in making incommensurability seem insurmountable. In practice, however, every description involves generalized categories—as any analysis of the nouns and adjectives of a description effortlessly demonstrates, and as postmodern theorists have argued at great length. No matter how much we trumpet the impossibility of overcoming incommensurability, therefore, we all routinely co-measure, co-relate, and translate by means of such generalizations in our descriptions and comparisons. There can be no thinking without generalization, just as thinking can never be adequate or useful without sensitivity to details. The philosophical challenge is to articulate the dialectic between particularity and generality in such a way as to manifest resources for managing the communication problems accompanying our attempts to co-measure.

The key resource in any useful philosophical account of the dialectic between particularity and generality is the dynamic social character of human rationality in all acts of inquiry. The account of problem emergence presented earlier in this chapter draws attention to the contextual conditioning of problems as they emerge reflexively from the flow of human experience. Relevant conditioning factors include socially formed expectations about how the world operates and how people ought to behave. Even cognitive factors such as basic ontological beliefs about natural kinds have a social component, as cultural variation of such beliefs shows. More profoundly, consciousness itself, from perception to emotion and from intelligence to self-understanding, depends on sociality. As neuropsychologist Leslie Brothers puts it, "the network of meanings we call culture arises from the *joint* activities of human brains. This network forms the living content of the mind, so that the mind is communal in its very nature: It cannot be derived from any single brain in isolation."[42]

Brothers goes on to present the evidence pertinent to her conclusion that the "deceptively humble behavior" of conversation, for which we are extremely well adapted, is the key to understanding human behavior from the individual to the social. Conversation bridges the gap between culture and the mind, enabling and constituting both. This perspective dramatically reframes the unidirectional model of functional, isolated brains cooperating to make a social world—a model for which there is scant evidence. A brain has nothing we can recognize as a mind without social interaction. With communication, however, the staggering potential of our brains to support practical intelligence, ordered feeling, and cultural creativity is unleashed. Everything we do is simultaneously neural and social, simultaneously a matter of biological causes and psychological reasons.

This is the framework for problem emergence. Sociality underlies not only our tendency to construct emergent problems in parochial ways but also our ability to enrich our understanding of problems with socially encoded wisdom. This is as true of the role of multidisciplinarity in the scholarly realm as it is of traditional wisdom in the realm of everyday practical problems. In the case of scholarly problems, we have seen how multiple disciplinary perspectives are necessary to complicate problems by drawing our attention to pertinent considerations that do not immediately appear in the naturally parochial way problems first show up for us. This is akin to the role that the shared wisdom of so-called common sense plays in enriching our understanding of ordinary problems in everyday life. Communication is not just the generic precondition for activating minds in a human way; it is also the means by which we work on puzzles as they arise from the flow of experience.

Overcoming the natural parochialism of problem definition is one of several ways in which sociality and communication feature in the way we handle an emergent problem. All aspects of "handling a problem" are inherently social and communicative. Even when we appear to be working alone, we read; we remember what we learned; and we make use of internalized communicative practices to unlock new perspectives on the problem that troubles us. Communication in all of these senses guides us to strategies for solving a problem, helps us intelligently arrive at promising hypotheses for solutions, draws attention to relevant resources for testing and refining our hypothetical solution, encourages us not to give up when we seem to be getting nowhere, and inspires us to branch out in a new direction when a key insight strikes us. Communication is both the key to preparing the mind for problem solving and the main strategic resource for actually constructing solutions.

In addition to all that, sociality and communication are the means by which we relate the abstraction of problem definition to the intricate particularities of experience. We internalize this dialectic when we ask ourselves whether the statement of a problem does justice to the experiences that gave rise to it, and when we assess the problem-solving potential of a resource for inquiry. We realize the dialectic socially when we take a problem statement, a strategy, or a solution into the public domain and ask others to evaluate it. If we have done our work well, the internalized version of this dialectic will have helped us to anticipate most of the criticisms that we will receive. That is, instead of being surprised when someone says that our formulation of the problem appears to be insensitive to how this problem takes shape in his or her distinctive context, the internalized dialectic in combination with information resources will have allowed us already to have registered certain aspects of this context. There will be no way to avoid abstraction, but refined judgment can produce abstractions that amplify salient details while muting peripheral details. And the key practices involved in acquiring and executing such refined judgment are communicative and social in nature, whether manifestly in public or internalized in private.

The moral quandary that incommensurability provokes finds its resolution in the artfulness of inquiry. We cannot avoid abstractions and would never want to if we cared about solving problems. But we can take responsibility for the abstractions we inevitably produce. Moreover, in a lifetime of learning from others in such a way that our abstractions are elegant and just, we can operationalize communication across the chasms of disciplinary and cultural and experiential differences. There is nothing simple about this, of course. But neither is it impossible in principle, as exaggerated versions of the incommensurability thesis suggest.

The final point to make about managing the moral difficulties of incommensurability is also the most obvious. Communication is dynamic. Social interests and resources are fluid. Human imagination and ingenuity are staggering capacities, which make the possibilities for solving problems virtually limitless. Even the best prepared human beings may not be able to solve every problem, and the most sensitive inquirers can never entirely eliminate the moral difficulties of incommensurability and abstraction. But challenges can be tackled as they arise, with surprising results. The dynamism inherent in the sociality of inquiry has several dimensions, including the following.

First, we can discover unanticipated resources that dramatically change the prospects of finding a solution to a problem. The Rosetta stone provided the key to translating many Egyptian hieroglyphic writing symbols. The discovery of the microscopic capillary system, which links arteries and veins, made the mammalian circulatory system intelligible. Anselm's discovery of the phrase translated as "that than which nothing greater can be thought" gave birth to bootstrapping arguments for the existence of God within the ontotheological tradition of religious philosophy. Inquirers working on complex problems routinely make discoveries of a more modest kind; insights learned from another discipline can dramatically change their perception of a problem. Discoveries of new facts and new ideas, both modest and stunning, have transformed and can still transform assumptions about what is possible in inquiries, within and beyond religious philosophy.

Second, we can arrive at new levels of efficiency in the social organization of inquiries, thereby changing the prospects for making advances in solving complex problems. Sophisticated databases have massively enlarged the range of tractable problems in both the sciences and the humanities by coordinating information that far exceeds what one person or even a small group of collaborators can assimilate. University-based disciplines and scholarly organizations help intellectuals focus their attention on particular issues—leveraging economies of scale that are necessary for advancing research on complex problems. Rapid and relatively accurate communication technologies—first through the printing and distribution of specialized academic journals and eventually through the Internet—have dramatically increased the probability that key results will be encountered by those whose research requires these results. These and other improvements in efficiency change the prospects across the board for problem solving.

Third, we can invent. Sometimes we invent technologies that solve medical problems or help us manipulate the physical world. Sometimes we invent conceptual objects in order to formalize knowledge and make it more widely and readily accessible. For example, the formal languages of logic and mathematics are abstractions that risk distorting the concepts and thoughts to which they are applied but also catalyze potent attention to problems that can be formulated by means of them. Technical terminology in virtually every field has the same disadvantage of distortion through prematurely fixing the imagination but also the same advantage of making disciplinary discourse more consistent and the associated inquiries more efficient.

Fourth, we can adjust to new information. Noticing and accommodating new experiences is the heart and soul of the empirical instinct in all human endeavors. We may feel attached to a hypothetical explanation because it has repeatedly proved its usefulness, and yet we can still train ourselves to notice its failures and thereby to gather the information required to correct and improve it, or perhaps to devise an alternative to compare with it. We can treasure the abstract formulation of a problem, and yet with the help of conversation, and often by means of other disciplinary insights, we can detect its liabilities and formulate a more satisfying version of the problem. We can register the way a generalized comparison distorts our understanding of a cultural artifact, especially in the sense that members of the culture in question cannot recognize what we say about that artifact. We can then accommodate information from this experience of failed communication to render our comparison more sensitive to the relevant facts.

Finally, we can bend social will to particular ends. The conservative political attitude to the approach of peak oil production is that, when the crisis is upon us, the well-attested ability of human beings to find solutions to urgent problems will kick in and we will find new and even more efficient portable energy sources. South Africa as a post-apartheid nation reorganized itself around more just economic and moral principles. Some of those who didn't like it emigrated. Most were determined to create a new arrangement and make it work. The Human Genome Initiative focused vast resources and energy on sequencing all human genes. Other projects have sequenced the genomes of several other species, with enormously important long-term consequences for biology and medicine.

These various manifestations of the dynamic sociality of inquiry produce the most direct answer to the problems of incommensurability. When communication is difficult, we need not accept the diagnosis that the problems are intractable. We can work on the difficulties and make communication more efficient and more accurate. The dialectic of abstraction and particularities, which is vital for formulating and solving problems, remains, but we can operate within its constraints more and less skillfully. When we focus our creative resources on generating new and better forms of communication, our skill set broadens, and our mastery increases. Understood in its proper moral sense, incommensurability is not a dead end but an invitation.

Chapter 5

Religious Philosophy and Comparison

Religious philosophy does not always involve explicitly comparing ideas. It is comparative in nature rather often, however, in a host of ways, and for good reasons. The themes treated within religious philosophy typically arise, appropriately translated, in several philosophical and religious traditions. When themes from one tradition are not found explicitly treated in another with roughly matching categories and terminology, they often subsist in differently angled questions and ideas. These explicit and implicit commonalities derive from the universal aspects of human nature, which are biologically rooted and evolutionarily stabilized in our species, and possibly also from consistent features of the environment, which inspire and constrain religious ideas. Yet cultural diversity is pervasive—to the point that identification, translation, and comparison are extraordinarily sensitive tasks. Thus, comparison is an inevitable and also a difficult aspect of religious philosophy. Some of the questions surrounding comparison are highly controversial. Within the field of religious studies, for instance, there is confusion and fierce debate about numerous aspects of the primary task—from how best to do it to whether to attempt the task at all.

I begin here with an abstract philosophical account of comparison. In an effort to keep things simple and to gain a clear grasp of the issues, I focus initially on the banal example of comparing fruit. Basic ideas in comparison often remain obscure, thanks to a tendency to rush to ideological posturing either on behalf of a kind of structuralism that guarantees that comparison will pay off in advance of trying, or on behalf of a type of skeptical deconstruction of all comparative meanings in honor of the exquisite distinctiveness of individual phenomena.

Under such charged circumstances, a patient analysis of comparing fruit might help. This general analysis of comparison then informs a discussion of comparison within religious philosophy, illuminating its inevitability and importance, and tracing the ways it can and does go wrong. This discussion establishes the criteria for what counts as an adequate and compelling account of comparison in the context of religious philosophy.

Subsequently, I lay out a series of views of comparison that are pertinent to religious philosophy. Each is an established point of view in the methodological literature surrounding comparative philosophy and comparative religion. The last view I discuss is the one I find most persuasive in the context of religious philosophy. This position holds that comparison should involve a self-correcting conversation between data and comparative categories, a conversation that cumulatively enhances understanding. Deriving from several sources, especially Edmund Husserl and Robert Neville, this "self-conscious dialectic" view takes a realistic stand on the inevitability and difficulty of comparison and accommodates the wisdom of existing approaches in a theoretically more satisfying account.

Finally, I explain how the self-conscious dialectic view of comparison operates within religious philosophy. The controversies surrounding comparison in religious philosophy cannot be evaded or avoided without self-deception. If religious philosophy is to get anywhere in this age of extensive crosscultural contact, it will need to take a persuasive and clearheaded stand on the comparison of religious practices and ideas.

What is Comparison?

Comparison is such a common activity that we routinely underestimate its complex cognitive requirements and conceptual structure. A close analysis of an instance of comparison (comparing fruit) discloses these features. Any serviceable model of acts of comparison must take account of comparative categories, their vagueness and specificity, and the ways by which perception and description can be distorted by comparison.

Comparison Generically

What is comparison? The Oxford English Dictionary's online definitions for the transitive verb *compare* are: "(1) To speak of or represent as similar; to liken"; and "(2) To mark or point out the similarities and differences of (two or more things); to bring or place together (actually or mentally) for the purpose of noting the similarities and differences." Both definitions are relevant to most kinds of comparison. We usually begin by noticing, thanks to our cognitive skills, that two things are curiously alike. Then we proceed to examine them closely, noting similarities and differences. To "bring or place together . . . for the purpose of noting the similarities and differences" is in effect to invoke a *respect of comparison*—I use this technical term consistently in what follows—and to use that respect in the cognitive process of comparison. We usually compare in respects that interest us, often neglecting respects that do not. The respect in which we compare constitutes a *comparative category* for the comparison.

When we seek to compare oranges and apples in respect of being fruit, we use "fruit" as a comparative category. As fruit, apples and oranges are similar in some respects and different in others; these more specific respects of comparison (more specific than the general respect of being fruit) are subordinate comparative categories. In respect of surface texture, oranges are dimpled whereas apples are smooth. In respect of rind qualities, most oranges have a thick and fleshy rind, while apple rinds are thin—and both are slightly bitter and both help protect the fruit from rotting. In respect of internal structure, oranges are segmented, and apples are not, but both carry seeds in a segmented arrangement. The respects of comparison thus define a complex array of categories—some subordinate to others, and each the basis for noting similarities and differences.

Every comparative category must be vague in order to register differences. Vagueness here does not mean failure, or perverse refusal, to be specific. Rather, vagueness refers to a logical characteristic of a category, namely, that the law of noncontradiction does not apply to what falls within it. For example, the comparative category of "fruit rind" must be vague to accommodate the quite different cases of apples, oranges, watermelon, avocados, and kiwi fruit. Propositions expressing the characteristics of fruit rinds—"Fruit rinds are thick and smooth" versus "Fruit rinds are thin and furry," for example—specify the category of "fruit rind" in contradictory ways and yet properly express the vagueness of the category "fruit rind." The vague category is a meaningful basis for comparison, and the many possible specifications of it fill out its content.

To say this is not yet to say that the comparative category is *useful* or *interesting*. In fact, I selected a mundane category just to make the point that we must distinguish the logical analysis of category vagueness from judgments about whether a vague category helps to detect anything interesting about important subject matters. In relation to fruit, rinds are interesting partly because of the functions that they perform, such as protecting the flesh and seeds, or making the fruit attractive to animals or improving the color of still-life paintings. This question about interesting categories is quite profound in the case of religious philosophy.

All comparison is interested—that is, it is an act conditioned by the interests of interpreting beings. We are rather often unaware of our interests, which is why meeting people with different interests can be so entertaining or disturbing: encountering the other heightens our awareness of our own particularities. We compare apples and oranges in respect of health benefits, cost, ease of production in a local climate, seasonal demand, shelf life, flavor, and what our kids will eat. We shift with ease among these various respects of comparison as our interests dictate and we think little of it because nothing of intellectual or moral significance seems to be at stake. But this is not always so; sometimes important moral or intellectual issues are at stake in our comparisons.

The vagueness and interestedness of comparative categories can combine in unexpected ways to produce bad comparisons. Specifically, we conceive categories poorly when: (a) they lead to uninteresting comparisons, (b) we fail to make them vague in just the right ways to accommodate the things we are interested in comparing, or (c) they depend on mistaken theories about aspects of reality. I will give examples of all of these in what follows.

(a) "Rind texture" is vague in just the right way to handle the varied surface characteristics of fruit, but it is not especially interesting in isolation from some theoretical account of why fruits have rinds and why the rinds vary in character. "Large-scale segmentation" is not much use as a comparative category if we are interested in comparing apples and oranges because the category only succeeds in registering apples negatively, as not having any large-scale segmentation. In fact, if we are not properly attentive, and our attention is focused only on large-scale segmentation, we may conclude that apples have no segmentation at all because they do not have the segmentation we see in grapefruits and tangerines and oranges. If we were to consider the broader category of "segmentation," however, we might happily make comparisons between apples and oranges with respect to several different kinds of segmentation (large-scale, sub-structure scale, seed scale, surface bump patterns, etc.) We handle vagueness of the "segmentation" category by specifying subordinate categories to flesh out the dimensions of meaning of segmentation that the data demand.

(b) There is nothing inherently wrong with comparative categories lacking the ideal level of vagueness. But two practical problems can arise, especially when we unthinkingly adopt existing categories for new purposes. On the one hand, too much vagueness gives undue freedom to our overactive pattern-recognition skills, permitting us to see similarities and differences that suit our interests, whether or not those interests are ideologically neutral. Thus, sometimes it may suit us to compare apples and oranges in respect of their reminding us of glorious summer holidays in the south of France. Far less neutral comparisons of the same sort are possible, especially in religious studies, though perhaps not in the domain of fruit. On the other hand, our comparisons can lack richness and insight when we use insufficiently vague categories to describe ill-suited subject matter. Consider again the comparative category of "segmented fruit structure," for example. This category must be vague to allow for the segmented macrostructure of tangerines, the segmented seed casings of apples, the fact that some apples have minor large-structure segmentation (in the form of bumps at the bottom of the apple) and others do not, the symmetry of peaches and nectarines, and the fact that some oranges have delicate internal substructures and others do not. If we unconsciously understand the comparative category of segmentation to refer only to comprehensive macrostructural segmentation, then our comparative category may lead us to overlook other types of segmentation in fruit—as when the claim that "Oranges are segmented but apples are not" can lead us to overlook segmentation of the apple core.

Consciousness of this problem is the first step in avoiding distorted descriptions of segmentation in apples. The most useful strategy is to develop an array of categories within which broader categories are specified by subordinate categories. This leads us to look for subtle features. It is precisely for this reason that classification schemes have been so important in the history of thought.[1] While promoting more detailed observation, however, classification schemes also carry hidden theoretical assumptions of which we must strive to be aware lest distortion of description and flawed understanding go unnoticed.[2] Thus, one of the tricks in improving comparisons is to allow the details of the process of comparing to make us conscious of narrowness in our comparative categories. Thereafter, we can either narrow the definition of a comparative category to conform to the way we were using it or broaden the definition to accommodate the features of the data that interest us. In either case, the categories of comparison should be responsive to the process of comparison. The danger of classifications is that they enshrine comparative categories and may make them seem to be beyond question.

(c) Some comparisons are invidious and lead to intellectual misunderstandings and moral disasters. When Aristotle compared human beings in respect of the independence and completeness of intellective soul, he concluded that slaves had none of these qualities and that women require a man's fully developed intellective soul to guide and complete their own partially developed intellective soul.[3] Aristotle seemed unaware of his powerful desire to rationalize existing social practices, yet his comparison reflects this interest in a way that is obvious to people with different interests, such as his teacher Plato.[4] It is still more obvious to people who live at a time when better data makes Aristotle's comparison seem silly, despite the fact that it was generous for its time in some ways (not everyone clearly distinguished women from slaves, as Aristotle did).

Where precisely does the problem with Aristotle's comparison lie? The mistake is in the meaning he gives to the comparative category by which he attempts to diagnose similarities and differences among men, women, and slaves—namely, the independence and completeness of intellective soul. The meaning of this category derives from mostly mistaken theories about human nature, the intellect, and human reproduction, and from mostly mistaken estimates of the power of social context to condition interpretations. Aristotle was empirically minded enough to recognize that some women did not fit his model but treated them as "contrary to nature" exceptions rather than as the few women able to realize some of their intellectual power despite the almost insurmountable difficulties they faced in their oppressive social circumstances. And Aristotle was just wrong about reproduction, as when he speculated that women had to be incomplete men because their bodies were unable to heat menstrual fluid to the point that it could become semen. Of course, he thought that semen was the source of the nonmaterial parts of a human being, including especially intellective soul. The theoretical framework for his comparative category of "the independence and completeness of intellective soul" was defective and we are entitled to wonder whether he did enough to test and improve the category.

The lesson here is that special interests interfere with the refinement of comparative categories. Interested comparison is inevitable but bad interested comparison is not. We can control for interests by seeking correction and refinement of our comparative categories. We can strive to make them sensitive to variations in the data for comparison, as when we have to avoid unconscious rigidity in our understanding of segmentation in fruit. We can also try to give comparative categories meaning through embedding them in superior theoretical frameworks. For example, we need sound theories of reproduction if we are to avoid Aristotle's mistakes in wielding the comparative category of the independence and completeness of intellective soul.

This discussion of interested comparison drives home the sometimes overlooked fact that behind every act of comparison there lurks an interpreter with only partially conscious interests and incomplete knowledge of the world. We have a prodigious capacity for making delicate discriminations to suit ruling interests, to rationalize desired actions, and to bring comfort and assurance that the "other" is comprehensible and controllable rather than alien or terrifying. The neurological conditions for comparison are important here. Human beings have highly developed pattern recognition skills, which are especially useful for recognizing the significance of facial expressions.[5] These skills misfire from time to time even in interpreting faces. They are also tuned to be slightly overactive, which can lead us to expect patterns where none exist, or at least none at the level we seek. This is one of the great liabilities that human beings bring to observation and inquiry, and psychologists have documented its effects in great detail.[6] It is equally a liability in comparison, where untrained human beings are too ready to find similarities on the basis of a quick glance. This tendency maximizes vulnerability to error due to overconfidence and marginalizes the careful checking needed to save comparative conclusions from becoming victims of casual hubris.

To summarize, comparison is a cognitive activity that involves construing multiple things as instances of a vague comparative category. Good comparison works empirically by keying categorial vagueness to comparative data, conservatively by allowing for overactive human pattern recognition skills, theoretically by attending to the way categories derive their meaning from existing interpretations of aspects of reality, and humbly by seeking correction of comparative hypotheses in light of changing observations and theories.

Comparing Religious Ideas and Practices

This theoretical model of good comparison applies to religious philosophy as well as to fruit. In fact, it helps us discern that we make comparative judgments more frequently in religious philosophy than we may expect, which indicates their *inevitability and importance*. This model suggests ways that comparison in religious philosophy might typically go *wrong*. It shows that comparison is *possible* because the focus on correction and self-awareness mitigates the perpetual problem of bias to an optimal degree. And it confirms practical experience that *methodological self-awareness* in comparison helps philosophers handle the peculiar complexities of comparison in religious philosophy. I remark on each of these four topics in what follows.

When religious philosophers speak of "theistic religions" or "samsaric worldviews," they invoke comparative categories. Even when limiting themselves to a single religious tradition, they require comparative categories to comprehend and relate concepts across cultures and eras, and across diverse sub-traditions of practice and belief. For example, when Christians speak of baptism, it is not one sharply defined practice but actually a host of practices stretching far and wide among contexts where Christianity has existed—accompanied by a similar host of theological interpretations voiced so differently that sometimes it is not obvious that the theologies describe the same practice. The question of whether these diverse practices are the same typically is prejudged by the unreflective usage of a comparative category. An anthropologist paying careful attention to differences in baptismal practices would rightly be puzzled by the inclusion within a single category of fully immersing in a river adults who have virtually no understanding of Christianity, dribbling water on the forehead of a newborn baby, or celebrating a rite of passage for teenagers who have passed through a period of intense educational preparation in the faith tradition of their community.

To call these diverse practices and associated beliefs "baptism" without any qualifications is to join them as a matter of principle, to assert their identity in important respects. This is an act of stipulation, in one sense, and such acts can be socially potent. Christian leaders use such stipulations to affirm the authenticity of their own baptismal practices in relation to a vaguely articulated larger tradition. Sometimes theologians use such stipulations provisionally to raise questions about authenticity. In that case, the comparative category of baptism sustains subordinate comparative categories that distinguish between those practices that are authentic and legitimate and those practices that are not. Sometimes ecumenical discussions use such stipulations merely to begin a discussion about the variant theological connotations of baptism within multiple denominations. All of these moves make use of comparative categories.

Decisions about how to translate key concepts into the languages that host influential traditions of religious philosophy can have far-reaching effects. Such decisions have influenced the understanding of students of religion for generations, for better and for worse. One of the most famous examples of decisions misleading subsequent interpreters was the use of the word *polytheism* in European languages to describe the array of Hindu Gods. It took some decades for scholars of religion and religious philosophers to correct the impression this gives of a disorganized pantheon. Most Hindus even in the context of popular religious practices believe that the God to whom they are devoted (Śiva, Viṣṇu, Gaṇeśa) is an aspect of Brahman, understood not as a High God trying to control a bevy of divine underlings but as ultimate reality itself.

Another example of the power of translated terminology is the use of *reincarnation* to describe Indian Buddhist versions of the South Asian samsaric worldview. In fact, the *anattā* (no-substantive self) doctrine of most forms of Indian Buddhism means that there is no *jīva* (soul) that persists from life to life through death and reincarnation, as there is in most forms of Hinduism. The consequences for *saṃsāra* and nirvana of this view are complicated, and perhaps mind boggling, and Buddhists have spent enormous effort in debate over them, both with Hindus and among themselves. So it is not surprising that many Buddhists do not hesitate to picture life and death in rather Hindu terms, as re-enfleshment of an enduring soul, despite their characteristic no-self doctrine. Many Buddhist intellectuals will not do this, however, and their more subtle approach is not registered at all when the word *reincarnation* is used as the comparative category to comprehend both Hindu and Buddhist visions of the implications of *saṃsāra* for living beings.

These two examples are interesting because of an important difference between popular and elite interpretations within a religion. In the first case, most ordinary Hindus concur with Hindu intellectuals that the Gods of Hindu piety are comprehensible and existentially meaningful aspects of ultimate reality. The comparative category of "polytheism" misleads religious philosophers about Hinduism at both levels. In the second case, most ordinary Buddhists can't make much sense of the no-self doctrine in relation to *saṃsāra* and so affirm a substantival interpretation of reincarnation despite the elite refusal to do this. The comparative category of "reincarnation" masks this difference. Elite interpreters can rightly point out the distortion involved in using the same word for this in Hindu and Buddhist contexts, but anthropologists of religion would be equally right to point out that Buddhism is always more and other than what elite interpreters are willing to say about it.

In response to these complexities, it would be understandable if religious philosophers were to follow the many religious studies specialists who seek to reduce their dependence on comparative categories, or to avoid comparison altogether. As we will see, such efforts are insightful in some ways but they are deeply mistaken in promising the impossible. It is simply not possible for students of religion, including religious philosophers, to avoid the use of comparative categories. They suffuse everything we say and think. Moreover, they often create understanding and a basis for refining understanding through further study. It is a mistake to interpret the distortions resulting from comparative categories in the study of religion as evidence of the futility of comparison. Rather, the undeniable distortions indicate the difficulty of the task of speaking about intricate, complex, dynamic, living phenomena such as religious ideas and practices. Discovering a distortion can immediately correct mistakes. Incorporating such a discovery into the way we wield a comparative category enhances understanding and improves the quality of future work. Comparative categories are inevitable and important, and they can be more useful than harmful within religious philosophy so long as philosophers self-consciously attend to the way they wield them.

What is the optimal way to manage the distortions that inevitably arise as we describe religious ideas and practices? I offer an answer to this question toward the end of the next section. But already it is possible to see that what the outlines of this answer must be. An optimal approach to the fact of distortion in comparative categories must be one of management. Purity is as impossible as comparison is inevitable. And the issues are so complex that we will need a corporate approach combining many perspectives rather than relying solely on the very few genius comparativists capable of storing and balancing every pertinent consideration in a single brilliant mind. But what kind of corporate management strategy is feasible for comparison in religious philosophy?

Comparing Approaches to Comparative Philosophy

Comparative philosophy and comparative religion have tried to understand their tasks so that distortion is minimized while the usefulness of comparison for understanding is optimized. Some of these self-understandings are better than others, and the associated debates are surveyed here. The conclusion is that comparison is best understood as a dynamic dialectic of data and categories. This understanding of comparison is more coherent with the prior analysis of acts of comparison and makes better sense than the alternatives, all of which take unduly pessimistic or optimistic stances in the debate over the possibilities and prospects of comparison.

In this section, I classify a number of attitudes and approaches to comparison according to how they would answer an increasingly detailed sequence of considerations. Some reject the possibility of comparison whereas I argue for its possibility. Others reject explicit categories for comparison whereas I argue that explicitness about the inevitability of comparison in categories (or respects) is overall a virtue. Still others justify categories from existing theories whereas I argue for limiting (not eliminating) this kind of justification in order to make categories more vulnerable to correction and more easily able to change in response to the process of comparison. And yet others justify categories directly from similarities in the data whereas I argue that this is too arbitrary a procedure. This compact survey of approaches to comparison is intended primarily as an argument for the self-conscious dialectic method for comparing religious ideas, which I describe last.[7]

Comparison as Impossible

We begin with the basic question reflecting the contention surrounding comparison in contemporary religious studies: is comparison possible? If we take this question in its narrowest sense, as asking about the sheer possibility of comparison of religious ideas and practices, it is unproblematic. I think it undeniable that comparison has actually occurred, whether well or badly done.

The question is more interesting if understood as a question about the possibility of successful comparison. The ideal of "success" is contestable, but I think the prior discussion reflects what success should mean: (1) allowing for overactive human imagination, (2) minimizing the effects of biased and only partly conscious interests, (3) identifying important features of the things compared, and (4) winning approval of descriptions from qualified adherents (where "qualified" means experts trained in the disciplines of comparison). There is also the metaconstraint that (5) the purpose of making comparisons should be morally legitimate. Understanding success in this fivefold way, I contend that relative success in comparing religious ideas is possible, at least some of the time. The views denying the possibility of successful comparison do so in at least the following three ways.[8]

First, as we saw in Chapter 4, some are so impressed by the differences between cultures and religions that they deem the corresponding discourses incommensurable, in the strong sense that denies the meaningfulness of talk about the vague categories that express respects of comparison. Even when common respects of comparison seem to be present, according to this view, we cannot assure ourselves that real commonality exists because intricate cultural embedding makes the ideas involved incommensurable. I already gave an answer to this strong form of the "incommensurability objection" in Chapter 4. In summary, the very real communication difficulties underlying incommensurability can be mitigated with attention and skill. What is difficult to communicate or translate at one time and place may not be so always and everywhere because language and culture are mutable, dynamic phenomena.

More specifically, to say that comparison is a social and political act is precisely to allow that it can change circumstances, including by creating previously nonexistent possibilities of communication and crosscultural understanding. This does not automatically assure the meaningfulness of speaking about common respects of comparison but it does check objections that would arrest from the outset all attempts to identify meaningful respects of comparison. Once the comparative process has begun, on most understandings of that process, the existence or creation of common respects of comparison is largely a creative matter of empirical responsiveness and social engineering. Comparison can draw on the way that the biological structure of human life limits the problem of cultural impenetrability and gives a solid basis for speaking of common features of human culture. Comparison can also make use of the phenomenon of multiple religious and personal identity (for instance, Confucian Christians, Jewish Buddhists), which shows how creativity, skill, and circumstances can combine to stimulate new forms of communication, include robust comparisons.

Second, some are so impressed by the human tendency to become attached to familiar ways of interpreting the world that they view the problem of bias as intractable. They deny that we can treat religious practices, texts, and traditions as specifications of comparative categories without fatal distortion, no matter what pains are taken to be fair. Perhaps we can imagine creatures capable of fair interpretation through being less thoroughly indebted to biologically congealed habits of understanding than human beings are. According to this view, however, we cannot imagine how we ourselves could be capable of overcoming the limitations of imagination and perspective that plague our attempts to be fair-minded in human affairs.

My reply to this "bias objection" turns on a difference in judgment regarding the degree to which bias is problematic. The existence of adaptable forms of inquiry such as the natural sciences is evidence that people are capable of establishing social arrangements wherein criticism and improvement of interpretations is prized. It is futile to seek perfect objectivity that eliminates bias, but it can be practical to construct a method for diagnosing and managing bias. Moreover, the already mentioned "qualified adherent approval" test—whereby we expose our descriptions to the evaluation of experts internal to the traditions we compare—can assure us that our efforts to be fair are sometimes relatively successful. Once again, however, nothing in this reply guarantees fairness, or even a recipe for achieving it. Fair interpretation is an art form in which success turns on skill and effort as well as on a clearheaded method.

Third, some might grant the meaningfulness of respects of comparison and even the possibility of managing bias, yet view the purpose of comparison as essentially immoral. In this case, comparison could not be successful in the sense of worthy. Whether the goal of comparison is to satisfy curiosity, to enhance understanding, to build theories, or something else, the "morality objection" insists that comparison is an exercise of cultural power for which it is hard to take full and fair responsibility. If not a blatant exertion of cultural force, then it is at the very least a dangerous form of transformative praxis: comparison changes things, both the things compared and those making the comparisons.

My reply to the morality objection begins by repeating that comparison is indeed interested and transformative praxis. Indeed, the very purpose of comparison in the social context of interreligious dialogue is to bring about cultural and personal change through mutual understanding. I think that purposes in making comparisons of religious ideas are often and perhaps usually morally legitimate. There are no guarantees, however, because moral judgments of this kind change with time and place. I have no trouble imagining settings in which curiosity should be checked and understanding sacrificed for the sake of some relatively higher moral purpose, such as the protection from scrutiny of an exquisite and fragile cultural phenomenon.

The incommensurability, bias, and morality objections to the possibility of successful comparison are serious challenges. My reply in each case turns on the social process of comparison, which plays an essential role in making corrections and adjustments in comparative judgments. My resistance to nonempirical pronouncements about what is possible and what is impossible in comparison makes most sense in the context of a positive viewpoint that moves beyond hopeful speculation about comparative method. That alternative is a properly empirical procedure that prizes vulnerability of comparative hypotheses and actively seeks to improve them in as many ways and with as much skill and diligence as possible.

Comparison as Something Other Than an Explicit Cognitive Process

Positions answering the question of the possibility of comparison in the affirmative can be differentiated by their responses to a second question: to what extent should comparison proceed as an explicitly cognitive process, with the results of comparison represented as (hypothetical) ideas? The argument that an act of comparison presupposes a respect of comparison (a category) is sound; it is simply a part of the grammar of comparison that two things are similar or different *somehow*—and the *how* is the respect or category of comparison. Nevertheless, comparisons of religious ideas sometimes avoid any explicit mention of the operative categories. This may be because of lack of interest or because of inconsistency, which would be serious defects. Yet, this silence also may serve a constructive goal: resistance to making the act of comparison an explicit cognitive process. To suppress discussion of the category of comparison while still making comparisons is effectively to leave the results and categories of comparison implicit in the comparative act itself.

There are at least two reasons why this goal sometimes seems important. First, if we view knowledge as an event of illumination within a dynamic social process, we might feel averse rather than drawn to explicit hypotheses about religions voiced explicitly in terms of comparative categories. Rather, proper knowledge is attained when the results involve a seeing-as with transformative effects. Second, refusing to make the results of comparison explicit in the form of clear hypotheses is a hedge against so-called logocentrism. Vigilantly deconstructing comparative conclusions as fast as they materialize keeps the mind agile, avoids the ironic trapping of theorists by their own comparative conclusions, and most adequately respects differences among traditions. Some theorists deem these virtues so important that they willingly forsake the rather different virtues of self-consciousness of procedure, vulnerability to correction, and detection of bias, which pertain to acts of comparison structured as explicit cognitive processes.

There are a number of examples of this reticent approach to comparison. They vary in the degree to which they oppose representation of comparison as an explicit cognitive process and of comparative conclusions as ideas but they uniformly insist on the value of comparison in absence of a cognitive representation of the results as a third thing. Such approaches may use respects of comparison drawn from narrative structures[9] or metaphors.[10] Alternatively, they may juxtapose points of view[11] or facilitate intellectually illuminating play across differences.[12] These approaches avoid large-scale theories about categories of comparison (such as the human condition or ultimate realities). Moreover, they tend to be suspicious of accounts of causal factors that supposedly explain conceptual similarities between traditions or texts. The suspicion is understandable: theories about comparative categories and causal analyses tend to be significantly underdetermined by the comparative data, leaving ample room for speculation that is subject to biased or unevaluated assumptions.

I have great sympathy for these indirect approaches to comparison. They highlight a genuine weakness, albeit hopefully a manageable one, in the approach to comparison I advocate here. These views hold in common that successful comparison is a moment of genius insight in which an illuminating similarity is grasped intuitively and then expressed gracefully, avoiding the unattractive mistake of smothering the insights with an unwieldy theoretical apparatus. Almost any broad theoretical framework either will be too abstract to explain anything or will quickly predict not only the insight under investigation but a horde of other comparative conclusions as well. In fact, it will predict so much on the basis of such slender data that the theory will collapse under the weight of its own pretensions. A theory about a comparative category is, according to these views, drastically underdetermined by the data, and thus extensively stipulates what ought to be the case, invariably getting too much wrong to be attractive. Making comparison into an explicit cognitive process with a dialectical method of vulnerability, debate, and improvement seems too facile, too unrealistic about the complex data to be accounted for in comparisons, and too optimistic about the power of theories to coordinate the disparate data consistently. What is left for comparison, then, except to be the domain of genius insight? And what is the point of rendering comparison an explicit cognitive process except boldly to hide from the fact that we simply cannot regulate comparative efforts in the way the self-conscious dialectic approach claims is possible?

I find this objection to making comparison an explicit cognitive process appealingly modest. It does not claim that successful comparison is impossible on a priori grounds. Rather, it plausibly argues that a slender base of comparative data about religious phenomena and a worrying history of distortion and arbitrariness in previous comparative efforts combine with the irreducible complexity of the task to make the safest approach one of avoiding formalization and ambition in comparison. Leave it to those deeply initiated into several traditions. Let us be content with their moments of illumination and the comparative insights they produce. Let us avoid systematization and cognitive fretting. It's just not worth it.

The relationship between the criticism and affirmation of comparison as an explicit cognitive process in terms of comparative categories is subtle. To resort to a simile, it is akin to the relationship between Mahāyāna and Theravāda sensibilities in Buddhism. In Theravāda, the focused journey toward enlightenment is for the monks, for the genius experts. In Mahāyāna, enlightenment is also for the masses; not being genius experts, however, they must find ways to work together. In the same way, I am urging that the process of comparison should be made more public, that many kinds of people should combine forces to search for stable comparative hypotheses, and that the key to this approach is an explicit method. This method must prize stability and vulnerability to correction in comparative hypotheses, render its provisional conclusions as ideas on the way to theories about religious matters, and demand careful justification for the comparative categories that make stable comparative hypotheses feasible.

More than this, an explicit, cooperative approach to the comparison of religious ideas and practices may be able to improve on the creative insights of the individual comparative genius. Human beings routinely cooperate to make complex problems tractable. The complexity of comparing religious ideas and practices is not different in kind than other complex problems, such as understanding the natural world or building civilizations, both of which depend absolutely on a high degree of methodological explicitness and cooperation. There is every reason to expect that a methodologically explicit, cooperative approach should prove feasible for comparing religious ideas and practices, particularly as pertinent data become more readily available. In fact, it is arguable that the intuitive, genius-insight approach to comparison was never sufficiently productive of deep insights and that such insights as were won were never made as fruitful as they might have been for the work of others. In short, there is a corporate approach to comparison that promises better results due to the coordinated work of many in place of the rare, uncoordinated insights of the few genius comparativists.

The question becomes, therefore, whether a corporate, methodologically explicit approach to comparing religious ideas and practices can work in practice. As sympathetic as I am to the criticism I have been discussing, I do think that a corporate, methodologically explicit approach can achieve more than this criticism allows. The dispute over this issue suggests an amusing image, flattering to both sides in different ways yet also gently mocking both. What begins as conflicting bets over what would be gained by self-consciousness about method in comparison ends with the reticent, Theravāda approach having nothing to do but watch while the enthusiastic Mahāyāna crowd uses every available resource to maximize the impact of their combined efforts. The members of the disciplined monkish group, amazed at the innocence of their nonadept friends, with some justification predict that the corporate experiment will begin in optimistic methodological stipulations and, chaotically stumbling along a host of mistake-ridden paths, end in utter failure. The large, noisy group, for its part, is unconcerned with the adepts' opinions because time is on its side. The adepts can only watch in amusement, already pressed hard up against their self-imposed limits for what is possible in comparison. But the corporate experimenters refuse to accept any limitations a priori on what comparison can achieve. That gives them time and opportunity to learn from their many mistakes and to generate new approaches and new forms of cooperation. The outcome remains an intriguing question. (I bet on the mob.[13])

Comparison Based on Categories Justified by Theories of Religion

Many approaches to comparison produce explicit cognitive representations of results. This is a diverse group, however, and it produces results of uneven quality. We can distinguish these approaches based on the answers they provide to the question about how we should justify the categories used for comparison. Some approaches attempt to justify categories directly from "similarities" in the data of religious ideas and practices; this is an extremely dubious procedure but it has its own special virtue, as I will show later. Here I discuss approaches that borrow or deduce categories for comparison from existing theories of religion and justify the use of those categories by virtue of the plausibility they gain from those theories. We can distinguish such approaches, though not without overlap, by the nature of the theory of religion that furnishes and justifies the categories. I present them here for convenience in family groupings.

One family of approaches begins from a particular religious perspective, approaching other religious traditions in terms of categories dominant within the home tradition.[14] An important social phenomenon connected with this is interreligious dialogue, in which representatives of religious traditions join in discussion over shared issues of practical importance or simply to increase mutual understanding. Surely this is the simplest and most direct way to approach the task of making comparisons among religious ideas. What could be more straightforward or more morally satisfying than to approach the plurality of religions from one's own perspective? I heartily affirm the moral and existential naturalness of this approach to comparison. Yet it has an obvious downside in that the categories for comparison are so heavily indebted to a particular religious perspective that they cannot be as responsive to the data as scholars and theorists of religion require. A deeply moving dialogue encounter for many religious-believer comparativists may not be ideal for comparativists with scholarly purposes—experts who believe that the inflexibility of categories derived from and justified by religious commitments interferes with the scholarly task. An approach with inherently flexible, data-driven categories would be superior because comparative categories always need improvement, and any theory that produces and justifies categories always needs refinement.

A second family of approaches justifies the key categories for comparison by means of a theological, mystical, or metaphysical theory. This is true in very different ways of the perennial philosophy,[15] various archetype and Jungian approaches,[16] and even certain contributions in the philosophy of religion.[17] The theory in question may be more or less complete and more or less empirically driven, yet is it persuasive enough to commend its principal theoretical categories to the comparativist? There are many examples that we might consider here. For the sake of specificity, I discuss the perennial philosophy.

The perennial philosophy offers a way to see how adepts of all religious traditions hold certain key ideas in common, albeit under sometimes radically different descriptions, while explaining why nonadepts could flatly disagree with each other about religious beliefs and practices. The existence of this purported common core is the reason the perennial philosophy is sometimes called the "primordial tradition." It is defended by thinkers who in some cases—and preeminently in the case of Huston Smith, its best known contemporary representative—have spent a great deal of time learning about religious practices and texts from all over the world while living for many years with adherents.[18] Its advocates would say without hesitation that its plausibility derives mainly from the fact that it can make sense of a great deal of data. Just because of this, we are told, we should not hesitate to adopt categories from the perennial philosophy for the sake of making detailed comparisons.

From the perennial philosophy's hierarchical ontology, the great chain of being, we receive the categories of Godhead (*nirguṇa* Brahman), God (*saguṇa* Brahman), discarnates and other intermediate beings, human beings, animals, plants, and inanimate objects. Its cosmology offers categories such as the human condition, ultimate and proximate religious truth, savior figures and bodhisattvas, ignorance and liberation. Its view of the religious quest leads to other comparative categories such as morality, ritual, sacred texts, and special revelations, each of which is interpreted through the lens of the ontology and the cosmology of the perennial philosophy. Perennialists urge that, when a powerful large-scale theoretical interpretation of religion furnishes categories, comparison can proceed untroubled by the problem of categorial justification, focusing instead on comparative details. Ultimately, on this view, the result is the further illumination and consolidation of the theory of religion furnishing the categories in the first place.

What happens, however, when some data beg for comparison in fundamental categories other than those served up by the perennial philosophy? The perennial philosophy approach expects such awkward data and explains them by means of the distinction between what is ultimately and proximately true, thereby containing their contraindicative force. Ultimately, the contraindicating data are really not so important even if, proximately, they are pervasive and central. Going further, what happens if, by following this procedure, most of the interesting details of religious practices and ideas are effectively eliminated from having a say in what the fundamental categories for comparison should be? For example, the majority of scholars in religious studies simply cannot accept that pervasive themes in religion such as purity and social organization can be marginalized in the way that the perennial philosophy does.

As beautiful as the perennial philosophy is, and as influential as it has been, it has few completely persuaded followers. This is partly because of an ontology that is opposed to the naturalist tendencies of modern Western science but also because its handling of comparative data is felt to be arbitrary. The sense of arbitrariness derives from the fact that the theory furnishing the categories for comparison is too neat, too easily able to deflect objections—and thus too convenient, too invulnerable, too unresponsive to criticism, and too uninterested in correction and improvement. For all that, of course, the perennial philosophy might be correct, at least in its essentials. The point here, however, is that the vulnerability of comparative categories is a virtue at least as important as the coherence and simplicity of the theological-mystical-metaphysical theory that might produce them. The same goes for other members of this family, including especially the various archetype theories of religion, regardless of whether we provide metaphysical or other explanations for the universality of the archetypes; correctability of categories is an essential hedge against ignorance about religion and the wider reality in which religion exists.

A third family of approaches justifies comparative categories by virtue of a scientific-causal theory about the origin and nature of religion, or of a feature of religion. Such approaches, including many of the brightest stars in the sky of the scientific study of religion, usually begin from particular scientific or social-scientific disciplines, thereafter leading out into proposals for more or less comprehensive theories of religion. Examples are legion, and usually emphasize a particular discipline such as evolutionary biology,[19] anthropology,[20] sociology,[21] neuroscience,[22] cognitive science,[23] or psychology.[24]

The word *causal* in *scientific-causal* is helpfully vague. On the one hand, it refers to naturally occurring limitations on how religious ideas fit together. This strategy is similar to that of the second family of theoretically driven approaches to justifying comparative categories, except that the third family explains these limitations in terms of the sphere of interest of the leading scientific discipline (social patterns, brain structure and function, psychological mechanisms) rather than in the second family's more metaphysical or mystical ways. For example, human brains evolved sensitive causal-detection and intention-attribution systems to aid in survival, but these systems have side effects in the form of a vulnerability to superstition and a preference for anthropomorphic conceptions of ultimate realities.

On the other hand, causation refers to historical influences that bring a high degree of natural applicability to certain comparative categories. For example, the historical emergence of Buddhism and Hinduism from earlier Brahmanic religions means that *saṃsāra* and *mokṣa* are natural categories for both, despite important differences of meaning. The historical influences in question might vary widely, from the effects of trade contacts or missionary zeal to planned cultural engineering.

Some approaches in the third family appeal to both kinds of causation for justifying comparative categories. This is true especially of approaches to comparison that allow the philosophy of history to play a role equal in magnitude to that of historical details.[25] Unfortunately, sometimes these views presuppose influence where none has been shown to have any historical-causal basis. Alternatively, they presuppose an evolution of ideas where the close-knit cultural competition needed for the natural selection of ideas cannot be demonstrated.

The third family displays relatively less interest in the first family's approach to religious pluralism, beginning from one's personal religious point of view. It also contrasts with the second family by limiting attention to recognizably scientific theories or to historical causation, at least in intention if not always in practice. The problem with the third family of approaches, however, is the same as the problem in the first and second families: comparative categories need to be more vulnerable to correction than these approaches allow. We must be able to take account of all that is learned about religious traditions in the process of making comparisons.

It would be churlish to criticize the many instances of creative genius in the study of religion, which abound in these three families of approaches. In no case is it the source of comparative categories that troubles me. Each of these types of theories of religion has bequeathed valuable categories for comparing religious beliefs and practices. The problem is rather the rigidity that categories suffer when we justify them mainly with reference to large-scale theories of religion. These theorists themselves, and I daresay the bulk of those making use of their comparative categories, have not said clearly enough how these categories can respond to resistant data. My contention is that, regardless of the source of categories for comparison, the methodology of comparison must prize vulnerability of comparative categories and of the comparisons they permit.

Comparison Based on Categories Justified from Similarities in Data

When comparative categories receive their justification from an existing complete or partial theory of religion, they are even less flexible and responsive than the theories themselves. When too much data is not registered well enough by an array of categories, the dependence on a background theory makes flexible correction of categories almost impossible. This has long been sensed within the study of religion and by reaction has produced a fundamentally descriptive group of approaches to comparison. In this group, the justification of comparative categories derives from how well they express the relative importance of the data and of the relations among data.

Justification of comparative categories in this way is a delicate procedure. Sometimes comparativists have justified comparative categories merely on the putatively self-evident character of the similarities themselves. Yet the failure of "what just seems similar" to justify categories of "the similar" is notorious.[26] This is so for two reasons. On the one hand, the role of the interpreter is so powerful in appeals to the obvious that it can overwhelm the ideal of descriptive impartiality. On the other hand, it continues to be difficult to figure out when phenomena are "essentially similar"; comparison seems not to advance this phenomenological task so much as codify persistent perplexity about it (but see below for a brief account of how philosophical phenomenology is supposed to overcome this challenge). Despite these problems, something like an appeal to the obvious is indispensable to the justification of categories in these approaches because of their insistence on allowing data to speak for themselves. The problem is unavoidable, therefore; it must be managed rather than avoided. I cluster the views in this group into families based on strategies for managing the challenge of impartiality in judging supposedly obvious similarities.

First, experience and brilliance matter, and thus one family of approaches simply does the descriptive task well. That is to say, some writers adduce descriptive categories on the basis of intensive personal grounding in multiple religious traditions, benefiting from ongoing discussions with a wide variety of people. The result is descriptions of religious phenomena and ideas that win the grudgingly appreciative approval of large numbers of experts. Under this heading, I include the luminaries of description in the study of religion. Some of these could be called descriptive phenomenologists of religion, in order to distinguish their expertise from that of the philosophical phenomenologists to which I will return presently.[27] For others, the phenomenological label is less apt but they are nonetheless expert observers and describers of religious phenomena.[28] There are many others of both sorts.[29] There are also many figures from the previous sections whose projects crucially depend on expertise in description, so it is as well to remember that this group is distinguished primarily by a commitment to descriptive adequacy as primary justification for comparative categories.

Second, another family of approaches to comparison manages the problem of bias in description by partially relying on the lines of justification already discussed. This has to be done in precisely the right way, however: the aim is to relieve pressure on descriptive adequacy as the sole justification for comparative categories, while still avoiding reliance on large-scale theories of religion in order to maintain the close ties between categories and data. One example of such a judicious hybrid approach is the comparative strategy advocated by Rudolf Otto in *The Idea of the Holy*.[30] In that work, Otto blends phenomenological description with a partial theological viewpoint. There is no fully worked out theory of religion underlying Otto's categories of *mysterium* and *tremendum*; he himself says that he only focuses on the irrational element in religion, which leaves out an enormous amount of data. Yet the categories achieve justification not only by observations of the recurrence of phenomena that are arguably identical in substance, but also by a partial worldview that postulates the religious potency of reality.

Third, another hybrid family of examples uses various kinds of higher-order classifications of the data to supplement justification of comparative categories by means of their adequacy for describing data. Examples are plentiful, including the classification systems of Watson and Dilworth[31] and Paul Tillich's analysis of God concepts.[32] In such cases, structural similarities in the ideas of diverse religious traditions suggest a classification. This classification is then supported in at least one of four ways: by elimination of alternative classifications, by the theoretical beauty and economy of the classification, by the classification's efficacy in organizing further data, and by the classification's production of new insights. These classifications may or may not be ideal, in the sense of being defined by key features that are rarely realized purely in actual instances, and they may be partial or exhaustive.

All of the approaches to justifying categories discussed in this section reject heavy reliance on well worked-out theories of religion. They cleave to whatever relevant data is available, without the aid of much in the way of a theoretical superstructure to add authority to the classifications and categories that result. This is so even in hybrid approaches to justification (the second and third families). The attempt to stay closer to the data by resisting the potentially blinkered influence of large-scale theories is to be lauded, in spite of the problems of justification merely from impressions of similarity.

From this, we learn the crucial lesson that, difficult though it may be, we must limit (not eliminate) the role that theories of religion play in the justification of comparative categories. Yet antitheoretical, data-driven comparison is too arbitrary, so we must not exclude large-scale theories of religion altogether from the justification of comparative categories. We must maintain a distinction—it can never safely be made rigid—between the task of comparison, which produces and justifies comparative categories, and the task of theory building, which receives or suggests the categories as well-attested ways of organizing data. In this way, we arrive at the necessity for a dialectical approach, which is the approach to comparison defended here.

Comparison as a Dialectic of Data and Categories

The self-conscious dialectic approach to comparison holds that there should be a dialectical collaboration between data and comparative categories whereby the task of understanding through comparison can build progressively on previous results. This conception of comparison calls for procedures that gradually refine categories, which helps us fret less over the impurity of the way they are initially produced. This is a particularly important point in comparative religions, where many contemporary comparative categories reflect originally colonial and anticolonial perspectives. Purity of origins is a vain ideal for comparative categories, much as perfectly certain knowledge is a vain ideal in epistemology.

By contrast, the goal of improvement is feasible. The most practical procedure for improvement is a thoroughgoing dialectic between the raw data and the categories used in making comparisons of the data. In practice, this entails a corporate approach that eschews exclusive reliance on the genius insights of brilliant comparativists and instead builds these into a wider and messier coordination of the work of many more ordinary scholarly experts. The emphasis on improvement makes this a corporate method. It may seem untidy but, like the natural and social sciences, it may be able to achieve results where nothing else can.

Self-conscious dialectic approaches tend to be unwieldy because of the number of variables involved. Not only is there a large amount of data to manage but the data also need to be organized for the effective correction of the categories in use. The theories guiding interpretation of the data are themselves complex and subject to correction, so this needs to be managed also. And the large number of people involved in traditions of comparative inquiry must have a shared understanding of their obligations and tasks. It is a complex method. But no other approach to comparison can do justice to the actual complexities of the task. Most approaches pick up on just one aspect of comparison and elaborate it into a method, with inevitable one-sidedness.

There is great practical advantage in allowing that categories can come from anywhere so long as a dialectical process of improvement and correction is in place. It encourages us to see our comparative categories as mutable, and the task of comparison as in part the creation of a language for communication and translation across cultures, mitigating the moral difficulties of incommensurability described in Chapter 4. We may use familiar terms but they get semantically stretched in the process, and the scholars involved in the comparative effort gradually learn how to make good use of the newly configured categories and terminology. Translation across cultures is a famously difficult task but comparative categories can be responsive to the comparative conversation.

The first and most famous source for the self-conscious dialectic approach to comparison is Edmund Husserl's philosophical phenomenology.[33] Husserl's attempt to allow phenomenological generalizations to respond to data is truly impressive. Yet his program is burdened by awkward philosophical assumptions. In particular, his foundationalist epistemic project seems unduly optimistic and it produces confusions in his method that obscure the details salient for a general theory of comparison. His elaborate procedure for guiding phenomenological reflection is both too little in respect of attending to too few sources of corrective wisdom, and too much in respect of being thoroughly overbearing and impossibly demanding. If ever there were a comparative method for adepts, it is Husserl's. That said, I do admire his attempt to found a discipline of comparative phenomenology, his scientifically minded respect for vulnerability of categories inferred from data, and his use of a dialectic of data and categories to drive his phenomenological method.

The second source also focuses on phenomenological reports: the so-called heterophenomenological method advocated by Daniel Dennett.[34] Dennett's approach can be regarded either as an attempt to correct some of Husserl's excesses or as a simplified version of Husserl's own procedures. Unfortunately, Dennett does not say enough about Husserl's method to enable a detailed judgment of the relationship between the two. Suffice to say that Dennett sees clearly the philosophical problems associated with the comparison of phenomenological reports. He is as keenly aware as Husserl was of how splendid it would be to have a way to know when apparently different descriptions were in some sense essentially about the same phenomenon.[35] I heartily agree. I am betting, however, that the vision of effective comparative phenomenology capable of meeting this goal will never be realized until neurophysiology advances to the point that it can make meaningful contributions to judgments about the essential similarity and difference of the experiences underlying the phenomenological descriptions being compared.[36]

With this complex heritage, the self-conscious dialectic approach to comparison might seem a hybrid beast, with incommensurable contributions from several philosophical traditions. On the contrary, however, this approach to comparison is powerful evidence that diverse philosophical traditions sometimes deal with the same problems and come up with similar solutions, even when they rarely communicate.

The most fully developed and tested version of a self-conscious dialectic approach to comparison is the comparative method implemented in the Comparative Religious Ideas Project (CRIP). This was a Boston-based research effort running from 1995 to 1999.[37] The double aim of this project was to test a methodology for comparing religious ideas by actually using it to make comparisons, and to explore a small-community-based approach to the formation of current and potential future experts in comparative religion. The seeds of the project's approach to comparison were planted in Robert Neville's *Normative Cultures*.[38] To the extent that it is an instance of the self-conscious dialectic approach, it also has the other roots described above. Several remarks about the CRIP's implementation of the self-conscious dialectic approach to comparison in religious philosophy are in order.[39]

First, the CRIP approach focused on religious ideas, rather than religious practices or religions in general. Focusing on ideas is not as limiting as it may seem at first because even religious practices are available for comparison as ideas when they are described verbally and framed theoretically. In fact, comparing practices in isolation from the ideas that make them important and relevant to people is probably futile. The point of focusing on ideas is to keep elements of interpretation in the comparative picture. Comparative categories derive their meaning from theoretical interpretations of aspects of religion and the comparative venture collapses into mere impressionism if we pretend that comparative categories somehow appear from nowhere—contextless and free of the distortions of history and the colorings of interpretation. When texts do not exist to document aspects of the meaning of religious beliefs and practices, as is the case for many modern tribal religions, cultural anthropologists and other observers of these religions must create interpretations of what they see to guide subsequent comparison.

Second, the CRIP approach was committed to a particular interpretation of the history of comparative categories. As noted earlier, many common comparative categories owe their origins to translation decisions about how to render in European languages key terms in the sacred texts of the world's religions. From there, those categories have had a huge impact on subsequent discussions. Even apparently neutral description makes use of available terminology and so is inherently comparative in nature. When some activity is identified as a ritual, some person as a priest, some place as sacred, or some time as propitious, the descriptions presuppose comparative judgments. The comparative categories of "ritual," "priest," "sacred place," and "propitious time" are stretched in these new usages and they also lead interpreters and subsequent readers of these descriptions to interpret the things described in terms of existing patterns of usage of the key categories. Comparison suffuses description and thus the only way forward even for description is to take responsibility for comparative judgments wherever they arise.

Third, the CRIP approach proposed that taking responsibility for a comparative judgment involves explicitly thematizing the category involved, subjecting it to scrutiny regarding its origins and existing usages, examining the theoretical frameworks that give it meaning, and testing to see whether it leads to distorted readings of the things described by means of it. In other words, comparative judgments are inevitable, so we must create a process whereby we can correct comparative judgments and the categories they involve. This commitment to constant correction and improvement requires us to treat comparative judgments as fallible hypotheses, not indubitable propositions. Moreover, this commitment to correction, while freeing us to work with comparative categories regardless of their convoluted histories, leads us to be suspicious of all comparative categories. This drives attempts to identify problems such as categories suffering from theoretically suspect framing, categories insufficiently vague to avoid distortion, and categories so vague that there is insufficient resistance to our tendency to form hasty impressions of similarity.

Fourth, the CRIP approach assumed that comparisons aim to be true, in the dyadic sense that locates the truth or falsity of a proposition in the accuracy of interpretation of its subject matter. Famously hidden within this apparently simple dyadic understanding of the meaning of truth is the far more complex process of interpretation, which associates a claim with a subject matter *in a particular respect* and locates the act of interpretation itself in a concrete social and political situation. It follows that we must evaluate the truth of a proposition expressing a comparative judgment about religious ideas in relation to the way the respect of interpretation—the comparative category—forges a link between the comparative judgment and the subject matter. And we must concern ourselves with the effects of comparing religions because comparison inevitably is a socially and politically contextualized act of interpretation.

Fifth, the CRIP approach insisted that justifying comparative categories was important. Justification begins with using the category to describe and compare religious ideas fairly, where fairness is judged by the standards of "qualified expert approval" and "qualified adherent approval," discussed above. But the CRIP approach also involves taking responsibility for the fact that a category derives its meaning from large-scale theories of the subject matter. That is, a category such as "ultimate reality" is not just an empty vessel containing other ideas such as Allah, Brahman, Chance, Dao, Emptiness, Form, God, the Holy, or the Inscrutable. Ultimate reality is itself an idea with meaning that derives from the various ways it is specified in comparisons and by theories that explain how these various specifications are related to one another (in Max Weber or Paul Tillich, for example). Some comparativists balk at entering the theoretical territory limned here but I think it is futile trying to avoid theoretically loaded comparative categories. The most prudent course of action is to make these theories explicit and to seek to refine them as opportunity allows.

Finally, in every aspect, the CRIP implementation of the self-conscious dialectic approach to comparison achieves objectivity and accuracy not by trying to avoid the many hermeneutical difficulties of comparison but rather by embracing them as inevitable and seeking, indeed constructing, a socially borne procedure whereby we can locate mistakes, overcome distortions, and improve the theoretical frameworks underlying comparisons. In this sense, the CRIP method exemplifies—and here at last I offer a compact definition of the self-conscious dialectic approach—a dialectic of theory and data sustained within a large-scale social process devoted to the discovery, improvement, and correction of comparative hypotheses. In this way, the self-conscious dialectic approach to comparison in religious philosophy answers the challenges issued by other approaches to comparison, both those that are more skeptical and those that are unduly optimistic.

Learning from the Past

I have claimed that the self-conscious dialectic approach to comparison in the domain of religious philosophy takes solid account of the insights of other approaches, while coordinating them all at once into a more satisfying theoretical model of comparison in religious philosophy. In order to support this claim more completely, I here recite a list of debts and corrections to existing comparative approaches, indicating in each case how the self-conscious dialectic approach has learned from the past.

First, comparativists borrowing categories from existing theories are exercising a kind of wisdom. They are backing categories that are at least partially attested by the theory that gives them meaning and they seek in that way to extend the core theory itself to new tracts of data. That is why I can admire the perennial philosophers' dogged adherence to their interpretation of the world religions. Without fidelity to core hypotheses, even sometimes to the point of prejudicial or arbitrary handling of data, we will almost certainly overlook some special virtue of the core hypothesis that guides and inspires our interpretation. Such devotion to research programs is vital to the stability of interpretative theories. Without stability, vulnerability for the sake of progressive correction is impossible. From these laborers in the vineyards of religious philosophy, we can learn to take good categories from wherever we find them and to be unafraid of the need for persistence in testing any theory of religion against data. However, we will still seek a fairer and more flexible approach to the data itself.

Second, comparativists that refuse to make explicit the categories in respect of which they make comparisons could well be exercising another kind of wisdom. In this case, it is the recognition that analogues of scientific theories of instrumentation do not exist in the study of religion to any great degree, at least not yet. Thus, they prefer moving gracefully within the forest of data rather than trying to map and regulate the data's wildness for the sake of evaluating its force for or against the particular interpretations of it implied in the explicit use of comparative categories. From these fellow workers, we can learn not to underestimate the complexity and disarray of the data of religious studies. It may be, however, that we can develop within the scientific study of religion decent analogues for data-handling theories of instrumentation in the natural and human sciences.

Third, comparativists who try to maximize the virtue of empiricism in generating comparative categories from data are wisely recognizing that there must be some degree of self-conscious distance between the comparative task and the task of larger theory building in religious studies. From them, we can learn that categories are a middle-level beast. They help to organize data for the sake of big-deal theory construction, yet they derive their justification as much from their polished data management as from the theories that use them. However, I remain sharply aware of the problem pointed out by J.Z. Smith of justifying comparative categories on the basis of apparent similarities in data.[40] The CRIP implementation of the self-conscious dialectic approach proposed a solution to this problem. This solution combines theory-side criteria for justifying comparative categories with data-side affirmation of the usefulness of phenomenological intuition for discerning respects of similarity and difference, though only when the phenomenological imagination is properly prepared. Categories derived from theory for classifying data need to be checked against independent phenomenological analyses of the data to determine their suitability.[41]

Fourth, in addition to the important critique of intuitions of similarity just mentioned, J.Z. Smith also argued that, at the date of writing *Imagining Religion*, there was no approach to comparison that produces or discovers, as against constructs or invents, comparisons,[42] and further that there was no satisfactory approach to comparison under discussion anywhere.[43] I agree on the second point but demur, slightly, with regard to the first. In Smith's language, nobody "has presented rules for the production of" discoveries in the domains of the natural and human sciences either, yet discoveries happen. Moreover, the insights of well-trained describers and comparers of religions can be novel, at times, and those insights can transcend the level of the flimsy associative connections that Smith rightly attacks. I agree, however, that discovery occurs too rarely. The scarcity is because it is so difficult to acquire the competence that makes novel insights also profound ones.

The self-conscious dialectic approach helps here by reducing reliance on the genius of comparative adepts in exchange for depending more heavily on the scrupulous hard work of ordinary expert comparativists. Many of the novel ideas that can be inserted into the dialectic of categories and data may turn out to be of little use; certainly the CRIP implementation of this approach disposed of a lot more categories than it kept. Similarly, some categories and comparisons may never achieve the fivefold standard for justification on which CRIP insisted (see below for a detailed account of these five criteria). We can fairly describe those categories that do make the grade as profound, however, and at least in some cases, novel. After that, discovery is a matter of learning to apply what worked elsewhere in new situations, tentatively extending the reach of data management that the web of comparative categories enables, and always seeking for the kinds of dissonance that should force revisions. The self-conscious dialectic approach answers Smith's call for a comparative method that can escape the weakness of extant approaches.

Finally, I also take seriously the alternatives to explicit methodologies of comparison discussed above by trying to incorporate their strengths into the corrective procedures of the self-conscious dialectic approach. This is present, for example, in the way that theoretical justifications for categories help to deconstruct assumptions about what seems obvious. Moreover, judgments of similarity, for all their dangers, can call forth theoretical efforts of justification—and all this for the sake of fidelity to the data. Nevertheless, the self-conscious dialectic approach is explicit about the categories and the provisional results of comparisons. In most domains of comparison, including religious philosophy, I enter my wager in favor of the loosely coordinated march of many feet, all contributing to the task of generating and improving comparative hypotheses. This bet includes the gamble that the chaos will in time yield to something more like the organized frenzy of the natural and human sciences.

I do see reasons to think that such a transformation in religious philosophy will be difficult. After all, forging the CRIP community of inquiry was a demanding, drawn-out process.[44] And then there are the intimate existential entanglements that routinely link comparativists to their subject matters in ways that do not often occur, say, for physical chemists. That is the nature of religion: its study is often profoundly self-referential. These difficulties notwithstanding, I see no reasons to think that my bet on the future of the self-conscious dialectic approach to comparison is likely to lose. On the contrary, especially because of its promise for aiding a more critical, data-aware era of theory building in the scientific study of religion and comparative theology, we have every reason to be hopeful.

The self-conscious dialectic approach absolutely demands a community of inquiry—one that stabilizes comparative judgments for investigation, capitalizes on diverse insights and types of expertise, and inducts novices into procedures and habits of thinking that facilitate effective comparison of religious ideas. In one sense, all scholarly learning is initiation into ways of thinking, key literatures, and disciplinary meta-questions of method and value. Initiation means something more concrete in the case of the self-conscious dialectic approach to comparison, however, because the community of inquiry is indispensable. In this case, initiation is not just learning the ropes and sails, after which the student can go off sailing solo. It must also mean accepting a place within a community of investigation that has differentiated roles and a common goal. It means being apprenticed not just in a specialty with its languages and literatures, but also in general theoretical issues in the study of religion, in the philosophy of comparison, and in both the theory-oriented and data-oriented aspects of the task of justifying comparative categories. It means committing to an ideal of scientific comparison for which mutual reliance and information sharing are crucial.

The most perplexing problem facing the construction of communities of inquiry that can make feasible a comparative approach to religious philosophy is the fractured state of the community of religious studies scholars. This slightly desperate situation makes building actual working groups of comparativists more difficult than it should be, and calls for significant social engineering efforts. As long as comparativists want to work only with ideologically like-minded colleagues, the ideal kinds of communities will remain rare. Scholars of religious studies need to initiate each other into the central tasks and problems of comparative religion, even if this means reaching uncomfortably beyond the narrow confines of their disciplinary specializations. Yet such groups can achieve jointly what no one member can achieve alone, despite individual brilliance.

Comparison and Religious Philosophy

A deeper understanding of comparison produces better descriptions of religious phenomena, and this is a key aspect of organizing the data needed for inquiries in religious philosophy. The way comparison works in such inquiries is similar in some respects to the way comparison operates in the scientific evaluation of competing research programs. Specifically, comparative categories organize data for inquiries in religious philosophy in much the way that theories of instrumentation organize data for inquiries in natural science. The justification of the comparative categories, which organize the data of religious beliefs and practices, is tightly linked to the justification of first-order theories in religious philosophy, which centralize those categories, just as theories of instrumentation and first-order scientific theories are locked in a hermeneutical circle of mutual justification. The descriptive database made possible by robust comparative categories can be activated for philosophical argument in a complex process of inference to best explanation. This kind of argumentation cannot be effective without a sophisticated database that surfaces alternative hypotheses, which traditional philosophy of religion may simply overlook.

Comparison in Religious Philosophy and the Philosophy of Science

This proposal for a comparative approach to religious philosophy has complex connections with the philosophy of science, which has struggled mightily with the question of comparison. In the 1960s, Imre Lakatos proposed a fairly detailed model for the operation of the natural sciences (the so-called methodology of scientific research programs).[45] It succeeded in overcoming to a significant degree the problem of discontinuity that arises when scientific work transitions from one paradigm (in which science is "normal") to another paradigm—what Thomas Kuhn had identified as "paradigm shifts."[46] The discontinuity associated with scientific revolutions had proved awkward because the history of science suggested on the whole that paradigm shifts fit into the flow of science more easily than Kuhn's proposal allowed. However, Lakatos's own proposal was also controversial. Though it allowed for paradigm shifts, it tended to make them more rational than the history of science suggested has been the case.

The controversy between Lakatos's relatively rational account of theory change and Paul Feyerabend's insistence that changing between scientific research programs cannot finally be given exhaustively rational justification is one of the great debates of twentieth-century philosophy of science.[47] It appears that, although reasons can be given for abandoning an apparently degenerating scientific research program in favor of a more progressive alternative, the decision remains a judgment call that cannot be made completely rationally. As with the problem of incommensurability discussed in Chapter 4, the impossibility of a fully rational decision is due to the incommensurability of frameworks, which makes their comprehensive comparison difficult.[48]

This shows that the dialectic between data and theoretical categories is a delicate one even in the natural sciences. Its management depends on having stylish good judgment about one's work. This virtue may be akin to what English religious philosopher John Henry Newman called "illative sense."[49] By means of it, one balances the virtue of switching to a promising new hypothesis that (hopefully temporarily) contradicts important data, on the one hand, and the virtue of staying loyal to a trusted old hypothesis that might be more consistent with data but seems to be running out of predictive steam, on the other. Newman's illative sense is the key to efficient, potent argumentation as much as it is the key to making decisions between two competing hypotheses, each of which calls for the investment of time and energy. This ineradicably artistic dimension of human reason is a sharp reminder that any dialectic between data and categories will be as subtle as it is complex, and that any account of such a dialectical process has to make room for intuition and judgment.

Perhaps Lakatos's most important insight was his detailed account of the complex path from data to theory and back again, in contrast with Karl Popper's more straightforward focus on the role of falsification.[50] In the natural sciences, data is incomprehensible apart from theories of instrumentation, which themselves are justified both by the sense they make of measurements and observations and by their derivation from active theories about how nature works. Additional essentially interpretative theories are also needed for guiding the relating of data to theory, and for picking out essential features of the gathered masses of data. Most important is the way that the data, already multiply interpreted in these ways, can have an impact on the central hypotheses guiding the research program. No good scientist would ever throw over a well-tested hypothesis because of one piece of contraindicating evidence. Rather, attempts would be made—frantic attempts, perhaps—on the one hand, to test the data by replicating an experiment or confirming theories of instrumentation, and on the other hand, to explain the data with an auxiliary hypothesis, which effectively protects the central hypotheses from falsification. It is partly the extension of theories to new data, even to potentially threatening data, by means of auxiliary hypotheses that helps to make research programs in the natural sciences seem progressive. Another sign of a progressive research program is its ability to predict novel facts. Of course, if novel facts are no longer forthcoming and explanations of threatening data seem contrived and merely face-saving, then the operative research program would be judged, sooner by its critics than by its advocates, to be degenerating.

What is true in the natural sciences is no less true in the study of religion: the relationship between data and theoretical terms, including comparative categories, is exceedingly complex. Determined recognition of complexity is the precondition for resisting the extremes of data-blind enthusiasm and theory-blind confusion. This acknowledgement also involves a discriminating appreciation of similarities and differences among the various kinds of inquiries we see around us. The subject matters of religious philosophy are very different from those of the natural sciences or economics or literature. Nevertheless, Lakatos's methodology of research programs, when appropriately generalized, fairly describes the way effective inquiry works in any context from the natural sciences to the humanities and even to commonsense problem solving. The same characteristics are crucial: a conservative approach whereby a feasible hypothesis is relinquished reluctantly, and a sense of adventure that prizes vulnerability to correction by whatever means are available given the nature of the inquiry.

Charles Saunders Peirce and then John Dewey first appreciated the potential generality the sort of theory of inquiry appearing much later in Lakatos.[51] Peirce actually anticipated Lakatos in many details relevant to inquiry in the natural sciences.[52] Peirce's more impressive achievements in this area, however, were his rich awareness of the complex relations between data and theory and his vision for extending a generalized theory of inquiry from the natural sciences all the way into the humanities and metaphysics. I share Peirce's and Dewey's basic intuition about this, and I will elaborate a theory of inquiry of this sort in Chapter 6, though modified to account for the underemphasized realities of embodied practices and social organization of inquiry.[53] I see no reason why the confusing data of religious beliefs and practices cannot be given flexible interpretative structures, which render them able not only to inspire but also to correct theories of religion and theories of religious topics such as the human condition, ultimate realities, and religious truth.

What form should such flexible interpretative structures take in religious philosophy? They should take the form of provisional conclusions in the study of crosscultural comparative religious ideas and practices. That is to say, the results of an effort at running comparative religious philosophy as a self-conscious dialectic of data and categories constitute the first step in a more effective approach to the generation and testing of theories of religion and religious topics. The categories within which comparisons of religious ideas and practices take place are precisely the flexible means of organizing data that constructive theoretical efforts require. These comparative results are the analogue of theories of instrumentation and interpretation in the natural sciences; they allow theorists of religion to do better work by stabilizing data in a flexible network of correctable comparative categories.

The self-conscious dialectic approach thus conceives comparative categories as mutable interpretative structures (or theories of instrumentation), which make data available to wider theory-building efforts in religious philosophy, while maintaining a dialectical relationship with data that is strong enough to force changes in the comparative categories and in the theories that make use of them. This explains why religious philosophers must justify the comparative categories they use with reference to both data and theory.

Mutual Justification of Categories and Theories

The relation between comparative categories and the philosophical theories that both furnish and use comparative categories produces the possibility of simultaneous justification of both categories and theories. In fact, the dialectic of justification is more than an opportunity; it is inevitable that we use a single process simultaneously to justify both comparative categories and theories in religious philosophy. Comparison cannot afford to be blind to the sources of its categories, which often include theories about religion, and religious philosophy cannot afford to be naïve about the fact that its leading theoretical categories are often the deliverances of vast processes of comparative reflection. This dialectic of justification resembles the dialectic between data and categories in that both can be made progressive by formulating canny hypotheses and then seeking to correct those hypotheses in every way possible. In the long term, philosophical theories of aspects of religion that centralize the best attested comparative categories will have an advantage over rival philosophical theories.

To be more explicit about the dialectic of justification, I offer the following parsing of the task of justifying comparative generalizations, embracing both comparative categories and philosophical theories. Each part of the task of justification corresponds to an impulse present in one or more of the approaches to comparison that I have discussed above. Coordination of these lines of justification is essential, as is remembering that we speak here of justifying categories for comparing *religious ideas*.

First, there needs to be a delimiting of possibilities whereby the ideas of interest within a comparative category are set in a wider framework of plausible religious ideas of the same sort, so as not to overlook vital alternatives. For example, if we are working with the comparative category of ultimate realities, and simultaneously with a philosophical theory of ultimate realities, then we need to know what sort of things have been and might plausibly be said about ultimate realities. If we think the category of ultimate realities can only be filled plausibly with God ideas, then both our comparative category and our philosophical theory of ultimate realities will suffer. Once we recognize the correct range of possible specifications of ultimate realities, both the category and philosophical theories that use it will be more robust.

Second, there must be an account of the dynamic logical connections among these various possible ideas so that the category is specified not merely by a list of ideas but also by relationships among the ideas themselves. For example, it is not enough merely to list specifications of the comparative category of ultimate realities. We need to know that these specifications logically interact and so constrain one another. A personal divine being (*saguṇa* Brahman) and an indescribable God beyond the personal God (*nirguṇa* Brahman) should both appear on any list specifying the category of ultimate realities but it is also important to know that both can be affirmed only if *saguṇa* Brahman is ontologically subordinate to *nirguṇa* Brahman. Such logical relationships of constraint deeply affect any philosophical theory centered on the conception of ultimate realities.

Third, there should be a genetic analysis of specific symbolic representations of these religious ideas, so that historical influences among ideas and social-cultural influences on the origins of the ideas are explicit. For example, we need to understand the origins of monotheistic ideas of ultimate realities—including the roles of polytheistic folk beliefs and practices, political monarchies, social needs, and cognitive instincts toward unifying and intentionalizing reality. Fleshing out these connections allows us both to stabilize the comparative category of monotheism and to discern what would count as a good philosophical theory of monotheism. All other considerations being equal, a theory that takes proper account of these factors will be stronger than one that does not, and the strength of the theory confers robustness on the comparative category.

Fourth, there ought to be analyses of the circumstances that accompany the key shifts in symbolic representation during the history of the religious ideas within the category. For example, monotheistic symbolic imagery has changed from time to time, often along with shifting cultural norms about power and politics. One of the Hebrew Bible's monotheistic images, God as king of a kingdom, was vital in the period of the unified Israelite monarchy. It became problematic in the divided monarchy and subsequently was the root of severe cognitive dissonance during the period of the Babylonian exile, and later under Persian, Greek, and Roman occupation. These cognitive pressures produced a range of alternate monotheistic symbolic structures, from God as faithful spurned lover to God as lord over all nations. Understanding the pressures that produced novel forms of representation, or resuscitated neglected symbols for God, is essential to understanding what a philosophical theory of monotheism would have to explain. A theory that can comprehend dynamic symbolism against the relevant causal features will be more persuasive than one that cannot, and the category of monotheism as developed in the explanatorily more powerful theory is thereby made more convincing.

Fifth, our sense of what is similar, when carefully conditioned by scrupulous preparation and exposure to many variations, really should count as partial justification of comparative categories. The first four criteria for justification are theoretical in nature. If they are met convincingly, with no detection of excessive arbitrariness or distortion, then we will have good reason to think, from the theory side at least, that our comparative category is doing useful work and that philosophical theories using it will be stronger. To these theory-side considerations, we must then add the basic phenomenological point on the data side, as a fifth criterion. For example, if we are fairly confident that our account of monotheism is sound in respect of the first four criteria, then we can meaningfully claim that the similarities among Judaism, Islam, and Hinduism justify the comparative category of monotheism and the theories that use it. That is, if we were to refuse to use that category, we would be overlooking a genuine structural similarity in the data of comparative religious ideas.

These five requirements for justifying comparative categories and the philosophical theories using them reflect standard commitments within the history of religions, the philosophy of religion, and the phenomenology of religion. They are the tests by which we determine whether comparative categories organize the data well and thus whether the categories themselves are adequate and the theories that centralize those categories well placed to be sound theories. These tests are theoretical endeavors related to the larger theories of religion for which comparative categories serve as the organizers and mediators of relevant data. With all of those lines of explanation and justification in place, the self-conscious dialectic approach to comparison leads out in interesting directions: to systematic comparative metaphysics; to a strengthened, potentially progressive, multidisciplinary investigation of religious phenomena; and to a more unified approach to the scientific study of religion that coordinates the typically more isolated disciplines of the history of religion, the phenomenology of religion, and the philosophy of religion.

Comparison and Inference-to-Best-Explanation Arguments

The final point to be made here about the role of comparison in religious philosophy is that many philosophical arguments are blind without a comparative dimension. Consider so-called natural theology, understood as strictly philosophical argumentation about religious realities not drawing on purportedly revealed sources of information.

Traditional natural theology investigates entailment relations from experienced reality to, say, a preferred metaphysics of ultimacy. But most arguments of this direct-entailment sort have fallen out of favor, mostly because they are undermined by the awareness of alternative metaphysical schemes that fit the empirical facts just as well as the preferred metaphysical scheme. By contrast with this direct-entailment approach, natural theology ought to compare numerous compelling accounts of ultimacy in as many different respects as are relevant. In this comparison-based way, we assemble the raw materials for inference-to-best-explanation arguments on behalf of particular theories of ultimacy, and we make completely clear the criteria for preferring one view of ultimacy to another.

For example, we might observe with a number of cognitive scientists that human beings are cognitively predisposed by the evolutionary process to appreciate stories that are minimally counterintuitive—that is, stories that conform to the intuitions of folk psychology and folk physics, save for a few colorful details.[54] These ill-fitting details give the story a strange and perhaps whimsical character, which helps it stick in the mind. Human beings are such that memory and attention are limited resources. In the battle for story space within human cultures, therefore, minimally counterintuitive stories tend to win out over both absurdly counterintuitive stories (ridiculous!) and stories that are utterly consistent with existing folk beliefs (boring!). This battle for story space is naturally fiercest when there are few empirical resources available to settle disputes among proponents of conflicting stories. Thus, in religious attempts to understand reality, it is the minimally counterintuitive beliefs that will capture the human imagination most powerfully. The cognitive role of minimal counterintuitiveness is a fairly sturdy theoretical edifice at this point, with empirical evidence from social psychology as well as more speculative theoretical support from evolutionary psychology.

On this basis, we might attempt to build a philosophical case about certain religious beliefs. We might argue, for instance, that beliefs having a minimally counterintuitive character—such as spirits who are just like people except that they are invisible, or Gods who are just like people except that they are superpowerful—are false. We are predisposed to such beliefs, just as we are predisposed to superstition by overactive pattern recognition. And just as superstitious beliefs are false, so are these more religious fruits of our cognitive apparatus.

Most religious philosophers would immediately object to such a facile argument. They would rightly point out that being predisposed to believe something does not make it false. Indeed, we may be predisposed to believe it precisely because it is true and it proved adaptive for human beings to believe it in the evolutionary past. Though the counterargument is weaker than the argument it seeks to refute, there is no question that the first argument overreaches. Perhaps, then, we are at a stalemate and can make no philosophical use of the cognitive psychology of minimally counterintuitive beliefs.

Such a despairing conclusion is equally out of place. It is possible to make use of the well-supported theories about minimally counterintuitive beliefs that cognitive psychology has produced, but only in the presence of a sophisticated comparative database. What we need to do is to line up a series of hypotheses about religious ontology. Here are four for the sake of argument. One view says there are supernatural spirits and Gods, just as so many sacred religious texts describe them. A second view says there is nothing of the sort but only physical reality. A third says that there is nothing at all, ultimately speaking, neither a physical world nor a spiritual realm. And a fourth says that there is an as-yet only partially understood physics that explains how spirits and Gods operate in the world of nature. Once these four hypotheses have been enumerated, we need to mount a comparative competition among them.

One of the criteria in such a competition is that each hypothesis needs to explain the sturdy theories from cognitive psychology about minimally counterintuitive beliefs. Some of these hypotheses will meet that criterion more easily than others. Specifically, while there is good evidence for the adaptiveness of some religious beliefs, there is a decided lack of persuasive evidence that religious beliefs are adaptive because they are true. Thus, any hypothesis about religious ontology that needs to presume this in order to make sense of minimal counterintuitiveness—as the first and fourth hypotheses do—will struggle for credibility relative to their competitors. In respect of this one comparative criterion, therefore, the second and third hypotheses are stronger. But there will be many other criteria to take account of in this comparative competition, and the overall judgment will depend on all of them, not just one. For example, it would be necessary to explain purported experiences of discarnate entities, to make sense of the efficacy of the natural sciences, to explain the dominance of the first view in the history of human cultures, and to assess how each view fares in making coherent sense of every existing thing.

This example illustrates both why traditional inferential natural theology is rarely feasible and how complex the reconstructed arguments become in comparative natural theology. This complexity is not excessive, but merely what the conceptual content of the issues require. Anything less short-circuits the debate. The case study on the existence of God in Chapter 4 showed how multidisciplinarity is essential even for traditional themes in religious philosophy. In much the same way, a comparative dimension is also necessary. While Swinburne's argument (discussed in Chapter 4) has a comparative dimension—comparing personal theism with a flattened-out atheism, which essentially refuses to address metaphysical origins and ontological dependence—it is drastically short-circuited. If we were to reconstruct his argument along the lines of a full-blown comparative natural theology, we would assess numerous sophisticated hypotheses against numerous comparative criteria.[55]

This is a dramatically different concept of natural theology.[56] It is much more persuasive but also much more complex than traditional natural theology because it depends crucially on a descriptive database of religious beliefs and practices, organized by means of robust comparative categories. And this is why most types of religious philosophy require a comparative dimension.

Chapter 6

A Pragmatic Theory of Inquiry

The argument to this point has surveyed the tasks and styles of religious philosophy. It has given a strong reading of how religious philosophy fits into the various cultural and academic contexts of which it is a part. And it has shown how religious philosophy, properly conceived, requires multiple disciplinary perspectives and a comparative dimension. Along the way, I have spoken of religious philosophy as inquiry and I have introduced elements of a theory of inquiry, or a theory of human rationality. In fact, this theory has functioned as a framework for my interpretation of religious philosophy in each of the previous chapters. In this chapter, I draw together the already introduced elements into a brief but systematic statement of this theory of inquiry.

Much of the argument of this book, including the strong reading of religious philosophy as multidisciplinary comparative inquiry, does not depend on the details of this theory of inquiry. Yet many of the key arguments, while sound regardless of the enclosing epistemological framework, only achieve their full strength in the presence of a pragmatic theory of inquiry. This is especially true of arguments from Chapter 4 and Chapter 5 concerning the necessity of multiple disciplinary perspectives and a comparative dimension even in the most traditional subject matters of religious philosophy, and concerning the value of cooperative approaches to inquiry and the complex role of cognitive assets and liabilities in inquiry. It is also true of the argument in Chapter 3, which assessed modern and postmodern instincts about the epistemology and morality of inquiry, and the various arguments in Chapter 1, which addressed objections to the possibility or feasibility of religious philosophy from the perspectives of philosophy, religious studies, and theology. The theory of inquiry presented in this chapter makes each of those arguments more compelling.

Problem Solving and Inquiry

A pragmatic theory of inquiry treats inquiry fundamentally as a kind of spontaneous interest-driven problem-solving instinct in organisms. Among human beings, the problem-solving instinct can be systematized where the desire and resources exist to do so.

What Is a Theory of Inquiry?

A theory of inquiry is a systematic interpretation of the way human beings ask and answer questions. It explains how problems show up for people, how people settle on reliable beliefs and wise actions in relation to them, why inquiry succeeds or fails, and how problems stop being problematic. It pays close attention to the cognitive resources made possible by intelligent brains, the social resources activated by cooperation, and the empirical resources accessible through contact with a world that is not always passively compliant in response to our problem-solving efforts but rather sometimes resists our hypotheses. A good theory of inquiry takes account of what we know from the natural and human sciences about brains, groups, and the world. But a very good theory of inquiry does not fall prey to a careless reductionism that eliminates truth, reality, and value in the name of confining the theory to the impressively detailed but sorely limited reach of the sciences. That is, a compelling theory of inquiry is a philosophical theory that integrates knowledge from the humanities with scientific understanding into a coherent and consistent interpretation—an interpretation properly applicable to its subject matter, adequate to all relevant considerations, and appropriately fruitful.

There have been many theories of inquiry in the history of philosophy. In fact, human reason has been one of the most prominent themes within all philosophical traditions. This is not surprising. Rationality is a wondrous phenomenon, which appears to be rare in nature and certainly is precious to human beings. It naturally begs for an explanation. Martin Heidegger was right that human beings are definitively those beings who are a mystery to themselves, perpetually a puzzle to be understood. Part of that puzzle is a curiosity about why we are so curious, a quest for an intelligent interpretation of our own intelligence.

One of the reasons we are a puzzle to ourselves is that our surface self-understandings are often misleading and do not survive rigorous scrutiny. Philosophers throughout history in all traditions have recognized this, in quite varied ways. In ancient Greece, we find Plato's depiction in the *Republic* of human self-deception in our cave-bound life of shadows and Parmenides' vision of changeless being behind every kind of reality. In South Asian philosophy, we have the Buddhist philosophical portrayal of human self-delusory attachment to the world of appearances, which prevents us from seeing that *saṃsāra* is nirvana, and the orthodox Hindu construal of life within the karmic ambit of *saṃsāra* as divine play (*līla*), and thus as self-deluded ignorance (*avidyā*) for human beings. In East Asian philosophy, we find philosophers such as the Daoist sage Zhuangzi (Zhuāng Zǐ or Chuang Tzǔ or 莊子 or 庄子; c. 369–286 BCE) emphasizing the deceptive quality of our experience due especially to our tendency to fail to notice the way we take perspectives, and the direct attack of Confucian philosopher Xunzi (Xúnzǐ or Hsün Tzu or 荀子 or 荀子; 310–238) and others on the human tendency to interpret world events in terms of the actions of supernatural agents.

Despite this longstanding awareness from all over the world that human beings do not necessarily interpret accurately matters of philosophical importance, including particularly their own rational operations, something important has changed in this striving for self-understanding. We now know a great deal more than we ever have known about human minds, human sociality, and human experience of the world. Few classical theories of inquiry are adequate to these bodies of knowledge, not least because many of the new insights are deeply counterintuitive. Most importantly, we can discover more or less precisely which sorts of misunderstanding we are prone to and also how and why misunderstanding occurs. This dramatically changes the terms for an adequate theory of inquiry. No matter what we go on to say about human rationality, inspired by classical philosophical theories from any number of sources, an adequate theory of inquiry in our time must at least make sense of what we actually know about how human beings form, hold, evaluate, correct, and reject beliefs—and why they sometimes do this successfully and other times unsuccessfully.

This is not the place for a comprehensive discussion of epistemology and ontology. Rather, I will work in the mode of constructive philosophy, elaborating a promising hypothesis about inquiry that satisfies the criteria for adequacy that I have presented. The primary context for this hypothesis is the pragmatic-naturalist tradition of American philosophy. This refers especially to the pragmatists Charles Saunders Peirce,[1] William James,[2] John Dewey,[3] and their descendents—through Alfred North Whitehead[4] and subsequent thinkers in the process lineage; and through Henry Nelson Wieman[5] and others in the Chicago School of religious naturalism. These elements of American philosophy were deeply entangled throughout the twentieth century and combine naturally in diverse philosophers and religionists such as George Allan, Justus Buchler, Jack Joseph Cohen, Robert Corrington, Donald Crosby, Frederick Ferré, Nancy Frankenberry, Charley Hardwick, Mark Johnston, Paul Kurts, William Murry, Robert Neville, Kai Nielson, Creighton Peden, Karl Peters, Jack Ritchie, Loyal Rue, George Santayana, John Shook, Jerome Stone.[6] The theory of inquiry I sketch here is a pragmatic one in the tradition of the original pragmatists, but it resists what I consider to be James's relativizing view of truth[7] and even more so the narrative-perspective approaches to truth in neo-pragmatists such as Richard Rorty.[8]

The pragmatic theory of inquiry has six main emphases, and I will explain each in what follows.

- Biology: inquiry is an embodied activity made possible by senses and brains.

- Evolution: inquiry serves survival through helping human beings solve problems.

- Sociality: inquiry is a social process depending on cooperation and consensus.

- Correction: inquiry is tentative formulation of hypotheses, continually seeking correction.

- Fallibilism: beliefs are always subject to correction.

- Critical realism: the source of correction is a feedback potential or an experienced resistance to hypotheses; this is the proper empirical basis for speaking of sensible, structured reality external to human experience.

The promise of the pragmatist-naturalist tradition for a theory of inquiry is simple but dramatic. This was the first tradition of world philosophy, and is still the principle philosophical tradition, that takes full and nonreductive account of the emerging evolutionary view of human minds, human sociality, and human experience of the world. It has proved far more adaptable than other philosophical traditions to new knowledge from the natural, human, and cognitive sciences. It has shown itself to be more resilient than other traditions in the face of an aggressive species of ontological reductionism—specifically, a reductionism that pretends at satisfaction over a half-hearted solution to the problem of human inquiry solely on the terms of the natural sciences, instead of laboring philosophically for an integrated interpretation that keeps classic philosophical categories of truth, reality, and value in full contact with the empirically based theories of the natural and social sciences. This tradition has also demonstrated richer connections with the standing insights of world philosophical and religious traditions, especially those that are the most directly experience based, such as most forms of Buddhist philosophy. These virtues are the reasons why I elaborate a pragmatic theory of inquiry—rather than an Aristotelian or Lockean or Cartesian or Kantian one, or one based on Śaṅkara or Rāmānuja or Madhva, or one rooted in Mādhyamaka or Yogācāra or Tibetan or Zen schools of Buddhist philosophy. Nevertheless, many insights from these and other theoretical interpretations of human rationality are registered in the pragmatic theory of inquiry, particularly as I elaborate it here.

Problem Solving and Inquiry

Human beings are the best suited among earth animals for problem solving (inquiry). We have the right sort of brain, with its massively expanded cortex relative to other animals. We are poor fighters so we have to solve problems to survive; compare our physical vulnerability with the hunting perfection of sharks. We are communicators so our problem-solving efforts can be made more effective both by teaching new solutions to others (education), and by combining efforts to solve problems (cooperation).

Yet human beings are far from being ideally suited for problem solving. We have many psychological and neurological characteristics that lead us consistently in the wrong directions—characteristics such as selection bias (noticing only confirming evidence), over-active pattern recognition skills (seeing patterns where none exist), and a tendency toward insecurity and anxiety that leads us to rationalize contrary evidence to an imprudent degree.[9] Good thinking requires a lot of training both to capitalize on our natural aptitude for inquiry and to compensate for our natural liabilities in inquiry.

The benefits of successful inquiry are enormous. Our survival depends on it, as does our thriving as a species. We may not be able to swim and hunt like sharks, but we don't have to live in the water and we have discovered ways of going into the water to hunt using tools that allow us to find food, including sharks, without unduly risking life and limb. We may not be able to run as fast as lions, but through trial and error we can figure out how to hunt lions with acceptable risks to ourselves and eventually how to restrict lion habitats and even how to confine lions in zoos as objects of curiosity. Beyond mere survival, our capacity for inquiry has been the key to the flourishing of our species through the construction of cultures and civilizations. Successful inquiry underlies architectural, artistic, publishing, medical, and technological achievements of every kind. The failure of inquiry or the failure of the will to solve problems creatively through inquiry similarly underlies much pain and suffering in our world, from wars of revenge and frustration to the ongoing disasters of unnecessary disease and starvation. It also lies at the root of much human stupidity and gullibility, in which victims of our biological limitations for inquiry are never educated to the point that they can compensate for those weaknesses and protect themselves from people who would exploit them.[10]

We can appreciate the importance of inquiry for human survival and flourishing, and yet also grant that systematic inquiry is often a socially costly luxury incompatible with the hard realities of politics and economics. Thus, we need to know not only how to inquire well but also when to solve problems through careful inquiry rather than through low-energy interventions and intuitive rulings. Should the U.S. government fund a super-conducting super-colliding accelerator in order to investigate the fine structure of matter? When is the right time for such a massive investment of time and expertise and financial resources? Which disputes should nations try to resolve through negotiations, which through threats and intimidation, and which through joint efforts to solve problems in rational ways?

These are among the most important questions facing a world whose technology gives unthinkable power to small groups of extremists, whose increasingly globalized economy increases opportunity and wealth but also injustice and poverty, whose political and cultural interactions are usually clumsy and often violent, and whose galloping technologies have potentially disastrous effects on the habitat on which we depend for our very lives. When do we solve these problems through patient inquiry and when do we deal with them through force or art or neglect? The problem of the *will to inquire* is an enormous one and morally one of the deepest questions we must answer. My interest here, however, is in the more modest but also important issue of the methods that will produce the best results when we decide to solve problems through determined inquiry, if indeed there are such methods. It is this question that most illumines the diverse expressions of human rationality, and also the deep structures of the world that account for why inquiry works in the particular ways it does.

So what method of inquiry will work best for creatures like us? Efficient inquiry, regardless of how it is described in the context of specific methodological analyses, in fact follows a threefold procedure, with each phase deeply rooted in the biology and sociality of human life. Intuitive abduction and imaginative induction allow us to formulate hypotheses; deduction produces testable consequences and predictions by which we might try to correct and improve our provisional hypotheses; and finally a process of correction identifies errors and provokes adjustments to our hypotheses. This is the biologically basic hypothetico-corrective method. It generalizes the more traditional and science-focused hypothetico-deductive method by stressing that correction can be and actually is sought in any way possible. That is, correction might work even when deductions from working hypotheses are not experimentally testable, and also when the propositions that can be exposed to correction are logically relevant but not strict deductions from working hypotheses. This allows for inference-to-best-explanation styles of argument as well as straightforward correction to hypotheses by means of the falsification of propositions deduced from those hypotheses. It also differs from traditional proposals for theories of scientific inquiry by drawing out the inherently embodied and social nature of acts of inquiry.

The intuitive and imaginative abduction process is fascinating but poorly understood. It appears to derive from hyperdeveloped capacities in human beings for pattern recognition and similar cognitive processes. Unsurprisingly, it misfires a great deal of the time (witness the prevalence of false beliefs and superstitions among human cultures). But it is overproductive of hypotheses in just the right way to help us stumble across good guesses now and then, which is the fundamental reason why it was adaptive in the ancestral environment.

In practice, abduction depends crucially on the way problems arise in relation to our bodies and our groups. These contextual features influence the bodily feelings that give us our bearings around new problems, condition the traditions of expertise and practical techniques that stabilize our understanding of problems, and activate the choices we have when we ponder how to transform our imaginative leaps of insight into robust solutions. Without embodied technique, problems would rarely arise intelligibly and without social skill problems would rarely be tractable. The contemporary field of science and technology studies has helped to reverse a widespread pattern of neglect of these factors in earlier philosophical analyses of scientific inquiry, though often at the cost of injudiciously rejecting valid insights into the nature of human problem solving in the sciences. Bodies and groups, techniques and traditions are indispensable for making sense of the problems that arise in human experience. This insight can be generalized validly from the domain of science and technology to the study of human problem solving in every form.

The deductive phase of inquiry involves discovering what our hypotheses entail. This is enormously elaborate territory, particularly in disciplines such as mathematics and law. Human beings are prone to reasoning errors, as I have said, and avoiding them requires extensive training. The descriptive and analytical study of reasoning, or logic, remained fairly settled from Aristotle's description of the syllogism until the late nineteenth century, after which intricate investigation has been the standard. The philosophy of logic asks why reasoning works when it conforms to logical rules, and is an exceedingly complex and thoroughly controverted discipline. I discuss the biological roots of logic below.

The third phase of inquiry is the process by which hypotheses get corrected. It is here that the strongest argument for the superiority of this theory over its many rivals emerges: the hypothetico-corrective theory of inquiry optimizes the neurological, bodily, psychological, and social constraints on human inquiry, while taking full advantage of the empirically undeniable yet uneven power of reality (however understood) to suggest corrections in our hypotheses.

The Biological and Sociological Basis of Inquiry

The pragmatic theory of inquiry is rooted in biology. It is a natural extension of the dynamic interaction between interest-driven perception and embodied action in an environment that responds to exploration. The pragmatic theory of inquiry takes the sociality of inquiry as seriously as its biological rooting. It explains why different subject matters stimulate different kinds of social organization for the corresponding types of inquiry, ranging from specialized discourse communities to loose-knit groups with parallel exploratory projects. This explanation involves giving an account of the phenomenon of hypothesis correction as the power source for inquiry and as the chief determining factor in what methods and forms of social organization prove most useful in a given case of inquiry.

The Biology of Inquiry

The most natural way to begin a formal presentation of the biological roots of inquiry is to analyze the way that inquiry begins, which is to say, the way that something becomes an object of inquiry. The discussion of complexity and abstraction in Chapter 3 described the process of problem emergence, whereby something stands out from the flow of experience, captures our attention, and strikes us irritating or curious or fascinating. This intensely embodied approach to the phenomenon of problem emergence takes bodies-in-contexts for granted, treats the human mind as a feature of contextual embodiment, and pictures contexts as social as well as physical. These are the keys to recognizing the interestedness of problem emergence and the inquiries it stimulates; everything we ponder is, in the first instance, an intrusion that draws precious resources of attention and thought. Yet thinking in response to an emergent problem is also the source of the greatest human achievements, and thus an activity of the greatest moment for societies and civilizations, as well as individuals. Inquiry is always interested but interestedness makes inquiry profoundly useful even though it sometimes has problematic side effects.

Unlike most theories of inquiry, the pragmatic theory stipulates neither the form of a problem nor the resources relevant to an inquiry. Inquiry is problem solving. It begins when we sense a problem, and it ends when that problem no longer bothers us. This might be because we solve the problem, because we lose interest in it, or because our attention becomes dominated by something new. Problems can be physiological challenges such as a baby learning to walk, social tasks such as figuring out why someone is angry, or intellectual puzzles such as thinking of a five-letter word beginning and ending in x to fit into a crossword. They can be anything and everything because their distinguishing feature is not their scope or topic but the fact that they are irritants to catalyze attention and initiate inquiry. The circularity here—inquiry is problem solving; a problem is whatever initiates inquiry—is not vicious. It merely reflects the biologically basic status of the phenomenon of problem emergence and instinctive human reactions to it.

Framing the varied phenomena of problem emergence and inquiry broadly in this way naturally places them in the heart of the natural world as activities of many species, not solely of human beings. If a being is complex enough that its attention can be arrested and intelligent enough that it can strive for solutions, then there will exist inquiry in response to emergent problems. Inquiry and problem emergence in this biologically basic sense jointly shade off into irrelevance as organism complexity decreases—and this in two ways.

On the one hand, the behavior of simpler organisms is dominated by purely programmed activity and there is neither the flexibility for behavioral adaptation, nor the attentional sophistication for problem emergence, nor the intelligence for inquiry. For example, the sophisticated collective behavior of ant colonies depends on dominantly programmed activity. It is possible to construe an ant bridge across a small stream as the result of inquiry in response to a problem, but this stretches the meaning of inquiry too far to be useful.

On the other hand, even in the most complex organisms, including human beings, consciousness is differentiated to the point that a kind of problem emergence and problem-resolving organism behavior can occur without a major arresting of attention. For example, it is possible for a human being to habitualize behaviors to the point that driving a vehicle relatively safely can be accomplished without a high degree of attention to the task. It is possible to describe negotiating a turn under such circumstances as inquiry that resolves a problem, just as it is possible to think of biological reflexes such as heart-rate adjustments as types of problem solving, but such usages stretch concepts beyond my immediate interest.

There is no sharp demarcation between situations where inquiry can occur and those where it cannot in either of these two gray areas. But this indeterminacy is a virtue, not a liability. It frames problem emergence and inquiry in exactly the right way—as a set of capacities that human beings share in some respects with some other species, and as subject to variations of intensity of attention and intelligent expertise. It is possible to develop a highly general metaphysics of complex systems by extending the concepts of problem emergence, inquiry, and programmed behavior into biological domains to which we would not normally apply such concepts. My interest here is in high-attention, high-cost, high-intelligence instances of problem emergence and inquiry, of the sort that we most associate with the word *inquiry*. But it is important to note that this limitation is in fact an abstraction from the enormously varied conscious and automatic activities of natural organisms. We do well to recall this abstraction in order to avoid imposing a sharp line of demarcation where none properly obtains.

The neurophysiological conditions for high-attention, high-cost, high-intelligence inquiry are fascinating, involving diverse brain functions operating in a tightly integrated system. If analytical detection of causes is excellent but memory is poor, then problem solving efforts will be frustrated. If sensory inputs are refined but cognitive categorization is weak, then interpretation necessary for problem solving is hobbled. The adaptive benefits of a high level of diversity and integration of the cognitive components relevant to problem solving suggests that brains are selected for their ability to support effective inquiry. Note that diversity of brain functions by itself does not suggest adaptation; religious behavior illustrates such diversity but may well be a loosely coordinated set of side effects of traits originally selected for other, nonreligious reasons, and only ever become adaptive later in newly emergent forms of social organization. It is the *tight integration of diverse brain functions in inquiry* that suggests selection.

The specifics of the neurophysiology of inquiry need not detain us. The adaptiveness of inquiry is what matters. Through the more recent stretches of the evolutionary process—at least since brains had highly adaptable cortical regions capable of prodigious feats of learning and memory—organisms have been subject to selection pressures for which the skill of inquiry confers a differential fitness advantage. Inquiry directly helps organisms to solve the sorts of problems that enhance their survival—from avoiding predators to finding and eventually growing food, and from building the skills for cooperation to controlling life niches and constructing habitats.

The proper philosophical interpretation of the adaptiveness of inquiry is a complex matter. Most interpretations of inquiry assign a foundational place to logical laws. Perhaps this is a gesture of Platonic trust in the ontological primacy of the conceptual world, but it is certainly an acknowledgement of the apparent definitiveness of logic in human reasoning. By contrast, a biologically based theory of inquiry such as the current one takes not logic but the dual phenomena of problem emergence and problem solving as fundamental. Both types of interpretation must negotiate an epistemic chasm between the apparent definitiveness of logic and the messy tentativeness of experience, approaching the chasm from opposite directions.

The primacy-of-logic interpretations of inquiry attempt to bridge this chasm by positing an epistemological foundationalism whereby human nature includes built-in access to certainty rooted either in clear and distinct ideas or in the indubitable quality of the basic elements of experience. But developments in modern philosophy demanding a nonfoundationalist approach to epistemology, as described in Chapter 3, make all such approaches deeply problematic. The pragmatic theory of inquiry surrenders certainty in order fully to recognize the embodiment of minds and the biological roots of inquiry. The result is epistemological fallibilism: all beliefs are formed in uncertainty; all are subject to correction; none can be placed beyond the possibility of error; and we achieve warranted confidence in them through living with them and testing them. The epistemological fallibilism at the heart of the pragmatic theory of inquiry is deeply at odds with interpretations of inquiry that depend on certainty, whether this certainty lies in the foundational elements of experience or in the laws of logic.

The sheer fact of the adaptiveness of inquiry supports neither the pragmatic theory nor its competitors. For the primacy-of-logic interpretations, the adaptiveness of inquiry is interpreted as a matter of aligning the human mind through the evolutionary process with preexisting logical forms of reasoning. Getting logic correct is a necessary condition for adaptiveness. For the pragmatic theory of inquiry, by contrast, logical laws are abstractions from experience, as it is honed through the processes that make inquiry adaptive. The adaptiveness of inquiry is the necessary condition for formulating generalized principles of logical reasoning, and different evolutionary settings might in principle—but not necessarily in actual practice—produce different principles of logic. At this level of analysis, both types of interpretation can make sense of the adaptiveness of inquiry and thus seem to be on equal footing.

Once we accept the sheer fact of the adaptiveness of inquiry and press for a more detailed account of the relationship between biology and inquiry, the pragmatic theory of inquiry appears considerably stronger than its competitors. Twentieth-century philosophy has discovered many systems of logic, some of which cover different kinds of reasoning and some of which are conflicting accounts of the same type of reasoning. It strains plausibility to conjecture, with the primacy-of-logic interpretations, that human beings generate conflicting logics because they cannot discern with perfect clarity ontologically independent laws of logic. It is far more plausible to suppose, with the pragmatic theory of inquiry, that conflicts arise because the vagueness of processes of inquiry permit different and conflicting abstractions of the basic principles of inquiry.

The case that logic has biological roots is a complex and controversial one. It has been made best by William Cooper in *The Evolution of Reason: Logic as a Branch of Biology*.[11] Cooper's case is deliberately extreme, in the reductive sense suggested by the subtitle. But a clear statement of an extreme view can help set up the debate needed to refine the hypothesis at stake. In one or another form, the pragmatic theory of inquiry must be committed to the thesis that biology and inquiry precede logic experientially and not the other way around. The early pragmatists explored this possibility—the most developed presentation is John Dewey's *Logic: The Theory of Inquiry*[12]—but they never achieved the degree of clarity that Cooper does. Yet it is odd that Cooper does not recognize his pragmatist precursors. Writing out of the analytical tradition of philosophy of logic, Cooper gives no sign of being aware that his central thesis about the biological rootedness of logic was already extensively discussed a century earlier. Among the philosophers who claim these early pragmatists as their heritage, Cooper's argument is not the controversial spike in the heart of contemporary philosophy that he thinks, but merely the unfolding of insights that inevitably follow from fully recognizing the biological character of inquiry.

The difficulty of accepting a fully biologically based theory of inquiry seems to be due to the chasm described above between the definitiveness of logic and the messy tentativeness of experience. In the context of a pragmatic theory of inquiry, honoring the apparent definitiveness of logic requires a richly developed view of habits that are grounded biologically in adapted cognitive mechanisms and then refined culturally through education and experience. It seems as though anything that depends on cultural refinement ought to feel more tentative than the laws of logic and mathematics do. But the power of excellent abstractions is that they are rarely contradicted in experience. This is how principles of logic and mathematics become habituated to the point that they seem beyond question. As Dewey pointed out, "the interpretation of them as *a priori* is not necessary."[13] The biology of inquiry and the interpretation of logical principles as abstractions from consistent experience are jointly sufficient to explain the *apparently* a priori character of principles of logic.

The Sociality of Inquiry

We have seen that problem emergence is interested, and indeed initially self-interested, because problems show up as irritations or curiosities within an organism such as a human being. But complex organisms have intricate social relationships and hardwired behavioral tendencies that cause most problems to have social relevance. The problem of how to find food is not just a matter of alleviating personal hunger but also of cooperation that helps others do the same. The problem of loneliness is not just about easing individual existential pain but also about making a friend. Even the problem of a headache is typically not just a pain management issue but also a search for comfort from a loved one. The social dimensions of problem emergence are so obvious that we are apt to overlook them or underestimate their importance.

A convenient way to surface the profoundly social character of processes of inquiry is to study the phenomenon of conflicting truth claims. Conflicts over what is true appear in many human activities—from parents having to settle the competing allegations of fighting children to the complex political and moral debates of social life. On most occasions, settling conflicts is largely a matter of expediency. Rarely is there the leisure to investigate conflicting claims with the patience required to get to the root of the disagreement and to decide the question with complete consideration and full fairness. The energy costs of rational inquiry must be weighed against the virtues of clear understanding and just action. The fact that expediency is a large factor in any resolution of conflicting truth claims illumines political processes and the exercise of authority within human societies, but it generates few insights about the rational elements of human inquiry. The focus here is on those few occasions when we can inquire with leisure into the problems posed by competing truth claims, without fear of constraints on time and energy.

Of course, relative to the whole fabric of human rational activity, much of which is reflexive and quite successful, the phenomenon of competing truth claims is actually quite rare.[14] So we narrow the focus a great deal when we move from human rational activity to conflicting truth claims, and a great deal further when we move from such conflicts to situations in which we have the luxury to examine and resolve them through rational inquiry. Yet this tiny corner of the fabric of human reasoning—I shall henceforth call it "serious inquiry" or just "inquiry" where the qualification is safely understood—is a useful place to go if our aim is to gain a philosophical understanding of human rationality. Rationality rather than social expediency is most prominent in the domain of serious inquiry, yet even here the social features of inquiry are unmistakable.

Serious inquiry requires a civilization, stable social life, and complex institutions devoted to the creation of culture and refinement of knowledge. Efficient inquiry is fundamentally a social process, requiring high cooperation and the possibility of strong consensus. In special circumstances, individuals can mount and complete inquiries alone, but such achievements are nonetheless woven into the social fabric of human life. In fact, all conceptualizing—in language and tool making, in self-understanding and problem solving—assumes a social group as its context and condition.

Primate studies have proved important for understanding the social intelligence of human life, particularly as the product of a long evolutionary process.[15] Understanding the social dynamics of a troop of chimpanzees, our nearest surviving evolutionary relatives, casts human social behavior into an eerie light. We seem to share many of the chimps' fundamental social instincts and strategies, even though we are accustomed to reframing these instincts unconsciously in the conceptuality and constraints of civilization and culture. The neuropsychological implications of this working picture of the emergence of our species are equally thought provoking.[16] Primate brains evolved under inherently social conditions. We are only selves in a social context. We communicate as social creatures. We solve problems corporately. We simplify social life by finding or constructing shared assumptions to guide belief and behavior.

Even a little exposure to the complexity of chimpanzee social life drives home these points. There is an enormous amount for researchers, and the chimps themselves, to track, including biological relationships—who is likely to help or threaten who, when and how the limits of hierarchy can be tested, and how to improve the chances of mating. The complexity of the resulting behaviors and strategies is prodigious, and shows how valuable it would be to have a brain better suited for conceptualizing, generalizing, and symbolizing than chimpanzee brains are. This environmental fact of life among intelligent social animals confers a significant advantage on animals with greater brain power of the special kind we have. This is the evolutionary trajectory propelling language, art, and self-consciousness.[17]

Social life is significantly about the presence and absence of shared assumptions. When we share assumptions widely with others, we greatly reduce the stress and energy associated with encountering strangers, feeling at ease, protecting ourselves and our families, and predicting the future. Shared assumptions also enable cooperation in inquiry, and with the right kind of organization they help to make inquiry more efficient. Sometimes many people share the same irritation that triggers inquiry. Whether it is how to catch fish or how to control a belligerent neighbor, corporate inquiry presupposes shared concern with a common problem.

As approaches to inquiry go, many people trying simultaneously to solve a shared problem is often more comical than effective. Efficiency of corporate inquiry requires much more than merely joint effort. The inquiring community needs a stable identity focused around the practices and procedures for carrying out inquiry, and also around the norms for judgment applicable to resolving competing proposals for solving whatever problem inspires the cooperation in the first place. Consensus on practices and norms can only emerge if mistaken proposals get corrected quickly. Otherwise, when proposals compete with no resolution, the focus of identity within the problem-solving group, as well as the goal of achieving consensus around the best solution, is frustrated. Human beings are only so patient.

On this view, then, rationality is the joining of consensus and correctability, which in turn crucially depends upon the impressive yet uneven power of reality to correct hypotheses (what I earlier called the "feedback potential" and about which I will say more below). The consensus part of this sacred union stabilizes group identity around norms and procedures for inquiry. This sort of consensus arises in many ways. Political, economic, and social needs are powerful factors influencing any group's identity, whether a group is committed to problem solving or not. When the leisure and resources for corporate inquiry exist, however, we can characterize the rationality of the process of problem solving in terms of the way the power of correctability fosters or frustrates the formation of consensus around norms and procedures for inquiry, as follows.

- An *efficient* rational process is one in which consensus arises because proposals for norms and procedures can compete, creating agreement about winners and losers.
- An *inefficient* rational process is one in which competing proposals for norms and procedures of inquiry do not produce widely accepted winners and losers.
- An *irrational* process is one in which resources for the correction of hypotheses are arbitrarily neglected.

Rapid correction of hypotheses fosters consensus around norms and procedures, and thereby efficient formation of identity in groups devoted to inquiry. By contrast, slow or no correction frustrates consensus around norms and procedures. This provokes social innovation to fill the space of possibilities for group identity, whereby people introduce hedges against the arbitrary imposition by other groups of norms and procedures that cannot win consensus. Under such circumstances, many socially supported modes of inquiry will coexist, battling the imposition of consensus, unable to resolve contradictory hypotheses, yet portraying a host of potentially valuable but uncoordinated perspectives on the underlying problem.

The differences among the various ways that hypothesis correction works in practice are significant especially because they provoke these contrasting social strategies. We can see this in the various types of inquiry around us. Modern science enjoys a strong corporate identity, despite fights around the margins, because it specifically confines itself to the parts of reality that promise relatively rapid correction of hypotheses. By contrast, the intellectual wing of religion is often governed more by the expediency of providing credible accounts of beliefs vital to religious institutions than by serious interest in rationally resolving conflicting truth claims about religious topics using all available resources. This is largely because resources for correcting hypotheses about religious topics seem relatively weak or absent—or too plentiful and inconsistent, which amounts to the same thing. Yet most major religions have sub-traditions within which the devotion to truth through inquiry is strong, which in turn redirects and controls the obligation to rationalize existing institutional religious practices and beliefs. Thus, both science and religion yield many instances of serious inquiry, and the contrast between the social character of inquiry in these cases has a lot to do with what sorts of hypotheses can be corrected.

The Power Source for Inquiry

It is deeply puzzling that we can correct some hypotheses more easily than others—and some seemingly not at all. A pragmatist theory of inquiry is critically realist in its approach to this profound question. This means that the explanation will make central reference both to the way the world is and to the way human beings function in their embodied and social ways as inquirers in the world.

On the one hand, regarding the way the world is, the differences in the correctability of hypotheses correspond to the contours of what I shall continue to call the "feedback potential" within reality (first discussed above in Chapter 3). Experience has domains where the feedback potential does not work clearly, which leads to multiple interpretations whose mutual contradictions seem irresolvable. This occurs most famously in metaphysics and the theoretical aspects of religion, in matters of taste and moral judgment, and also in some of the more speculative areas of the sciences such as quantum cosmology. Reality also has more definite parts where the feedback potential "speaks" clearly. This makes possible the correction of hypotheses within social processes of inquiry, and thereby consensus around norms and procedures for inquiry. This occurs most prominently in many parts of the natural sciences and also in many commonsense inquiries.

On the other hand, regarding the way human beings are, the differences in the correctability of hypotheses also express how well adapted human beings are, and how well optimized their social organizations are, for taking advantage of the feedback potential of reality. Areas of correctability have to be discovered in inquiry because it is difficult to know in advance where the feedback potential works well and difficult to organize human efforts to leverage corrective resources. Indeed, the history of human inquiry shows that many previously unknown areas of efficient correctability have been discovered—the modern natural sciences are the standing examples but the same is true to lesser degrees of sociology, psychology, economics, and other human sciences. It is likely, therefore, that we will discover further areas of correctability and that currently intractable debates might prove to be resolvable after all.

It is never easy to adjudicate the question about how much of the difficulty of a given inquiry is due to the feedback potential and how much to the cognitive and social limitations of human beings as inquirers. This question takes its most challenging form in the case of lifestyle and moral inquiries that are independently successful within more than one context yet produce strikingly different results. In such cases, the multicontextual version of the same inquiry seems intractable in a particularly frustrating and painful way. For example, child-rearing practices differ widely among social and cultural contexts yet there is significant consensus around them in many local groups, to the point that what seems deeply satisfying in one place and time can seem shockingly cruel or neglectful or indulgent in another. When a child-rearing problem arises in a local context, a solution can often be found and implemented with confidence born of social consensus, yet in a larger context no solution that wins strong consensus is (or would be) forthcoming.

Is the success of inquiry in local contexts due to the contextual sensitivity of the feedback potential or to the culturally aided neglect of relevant data and hypotheses? A pragmatist typically believes that there is an empirical answer to this question. To find the answer, perform the following test: what happens when new data and hypotheses are introduced into the debate over the child-rearing challenge that triggered inquiry in the first place? A maximally rational process strives to accommodate the new perspectives. But that does not always happen. It follows that many such debates are in fact aided in their efficiency, and consensus norms buttressed, by simplification and neglect of relevant data and useful hypotheses. It also follows that a fully rational process of inquiry may be maximally efficient in respect to winning consensus in the long run among all qualified inquirers but often socially disruptive and practically unhelpful in the short run within local contexts.

The capacity for correcting hypotheses, the feedback potential, is a basic ontological hypothesis within a pragmatic theory of inquiry. This feedback potential is the heart of what we mean by reality; it is that which presses back against our physical and conceptual self-assertion, forcing us to adjust our behavior and refine our ideas. From a strictly empirical point of view, it is difficult to introduce the idea of reality in any other way because the feedback potential describes our actual inquiry experiences simply and directly. Yet the textured character of the feedback potential—varying from rough to refined, from powerful to absent—is deeply impressive. We can describe these variations based on our experience more easily than we can explain them. Scientists often find the feedback potential to be quite awesome and mysterious. For example, Stephen Jay Gould expressed such sentiments in the following passage:

> Something almost unspeakably holy—I don't know how else to say this—underlies our *discovery and confirmation* of the actual details that made our world and also, in realms of contingency, assured the minutiae of its construction in the manner we know, and not in any one of a trillion other ways, nearly all of which would not have included the evolution of a scribe to record the beauty, the cruelty, the fascination, and the mystery.[18]

There are many other moving expressions of the same sort scattered among the writings of thoughtful inquirers. They are right, surely. The operation of the feedback potential in human inquiry, including its powers to forge group identity through generating consensus around norms and procedures for inquiry, is one of the primal instances of human beings encountering the *other*. The corrective feedback potential is something uncontrollably beyond us, which has a kind of awesome power and evokes wonder and awe.

This pragmatic line of interpretation bears a close similarity to James Gibson's theory of perception.[19] Gibson conceived perception as an essentially exploratory and hypothetical system by which organisms could interact with and manipulate the surrounding environment. The organism reflexively and sometimes deliberately samples the environment for information about interactive possibilities, which Gibson intriguingly and aptly called "affordances." This means both that the environment is perceived according to the organism's interests and that the environment's affordances are disclosed according to both the way the organism is prepared to interact and the way it actually behaves in its surroundings. If a hypothetical, exploratory move in relation to an object or circumstance yields no affordances—no way to manipulate it, no way to navigate it, no way to comprehend it—then that interactive hypothesis is abandoned in favor of an alternative. Experience and memory, as well as observational and interpretative skills, determine how efficient the production of workable hypotheses is. Smart mice learn to sense in the most useful way more quickly than less smart mice, and the same is true for humans. Cooperation helps here, as the imaginative contributions of many organisms are more likely to unlock the environment's affordances.

The parallels with the pragmatic theory of inquiry are clear, and establish the biological credentials of that theory. In fact, there are traces of influence from James's radical empiricism to Gibson's own intellectual formation.[20] The exploratory perceptual interaction within an environment is the means by which human beings both perceive and act effectively, and thus also the means by which they gain understanding of every kind, including in inquiry. The encounter with a world that possesses an "affordance profile"—what I have been calling a "feedback potential"—reflects organism interests and social organization and also determines accuracy and fidelity of perception and understanding alike. To reach out for the handle on a photo-realistic painting of a door, expecting to open the door and pass through, fails to produce an affordance that matches organism interest. This in turn refines perception, modifies action, and rectifies understanding. The biologically basic character of exploratory, hypothetical interactions with the ambient environment explains why inquiry, from the commonsense to the sublime, has the structure of a dynamic dialectic between perception and action. It also explains the philosophical symmetry between the commonsense argument for realism based on the relative usefulness of perception and the more high-powered argument for critical realism based on the encounter with corrective resources in acts of inquiry.

Several decades have passed since Gibson's research efforts, and that is a long time in the fast-moving worlds of empirical psychology and theoretical psychology. These days, Gibson's ecological theory of environmental affordances and organism sensing persists primarily in the field of ecological psychology. The formal conceptuality of ecological psychology has not proved irresistible to the field of perception and action psychology as a whole; presumably this is due in part to the heavily philosophical overtones of the central categories, which tend to make empirical psychologists uncomfortable.[21] Yet the general perspective of embodied perception and an appreciation for the mutually constraining relation between action and perception is a dominant theme of contemporary perception psychology, albeit in less metaphysically modulated terminology than either Gibson or ecological psychology as a whole tend to use.

The idea of ecological perception has also become central in cognitive psychology, the neurological study of perception, and artificial intelligence research, where it underlies many approaches to computer modeling. Moreover, ecological psychology has had a vital impact on artifact design, software-interface design, architecture, and other fields that focus on design, usability, or both. There are important lines of critique to contend with, but these apply at a more detailed level than the general points relied on here.[22] In all, the Gibsonian theory of perception, at least in the generic sense of an ecology of perception-action, remains empirically robust and has proved an important corrective to more one-sided and abstracted theories of perception and action.

Gibson battled against several alternative accounts of perception during his lifetime, and each battle had profound philosophical implications for him. Early in his career, Gibson fought against the strong behaviorist program according which the only properly scientific subject matter for psychology is publicly observable behavior. Behaviorists of this and even some other less extreme kinds saw no reason to speak about the human mind (or animal minds), intentions and decisions, interests and desires, or even perceptions and ideas. But Gibson's experimental work had convinced him that visual perception, at the very least, was incomprehensible within the framework of behaviorist psychology. Some of the tools necessary for an adequate explanation of organism-environment interaction were not present in the behaviorist's toolkit: interests, emotions, desires, expectations, plans; imagining, trying, failing, succeeding, modifying; and determination, irritation, frustration, resolution, satisfaction. Of course, from a certain point of view, Gibson's own approach owed a lot to the behaviorist program, particularly in that he, too, stressed organism-environment interaction in his account of perception. But his account of that interaction required minds with interests and emotions as well as external stimuli and organism responses.

Later in his career, Gibson had to take the measure of the information-processing view of perception proposed by the cognitivist program in psychology. According to this view, perception is an information-processing mechanism, which can be modeled with computer programs capable of analyzing information from the equivalent of sensory inputs (cameras, pressure sensors, microphones) to produce valid, organism-like inferences about how to act. The problem here is that the infinitely variable quality of the environmental context could not be captured in a computer model of perception, let alone the complex behaviors that rely on perception. If the behaviorists neglected the necessary role of internal states of mind, then the information-processing cognitivists and artificial intelligence researchers neglected the thoroughgoing embodiment of human minds in a dynamic environment. The brain's environment constitutes an intensely intricate ecology of relations.[23] Here, too, Gibson's approach owes something to the cognitivist program he fought against. He was targeting not so much the idea of information processing, to which his analysis of perception lends itself, but rather the relatively environment-independent and disembodied way information processing was conceived in his day.

Gibson also battled the cognitive psychologists who urged that perception was strictly indirect—that is, that we perceive not the world itself directly but rather only internal cognitive representations of the world. Immanuel Kant argued for the inaccessibility of things in themselves to direct rational inspection because of the way that knowledge is always necessarily mediated spatially, temporally, and by the categories of the understanding.[24] The indirect theory of perception in psychology drew support from this influential account of mediated knowledge, and also from Sigmund Freud's and other accounts of unconscious psychic processes that can distort perception and understanding. Gibson's direct theory of perception insisted that organisms perceived aspects of the environment directly, and not merely mental representations of the environment—just as the environment impacts organisms directly, and not by means of mental representations. Direct perception is the dynamic dialectic between perception and action that lies at the root of all understanding.

As with his other philosophically loaded battles, time has made the gap between the Gibsonian dialectical version of direct perception and the various theories of indirect perception seem smaller than it did at one time. Nothing about Gibson's direct theory of perception entails that we would have uncomplicated access to understanding of the world, or that we should be able to generate consensus in inquiry just by concentrating hard on what we perceive, either of which would be contrary to experience. On the contrary, organism interests and chance events determine what aspects of the environment are sampled for affordances to support manipulation or navigation. That means that things show up for sensing organisms as tentatively categorized, but also as capable of resisting hypothetical explorations. There is a causal basis for the generation and correction of categorical schemes, as well as for their application, and this basis is the dynamic organism-environment interaction itself. Therefore, this is not a theory of direct perception in the sense of naïve realism, but neither does it bear out Kant's strict prohibition of knowledge of things in themselves. The dichotomy between direct and indirect theories of perception is far from sharp in an ecological account of the dynamic perception-action relation operating between interested organism and ambient environment.

In the partial reconciliations of three debates that I have proposed, we see both how the biological basis for inquiry can be rooted in the direct causal interaction between organism and environment, and how the ecological texture of this interaction requires interpretation in the sophisticated terms of indirect theories of perception. The causal story of perception may be relatively direct despite the interest-driven and category-structured nature of perceptual cognitions. In the same way—and this is no mere analogy—the causal basis for inquiry is rooted in the corrective resources of the biological encounter of organism with environment. This is so even though the cognitive content of inquiry is thoroughly mediated through layer upon layer of categorization, symbolization, and interpretation.

The importance of the concept of correctability sponsors several theoretical tendencies in all pragmatic theories of inquiry, and certainly in this one. Pragmatic theories of inquiry tend to view the meaning of truth as correspondence between human ideas and the world, without oversimplifying this relation. They affirm a unified world, conceived of as the ontological condition for the possibility of the capacity for correction (the feedback potential in experience, which is the ground of both resistance to hypotheses and Gibsonian affordances). They are unitary theories of inquiry, in the sense that everything is known in the same basic way, with variations due ultimately to variability in the feedback potential, and proximately to subtle variations of social context and inquiry procedure. And they tend to be resonant with naturalistic forms of religious sensibility that register the "mystery" and "wonder" of the feedback potential. These characteristics arise differently in the varieties of pragmatic theory of inquiry, however, so there is a great deal to be gained for understanding both inquiry and pragmatism by a careful comparative study on this point. But that is a topic for another place.

Specialized Discourse Communities and Inquiry

Specialized languages and communities that nurture and depend on them advance inquiry in three markedly different ways. In each case, the social dimensions of inquiry are amply evident, as are the variable contours of the feedback potential.

First, in domains of inquiry where the feedback potential is weak, as we have noted, there is little agreement on procedures and norms for inquiry. Social innovation is necessary to prevent the arbitrary imposition of opinion masquerading as resolution of a problem. Social innovation often consists in communities built around different sides of disagreements, which is to say, around key hypotheses that compete without resolution. These communities develop distinctive practices and specialized languages, which enable them corporately to explore the hypothesis that defines the identity of their group. The politics of such groups often expresses commitment to the value of this core identity in the form of behaviors that coerce or convince outsiders to join, regulation of insiders' beliefs and practices, and maintenance within the group of a sharp awareness of the insider-outsider boundary.

In such situations, specialized discourses serve to elaborate and test the contested hypothesis that lies at the heart of the community's identity. Specialized discourses are also badges of membership. When tensions with competitor groups are high, it is particularly important to know who you can trust. Specialized discourses function as costly signals because they are difficult to master. That is, they are hard-to-fake signs of sincerity, signaling that a person's commitment to the group is authentic and that the person can be trusted. This function of specialized discourse appears to be a side effect of adaptive social instincts that promote costly signaling in order to weed out free riders and strengthen group solidarity for times when it really matters.[25]

For example, the Church of Jesus Christ of Latter-day Saints, popularly known as Mormonism, is an American religion with strong affiliations with Christianity. From its origins, it was distinguished by beliefs and practices that other Christians rejected, including belief in the supernatural provision and authority of the *Book of Mormon*, belief that the resurrected Jesus Christ visited ancient people in the Americas, and belief in the *Book of Mormon's* historical accounts of the struggles of the ancient American tribes. A specialized discourse developed around these distinctive characteristics of the Mormon community, rooted especially in reading and studying the *Book of Mormon*. The competition between Mormonism and other variants of Christianity is less pronounced than it once was, thanks especially to the official Mormon renunciation of lifestyle practices such as polygamy that disgusted or outraged or intrigued many other Americans. Nonetheless, mastering this specialized discourse continues to define what it means to be an insider in the Mormon community. By means of it, thousands of ordinary people explore the core hypothesis of their group and test their distinctive beliefs against ordinary and extraordinary life experiences.

Without the specialized discourse, there would be no elaboration, exploration, or testing of the claim that there is a distinctively American revelation of Jesus as the Messiah commensurate with American national identity. If the specialized discourse were to lose its power, it would be because the community that formerly nurtured it no longer found it valuable enough to expend the energy required either to initiate novices or to think through their experience in its terms. This has happened countless times in the history of religions—vastly more specialized discourse communities have perished than have adapted and survived. It also happens in other domains of cultural life where specialized discourse communities are defined fundamentally by intractable disagreement with competing hypotheses. Is one kind of art better than another, one style of photography superior to another, one approach to cooking tastier than the alternatives? For a while, such questions can be passionate targets of inquiry, with the absence of clear feedback prompting communities to consolidate around particular convictions. There they explore and enhance the specialized discourse through which they interpret their conflicted corner of reality.

Most specialized discourse communities do not last very long because the existential motivation to pay the cost of mastery is relatively low—they have the status of fads for most involved. The specialized discourse of computer users fanatical about the Macintosh computer platform is quite distinctive, with special words and phrases that underline their group's identity in contrast to competitors such as the generic PC platform dominated once by IBM and now by Microsoft. But that fight will pass away in time. The more existentially loaded and emotionally consuming the topic under debate, the more likely both that intense specialized discourse communities will develop around the endlessly competing hypotheses and that those discourse communities will adapt and persist. This is why specialized discourse communities with staying power are almost always religious, in some sense.

Second, in domains where the feedback potential is strong, specialized discourse communities develop specifically to take full advantage of the opportunities to advance inquiry that such situations promise. As in the perpetually conflicted scenario just discussed, such specialized discourses help those who get on the inside of them to elaborate and test hypotheses with a high degree of cooperative efficiency. But a specialized discourse is not as important for group identity in the strong-feedback context. There is little pressure on outsiders to join or on insiders to be loyal because disputes are tractable and inquiry can advance. Rather than being badges of membership, specialized discourses function as tools to get an interesting job done. Mastering a specialized discourse does define identity, of course, but the pragmatic value of the discourse for inquiry makes it worth the effort to gain mastery even though the discourse is neither existentially all-encompassing nor emotionally bracing.

For example, returning to the example of Galileo mentioned in Chapter 4, a specialized discourse community grew up around Galileo's approach to studying the natural world. This occurred in a strong-feedback situation that permitted rapid advance in inquiry. The new discourse was stimulated by the newly perceived possibility of developing mathematical models to describe natural phenomena, on the one hand, and using emerging technologies such as the telescope to produce new observations capable of falsifying claims about the natural world, on the other. Interestingly, Galileo's intense fighting with other natural philosophers appears not to have been the stimulus for the development of this new discourse. Rather, it seems to have enjoyed a life of its own, coming into existence and developing specifically for the purpose of advancing scientific inquiries. Much the same is true of most specialized discourses in the natural sciences. While there are fascinating boundary cases, most specialized scientific discourses came into being and continue to mutate according to their usefulness for inquiry, not to consolidate group identity over against competitors. The stronger the feedback potential in a given case, the more likely this is to be true.

A specialized discourse enhances the ability of expert inquirers to elaborate and test their hypotheses. It stabilizes terminology specific to the contours of the inquiry so that people can talk about what they need to without having repeatedly to define what they mean, which quickly becomes tiresome. While there are dangers in settling on terminology, due to fact that the judgments expressed in naming can distort that to which the names refer, shared terminology offers a huge advance in efficiency. Consistent terminology inspires close observation of parts of the world previously taken for granted—as when Galileo started observing objects falling down inclined planes instead of simply assuming that received natural philosophy had the physics of falling correct. With consistent terminology, the possibilities of stabilizing theories about key concepts and developing literatures on which experts rely to mark competence in a field also arise. This much is true of specialized discourses regardless of the strength of the feedback potential that power inquiry. In a strong-feedback context, consistent terminology and the attendant theoretical edifice sets up the possibility of high-level correction of hypotheses, which is impossible otherwise.

It is one thing for Galileo to point out, with the aid of a telescope, that there are craters on the moon, contrary to the then-prevalent assumption that the moon is a perfectly smooth orb. It is quite another for Edwin Hubble to make a sophisticated series of observations and calculations to show that the observable universe is expanding, contrary to Einstein's expectation that it is not. There was very little for Galileo's detractors to contest; besides lamely accusing him of using poor optics, the most they could do was stubbornly refuse to look through the telescope. But the theories of instrumentation underlying Hubble's interpretation of his observations, are prodigiously complicated. Without a specialized discourse built around astronomical observation, including concepts that relate star brightness to distance and the chemical composition of stars to their red-shifted light signatures, Hubble's conclusion would have been out of reach.

It follows that specialized-discourse communities stabilize not only terminology but also layer upon layer of mutually constraining theories. This is what enables expert inquirers to search out means of correction that would otherwise remain undiscovered. Most scientific discoveries are not merely observations of hitherto unknown features of the world; they are also, and perhaps primarily, probings of the corrective powers of reality, uncovering new possibilities for advancing inquiry. Specialized discourses are the means by which communities of inquiry discipline themselves to activate resources for correction.

This is why it is impossible to know in advance how effective inquiry in any particular domain can be. New forms of social organization disciplined by the possibilities inherent in emerging specialized discourses can bring the powers of correction to domains once thought permanently mired in intractable disagreement and intransigent opinion. This has happened over and over again, and not only in the natural sciences. As the disciplined development of specialized discourse communities activated new domains of correction, philosophy gave birth to one discipline after another in the course of its history in the West, in South Asia, and in East Asia. Fights between Buddhists and Hindus over the nature of the human soul (*jīva*) seem beyond the possibility of correction, as the millennia-long disagreement attests, but this may not always remain so.

Third, and finally, specialized discourse communities sometimes advance inquiry by means of technical and formal languages. This applies to all types of inquiry where the rigorous unpacking of dense semantic territory is crucial for making sense of the subject matter. I refer here not to the generation of specialized terminology fitted to the subject matter of an inquiry but to the wholesale fabrication of languages for special purposes. Such languages may have empirical roots, but they take on a life of their own as their disciplining effects on the communities that invent and master them take hold.

The difference between a technical language and specialized terminology is one of degree, and it is possible to debate how to classify marginal cases. The key defining characteristic of a technical language by contrast with specialized terminology is that a technical language internalizes within its own semantics a model of interesting features of a subject matter. The key distinguishing virtues of a technical language are rigor, clarity, and consistency. Both technical languages and specialized terminology have a sturdy empirical basis, which makes them potentially useful for inquiry in the ways already discussed, and so worth the effort required to master them. But a technical language picks up on systematically recurring features of the phenomenon under investigation and models those features in the semantic relations among technical terms in the language. The virtues of rigor, clarity, and consistency in a technical language emerge from the excellence of its modeling.

For example, while there are many domains of specialized terminology surrounding human languages, linguists also developed technical languages to express certain dimensions of language. At the phonetic level, the International Phonetic Association developed a technical language to express the various sounds that appear in human languages. This so-called International Phonetic Alphabet enjoys relatively high rigor, clarity, and consistency because it derives from deep knowledge of the sorts of sounds that an ordinary human voice can make—as modified by breath, throat, tongue, teeth, and mouth. Its physiological roots are what make it a useful descriptive tool in linguistics.

At the grammatical level, the transformational-generative grammar of Noam Chomsky and others is a technical language used to relate the surface structure of sentences in any language to a deep grammatical structure and ultimately to a hypothetical universal grammar transcending every particular language.[26] The coherence of the universal grammar hypothesis together with the flexibility and ingenuity of the transformational rules relating deep structure and surface structure promise the virtues of rigor, clarity, and consistency—though the extent to which transformational-generative grammar achieves these virtues is more strongly contested than is the case for the International Phonetic Alphabet.

At the semantic level, the Natural Semantic Metalanguage of Anna Wierzbicka, Cliff Goddard, and others posits a set of semantic primes that, in combination, supposedly produce virtually all meanings of all possible sentences.[27] As in the case of transformational-generative grammar, the virtues of this natural metalanguage depend both on the soundness of the core hypothesis and on the ingenuity of the translations of ordinary sentence meanings into the lexical units of semantic primes.

In relation to pragmatics, though strictly at the sentence level, the Speech Act Theory of John Austin, John Searle, and others proposes a technical language with which to analyze the illocutionary force of sentences in action (that is, what sentences *do*) and to relate this illocutionary force to the propositional content of sentences.[28] In relation to pragmatics at levels larger than the sentence, both semiotic theory in the tradition of Ferdinand de Saussure (rather than the very different tradition of Charles Peirce) and also the discipline of rhetoric use specialized terminologies in a way that resembles a technical language.[29] These are used to analyze entire acts of communication, especially with the aim of detecting the mechanisms and strategies that underlie its effects. At this high level, the specialized terminology can be called a technical language only in a loose sense because the tie to experienced reality is somewhat arbitrary. That is, it seems possible for many incompatible lines of analysis to produce valid insights into the same act of communication, so the reasons for selecting one candidate for a technical language over another candidate are not decisive.

The technical languages mentioned above all required a formidable amount of work to establish their empirical credentials, work that continues within specialized communities devoted to using and enhancing these languages. Each remains useful to varying degrees because of this empirical rooting and also because the core hypotheses—physiological, grammatical, semantic, and pragmatic features that are universal across human language use—are plausible, albeit contestable, interpretations of the subject matter. Post-structuralist philosophers find plenty to attack here, obviously, because language use is intensively complex and any analysis of it by means of the structuralist approaches fails to register the full subtlety of communication. Nevertheless, the common features of language across users and cultures do provide a meaningful basis for analysis using technical languages of one sort or another. This is a powerful asset for inquiry when conducted within communities with a shared interest in a common problem and the willingness and ability to create and master the technical languages needed to discipline their shared efforts.

The most structured of formal languages go further than technical languages in that they stipulate vocabulary and syntactical rules to support a sharp definition of well-formed sentences within the language. These artificial languages take on a life of their own, because sentences in the language can be manipulated more or less independently of semantics, and thus independently of the meanings and empirical considerations that inspired their invention. The most fascinating aspect of formal languages is that the abstraction of their syntax and vocabulary from semantic ties makes them quite portable. This allows inquirers to apply them to quite diverse subject matters in such a way as to produce relevant and valuable insights. The semantic interpretation of a formal language in application to a particular subject matter is a model in the strictest sense of the word. Modeling in a looser sense refers to representing a subject matter in any kind of conceptual framework, typically using specialized terminology.

A classic example of a formal language is symbolic logic. In fact, there are many formal languages in symbolic logic, inspired by the kinds of argumentation that human beings use such as deductive, inductive, and modal argumentation. According to the pragmatic theory of inquiry, human reasoning itself needs to be modeled, just as human bodies and human behavior need to be modeled, because biology and behavior and reasoning are conceptually prior to logic. Indeed, it is readily conceivable that what experts are willing to call valid reasoning cannot be translated perfectly and exhaustively into the terms of a formal language. For example, Kurt Gödel's first incompleteness theorem shows that a sufficiently complex, consistent formal language—that is, anything consistent that is complex enough to map onto basic arithmetic, which includes all of the formal languages of any real interest—will include true propositions that cannot be proven to be true within the system.[30] This suggests that formal languages can never express everything important in acts of reasoning. Nevertheless, the formal languages of symbolic logic are the supremely portable tools for modeling reasoning and thus for exploring many of the controversial questions that arise in human inquiry.

Controversial Features of the Pragmatic Theory of Inquiry

This pragmatic theory of inquiry comes into clearer focus when its distinctive relations with competitor viewpoints in the epistemology of inquiry are presented. It is radically empiri-

cist, finding no need for a priori judgments. It is sensitive to the full contours of experience. It reflects many elements of the critical theory of the Frankfurt School and its followers. It vests meaning in practical use, understood extremely generously. It understands the pragmatic meaning of truth to be correspondence. It adopts as a guide to truth the ideal of the long-run consensus of qualified inquirers. And it comprehends every type of inquiry.

To conclude this chapter, I offer a statement of the way that this pragmatic theory of inquiry relates to key questions in epistemology and the study of rationality.

First, the pragmatic theory of inquiry is radically empiricist, in the sense that it discerns no basis or need for synthetic a priori propositions. This is to say, roughly, that informational (as against definitional) propositions derive from experience, in the broadest sense. This is not to portray human beings as John Locke's supposed *tabula rasa* (blank slates) upon birth, waiting for experience to fill in the picture. On the contrary, many basic features of the human cognitive makeup are genetically fixed—including especially the sponge-like language learning and category absorbing capacities that give cultural context such importance in forming cognitive function. This blend of biological and social factors creates the capacity for abstraction, which works best when applied to the most general features of the ambient experiential environment. The indubitable quality of certain beliefs is due to the way that some abstractions express reflexively absorbed beliefs and are rarely or never contradicted in experience. Such experiences of certainty appear to demand explanation in terms of synthetic a priori knowledge, but this is in fact not necessary. Nor is it desirable, as a number of allegedly synthetic a priori intuitions have proven merely approximate or less than completely general—including especially Immanuel Kant's construal of space and time, and certain logical and mathematical ideas.

Second, the pragmatic theory of inquiry takes all of experience seriously. This does not imply a credulous approach to experience, as if there were no basis to detect delusions or to critique their cognitive reliability. Rather, it implies attentiveness to the rich contours of experience, acknowledgment that the full wealth of human experience needs to be explained, and an expectation that the experiential resources for explanation are wide ranging. A contrary view is that of positivists, of the logical-positivist sort or other varieties. Positivists propose strict rules governing what can count as a proposition—that is, a meaningful statement capable of being true or false. This supports a sharp divide between the rational and the nonrational even within discursive thought, and it certainly denies rational standing to the nondiscursive aspects of human experience. The pragmatic theory of inquiry fails to see the basis in experience for such strict rules. It regards them instead as the provisional expressions of moral commitments by means of which philosophers intend to regulate speech according to favored norms. But other provisional guidelines are also possible, and some of them presume that an extremely wide range of human behaviors participate in the domain of the rational, in the sense that they can appear in processes of inquiry. The pragmatic theory of inquiry regards the specter of intractable disagreement not as evidence of irrationality or as a reason to propound a rule to keep philosophical debate under control—but rather as a sign of the weakness of the feedback potential, the failure of creative social organization to support inquiry, or both. One basic motivation for positivist moralism evaporates in the presence of this analysis of intractable disagreement, and other methods of regulating speech in the presence of failed inquiry become more compelling.

Third, the biological and social rooting of the pragmatic theory of inquiry gives it a lot in common with critical theory, in the sense of the Frankfurt School and Jürgen Habermas. In particular, it demands the detection and criticism of ideology—in the negative sense of unreflectively accepted ideas with harmful practical consequences for individuals and societies. This is an essential component of the process of correcting hypothetical beliefs of all kinds. The pragmatic drive for correction is simultaneously a demand for psychological self-awareness, a call for diagnosis of social effects, and a flight in the name of the common good from arbitrary authorities that resist detection and criticism of ideology. The antifoundationalism and fallibilism of the pragmatic theory of inquiry are deeply resonant with the psychodynamic sensibilities of critical theory, whereby human beings are prone to grasp after certainty even where none is available.

The shared rejection of positivism expresses a common belief that diverse kinds of reasoning are necessary to foster the criticism of ideology and also of the societies and minds that give ideology its meaning and power. Rather than deciding in advance of concrete experience what is rational and adumbrating inflexible rules to express this preemptive conviction, critical theory and the pragmatic theory of inquiry alike accept all kinds of hypotheses as potentially explanatory and rely on a generous range of feedback sources to supply the correction that inquiry needs for its advance. In fact, the pragmatic theory of inquiry is even more open than critical theory in this regard.

This is because critical theory typically self-consciously limits itself to processes of inquiry and hypotheses that promote enlightenment and social emancipation.

Fourth, the pragmatic theory of inquiry is equally opposed to a simple realistic theory of meaning based on reference to an external world and to a simple relativism in which claims about the meanings of propositions can never be rectified. Both views settle a fundamental question in advance of sufficient evidence for doing so and when there is no need to do so. That is, their core programmatic hypotheses are unparsimonious.

On the one hand, a realistic, reference-based theory of meaning presupposes a world external to human minds as the causal basis for the achievement of meaning in human discourse. But the ontological definitiveness of such a world makes problematic the familiar experiences of uncertain meanings and failed inquiries, of irresolvable disputes and irreconcilable perspectives. These experiences quickly lead to the positivist's claim that the associated sentences are not after all meaningful. But this is merely a sign of overcommitting to the core ontological hypothesis at the outset. It is more elegant to conform the core hypotheses of a theory of inquiry to the basic contours of experiences of inquiry, in which correction is sometimes available and sometimes not. This yields reasons for the hypothesis of a world external to human minds but does not definitively tie the meaning of human discourse to that world. This in turn respects the wide range of meaningful sentences that appear not to be correctable even in processes of the most serious forms of inquiry, while also allowing those that can be corrected to flesh out our theories about this external world to which inquiry gives us some connection.

On the other hand, a relativistic theory of meaning locates the meaning of human discourse exclusively in the minds of individuals, as conditioned by the groups to which they belong and the contexts in which they express themselves. The associated skepticism about the causal effects of an external world on discursive meanings overreaches ontologically, in the opposite direction, to about the same degree as the simplistically realistic, reference-based theory of meaning. The associated defects include an unempirical rush to declare that we never can resolve disputes and that all knowledge is a matter merely of opinion, when this is patently not so.

The pragmatic theory of inquiry vests the meaning of discourse in its practical use. In suitable kinds of specialized discourse communities, we conform our discourse to statements that refer to an external world. But the meaning of such statements derives not from this reference as such, which is a mere artifact of the organization of discourse within the community, but from the function of the speech as this function is enabled by the special interests and disciplines of the community. Consider again the two extremes between which the current view splits the difference.

On the one hand, a realistic, reference-based theory of meaning results when we mistake a specialized function of certain kinds of discourse in discourse communities—namely, to help us refer to an external world—for the genesis of meaning. This fallacy can be corrected by varying the elements of the theory of meaning taken for granted, such as the discourse community's habits or the range of discourse communities that we are prepared to consider.

On the other hand, a relativistic theory of meaning results when we confine our attention to those discourse communities whose purposes and habits are such that language functions not to pick out features of experience that can be rectified, but to illumine features of experience *from a point of view*. The fallacy in this case mistakenly generalizes to every kind of discourse community the referential features of such discourse (especially the failure definitively to refer), and thus overlooks the contextual, functional features of discursive meaning (which include practical achievements of navigating and controlling environments and consensus in many inquiries).

Fifth, the pragmatic theory of inquiry has a distinctive view of the meaning of truth—one that opposes both the neopragmatist view of Richard Rorty and the pragmatic approach of William James.[31] Both supply a pragmatic account of the meaning of truth, by which they intend to rule out the commonsense meaning of truth as correspondence between word and world. As was just pointed out, the meaning of human discourse derives fundamentally from language use in social contexts, so there can be no objection from within the epistemic framework of the pragmatic theory of inquiry to a pragmatic determination of the meaning of truth. But what actually is the pragmatic meaning of truth? In fact, *truth* is used typically to indicate correspondence between a proposition and a state of affairs in the world to which the terms of the proposition refer. Admittedly, James and Rorty do not intend to use *truth* in this way but actually they seem to do so anyway, even against their principles and best intentions.

Charles Peirce realized that the meaning of truth could not be reduced to the means by which we evaluate truth claims. Peirce failed to convince his friend James on this point, however, and he felt so disgusted about this and other misunderstandings that he wanted to change the name of his viewpoint from "pragmatism" (which James could thenceforth keep) to "pragmaticism" (which Peirce quipped was too ugly for anyone to steal) so as to distinguish his view from that of James. Presumably he would have failed to convince Rorty as well. The strongest argument against James and Rorty on this question involves linking truth and meaning. Precisely because of the pragmatic theory of meaning, we need to recognize that *truth* usually means correspondence, even though the means by which we evaluate a truth claim might be many and varied, including involving correspondence, coherence, and pragmatic criteria. Surely there is no need to surrender the simple pragmatic meaning of *truth* as word-world correspondence, particularly within a philosophical framework that rejects naïve realism.

Yet perhaps there is some reasonable impediment to accepting this pragmatic analysis of the meaning of truth as correspondence. The usual critiques turn on noticing that some specialized discourse community (say, a poetry reading group) does not operate with a correspondence theory of truth, or that it is impossible to do so (because there is no world external to human minds). But there are two problems with this.

On the one hand, as we have seen, the existence of diverse specialized discourse communities can be misleading, and we must resist the tendency to generalize too quickly from the habits of a special subclass of those communities to the necessary conditions for all discourse communities.

On the other hand, such counterexamples typically turn on confusion between the meaning of truth and the means by which truth claims are evaluated. Obviously truth claims as advanced in some discourse communities, such as our poetry reading group, are not always susceptible to straightforward empirical confirmation or disconfirmation. In such cases, coherence or pragmatic criteria would be more important for an inquiry—if in fact inquiry were desired, if the corrective feedback potential were rich enough to permit a provisional determination of truth in any instance of inquiry, and if social resources were organized to take advantage of the feedback potential.

As we have seen, the pragmatic theory of inquiry sanctions determined creativity in regard to means of correcting hypotheses. But the question of the way we correct hypotheses is not the same as what we mean pragmatically by asserting the truth of an inquiry's hypothesis. Most of the time, we mean many things, including unstated ideas related to the rhetorical effects of announcing our claim. But at the center of those meanings, typically, is the idea of correspondence.

Sixth, if most of us typically mean word-world correspondence when we use the word *truth*, we also must recognize that there are specialized discourse communities in which we mean something more as well. In particular, within communities devoted to what I am calling serious inquiry, it is necessary to assess the state of inquiry, including the effectiveness of the corrective mechanisms necessary for inquiry to advance and the warrant for asserting the truth of the hypothesis under inquiry. This kind of scrutiny plays a key role in maintaining community identity and minimizing major disruptions that destroy the social conditions for serious inquiry. It is also important for decisions about ending inquiry and publicly announcing the results of inquiry. In serious-inquiry contexts, the meaning of truth remains correspondence, centrally, but in practice the meaning of truth is deeply entangled with the conditions for securing warrant for asserting that a proposition is true. When can we say something is true with confidence sufficient to meet the high standards of a specialized discourse community devoted to serious inquiry?

The answer to this question is given differently in different groups. The relevant factors in the answer will be social in character because this kind of judgment is always a social act when it occurs within a community devoted to serious inquiry, which is the context we are considering. The two relevant factors are authority and consensus, which are contrasting but correlated elements in many kinds of social transactions among human beings and other animals. Both have their dangers. Emphasizing authority endangers the core moral principle of openness in inquiry, while stressing consensus risks the core moral principle of assiduous effort in inquiry. Indulging either emphasis risks short-circuiting the process of serious inquiry, which crucially depends on the relentless quest for corrective resources for refining promising hypotheses. But deference to authority is needed because some people know more than others and expert opinion of the state of inquiry should be valued more highly. Similarly, consensus is important because it is vital not to overlook promising ideas that some may be able to see when others cannot.

Most groups devoted to serious inquiry find ways to balance authority and consensus in their procedures for assessing the state of inquiry, the effectiveness of the feedback potential, and ultimately the warrant for asserting the truth of the hypothesis under examination. Somewhere in the middle of the range of possibilities for balancing authority and consensus lies the ideal of expert agreement—that is, we don't take a poll of everyone interested in the inquiry but only of the qualified experts.

The least satisfying aspect of the "consensus of qualified experts" approach to judging the state of inquiry is that it risks insensitivity to considerations of timing. The consensus of qualified experts about the state of inquiry will be next to worthless in the early phases of inquiry, or at deeply contested periods within an extended process of inquiry. Thus, in practice we must rely on the "consensus of qualified experts at a propitious moment." In a fallibilist theory of inquiry the most propitious moment is far-off distant future where all factors relevant to the inquiry are fully understood. This is why Peirce originally propounded the ideal of expert consensus over the infinite long run. But this ideal is no more than a regulative principle to remind the community devoted to inquiry of its fundamental principles. In practice, there are and must be propitious moments along the way toward the infinite long run. Such optimally propitious moments occur when the inquiring community loses significant interest in a question, when there appears to be no prospect of further advance because all known avenues of correction have been explored, and when external circumstances (such as a social crisis or the exhaustion of research funds) demand a judgment.

Seventh, the idealization of the ultimate goal of inquiry as the long-run consensus of qualified inquirers is a fascinating feature of the pragmatic theory of inquiry. This regulative ideal expresses the pragmatic bet on reality as in some sense objective and truth as in some sense universal—objectivity and universality precisely sufficient for consensus of all relevant inquirers in the long run. Why this bet rather than an alternative—say, that reality is exhaustively a social construction and truth is nothing but relative patterns of agreement? The latter will not promote diligent inquiry in the way that the former will. Dogged work is necessary to make sure that we are not overlooking important new hypotheses or special virtues of existing hypotheses and the former view inspires us to keep striving for deeper insights and richer appreciation of complexities.

Philosophical movements have taken their rise over how to handle the entanglement of human rationality and the feedback potential in inquiry. On the side of some extreme forms of post-structuralist critical theory, we have the hypothesis that limitations in inquiry can be traced to the limited rational insight of human beings. Proponents of this view can be so extreme that the operation of the feedback potential within reality is almost entirely neglected—whereupon human beings have to be interpreted as wielding vast and dangerous powers of interpretation and social construction, and any distinction between hermeneutics and politics dissolves. Within this philosophical subculture, people can remake the "great discovery" that the world does indeed have a feedback potential, and this discovery can seem novel and groundbreaking. On the side of some extreme rationalist forms of philosophy, we see philosophers expressing such confidence in the feedback potential of the world that they assume it makes soluble every problem regardless of topic or difficulty. This has produced famous comical mistakes in the history of philosophy, from some of Descartes' bizarre proposals for "clear and distinct ideas" to the view that science can satisfyingly interpret every aspect of reality. This latter view is false on its face yet has some influential advocates among contemporary scientist intellectuals.

These mistakes confirm the view advanced here that consensus around norms and procedures for inquiry takes shape within social groups. But just for that reason they also give evidence of the value of multidisciplinary approaches when inquiry is complex, lest our limited perspective should doom us to quaint errors. Of course, most intellectuals of all stripes steer a middle course between these extremes. They realize that it is difficult to tease apart the functioning of the feedback potential from the functioning of human minds and contexts in inquiry, and understand that a theory of inquiry collapses under the weight of its own pretensions unless it attends to both aspects of the task of inquiry. Within this middle territory, a pragmatic theory of inquiry provisionally adopts the regulative, idealized norm of long-run consensus among qualified inquirers, betting on its special usefulness for exploring the entanglement of human rationality and the feedback potential in processes of inquiry.

Finally, one of the fundamental claims I make on behalf of this theory of inquiry is that it comprehends every sort of human inquiry, and among these identifies the most energy-efficient methods of fully rational problem solving. This identification is in terms of the capacities and limitations of human brains, the realities of social life, and the variability in the hypothesis-correcting feedback potential across diverse subject matters. I have already given reasons for this claim but consider further the following.

The hypothetico-corrective method has essentially conservative implementations. It fosters tenacious attachment to the core hypotheses being evaluated, seeking every way possible to avoid their falsification. In this way, the method manifests a means by which actual inquiry makes a virtue even of a potent feature of human emotional life that often interferes with inquiry in untrained and often highly trained minds—namely, insecurity and the longing for stability. It is because of such emotions that people both cling to treasured hypotheses against all evidence or in the face of fierce social pressure, and work so hard to find the time and energy to defend their working hypotheses. In the context of a social form of inquiry, this dogged attachment of some members helps the group feel more confident that it is not overlooking any hidden virtue of its core hypothesis, which in turn is essential to any decision finally to abandon it.

This theory of inquiry is quite general in its application. While it owes a lot to Peirce and Dewey, I pointed out in Chapter 4 that we can also understand Imre Lakatos's work as an application of the hypothetico-corrective method to the natural sciences.[32] In this construal, Lakatos's concept of a research program specifies the general framework of the pragmatic theory of inquiry and demonstrates how complex the sociality and logic of inquiry are even in situations where the feedback potential speaks relatively clearly, as it does in many parts of experimental science. And his debate with Feyerabend (also mentioned earlier) over whether the abandonment of a degenerating research program can ever be rational is a specification of the important role that criteria for theory choice play in all processes of inquiry.[33]

Some have applied Lakatos's work to metaphysics and theology, where the feedback potential rarely speaks clearly.[34] These applications strike me as contrived when Lakatos's work is the basic inspiration because his work depends on a strong feedback potential and takes no account of the social innovation and fragmentation that results from slow or no correction of competing hypotheses. Similarly, Lakatos's methodology of research programs is indifferent to special concerns in religious epistemology having to do with the existentially self-involving quality of faith. Such attempts to shine methodological light on metaphysics and theology would be more robust if they were to reach behind Lakatos to a more comprehensive and flexible pragmatic theory of inquiry—such as the one proposed here.

In any event, these applications of the methodology of research programs furnish preliminary evidence that the unitary theory of inquiry described in this chapter can work across the board from common-sense inquiries to physics, from metaphysics to mathematics, and from the social sciences to theology. Lakatos's optimism about the rationality of all phases of inquiry was unwarranted. He might not have succumbed to this extreme viewpoint—nor other philosophers of science to the opposite mistake of affirming fundamental irrationality at the root of science—had the broader perspective of a pragmatic theory of inquiry been the operative framework for understanding human rationality.

Chapter 7

Religious Philosophy and Inquiry

Religious Dimensions of Inquiry

This pragmatic theory of inquiry is capable of more or less indefinite extension and elaboration. Though always constrained by biology and sociology, its rooting in the basic realities of human life makes it broadly applicable to a host of human behaviors and cognitive processes. In particular, if the pragmatic theory of inquiry is correct, then the previous chapters' descriptions of the diversity and complexity of religious philosophy comes into clear focus as the predictable effects of attempts to mount inquiries into religious topics using every available resource. The pragmatic theory of inquiry helps to explain several distinctive features of religious philosophy, including the way it relates the religious inquiries of ordinary people, and the way religious philosophers can be existentially entangled in its subject matters.

The Emergence of Inquiry in Religious People

Most people experience the spontaneous emergence of existentially loaded questions of meaning and value. These questions might be prompted by life events that are difficult to assimilate into a functioning self-understanding such as illness or a violent attack; by impending decisions of great import; by persistent patterns of life that come to seem empty or self-destructive; or by curiosity about the natural world as the womb of our existence. After the fundamental puzzles of survival, reproduction, safety, and belonging are more or less settled by relatively civilized social arrangements, these questions become some of the most compelling problems of human life.

Partly because they are of such definitive subjective importance for us, and partly because their answers appear to lie at the far reaches of our cognitive and emotional capacities, Paul Tillich and others have called them questions of "ultimate concern." Tillich overlooked or played down the fact that people experience such questions in very different ways, being relatively insensitive to some dimensions of existential concern and intensely engaged by others. For example, the meaning of life is a big issue for some people, while repairing broken relationships is paramount for others. But Tillich liked the name because of the pun: according to him, questions of subjective ultimate concern find their proper answers only in objective ultimate concern, which is to say ultimate reality, which Tillich called "Ground of Being." This enabled him to launch an entire Christian theological outlook—not from ecclesiastical doctrines but from the correlation between experiences of ultimate questions and an interpretation of Christianity's answers to them.

In its social context, Tillich's existentially potent philosophical theology entranced people, especially some within the Christian tradition who felt dissatisfied with the supernatural narratives they were force-fed (so they felt) in local churches. It also captivated existentially alert people beyond the Christian tradition who were relieved to see a thinker registering their questions of ultimate concern and authenticating their creative cultural responses. Eventually, it became one of the foci of an active dialogue with Buddhists who saw in Tillich's existential framing of Christian theology many similarities with their own existentially loaded narrative arc. Though most Buddhists were not interested in stressing the objective meaning of ultimate concern, Tillich's refusal to think of ultimate reality as an existent divine being gave it a lot in common with Buddhist ideas of *śūnyatā*, which invited an intriguing ontological dialogue grounded in shared existential questions of ultimate concern. Because this category of "ultimate concern" has proved itself serviceable within several religions and also outside religious communities, I use it here with some confidence that I do not thereby distort the subject matter, so long as I recall the individual variations that are often elided in systematic discussions of ultimate questions.

The emergence of such ultimate questions is profoundly shaped by participation in a religious community. Religions nurture narratives and doctrines that furnish concepts and categories for expressing existentially loaded questions, as well as answering them. Religions also provide nondiscursive means of tolerating the psychically destabilizing effects of such questions. These nondiscursive resources include rituals and communal meals, which reinforce feelings of belonging and help participants internalize patterns of behavior that have proved healthy according to community norms. Beyond the borders of religious communities, these orienting benefits of religious wisdom traditions are probably not functional and neither are the powerful narratives that structure self-understanding in relation to ultimate questions—though there may be spillover effects depending on the personal history and cultural setting of the nonreligious people in question. This is disabling in respect of not supplying a body of well-tested wisdom to draw on but also liberating in that ultimate questions can be approached anew, free from the taint of their functional roles in specific religious communities, which inevitably include reinforcing social stability and legitimating religious authority.

Understandably, therefore, ultimate questions provoke the formation of loose social alliances among those outside organized religious groups—and also among those for whom religious answers fail to satisfy—in order to activate social resources for support and encouragement in the face of shared concerns. There are twelve-step groups, support groups for people with the same disease, book discussion groups, political activism groups, and groups for people with shared artistic interests. There are a host of specialized medical practices that enjoy strong communities of support. There are also economically sizable industries promoting products and activities around which enthusiastic audiences gather, sharing testimonials and offering support in the face of ultimate questions. Few of these social alliances are more than transitory. Involvement in them rarely extends across an entire lifetime and they typically do not posture at providing a total worldview that can claim to answer every ultimate question.

The existence of such groups is powerful evidence of the social aspects of the human handling of ultimate questions, even outside the direct shaping influence of religious groups. Yet the individual typically remains the locus of existential integration—making use of such groups as each sees fit, sometimes in combination with religious resources, to articulate and answer ultimate questions. This often produces creative results, possessing a degree of coherence fitted to the individual's sensibilities and intellectual style. For some, the incoherent mélange satisfies, while others demand a relatively rigorous system of ideas tightly integrated with moral commitments and life practices.

In all of these variations, ultimate questions trigger inquiry, which develops in the way the pragmatic theory of inquiry describes. People in the grip of a pressing existential puzzle formulate hypotheses that seem promising as provisional guides to action and self-understanding.

They then explore these hypotheses by living with them and unfolding them, effectively testing their capacity to orient and enlighten through the various experiences of life and in relation to the welter of competing ideas they encounter. These processes of testing are more and less systematic, just as the hypotheses themselves are more and less coherent, depending on individual taste. People frequently dispose of a serviceable hypothesis too quickly, in the sense that they do not explore all of its helpful resources before finding themselves captivated by an alternative hypothesis. They often fail to appreciate the weaknesses in an hypothesis because they are insensitive to the way its implications contradict other beliefs, or because the hypothesis is not elaborated in enough detail even to discern what its ontological or moral implications might be. Yet even under these imperfect circumstances, inquiry proceeds. Often enough, people feel content with such limited results, either because they are happy to bounce from one working hypothesis to the next or because they eventually land on something that stands the tests of time and experience.

From the limited point of view of optimizing the efficiency of inquiry, the great virtue of religious traditions is that they offer readymade, more or less carefully conceived and extensively elaborated hypotheses as answers to many ultimate questions. From the same efficiency point of view, the virtues of any corporate approach to an aspect of inquiry into ultimate questions, whether or not the group is religious, are the broadening of the base for potentially corrective experiences, the embrace of rich resources for imaginative adjustments, and the activation of nondiscursive practices that engage the whole person in the testing of hypotheses. In all things, however, the central integrating force remains the individual, because the individual is the locus of criteria for the progress and success of existentially rooted inquiry. It is his or her judgment about what counts as a good answer to ultimate questions that matters. Only he or she can assess what serves as a satisfying life world within with which to tolerate the existential disturbance of possibly unanswerable ultimate questions. But he or she does this in a social context that sometimes furnishes relevant and even precious resources for the task, and also sometimes attempts to impose constraints on cognitive exploration.

Religious Philosophy, Existential Entanglement, and Socialization

Religious philosophers are fascinated with the facts that such questions arise in the world, that people vary in their sensitivity to them, that religions promise incompatible answers to them, that people approach the existential task of answering them differently, and that the social embedding of such inquiries is crucial yet dramatically varied. These facts represent important entry points for philosophical inquiry, interfacing especially with the human sciences, in which ultimate questions play a second-order role. That is, inquiry in these cases focuses not on the content of ultimate questions but on the varied phenomena surrounding the asking and answering of ultimate questions. Yet ultimate questions can also become first-order objects of inquiry for religious philosophers.

Because religious philosophers are human beings, it is entirely natural that ultimate questions should arise for them at a personal level. The existential involvement of religious philosophers in their subject matter has been a virtue in respect to the way it has inspired some of the most beautiful and potent ideas in the history of the human species. But religious philosophers sometimes ask questions of goodness, truth, and beauty in relation to those ideas and they sometimes evaluate claims made on behalf of such ideas by religious traditions or great philosophers of the past. So the problem arises of how to deal with this entanglement of existential interests in relation to the ideal of impartiality in inquiry.

Scholars of religion often bracket the existential ramifications of ultimacy ideas for the sake of meeting professional obligations, and many times this can be done quite successfully. For example, social scientists studying religion may excuse themselves from the evaluative tasks of religious philosophy on the grounds that their disciplinary framework is committed to a neutral, descriptive approach in inquiry. But religious philosophers do not have the luxury of eschewing philosophical criticism and evaluation. At least some religious philosophers are obliged to take on these evaluative tasks, since nobody can do it better. The question then becomes whether these tasks can be pursued without enslavement to covert or explicit ideologies, and whether, in face of uncertain prospects, it is worthwhile making the attempt.

Is it the case that religious philosophers have their highly trained and refined judgment hobbled by personal attachment to particular hypotheses? Are they unable to function as evenhanded investigators or competent evaluators of religious ideas about issues of ultimate concern? In fact, there is evidence that these defects in impartial inquiry sometimes do occur, some of which was documented in one of Chapter 4's case studies. But *must* they occur?

The most extreme reply to this difficulty is that impartiality is impossible, and thus that religious philosophy is impossible. This is manifestly an overreaction. Surely such questions can be pursued in better and worse ways and in more and less impartial ways. If that is the case, then there is meaningful work for religious philosophers to do. A less extreme response is to acknowledge as legitimate only religious philosophy in styles that are supposedly easiest to pursue objectively—which means especially the historical and analytical styles, perhaps the phenomenological and comparative styles, and especially not the literary, theoretical, or evaluative styles, though the dividing line would vary among those willing to police it. But some of the most egregious and influential offenses of impartiality in the long history of religious philosophy have been in the historical, analytical, and comparative styles—in addition to the mistakes discussed in one of Chapter 4's case studies, think of the many historical misjudgments in the study of religion that required centuries to correct, or the comparativists who made dubious translation decisions that set entire arcs of inquiry in unsteady directions. Perhaps an alternative response would be to insist that, in order to qualify as a competent religious philosopher, it is necessary to be religiously unaffiliated and existentially unmoved by all ultimate questions. But this kind of social isolation and tone deafness to the existentially potent dimensions of human life would be deeply disabling, and such strange people are exceptionally rare.

The solution to the problem of existential entanglement with the subject matter of religious philosophy lies elsewhere—in the social organization of inquiry among religious philosophers, and in a less defensive attitude to the problem itself. To begin with attitude, as in any other kind of inquiry, special sensibilities are required for inquiry into ultimate questions. Philosophers need a refined grasp of the significance of questions about the meaning of life and the basis for values in order to give adequate phenomenological descriptions, insightful literary elaborations, and properly comprehensive systematic interpretations of the way such questions arise in human lives and the manifold ways they are answered. Objectivity is important, but not in the sense of remaining unswayed by the potent existential valences of ultimate questions. Rather, the sort of objectivity that matters involves a deep understanding of the actual existential potency of ultimate questions and a wide appreciation for the diversity of ways such questions are framed and answered. The twin abilities to understand deeply and to appreciate widely are difficult to acquire; they are the hard-won fruits of careful training and long labor in religious philosophy. In their immature forms, they amount to little more than enthusiastic wordiness but when fully developed they are enormously sensitive and powerful intellectual-emotional capacities.

The socialization of religious philosophers is a complex matter because it has taken numerous forms in many cultures. Often enough, religious philosophy in the specific sense of multidisciplinary comparative inquiry was not in view because religious philosophers functioned as philosophical theologians on behalf of the identity interests of particular religious institutions. In those settings, serious forms of multidisciplinary comparative inquiry were only achieved as select individuals reached beyond their local intellectual community in search of a wider and deeper interpretation of religious phenomena. The examples are notable, from Plato to Aristotle, from Śaṅkara to Nāgārjuna, and from Confucius (Kong Fu Zi or K'ung-fu-tzu or 孔夫子; 551–471 BCE) to Laozi (Lǎozǐ or Lao Tzu or 老子; probably sixth century BCE). In the modern era, however, there has been a steady stream of religious philosophers from many parts of the world not content with the deliverances of the religious traditions closest to home. They have instinctively sought after a more far-reaching form of inquiry—one that does not remain in thrall to purportedly authoritative traditions of revealed knowledge but that integrates the best of human knowledge across the boundaries of disciplines and religious traditions. Though they were still mostly self-taught, at least in respect to the elements of their work that extended beyond their formal training, they were inspired by their intellectual forebears with similar goals.

All this has changed in the last couple of decades. There are now recognizable lines of socialization into religious philosophy conceived of explicitly as multidisciplinary comparative inquiry. One line is through the emerging field of comparative philosophy and comparative theology. Another is through the emerging multidisciplinary fields of science and religion, which is outgrowing its Christian roots, at least in some circles, and reaching across religious traditions more effectively. Yet another is through the return to theology among some influential poststructuralist philosophers such as Jacques Derrida, Emmanuel Levinas, and John Caputo. Their sensitivity to lurking ideologies has made them suspicious of organized religion and reluctant to venture anything of a strongly systematic nature, but they consistently and profoundly register ultimate questions and their effects on social life. Communities of religious philosophers specifically devoted to multidisciplinary comparative inquiry are slowly forming within and between these three lines of socialization. In some places, this has made the training of religious philosophers materially different than in the past. Yet traditional forms of philosophy of religion operating within the confines of particular religious traditions continue to be influential, and indeed dominant, and this is part of the reason the number of philosophy of religion positions in colleges and universities is shrinking.

The socialization of a religious philosopher is notably different from that of a traditional philosopher of religion. There are demands to learn the key ideas of multiple religious traditions, expectations that students will follow inquiry into whatever disciplines it may lead, and scrupulous monitoring of depth of understanding and breadth of appreciation of religious ideas and practices. This kind of training produces philosophers who typically can teach the college "Introduction to Religion" course, without pretending that religion is all about ideas. They can usually converse with specialists in a wide range of disciplines, confident that there is a material connection to their philosophical interests. Regardless of their preferred styles of religious philosophy, they display a fine-grained sensitivity to similarities and differences among religious ideas and practices, they intuitively grasp the internal workings of numerous worldviews, and they respect the contextual factors conditioning religious ideas and practices. Most importantly, they understand the morality of assertion and correction discussed in Chapter 3. To assert is not necessarily to control; a ceaseless quest for correction of their fallible hypotheses prevents them from becoming coercive, oppressive, or blind to their intellectual and moral weaknesses.

The social organization of religious philosophy begins with socialization and training but continues in cooperative inquiry and mutual criticism. Most complex inquiries in religious philosophy obviously require active participation of scholars with different specialties because so many disciplines and traditions are involved. Indeed, in most instances, the religious philosopher has to seek out such alliances in order to work effectively. This diversity of partners in inquiry helps religious philosophers notice and control for bias due to their existential entanglement with the subject matter of an inquiry. This cannot be done perfectly, to be sure, but it certainly can be achieved at least to the degree that the same goal is achieved in the historical and social scientific study of religion—perhaps to a greater degree, in fact, given that inquiries in religious philosophy tend to be more explicitly cross-traditional than historical and most sociological inquiries.

Religious Philosophy and the Demarcation Problem

The pragmatic theory of inquiry helps to demarcate the various disciplines of human inquiry from one another, and religious philosophy from all of them. The principles of disciplinary

demarcation are the fundamentally unitary character of inquiry and the interpretation of advancing inquiry as contingent upon a social organization that allows inquirers to leverage feedback potential to correct hypotheses. These principles permit discrimination of the natural sciences, the historical and human sciences, the humanities, fine arts and practical crafts, metaphysics and theology, and finally religious philosophy.

Approaching Demarcation Problems

Religious philosophy is not much like physics, and especially unlike experimental physics. Why? The pragmatic theory of inquiry gives a powerful answer to the demarcation problem within the philosophy of science. This is the problem of defining the boundaries of science—of science as a whole, of a specific type of science (natural science, human science, etc.), or of a particular science (physics, chemistry, etc.). The pragmatic theory is equally adept at distinguishing disciplines in the humanities from the sciences and from each other, and for accounting for the emergence of new disciplines and the fights over boundary activities that occur in most disciplines.

The pragmatic theory of inquiry presents two crucial guidelines for solving the various types of disciplinary demarcation problems. First, at the most general level, there is only one way of finding out anything, only one process for inquiry in all forms, and only one kind of knowledge. That is, as noted above, the pragmatic theory of inquiry is a *unitary* theory of inquiry. Empiricist John Locke proposed a relatively sharp distinction between sensation and reflection, the heart of which is regularized in Kant's distinction between synthetic a posteriori and synthetic a priori judgments. From this flowed the dualist Kantian theory of inquiry, in which synthetic a posteriori judgments were made in one way and synthetic a priori judgments in quite another, and both are informative (synthetic rather than analytic). The method for making a posteriori judgments depended on the way synthetic a priori judgments organize experience. But only transcendental reflection, in the sense of reflection on the conditions for the possibility of knowledge, could yield a systematic appreciation of the synthetic a priori principles of reasoning. This is the burden of Kant's *Critique of Pure Reason*.

As we saw in Chapter 6, however, a radically empirical approach to inquiry interprets the distinction between sensation and reflection loosely, as related types of synthetic a posteriori judgments. It rules out synthetic a priori judgments altogether, treating their seeming definitiveness as an artifact of habits built around relatively stable generalizations. This means that there is no Kantian distinction between a noumenal and a phenomenal realm, and no questions or topics off limits for inquiry, at least not on Kantian grounds (there may still be social prohibitions against certain kinds of inquiry). Kant's over-crisp distinction between two modes of inquiry led him into the erroneous reasoning of the antinomy of pure reason, described in Chapter 1. On the contrary, all inquiry proceeds the same way, whether in the sciences or the humanities, whether in mathematics or metaphysics: we adduce promising hypotheses and test them in every way we can imagine, using the best social organization we can devise for the task.

The second guideline is this: inquiry advances when social organization allows inquirers to leverage the feedback potential to correct hypotheses. When inquiry does not advance, it is impossible to tell with complete confidence whether this is due to a permanent aporia in the textured fabric of the feedback potential, or to the failure to imagine or sustain a form of social organization adequate to take advantage of available corrective resources.

There are plenty of examples of the latter. Indeed, the birth of most disciplines, particularly those that evolved from the womb of philosophy, was due to the discovery that a particular kind of feedback could be accessed providing that specific social practices and commitments were in place, as discussed in Chapter 4. Galileo introduced mathematical models for observed physical phenomena and thereby pushed experimental physics out of the womb of natural philosophy. The natural philosophers of his day did not like it and fought him bitterly but the new social arrangement captivated researcher after researcher, initiating them into ways of thinking that allowed them to advance knowledge in ways they had never dreamed possible before. The feedback potential was ready to speak, but the social organization needed to hear and heed it did not exist—until it did.

Are there any examples of a permanent aporia in the textured fabric of the feedback potential? Of course not. How could we know for sure that there is a region of experience where the feedback potential is permanently silent, offering no correction to advance inquiry? Indeed, we should learn a lesson from the wealth of examples showing that innovative social organization, with novel priorities and practices, activates forms of correction that were previously unnoticed. We should not jump to conclusions about what kinds of correction we can leverage for inquiry. This is directly relevant to charges against the possibility of religious philosophy, of course: religious philosophy as multidisciplinary comparative inquiry in the contemporary period represents a relatively new form of social organization and is likely to leverage forms of correction that hitherto have been dormant.

From these two guidelines, it follows that a discipline is not chiefly a subject matter, or even a subject matter and a correlated method. Rather, a discipline is, first and foremost, a conjunction of social organization and operational feedback potential; secondly, a set of socially embedded values and procedures that activate correction for hypotheses; and thirdly, a subject matter. The first two elements of the definition will sometimes pick out a unique subject matter, making the third element superfluous.

Natural Sciences

Consider physics. Many aspects of the subject matter of physics appear in at least one other scientific discipline, so it cannot be the subject matter alone that determines the discipline's boundaries. Rather, physics is devoted to studying that region of experience which (1) offers powerful feedback so that hypotheses can often be corrected quickly; (2) is readily subject to mathematical modeling so that quantifiable features of experience can be leveraged for refining models; (3) is subject to reductionism, whereby simple systems can be analyzed exhaustively by studying their constituent elements and their interactions; and (4) is the least complex domain of reality serving as the basis for more complex emergent domains.

This definition of physics picks out a subject matter. It describes working principles and practices that are active in the socialization of physicists and operative in the daily work of physicists (other principles and practices are shared with many sciences, such as honesty, diligence, and functional naturalism). It also explains why the fights over the identity of physics as a discipline occur where they do: they are about these principles. For example, the reason so many physicists reject string theory, depreciating it as a kind of mathematical-metaphysical speculation, is that it defies (1), above; for now, at least, such critics say that it is not a part of physics. The border between physics and metaphysics is patrolled by people anxious to uphold (2); this is why physicists do not concern themselves with the philosophical implications of several of their key concepts, such as energy and cause. These concepts are a tangled mess of unreconciled, inconsistent usages but there is no way mathematically to model the topic so it must be someone else's problem—in this case, the philosopher of science has to worry about it. A physics graduate student spending a lot of time worrying about what a cause is would be told to shape up or ship out. Similarly, a student complaining that the full richness of a gas is not registered in the statistical thermodynamic reduction of macroscopic gas properties (pressure, volume, temperature) to the motions of individual molecules would be regarded as quite bizarre; they would be violating (3): physicists *as physicists* are only interested in those aspects of a gas that are so reducible, at least in principle. And the features of physics in (4) are manifested especially in the way that physics spawns new disciplinary ventures, such as information theory and complexity theory, which step beyond the bounds of the most basic level of theorizing.

The disciplinary police can be quite hostile to transgressors. For example, the attacks on string theory often display aggression borne of the instinctive awareness that the discipline's social identity is in danger when string theory has a home within it. Such vigilance is understandable because, without a clear social organization to activate correction, the entire enterprise of physics spins apart. Yet disciplines are dynamic, and their principles do change with time. The fourth principle, that physics confines itself to the most basic level of reality, was not operative some decades ago in the same way that it is now, because the problem of diffusion of effort induced by the explosion of new sub-disciplines in physics is relatively new. In all cases, the pragmatic theory of inquiry forces the social framing of inquiry into the open and that helps to make sense of disciplinary behavior such as policing boundaries, which members of the discipline themselves often take for granted.

The natural sciences in general affirm only the first of the four principles demarcating physics. That is, science is devoted to studying that region of experience which offers powerful feedback so that hypotheses can often be corrected quickly. This is joined with the general moral and theoretical principles already mentioned: honesty, diligence, and functional naturalism. The latter refers to proceeding with inquiry *as if* there were no supernatural realm, and *as if* all events were due to naturalistic processes subject to scientific study.

There are several other natural-science-wide principles that are debated with more and less energy, depending on the context. One concerns social responsibility. The Union of Concerned Scientists urges scientists to accept social responsibility as a core principle of natural science, just as it became central to medical research after the horrors of Nazi medical experiments, the Tuskegee syphilis experiment, and other disasters of medical science madness.[1] This urging is contested on the (dubious) grounds that science is pure inquiry and not responsible for its technological applications.

Another contested principle concerns the unity of science in a naturalistic worldview. In fact, natural science is a patchwork of semi-consistent theories and not a seamless garment, but many scientists feel that it points in a naturalistic direction nonetheless. That is, the functional naturalism of the natural sciences works so well, and encounters no clear contraindicating evidence, that it ought to be enshrined in a naturalistic worldview; natural science should claim ontological naturalism rather than mere functional or "as-if" naturalism. This metaphysically bold attitude is most evident in debates over creationism and evolution. But many scientists resist it on the grounds that this ontological hypothesis is not actually necessary for science, the "as-if" of functional naturalism being sufficient. Moreover, a significant number of scientists personally believe in a supernatural realm, though in such a way that studying the natural world is still an intelligible activity for human beings to pursue.[2]

Historical and Human Sciences

The historical and human sciences are distinguishable from other disciplines in the first instance by the partial failure of the first principle of the natural sciences: strong feedback and ready correction of hypotheses. In its place, there is empirically based correction joined by dramatic under-determination of theories by data. This produces heavier reliance than in the natural sciences on aesthetic and pragmatic criteria to discriminate among empirically adequate competitor hypotheses, as well as social differentiation to protect against the arbitrary imposition of authority and to activate particular nonempirical criteria for theory evaluation.

Historical, psychological, anthropological, sociological, and economic theories are enormously complex edifices. They contain points of traction with empirical data, to various degrees depending on the subject matter, and they also involve theoretical extrapolations linking these points in plausible arcs of interpretation. This is no different in principle from the natural sciences, of course, but in practice the data points are relatively fewer and relatively less decisive in their evidentiary import. Meanwhile, the interpretative arcs are much wider and more theoretically speculative than in the natural sciences. A measure of the breadth of interpretation is the fact that, for most people, theories from within the historical and human sciences are more interesting than those of physics, because they are (relatively speaking) simpler to understand, easier to evaluate against our ordinary experiences, and more likely to reframe our interpretations of self and world.

Every now and then empirically oriented human scientists demand that their colleagues rein in speculative theories and cleave more closely to available data; this is the only basis for earning the designation "science." By contrast, theoretically oriented human scientists demand that their colleagues recognize the centrality of interpretation to their discipline; the vast collection of empirical data on human beings and their social arrangements by itself tells us nothing about human reality. The critical theory of the Frankfurt School and its latter-day followers goes even further and actively seeks enlightenment and emancipation. It calls upon the human sciences to wield analysis as a spotlight that penetrates the fogs of self-delusion and deliberate deception that mask the dynamics of social power.

Regardless of these variations, inquiry in the human sciences works in exactly the way that the pragmatic theory of inquiry describes: hypothesis formation and testing in a social process geared to optimize the efficiency of correction. The internal debates within the human sciences suggest that the social principles and procedures are not completely settled. The pragmatic theory of inquiry explains this as a result of relatively less decisive feedback. Under such conditions, it is routine to encounter loudly expressed opinions with insufficient support. Is Sigmund Freud or Carl Jung or Donald Winnicott right about the psychodynamics of human life? Is Max Weber or Émile Durkheim or Peter Berger right about the way power is expressed in human societies? Most Freud enthusiasts would happily take over the discipline of psychology, if they could—controlling academic appointments and focusing resources where it suits them. And the same is true of every other important opinion. Under these circumstances, "schools" naturally develop as a hedge against the arbitrary exercise of power. Each school is built around distinctive core hypotheses and explores and develops those core ideas on its own terms, keeping them active when others would allow them to languish. Thus, they carry forward a research program, more or less well articulated depending on the clarity of the school's identity. Schools tend to have relatively distinct lines of communication and modes of socializing students. Each nurtures a distinctive set of values that theoretical speculation is supposed to embody. Each has some degree of empirical support but jointly they are unable to activate resources sufficient for deciding among the core hypotheses at the heart of the competing schools.

Schools in the historical and human sciences are distinguished in one dimension by major theorists and in another by methodological commitments. So empirical psychologists and theoretical psychologists and clinical psychologists operate in parallel. Similarly, empirically oriented sociologists, theoretically oriented sociologists, and critical-theory sociologists operate in parallel. In all cases, these alternatives arise in the presence of less than perfectly efficient inquiry due to weakness of resources for correction. Whether these weaknesses lie in social organization or in the feedback potential itself is difficult to discern, as usual. This is not how the schools represent the reasons for their existence, of course. But it is clear that something different is happening here than in the natural sciences.

It is relatively rare to have competing schools or research programs in the natural sciences. When it does occur, the battle is typically short-lived because corrective resources are strong enough that focused attention can resolve the issue by forcing one research program into face-saving degeneration to survive the threat of falsification while its competitor is predicting novel facts and seeing those facts confirmed by observation or experiment. When decisions are not rapid due to lack of empirical traction—as in the decision between the variations of theories that attempt to integrate gravitation and quantum mechanics—the natural-science identity police get nervous and begin fomenting threats to withdraw the "science" label. But the historical and human sciences tend to break into schools under such circumstances, because they are accustomed to the under-determination of theory by data.

When empirical resources cannot settle theoretical debates, other kinds of correction become more important. Aesthetic criteria such as elegance, parsimony, justice, and consistency with broader convictions about the natural world are clearly subordinate to empirical evidence in the natural sciences. But the under-determination of theory by data gives such criteria greater importance in the historical and human sciences. Schools in these fields sometimes emphasize particular approaches to wielding aesthetic criteria, inculcating students in those ways of thinking. For example, critical theory prioritizes emancipatory criteria for theory selection, which most other social scientists do not admit. Such social-organization values serve to consolidate school identity, to support the intensive exploration of a complex hypothetical outlook, and to leverage forms of correction to keep inquiry advancing in the absence of decisive empirical evidence.

Humanities

We now come to the humanities. Here the feedback potential is typically quite weak, which gives full rein to other kinds of corrective resources. In the earlier presentation of the pragmatic theory of inquiry, a distinction was drawn between efficient, inefficient, and irrational processes of inquiry. To recall, an efficient process of inquiry is one in which the feedback potential promotes consensus around norms and procedures for inquiry, creating agreement about winners and losers among substantive theories. An inefficient process of inquiry is one in which the feedback potential is not strong enough to resolve competing proposals for norms and procedures of inquiry, so agreement about winners and losers in substantive theories is more difficult to achieve, and social differentiation into schools occurs. An irrational process of inquiry is one in which resources for the correction of hypotheses are arbitrarily neglected.

The natural sciences make efficiency in this technical sense definitive for their work and scrupulously police the efficiency issue. The historical and human sciences are sometimes efficient and often inefficient, but they are never irrational in the technical sense of arbitrarily neglecting resources for correction. The humanities, by contrast, are rarely efficient and only occasionally do corrective resources permit even inefficient inquiry. In the battles of criteria for the selection of hypotheses that result, the humanities frequently face a plethora of incompatible ways of thinking about excellence in interpretation. A consistent pattern of interpretation typically requires making a tasteful selection among such criteria, elevating some and neglecting others. This is not the *arbitrary* neglect of corrective resources defining an irrational process of inquiry, however, because principles of taste and habits of communal interpretation govern the decision, and decisions about how to weight criteria are subject to debate. Relatively irrational processes of inquiry (again, in the technical sense) do occur in the humanities, particularly when communities of like-minded interpreters hold no respect for certain types of corrective resources that are relevant and would in fact help to advance inquiry. Ordinarily the operative corrective resources and the social establishment of criteria in the humanities are such as to make them highly inefficient.

The emotional valence of the term *inefficient* is such as to suggest that the humanities must be somehow ignoble or deficient, relative to the "efficient" natural sciences. But this is precisely why remembering the technical meaning of these terms is vital. There is nothing "wrong" with the humanities; they operate as efficiently as possible most of the time, given the existing forms of social activation of corrective resources. Indeed, the shifting world of kaleidoscopic interpretation characterizing the humanities is precisely what is so beautiful about them. The events and creations of human life are genuinely multivocal and it would be a disaster for understanding if this superfluity of meanings was artificially eliminated through a false consensus driven by artificial application of a clunky methodological procedure. Indeed, this prospect unnerves humanists and consolidates their resistance to rabid reductionists who elevate the scientific method as the only means of gaining understanding. Such reductionism betrays a profound ignorance of the subtlety and richness and range of human understanding. In fact, the sensitivities required to function as a competent humanist within a community of interpreters are more difficult to acquire than those required to function as a competent natural or human scientist. Radical reductionists often lack the temperament to appreciate the activities they seek to eliminate in the name of rescuing the venture of human understanding from the supposed confusions of humanists.

The pragmatic theory of inquiry has no difficulty moving across the boundary from the sciences to the humanities and still recognizing the humanist's quest for understanding as a form of inquiry. As I have indicated, the relevant types of correction are numerous, with attendant manifestations in social organization—and this plurality of corrective resources is as helpful in the humanities for uncovering salient insights and promising lines of investigation as it is disastrous in the natural sciences. But the hypotheses for such inquiry are also of many different kinds—unlike in the natural, historical, and human sciences—and this further complicates inquiry in precisely the right way.

Consider a community of literary critics examining an influential novel. One of them notices that the prose style has a surprising lack of adverbs and auxiliary verbs, a point that is subject to correction by means of direct inspection. She hypothesizes that (1) this is what gives the prose a robustly plain-spoken character, (2) that this in turn creates overtones of direct frankness that indirectly express the story's portrayal of simple people with hard lives, (3) that this helps readers develop a feeling for people living under such circumstances, (4) that this kind of writing is difficult to produce and so its effects must have been intended by the author, (5) that his authorial decision was a self-conscious attempt to model the writing techniques of a series of folk authors in his local community, (6) that this modeling move subverts the dominant literary style of the author's context, (7) that it expresses the author's alienation from his creative writing environment, (8) that it further reflects a longer-term alienation from the author's high-culture family, (9) that his earlier novels hint at this creative move as an incipient possibility, and (10) that all this makes the novel one of the great literary works of its era.

These hypotheses are very different in kind, as evidenced by the kinds of arguments necessary to support them and the modes of correction relevant to testing them. It is in the prosecution of such arguments and in the search for data and interpretations relevant to assessing them that inquiry occurs. The social differentiation of inquiry in the humanities has a fascinating influence here. Some schools of literary interpretation consistently reach for certain kinds of hypotheses that reflect large-scale working commitments—say, authorial intention is irrelevant to meaning, or personal biography is crucial for understanding literary style. While it is not clear that corrective resources are strong enough to decide these central theoretical debates in literary criticism, the instinct to hypothesize according to a particular interpretative strategy still discloses dimensions of meaning that might be cut off were all literary critics in thrall to the same paradigm of interpretation. In this way, the humanities remain faithful to the multivocal character of meaning within the human adventure. And we wouldn't want it any other way. Just as it is important to make use of corrective resources to the greatest extent possible, so it is vital to honor the ambiguity of worlds of meaning by resisting the intrusion of artificial clarities where none belong.

From time to time, we discover even in the humanities that previously unsuspected empirical leverage is available to assist inquiry. At these moments, the cry for revolution is in the air—the humanities can be more like the sciences!—but in practice these discoveries of additional corrective resources do not change the basic quality of inquiry in the humanities. Superfluity and ambiguity of meaning is still the rule. But it certainly is possible to make use of empirical resources to eliminate certain lines of interpretation as fundamentally implausible, thereby narrowing the range of serious hypotheses in any given inquiry. For example, philosophical ethics has traditionally been rather speculative and intuitive in character. But it is being revolutionized by engaging actual information from experimental social psychology and cognitive neuroscience about how people behave and make decisions. The experimental discovery that people typically use moral reasoning not to make decisions but to furnish post-hoc rationalizations for intuitive moral judgments should profoundly alter the way humanist ethicists mount arguments. Likewise, the discovery of distinct domains of moral intuition offers a far deeper interpretation of moral conflict and culture wars than ethicists were formerly able to produce.[3]

In much the same way, religious philosophy is a humanities discipline aligning itself with multiple fields in order to take full advantage of such corrective resources as are relevant to its inquiries. It does this without forgetting that the intense diversity of interpretations in the humanities is a virtue, in general, and that artificial consensus is dangerous in a world of multivocal meanings.

Fine Arts and Practical Crafts

Before moving any closer to religious philosophy, let us pause to consider how the pragmatic theory of inquiry might approach the demarcation of the fine arts and also of essentially practical crafts such as law, politics, and the helping professions of medicine, social work, and religious leadership. In all of these cases, value of one or another kind is the main source of corrective resources in inquiries associated with these fields. Aesthetic values matter most in the fine arts. Moral values—related to behavior, mental and physical health, group identity, efficacy of change, and justice—take the leading roles in the practical crafts.

Beginning with the fine arts, let us consider a simple example of a debate that offers in a microcosm some indication of the macrocosmic aesthetic battles waged in the fine arts. A question confronts the staff of a private museum as they ponder how to present a new exhibit of photographs. They have the dated photographs in hand, and they have already reached a consensus on where to hang them because they are focusing on a transformation in the photographer's style that is most evident when the photographs are arranged in a strictly chronological order. Their problem is that they have a team of five framers ready to go to work and they cannot agree on how to frame the photographs. In fact, the issue is much more specific: they have decided on a heavily geometric black wood frame, a simple double matte of the whitest color they can obtain, and expensive non-reflective glass for all of the photographs. The only remaining decision is how wide a matte to use for setting each photograph off from the frame. An unusually egalitarian outfit, everyone is involved in such debates regardless of seniority, and in this case some of the subcontracted framers with an interest in aesthetic debate have weighed in with their opinions as well.

They have discovered that their opinions divide into two groups. On the one hand, some want symmetry of the matte on all four sides, after which the debate reduces to the width question. Should the matte width be the same for all photographs, which are all rectangular but vary significantly in size? If so, what should that width be? Or should the matte width be set in strict proportion to the size of each photograph? In that case, what should the ratio be, and should the ratio be calculated relative to the height or width of the photograph or some combination of the two? On the other hand, others reject the ideal of four-way symmetry and prefer some variation of an asymmetric matte. One proposal is to make the matte wider on the bottom of the frame than on the other three sides—recalling a classic design principle—and to do this for the entire collection. After that, the same questions about width crop up as in the symmetric case. Another proposal is to set the frame sizes to be identical, which would speed things up for the framers, and to cut the matte for each photograph so as to place it in the middle of its one-size-fits-all frame, which would produce narrow mattes in some cases and shockingly broad mattes in other cases. A third asymmetric proposal is truly bizarre, asking for random mattes that situate each picture in a different place within the frame. The aim in this case is to challenge the viewers' expectations about the way a photograph should be framed, in order to draw their attention to the wildness of the photograph itself.

Having diagnosed all of these options—one of the analytically minded office staff even wrote them up on the conference-room white board—the conversation moved from the expression of preferences and ideas to argumentation. At this point, three of the outside framers excused themselves, saying they would eat lunch and leave pointless arguments over aesthetic opinions to people with time to waste, but the other two framers remained. It quickly became obvious that some of the gallery staff had no idea how to make a case for their preference. They found themselves reacting strongly for and against many of the proposals, but they had no idea why. After essentially repeating themselves a few times, and running the gamut of fairly strong emotions, they fell silent and listened to an emerging conversation about aesthetic values, which they found deeply surprising for its gentleness and sophistication. Some of the references were obscure because the four genuine experts in the group were recalling specific aesthetic traditions and key moments of the establishment and subversion of guiding aesthetic principles. One of them appeared to enjoy name dropping and never paused to explain the names he mentioned. But the four-way conversation remained on track, and even the novices in the group could follow what was happening in broad terms.

The decision about the mattes was being contextualized in traditions of aesthetic experimentation and debate that actually *made the decision nonarbitrary*. There were no absolute judgments about beauty or ugliness. Rather, the focus was first on appropriateness to the goals of the exhibition, which served to eliminate some of the proposals. Second, the surviving proposals were situated within traditions of aesthetic interpretation, which provided conceptual and historical context. Third, the aim was not to find the putatively best solution but rather to locate an interesting hypothesis that could guide the decision. The four experts were treating the eventual answer to the matte question as an aesthetic experiment, which would not only contribute to the aesthetic traditions that informed it but also provoke intelligible shifts in the way the photographs were received, especially by well-trained and sensitive viewers. All but one of the traditions discussed were Western in origin, and it is possible that a wider representation of aesthetic traditions from world cultures would have derailed the discussion due to the lack of knowledge about conceptual linkages or historical interactions sufficient to connect the diverse traditions together.

Eventually, the four experts reached a consensus about what kind of experiment to conduct and thus what kind of aesthetic hypothesis to explore. The consensus involved some compromise, as well as a commitment to try an alternative for another exhibition in which framing would be an issue. They then asked those who had been silent for their opinions. In one way or another, the preceding expert discussion enabled each participant to transcend his or her initial instinctive reactions. Those reactions persisted as preferences in most cases but appreciation for alternatives and especially for what could be seen to be at stake in adopting a particular matte style was enormously expanded. Each was able to accept the expert consensus with some degree of understanding, even if their initial preference had been different. Most importantly, each felt as though they were involved in the hypothetical exploration of an aesthetic landscape far more intricate and interesting than they had ever suspected possible. When the three absent framers returned from their lunch to discover the conversation winding up, their two colleagues conveyed the decision about the matte style and tried to explain what was at stake in the decision. Completely uninterested, the three returning framers cut their friends off, convinced that this was all arbitrary and meaningless, and insisted on getting on with the work.

The pragmatic theory of inquiry explains the role of the specialized discourse community in this story, and how it permits relatively nonarbitrary inquiries to operate even in domains of human experience where there is virtually no opportunity for uncontroversial empirical feedback. Specialized discourse communities in the fine arts are built around central hypotheses, just as all specialized discourse communities are. In this case, the core hypotheses concern aesthetic value and its expression in the visual arts, and those hypotheses are elaborated in a sophisticated conceptual language that is compelling to insiders because it registers faithfully what they experience as important in their encounters with visual art. The terms of the conceptual framework are stabilized by the narration of a series of historical episodes and by a kind of phenomenological aptitude, which some people possess in relation to the visual arts to a much greater degree than others. Corrective resources take the form of consistency tests within the articulated framework of guiding aesthetic values and also experiments in inciting particular kinds of reactions in both trained and untrained audiences.

In the elaboration of numerous aesthetic traditions and in the subtle debates over beauty that they adumbrate, experts in the fine arts succeed in uncovering depths and dimensions of meaning and value that any one tradition cannot register alone. The pragmatic theory of inquiry regards this unfolding of the realms of value as evidence for the reality of values external to human minds just as it regards the Milikan oil-drop experiment as evidence for the reality of a practical minimum unit of electric charge external to human minds. The reality of values can only become evident when nature is organized into sufficiently complex ways to register them, but they are no less real for being dependent on a process of emergence, any more than a macromolecule such as RNA is less real for being dependent on the lower reaches of the same process of emergence.

Practical crafts are similar to fine arts in respect to requiring multiple traditions for the articulation of the multifaceted meanings and possibilities of whatever domain is the object of practical mastery. They are different in two important ways.

On the one hand, they sustain different relations to allied disciplines. The fine arts have enjoyed a fruitful collaboration in the last few decades with cognitive neuroscience. What is learned about the way human beings recognize beauty and ugliness or process color and shape can impact the techniques of fine artists, particularly by inspiring them to manipulate perception and interpretation in light of what cognitive neuroscientists say about these aspect of human beings. But such questions of technique help neither to answer questions about the values guiding aesthetic traditions nor to resolve the power struggles among those traditions as they scramble for precious cultural resources and attention. Meanwhile, the practical crafts typically enjoy richly articulated relations with the historical and human sciences. Here, too, questions of value are not settled merely by knowing more about how a particular political philosophy was implemented in Andalusian Spain, or how a particular Islamic legal tradition handles the controverted question of fair water use. But because of these relations, the constraints on hypotheses within the practical crafts are far stronger than in the fine arts.

On the other hand, the fine arts are governed chiefly by aesthetic criteria, whereas the practical crafts draw mostly on roughly moral criteria pertaining to the practical effects of decisions, ideals of health in various dimensions, and criteria such as justice and compassion.

Practical concerns engage a far wider range of people than the more specialized aesthetic sensibilities, and are easier to reach consensus about. That is, while it is not completely obvious what mental or physical health is, or what fair access to basic resources is, it certainly is a lot easier to win an approximate consensus in those domains than in questions of aesthetic value. This is because the range of meanings that human beings can explore is relatively less dense and overloaded in practical domains of life than in aesthetic questions. This is so even though practical domains are enormously more complicated than the historical and human sciences, which are themselves significantly denser with overlaid meanings than the natural sciences. This difference in the type of criteria relevant to negotiating debates helps to create greater consensus around principles and procedures for inquiry in the practical crafts than in the fine arts.

Both the fine arts and practical crafts routinely cut short inquiry because of the attendant personal and social costs. As befits their name, the practical crafts call for the assertion of decisions for the sake of moving life forward in practical ways. Likewise, it is possible for a sculptor to feel quite impatient with intellectual debates over the aesthetics of form when he or she really only wants to press life into a chunk of rock. Practical decisions are rarely capable of perfectly satisfying all stakeholders, and artistic decisions are seldom intended to satisfy all those that may feel they have a stake in the work of art produced. At this first-order level of inquiry, therefore, inquiry itself must be curtailed in order to avoid wasting energy on frivolous activities (for example, certain lawsuits, medical treatments, psychotherapeutic methods, religious rituals, and debating aesthetic theories), energy that most feel would be more productively spent in other ways.

First-order inquiry can be contrasted with second-order inquiry, which aims not at the production of art or practical outcomes but at understanding. Indeed, second-order inquiry in these contexts can be defined precisely as inquiries that continue as long as curiosity persists and do not end just because someone has a music commission to fulfill, a legal case to decide, or a liturgy to complete in time for a religious ceremony. Second-order inquiries are often pursued in universities even when no first-order inquiries are. For example, law schools typically host legal theory rather than actual courts of law. In the fine arts, it is typical to have first-order and second-order inquiries pursued alongside one another, sometimes by the same person, just as some creative writers are also excellent literary critics.

The relationship between first-order and second-order inquiries is complicated, as these examples suggest. Judges trying a complex case may care a lot more about actual precedents than about the theoretical debates surrounding relying on precedents. Doctors trying to eliminate cancer may care a lot more about functional treatment options than whether primary oncology research should pursue RNA or viral approaches to curing cancer. A composer may care a lot more about expressing musical ideas than about the musicologist's interpretations of the heritage of those ideas. Yet first-order inquiry can also degenerate into rigid repetition without the flexibility of perspective afforded by second-order inquiry; think of the neglect of the oncologist who does not keep up with cutting-edge treatments, or the growing despair of the artist who keeps fulfilling plentiful commissions with derivative but popular paintings. In the other direction, second-order inquiry lapses into sterile abstraction without rich connections into the first-order inquiries that producers of fine art and practical crafts make possible. Ideally, the two types and levels of inquiry are interlocked, sometimes loosely and sometimes rigidly, depending on the kinds of inquiry underway. This distinction between first-order and second-order inquiries is no mere theoretical nicety. It is an intelligible response to the need for efficient production in creative and practical endeavors, which typically curtails inquiry prematurely, and leaves some people—those temperamentally angled toward satisfying curiosity rather than producing goods—persisting in inquiry against the pressure toward expediency.

Metaphysics and Theology

What has been said about the humanities applies also to metaphysics and theology: inquiry in these disciplines operates within the ambit of relatively weak corrective resources, uses social differentiation to deflect arbitrary imposition of unduly narrow principles and procedures, profits here and there from empirical resources to prune the tangle of competing hypotheses and constrain the survivors, and deals with the reality of ambiguous and multivocal meanings compressed together into dense and fascinating human phenomena. Like the fine arts, moreover, aesthetic values bearing on subtle qualities of hypothetical theories play a role in defining active traditions and articulating the dimensions of meaning that make the world as we encounter it such a potent domain for metaphysical and theological reflection. For example, should we prefer the affinity of the Neoplatonist Plotinus and the Advaita-Vedāntan Śaṅkara for a metaphysics that resolves the problem of the one and the many despite being morally impenetrable, or the Middle Platonist and the Dvaita-Vedāntan affinity for a morally intelligible portrayal of reality that cannot answer the problem of the one and the many as convincingly?

Like both the fine arts and the practical crafts, metaphysics and theology display the distinction between first-order and second-order levels of inquiry, though the pressure that drives this distinction is different. The first-order inquiries are attempts of ordinary people to make sense of their lives in theological and metaphysical terms. These are the construction of worldviews and patterns of practice that address the existential pressures related to coping and flourishing. Such first-order inquiries routinely involve curtailing inquiry prematurely for the sake of managing life with a minimum of cognitive dissonance and upsetting ambiguity. The second-order inquiries refuse the curtailing of inquiry even though most regular people immediately lose interest in the elaborate specialized discourse communities and traditions of debate typical of second-order inquiry into metaphysical and theological questions. Even so, the connection between first-order and second-order inquiry is as important in metaphysics and theology as it is in the fine arts and the practical crafts, and for the same reasons of mutual fecundity.

A vital difference between the fine arts and practical crafts, on the one hand, and theology and metaphysics, on the other, is that almost all human beings are involved in first-order inquiry of the theological or metaphysical kind. This means that virtually all second-order inquirers in metaphysics and theology are existentially entangled in their subject matter, the phenomenon that was discussed earlier in this chapter. Another vital difference is that the criteria relevant to assessing inquiries in metaphysics and theology sometimes include those related to the first-order quest for spiritual enlightenment and authentic lifestyles. The strong attachment human beings routinely feel toward their working answers to spiritual questions of enlightenment and authentic living can influence second-order inquiry more in metaphysics and theology than in the fine arts and practical crafts. This influence can be helpful for increasing sensitivity within second-order inquiry to the intricacies and intensities of first-order spiritual quests. But it can also interfere with inquiry by substituting prejudice for reasoned argument and by supporting the assumption that alternative hypotheses have no bearing on an inquiry whereas in fact they do. We saw in this in the first example on multidisciplinarity in Chapter 4.

Some philosophers treat metaphysics as having nothing to do with existentially loaded spiritual quests or with hypotheses about the ultimate concerns of human life. For them, metaphysics is merely the enclosing designation for inquiry into questions such as "What is a thing?" and "What is a cause?" and "What is a relation?" To a large extent, they can effectively abstract such questions from the wider context of metaphysical concerns. But it is quite unlikely that whatever might count as an ultimate reality would have no theoretical impact at all on what is said about what are things, causes, and relations. Indeed, the history of philosophy in all traditions suggests that one's view of ultimate reality has a profound effect on the way one interprets the rest of the world.

A similar limitation in the scope of theology is recommended by some theologians. They treat theology as second-order reflection on the first-order beliefs and practices of a *particular religious community*. The primary goal is *to support that community's institutional interests* through giving a rational account of beliefs and practices—an account broadly consistent with the community's internal authority structures and capable of nurturing the faith of its loyal members. Such community-oriented, confessional inquiries can have a broad range of effects beyond those envisaged in the primary goal. For example, what another religious community has to say about a point of shared interest might trigger mutually transformative dialogue. Reflection on an aspect of contemporary science might lead to the reconstruction of a theological doctrine. Or cultural changes might lead theologians to ask large-scale questions about the plausibility of the theological system as a whole.

Despite the flexibility of this form of theological inquiry, there are many natural theological questions that cannot receive proper treatment because they are inconsistent with the essentially confessional institutional starting point. This fact provokes a specialized discourse community of theologians operating independently of the institutional interests of specific religious communities. Such theologians reject the constraints of authority and revelation that operate internally to each religious community. They construct categories and conceptualities capable of registering ideas from across traditions with minimal distortion. They pay close attention to the historical and social contexts of the ideas they study so as to register nuances of difference as well as structural similarities. And they develop theories about theological topics that belong to no one religious tradition but rather take their specialized academic discourse community itself as home turf.

The existence of this form of inquiry, with its independence from the authority structures and institutional interests of particular religious groups, entails that metaphysics and theology, appropriately conceived, need not be restrained by religiously skittish philosophers and metaphysically defensive theologians. Doing metaphysics and theology to some degree independently of the constraints imposed by determinate religious institutions allows inquiry to press in quite novel directions, and in some respects much further than confessionally obliged forms of theological and metaphysical inquiry allow. But it is necessary to work comparatively, to attend to multiple disciplines, to eschew external authorities acceptable only to religious groups, to construct specialized discourse communities that facilitate inquiry, and to sustain multiple inquiring traditions built around core hypotheses just as the humanities do. This kind of metaphysics and theology is one style of religious philosophy, to which we turn next.

Religious Philosophy

This discussion of a variety of disciplinary demarcation problems helps to frame the distinctiveness of religious philosophy. But religious philosophy actually involves a variety of types of inquiry, so it is not a discipline with a unique relationship to the issues we have been discussing. Recall the seven styles of religious philosophy first discussed in Chapter 2: phenomenological, comparative, historical, analytical, literary, theoretical, and evaluative. The styles of inquiry operative within physical sciences are diverse—arcing from the historical sensibilities of geology and evolution to the experimental approaches of biology and mechanics, and from the speculative theory building of contemporary theories of gravitation to the concrete mathematical modeling of observable processes in chemistry. The characteristic approaches to inquiry demanded by the varied styles of religious philosophy are even more diverse. Yet, in the natural sciences and religious philosophy alike, the relevant types of correction depend on the style of inquiry, the decisiveness of the feedback potential changes with the specific subject matter in a given inquiry, and the social organization for leveraging corrective resources varies across the range of activities pursued.

These similarities are important. But there are field-wide differences distinguishing religious philosophy from other intellectual ventures. These include the following.

First, the existential entanglement of the expert inquirer in the subject matter of the inquiry is common within religious philosophy and rare elsewhere. It has to be managed to avoid distortion through the effects of unexamined prejudices. When properly regulated, however, it is a great asset for inquiry because it engenders a range of sensitivities that are indispensable for sophisticated interpretation of religious subject matters.

Second, the distinction between first-level inquiries pursued informally in communities of nonexperts and second-level inquiries prosecuted by experts is also common in religious philosophy and less pronounced outside religious philosophy. The intimate linkage between first-order and second-order inquiry is problematic for religious communities because the results of religious philosophy can disturb religious people more than they might like. But this linkage is also an asset because religious philosophy depends on access to first-order religious behaviors, beliefs, and experiences for much of the raw material for its inquiries.

Third, religious philosophy sometimes involves formal inquiry into ultimate concerns and ultimate realities, which is relatively uncommon in most other human intellectual endeavors and strictly out of bounds for the natural and human sciences. These are among the most exciting and seductive "big question" inquiries in the history of human intellectual effort and people both treasure and condemn them because of that heritage. The multivocal quality of the feedback potential has sponsored numerous individually coherent but mutually inconsistent hypothetical interpretations of ultimate concerns and ultimate realities. Whereas theology oriented to specific traditions focuses mostly on articulating and refining a particular hypothesis, sometimes in response to competitors, religious philosophy takes on as much of the conflicted domain of ultimacy interpretations as a given inquiry can manage.

Fourth, and connected to the third point, religious philosophy is inherently crosscultural and comparative in character. This is relatively uncommon in other domains of human inquiry—though comparative linguistics, some types of cultural anthropology, and some forms of sociology and religious studies do attempt to comprehend a wide range of cultural phenomena within a single interpretative framework.

Fifth, religious philosophy is implicated in making sense of multiple disciplines to an unusual degree. Almost everything that religious philosophy takes up is the primary subject matter for some other type of inquiry. It is vital to absorb those specialized disciplinary perspectives in order to avoid simple mistakes in interpreting religious behaviors, beliefs, and experiences from a philosophical point of view.

Special consideration should be also given to demarcating religious philosophy from other domains of inquiry in which ultimate concerns and ultimate realities become objects of inquiry.

First, some works of literature are among the most powerful explorations of the worldviews that are the stock in trade of the religious philosopher. The ability of a novel to connect such worldviews to the existential intricacies of literary characters furnishes a powerful basis for evaluation of a religious outlook's capacity to satisfy, for exhibiting its virtues and incoherencies, and perhaps for refining it. At this point, literature merges with the literary style of religious philosophy. The more useful the literature is for advancing inquiries in other forms of religious philosophy—which usually means the more systematic and refined its appreciation of philosophical details in a literary form—the more likely it is to count as religious philosophy in the literary style.

Second, there are numerous issues that arise at the boundaries of the natural and human sciences for the sensitive interpreter, but that cannot and should not be answered as scientific questions. For example, physical theories of the origins of the universe have well-understood relations to questions about the unity and meaning of the universe and its ultimate dependence on a divine reality. These are not questions for cosmologists to answer but most cosmologists seem to sense the presence of such boundary questions and many pause to reflect on them outside the boundaries of formal scientific work.[4] Many such boundary questions are matters for religious philosophy, and almost all such questions already have received significant discussion in the history of the various traditions of religious philosophy. When ultimate questions arise at the boundaries with the sciences, they are no more scientific than anything else in religious philosophy, in the formal sense of "scientific." Such questions can be pursued casually or expertly, according to the distinction between first-order and second-order inquiry already mentioned, and the resulting inquiries can engage a variety of traditions and disciplines, as usual.

Third, metaphysics is related especially to religious philosophy in the theoretical style. It is easy for metaphysicians to assume that their theoretical adventures capture everything of possible interest to religious people but this is manifestly not the case. Some technical metaphysical questions are intelligible in isolation from religious and existential questions, such as the best ontology for handling the rigors of the contemporary emergentist account of the natural world. But others are deeply entangled with religious and existential questions. For example, the metaphysician's problem of the one and the many involves consideration of the religious themes of creation and dependence, which are pointed existential issues for many ordinary people, at least when translated into more familiar categories such as "meaning of life and purpose of reality" and "coping with sickness, decrepitude, and death." Similarly, the metaphysical problem of the origins and reality of values is question loaded with practical religious import. It follows that religious philosophy in the theoretical style overlaps significantly with metaphysics. But just as there are metaphysical questions to which most religious philosophy can remain neutral (such as the nature of physical causation), so there are theory-building efforts in religious philosophy that are not necessarily strongly metaphysical in nature (such as a theoretical account of religious authority structures).

Fourth, the relations among religious philosophy, theology, and philosophy of religion (discussed in Chapter 1) demand discussion in terms of demarcating religious philosophy in the evaluative mode from the way evaluation arises in tradition-specific theology or philosophy of religion. Evaluating truth claims in religious philosophy—for example, "God exists" or "*saṃsāra* is nirvana"—is a complicated task, by any measure. These complications are much reduced by limiting the outlook to one particular religious tradition, as tradition-specific theology does. But this involves foregoing comparative resources capable of inspiring corrections in processes of inquiry. In respect to actually striving for the truth as against answering concerns of adherents, therefore, the monotraditional limitation makes things more complicated not less. Similarly, introducing a body of putatively revealed knowledge against which to assess religious truth claims promises to simplify evaluative inquiry, and indeed this is how things work within a monotraditional, faith-supporting approach to theological inquiry. But the religious philosopher's perception of multiple tradition-borne sets of evaluative criteria forces a different approach. The religious philosopher considers the operations of such criteria in theological reasoning as more data for analysis and does not rely directly on such bodies of normative doctrinal statements for evaluating religious truth claims. It is important to note that some forms of theology are not monotraditional and faith-supporting in this way, and such (atypical) theological ventures have a great deal in common with religious philosophy.

Thus, the principle line of demarcation is not that theology is evaluative and religious philosophy is not, or that theology is necessarily limited to a single religious tradition and religious philosophy is not. Rather, monotraditional and faith-supporting theology and philosophy of religion accept tradition-authorized bodies of normative doctrine as criteria for evaluating religious truth claims whereas religious philosophy does not. Religious philosophy is socially and intellectually and ideologically located not in a particular religious tradition but in the modern academy. The modern academy operates with normative assumptions of which it sometimes seems humorously innocent. These include the value of expert consensus, the value of public debate and objective evidence, and the value for inquiry of its functionally naturalistic ontological framework. Religious philosophy accepts those normative assumptions and operates within the orbit of inquiry that they support. In that sense, religious philosophy is just as vulnerable as any other evaluative enterprise to critique based on ideological tainting. But the ideological and procedural particularity of religious philosophy offers special benefits for taking account of multiple competing hypotheses about religious matters. Hopefully, self-awareness prevents the ideological assumptions of religious philosophy, shared with the rest of the modern academy, from operating in a covert and unconsciously destructive way.

Case Study: Religious Philosophy, Religion, and Secularism

A case study on the resilience of religion in secular environments demonstrates the usefulness of the pragmatic theory of inquiry for understanding both religious philosophy and religion itself. Where secularization theorists predicted the decline of religion in secular environments, the pragmatic theory of inquiry predicts that religion in secular settings should prove rationally flexible and socially resilient.

Secularization Theory Revisited

The pragmatic theory of inquiry, as applied to religious philosophy and to inquiry within living religious traditions, is exceptionally useful, especially in that it enables interpreters to rise above traps to which other theoretical frameworks fall prey. To see how this works, I present a case study explaining from a philosophical point of view the surprising resilience of religion in its confrontation with secular culture and scientific rationality. I begin by explaining this resilience and describing the point of view from which it has seemed surprising—namely, so-called "secularization theory."

Standard secularization theory predicts a double problem for religion. On the one hand, regarding institutional differentiation and change, religious institutions should fail to thrive in secular contexts. On the other hand, regarding knowledge claims and plausibility structures, religious intellectuals should be unable to make religious beliefs credible in an era of secular social life and scientific rationality. The theoretical framework for this envisaged "problem of religion" is an account of the development of Western religious (especially Jewish and Christian) institutions and theology since the Enlightenment. Most sociologists of religion and some historians of religion held to this interpretative framework during the last third of the twentieth century. A classic historical analysis is Owen Chadwick's *The Secularization of the European Mind in the Nineteenth Century*.[5] Peter Berger gave an elegant statement of the sociological version of secularization theory toward the end of his book, *The Sacred Canopy*,[6] and many other sociologists have developed it in detail.

This standard view of post-Enlightenment religion presupposes such propositions as the following.

- Vital religion is dependent on widespread ignorance about the world's workings.

- Secular nation-states create freedom of opinion, loosening the vice grip of religious authority.

- Science creates knowledge about the world that contradicts religious truth claims.

- Thus, religion is increasingly irrelevant to educated people from all classes and cultures.

Within this framework of analysis-guiding assumptions, the "problem of religion" has the following three aspects.

- Religion is dying wherever secular social orders thrive because *religion is about authority and social control*.

- Religion always retreats from intellectual confrontation or else engages it merely with reactionary authoritarianism because *religious beliefs can't compete on rational terms with scientific beliefs*.

- Flourishing, stable economies create lifestyles that render religion superfluous because *religion compensates for lack of perceived goods and needs poverty to make people willing to submit to its authority* (so-called deprivation theory).

Based on this view, therefore, it is only a matter of time until religion is reduced to a cultural curiosity.

Moving from its theoretical framework to the question of evidence, standard secularization theory plausibly models the relations between religion and secularity in certain social contexts—especially Western European countries where traditional forms of religious involvement have declined precipitously through the twentieth century. As soon as we begin to attend to other contexts, however, secularization theory falls apart. Most parts of the United States do not fit the predicted pattern at all, and the rest of the world even less so.[7] Even so-called secularized European countries display a tremendous amount of religious activity and interest, albeit often beyond the boundaries of traditional Jewish and Christian religious institutions—such as the widespread interest in new age spirituality in many parts of Western Europe, and the growth of Islam in Europe since World War II, due in large part to immigration (as of 2005, there are about 1.6 million Muslims in the United Kingdom; about 3 million Muslims in Germany; about 6 million Muslims in France; and about 7 percent of the European population are Muslims).[8] In short, the data contradict most of the major predictions of standard secularization theories: the vitality of religion has persisted even among educated Westerners, religious fundamentalism is a powerful global phenomenon provoking unanticipated resistance to secularism, and spiritual enthusiasm thrives even when interest in organized religion flags.

The disintegration of standard secularization theories has triggered a determined effort on the part of sociologists and historians to study particular contexts more thoroughly. The relationships among religion, scientific rationality, and secularizing trends are evidently dynamic, varied, and culture-specific in their outworking. As one of the influential proponents of secularization theories, Berger has also been one of the sociologists leading the call for more detailed study of religion, politics, economics, globalization, and secularism in particular contexts. He presents a brief but honest explanation of where secularization theory went wrong in his lead essay for the volume, *The Desecularization of the World: Resurgent Religion and World Politics*.[9] There he writes, "The world today is massively religious, is *anything but* the secularized world that had been predicted (whether joyfully or despondently) by so many analysts of modernity."[10] He does note two exceptions to this generalization. On the one hand, the case of Western Europe really does display an increase in secularization indicators spreading south from the northern countries since World War II, though even this case is ambiguous, for the reasons noted above. On the other hand, a secularized subculture of intellectuals with Western-style educations pervades the world. Consisting of both humanists and scientists, "this subculture is the principle 'carrier' of progressive, Enlightened beliefs and values." Though relatively few in number, these people tend to be influential and constitute a "globalized *elite* culture."[11]

This is a fascinating turn of events. Just as globalization has turned out to be unexpectedly reconcilable in diverse ways with a wide range of local cultures, so secularization turns out not to be the triumphal defeater of religion that many theorists anticipated, but instead provokes religious resurgence in a host of ways within diverse cultural contexts. We can tentatively hypothesize from this sea change in the sociological study of religion and culture that religion is more basic to human nature and society than once typically thought, that it is extremely adaptable and rationally flexible, and that it is capable of existing with and even within secular societies.

The study of the intellectual aspects of this confrontation between religion and secular scientific rationality has also undergone a reversal in recent times. Since this question began to receive intense scholarly attention at the end of the nineteenth century, scholars have often characterized the relationship between theology (thought of as the intellectual wing of religion) and science in terms of conflict.[12] Famous instances of conflict attributable in significant part to differences in the rational structures of theology and science do exist—from the Galileo affair to some aspects of the reception of Darwin's theory of evolution. Recent studies of these and other episodes have revealed a much more complex picture, however. In fact, it is fair to say that careful historical scholarship has been nuancing and overturning conflict interpretations of theology and science.[13] Just as in the case of the mistaken interpretation of secularism by early social theorists, so the pervasiveness of oversimplified conflict interpretations between theology and science calls for an explanation. It is tempting to account for this mistaken scholarly consensus with reference to the likelihood that some sociologists and historians are unduly influenced in their analyses by their own experiences of meeting people like themselves all over the world (Berger mentions this as a factor[14]). Then there are the facts that conflict is remembered more clearly than moments of harmony or compromise, and that colorful accounts of conflict sell newspapers and books.

Another reason for the pervasiveness of intellectuals with little confidence in the resilience of religion may be the prevalence even among such intellectuals of inadequate interpretations of rationality. If this is indeed part of the problem, then philosophical analysis may have a relevant contribution to make. Of course, sociological and historical approaches are better suited to most aspects of the task of analyzing the complex and often local dynamics of the relations among religion, secular cultures, and scientific rationality. For example, sociologists and historians can revisit the history of modernity to construct a more nuanced account of religion and secularism, which promises far more for an understanding of the broad range of relations among religion, culture, and science than a philosophical approach could hope to offer. Yet philosophers have something distinctive to contribute: an appreciation for what is *possible* in relations among religion, scientific rationality, and secular culture—and, on that basis, some deep reasons for the resilience of religion and the rational flexibility of religion in the face of secular social environments.

A Philosophical Analysis of the Resilience of Religion

The pragmatic theory of inquiry sketched above registers subtle differences in the ways beliefs are formed and justified in various intellectual activities, which makes it a powerful philosophical tool with which to analyze and compare the rational structure of inquiry in science and in religion. It generates insights into the rational flexibility and practical importance of religion, including its abilities to resist and transform secular contexts. Indeed, religion, on the theoretical grounds furnished by the pragmatic theory of inquiry, should be exactly as rationally flexible and robust as its impressive reactions to secularism have demonstrated it to be. Consider basic contrasts between science and religion in the framework of the pragmatic theory of inquiry.

On the one hand, the pragmatic theory of inquiry predicts that a stronger feedback potential provokes stable practices of inquiry, which can work across cultural boundaries. The stability of these practices is the result of the way that rapid correction of hypotheses promotes consensus around procedures and norms for inquiry. Inquiring groups formed in this way will accept limitations in the scope of inquiry and in the resilience of hypotheses in exchange for the satisfaction of progressive knowledge—as always, hypothetical theories are corrected and improved and replaced by better theories. This describes the community of modern scientific inquiry, which is global in scope and in which people of many different cultures and religions can participate without much difficulty. Consensus around procedures is stronger than consensus around norms. Because experimentation occasionally can directly falsify some claims, there is strongest agreement on procedures and norms in those branches of science where repeated experimentation is possible. In other branches (such as high energy particle physics), the theories of instrumentation needed to make sense of experimental results are so prodigiously complicated that there needs to be constant scrutiny of results, which produces manageable controversies over interpretation of data.

The real disagreements within science appear when experimentation is difficult or impossible—as with historical inquiries such as cosmology and evolutionary biology, or extremely speculative inquiries such as quantum cosmology. In these cases, inquiry operates much as it did for Aristotle, though with more in the way of mathematical modeling: subtle and contestable observations are the only direct constraints on theoretical proposals, experimentation is almost irrelevant, and the criteria for theory choice are aesthetic (such as conceptual simplicity, mathematical elegance, and consistency with metaphysical or religious beliefs) as often as they are in any sense empirical. For example, a few decades ago, Stephen Hawking advanced his quantum cosmology in part specifically to rebut claims that big-bang cosmology entails a universe with a finite age, which to some suggests a deliberate act of divine creation.[15] At this point, consensus around procedures and norms for inquiry breaks down and complicated disputes ensue over what counts as science, all with the effect of maintaining group identity in face of a threat to precious consensus around group values.

On the other hand, where the feedback potential is weaker, as it is in religion (and theology, understood as the intellectual wing of religious communities), we expect to find social innovation to secure group identity against the inevitable conflict that springs up in the face of intractable disagreements. Religious faith is a complex concept but we would not be far from the mark were we to understand its cognitive aspect as the act of making vital assumptions that guide life by furnishing a moral and spiritual orientation through identification with a particular community of like-minded believers. People make these "faith assumptions" consciously or unconsciously in situations of this epistemologically intractable sort not only because they want and need to but because they are forced to by the relative vagueness of the operative feedback potential. Such faith decisions are forced in the sense William James described: refraining from deciding is in effect to decide anyway, yet decisive rational grounds for a decision one way or another do not exist.[16] Under such conditions, people make faith decisions with reference to existing options presented by social groups whose existence and identity is ultimately the result of innovative responses to the under-determination of faith decisions by the feedback potential. The result is faith-based identification of like-minded individuals with one another—all engaged in a corporate venture having the historical dimensions of a grand social and moral experiment even though its immediate significance for participants is the provision of a moral orientation and a social framework for daily life. This kind of social embedding of existentially powerful faith decisions produces superior resilience of working beliefs through subgroup-based social control of the criteria for plausibility that determine whether beliefs flourish. The basic experience for members of successful religious groups is that their beliefs work for them and for their community. If it were not for this compelling fact, the strategy of social innovation in the face of intractable disagreement would not prove to be effective in the long run. Yet this basic experience has many social packages: large and diverse religions splitting formally or informally into subgroups within which the working power of a community's shared faith assumptions manifests itself, the constant emergence of personality cults, the modification of sacred rituals for new purposes, heresy trials, and sometimes wars.

Thus, Christian churches have national, denominational, cultural, political, doctrinal, and liturgical divisions. Judaism has deep divisions among orthodox, conservative, reform, and even more progressive fragments. Buddhism has two ancient and many more recent divisions; Islam has two major early politically distinct subgroups and, in any given era since its origins, many practically distinct legal traditions and many culturally and personality-driven subgroups. Hinduism enumerates six orthodox schools and several unorthodox schools, while practically it takes the form of a veritable horde of often local sects and independent gurus. Daoism is similarly diverse. The diversity of theological reflection within each of these groups produces finer distinctions and subtler forms of social division.

Sometimes these religions have unifying ritual practices that continue to work despite widely divergent interpretations—as when Muslims go on the Hajj, or pilgrimage, to Mecca; Hindus of many different kinds appreciate major festivals, especially along the Ganges and other major rivers; and most Christian sects celebrate a sacramental memorial meal in memory and invocation of Jesus Christ. The massively complex and chaotic social process of splitting and clumping decentralizes authority and hands social control of groups to subgroup leaders, who are often local personalities, operating with or without the authority of idealized, nonlocal leaders. This pattern of local leadership and local identification allows religions to work for people as social homes, orienting forces, sources of inspiration and moral authority, convenient means for expressing compassion through social work, and founts of plausibility structures—all this despite the disagreements among even culturally and geographically similar groups.

The local character of plausibility structures and the social effectiveness of religion are the secrets of the great adaptability of beliefs in the face of competing accounts of reality, the refusal of most people to accept an elitist secular subculture, and the power source for the self-renewal of religious groups. It follows that secularity as a social option should be fairly easy to coexist with, and secular scientific worldviews should be relatively easy to resist. In fact, religion can simultaneously adapt quickly to certain aspects of secular worldviews and yet energetically contest others more or less indefinitely, so the secularity of a social environment may be a relatively unimportant factor in the survival of religion. From the point of view of this philosophical analysis, far more important factors in religious survival and flourishing are the social functions that religion performs.

In short, it is when religion stops inspiring and convincing people that they give it up, not when someone disagrees with them or judges them backwards or superstitious. Some evolutionist scientists arguing against the teaching of creationism in U.S. schools give painful or comical evidence of their utter failure to grasp this point about the way religious beliefs work for people in local groups. Their amazement that Christians could be so backward smacks of the same kind of parochialism they criticize—only in the scientists' case it is the simplistic and improper projection of their own way of working in a group onto conservative Christian communities.[17] Those communities do not work the way scientific communities do. The evolutionist cause is better entrusted to scientists who have the imagination to grasp the sociology of group-based plausibility structures in religion. The sociological task of understanding the survival, and even the resurgence, of religion in the face of secularism and globalization calls for sensitivity to variations in the workings of inquiry. The pragmatic theory of inquiry registers these variations exceptionally well. Of course, historians and sociologists would have to track down the all-important details in each context.

I have presented a philosophical analysis of the way religious diversity and fragmentation in face of intractable disagreement promotes local control over plausibility structures and makes feasible the survival of religious groups in secular environments. This analysis is not novel in its social implications. With some variations of emphasis, and perhaps with adjustment of sociological details, probably many sociologists of religion would accept much of this description of some of what happens in the confrontation between religions and secular scientific worldviews. My fundamental claim here concerns some of the basic reasons for all this, reasons whose detection and description require a philosophical analysis of the sort I have furnished. A pragmatic theory of inquiry explains differences in the social arrangements of groups in terms of the efficiency of the feedback potential that we rely on to solve problems, whether commonplace existential challenges, intricate theological conundrums, or scientific puzzles. This connection between social structures and the way the feedback potential works is in turn a direct reflection of the deeply, inevitably social character of human inquiry and of the human species itself.

Chapter 8

Traditions in Transformation

Religious philosophy has given birth to a variety of distinguishable traditions of inquiry and debate (for the reasons described in Chapter 2). These traditions have sometimes overlapped, and some of them have appeared in all of the world's philosophical cultures. Admittedly, the philosophers who contribute to these traditions may not identify them as such. Rather, they are the results of a strong reading whereby elements of many philosophic activities are united together for the sake of constructing distinctive arcs of inquiry with common features.

    This construction is problematic in respect to historical nuance and I stress here again the importance of paying close attention in a given inquiry to cultural and religious contexts that frame acts of religious philosophy and give them much of their meaning and relevance. Nevertheless, the virtue of constructing loose traditions in the way I do here is that it invites us to consider the way that similar strategic moves and conceptual tools recur across cultural and religious differences. This way of speaking implies the claim that certain categories (such as being, causation, physical nature, the psyche, value, and cognitive breakdown—corresponding to the six traditions to be discussed) are robust and flexible enough to register what is happening in a variety of traditions without undue distortion. This claim is difficult to justify but comparative philosophy suggests that it is a reasonable supposition nonetheless. In the model of comparison employed here, this claim amounts to a hypothesis that has to be subjected to the tests of comparative philosophy, as described in Chapter 5.

    At least six traditions have been especially important in several or all of the various styles of religious philosophy. In what follows, I briefly discuss each one, distinguishing them by means of principal focus of attention, fundamental intellectual instinct, distinctive conceptual and linguistic techniques, major exponents, and chief liabilities. I will not attempt a literature review, which would be an absurdly large task. Rather, I will estimate the health and status of each tradition, in the sense of measuring promise in light of the way the constitutive elements of each are undergoing transformation in the contemporary situation. I will conclude that, having passed through a fiery period of criticism and self-questioning, each tradition is in a process of transformative reconfiguration in which new questions are supplanting old ones, even while the key intuitions and classic problems persist at the root of the intellectual effort. In short, though there may have been health problems lately, each tradition is currently regaining strength and bursting with promise, precisely to the extent that it engages the academic study of religion and as many scholarly disciplines as are relevant—that is, to the extent that it operates as religious philosophy in the sense this term has here.

The Ontotheological Tradition

The ontotheological tradition focuses on being. Its fundamental intellectual instinct is that we can gain an understanding of ultimacy by investigating being, thought of as the single most fundamental characteristic of everything that is.

Every living thing, every inanimate object, every idea, and every cultural creation has being—and has it in some sense in common with everything else. The word *being* and its translations are in such common usage that their meanings seem obvious and their constructed character difficult to recall. In fact, *being* is just "be"-ing—the act or process of continuing to be. It conveys nothing more than this until philosophers go to work on it—nominalizing it, imputing a wondrous aura to it, and building up around it conceptual scaffolding that articulates and supports the meanings they assign to it.

The most adventurous conceptual invention is imputing such coherent power to being that "Being Itself" can function as a name for God. After this, when anything exists, it manifests Being Itself and thus becomes a potential means of understanding God. All being is transparent—well, translucent—to the transcendental qualities of goodness, beauty, and truth that mark the divine presence. *God* is a word with fabulous connotations, but they are also deeply inconsistent. I will sometimes use the less overdetermined word *ultimacy* to avoid prejudging too many issues about the character of Being Itself. Ultimacy is the backstop of reality, the most profound truth and the last word.

The sense in which beings might "manifest" Being Itself is a vexed issue. It is also one of the keys to assessing the reliability of inquiry in philosophical theology. One wing of the ontotheological tradition has interpreted this manifestation through more or less causal concepts such as participation, engagement, or purpose expressed in function (a combination of Aristotle's formal and final causes). If the relation between beings and Being Itself does in fact possess a causal aspect, then we can reasonably hope to inquire into the latter by means of the former. This hope conjures the exciting vision of reliable knowledge from a meaningful process of inquiry—the religious philosopher's dream! The standard bearers in the West for this wing of the ontotheological tradition are Platonists and Neoplatonists, especially Plotinus and Augustine, and also Aristotelians, especially Thomas Aquinas, all of whom have a rich network of antecedents and followers.

Another wing of the ontotheological tradition has interpreted this manifestation not in causal terms but in terms of its cognitive characteristics. This phenomenological-cognitive approach treats manifestation as a kind of luminous disclosure or revelation. The metaphors in this case are of light rather than friction, of vision rather than action. But the conviction that the luminosity of Being has the power to guide philosophical and theological inquiry into the nature of Being Itself still inspires epistemological optimism. Classic modern Western examples are Jean-Paul Sartre's view of being as revelation, and Emmanuel Lévinas's view of being as the milieu for the revelation of moral obligation through encounter with the Other. The antecedents of these views run far back through the Gospel of John and beyond. Mullā Sadrā is a prime example of a similar view from modern Islamic philosophy, and the entire Vedānta tradition is a storehouse of debate over these issues in South Asian philosophy, as are Buddhist traditions of metaphysics evolving from the core concept of *pratītya-samutpāda* (dependent co-origination).

The great problem with the ontotheological tradition is that the manifestation of Being Itself in and through all being,—whether construed as participation or as luminosity or in any other way—has not delivered on its promise of reliable fruits of inquiry. The ontotheological tradition swept into the modern period with a lot of momentum and strong consensus around its main claim—that careful analysis of being showed the kind of coherent power in Being Itself that raised it above a mere abstraction to the most honored level of a name of God. But this consensus covertly drew on the power of active religious traditions. Modernity's loosening of the bonds between philosophical theology and religious piety caused the consensus to begin breaking down.

Philosophers of a nominalist mindset, already skeptical of the reality of universals, pointed out that *being* was merely the most abstract of all universal terms. Thus, we have no reason to ascribe to it determinate character, let alone any sort of transcendent ontological standing. Moreover, in due course the most scrupulous inquiries, such as Heidegger's *Being and Time*, failed to uncover the degree of coherence in the analysis of *being* that the linkage between Being Itself and God requires—at least when "God" is understood as having coherence sufficient to ground the sorts of divine personality, awareness, intention, and action presented in many sacred texts of the world's theistic religions.

Unsurprisingly, there is now widespread disillusionment about the ontotheological tradition of philosophical theology. While this inevitably involves some unreflective criticisms of ontotheology, the better expressions of this disillusioned response argue for the scrupulous avoidance of ontological categories in theological reflection. One contemporary expression of this response is Jean-Luc Marion's insightful book, *God Without Being*.[1] Yet the disillusionment over ontotheology is hasty. We can no more cast aside an entire tradition of philosophical theology than we can allow ourselves to become enslaved by it.

The failure of consensus within the ontotheological tradition is merely a transitional phase, like a momentary shaking of the head to refocus concentration. It is a sign that the ontotheological tradition is freeing itself from unduly anthropomorphic conceptions of ultimacy and unnoticed indebtedness to religious practices and pieties. Ontotheology was robust when its analyses of Being Itself seemed to line up with the anthropomorphic imagery of God that dominates living religion. This happy consonance appeared preeminently in Augustine's writings. The tradition began to struggle when careful analysis of being made us aware of this anthropomorphism and disclosed the way our confidence in the results of philosophical argumentation profits from prior religious convictions.

In fact, the problem with the ontotheological tradition was never its focus on being. Indeed, being is as sensible a category as any other for approaching the task of ultimacy talk. Rather, the problem was lingering anthropomorphism and reification of Being Itself as a determinate entity, which inquiry into being appears not to sustain. In other words, the ontotheological tradition of philosophical theology is actually advancing even now. It is transforming toward greater empirical adequacy and methodological consistency. And it is paying for this advance in the currency of decreasing harmony both with the anthropomorphism of much living religion and with the tendency to reify the terms of commonsense human cognition.

The ontotheological tradition boasts a centerpiece argument known as the ontological argument. It is far from clear that this argument is well named, as it seems to dwell in the borderlands of language, modal logic, and ontology. Medieval philosopher-theologian Anselm gave two complex versions of the argument in his *Proslogion* and a related version in his *Monologion*, mentioned earlier in Chapter 4. Immanuel Kant's account of it is simpler, deriving from Gottfried Leibniz's version rather than from either of Anselm's.[2] Indeed, Anselm's main detractor at the time, a fellow monk named Gaunilo, simplified Anselm's argument in the direction of Leibniz's form of it.[3] Contemporary logical analysis of the argument in its numerous forms involves recondite debates over what counts as a good axiom in a system of modal logic. This is a sign that the debate has degenerated into an unattractive kind of scholasticism, which excites only a few connoisseurs.

The argument in its simplest forms posits that existence is a property of beings and supposes that possessing the property of existence makes a good thing more excellent than it would be otherwise. The conclusion is that the most excellent being would have to exist. This argument is generally taken to be logically sound but marred by the severe, serene fact that at least one of its major premises is false. Kant's critique has been the most persuasive. He identified the problematic premise as the one that treats existence as a property. Some reformulations of the ontological argument aim to evade Kant's criticism by finding modal concepts (such as necessary existence) that seem to be properties in a way that sheer existence is not. But each variation faces similar criticisms.

Can the very idea of God contain unanalyzed within itself the idea of existence, or necessary existence? In my view, any such idea of God is incoherent, so the ontological argument can never get started. The basis for the coherence of the idea of an omnipotent, omniscient, omnibenevolent, necessarily existent deity is anthropomorphic analogies that always prove unsteady. The ontological argument was born in anthropomorphism and reification, and its discussion remains bogged down by anthropomorphic religious instincts even today.

If the ontotheological tradition of religious philosophy were to be judged solely by the ontological argument, most philosophers would probably consign it to the dustbin of history—and not without reason, despite the ballooning contemporary literature on the subject. So consigned, the argument would continue to fascinate historians of philosophy without making any claims on the energy of contemporary philosophers. As I have suggested, however, the ontotheological tradition is far broader, and it flourishes today independently of the ontological argument's fortunes. Indeed, in its most promising forms both past and present, it flourishes without the ontological argument's heavy reliance on anthropomorphic modes of thought. The key to this flourishing in all cases is, as I have suggested, the idea of being as manifestation, with manifestation typically understood either in causal or cognitive terms.

A premier example of the former—the ontotheological tradition renewed under the banner of being as manifestation, with this understood in causal terms—is the vast project in religious philosophy begun by American religious philosopher Robert Neville in 1968 with *God the Creator*.[4] This effort now extends to more than twenty books on a wide range of topics, including that rarest of beasts in the twentieth century: a multivolume systematic philosophy.[5] Neville has no particular interest in the ontological argument, and yet his work from beginning to end belongs in the ontotheological tradition because it treats being as manifestation. His central metaphor for the link between determinate beings and Being Itself is engagement, where Plato's was participation, but the ideas are similar and the shared emphasis on a causal concept of relationality-in-being is unmistakable. The world engages God by virtue of an eternal divine creative act, so we find out about God the creator by studying the determinate beings of our experience. Moreover, for Neville, there is no other way to discover the character of God. In particular, in a vast philosophical gambit that is rare among practicing religious people, he rules out supernatural revelation. This indicates how vital the ontotheological instinct is within his thought. It is the first and the last hope for religious knowledge.

Neville's work is not as well known as it deserves to be, in part because it does not fit existing projects within religious philosophy. It is stranded between two islands of busy religious philosophers. One island houses the Anglo-American philosophers of religion, with their analytical habits of mind. They tend to neglect Neville's root sources in the early American philosophers Peirce and Dewey and Whitehead. The other island is home to European religious philosophers, with their literary and phenomenological habits of mind. They tend to turn away from an explicit treatment of classical Western themes in religious philosophy, such as the problem of the one and the many that so captivates Neville. Both major traditions are skeptical about the theoretical and evaluative styles of religious philosophy, which are prominent throughout Neville's writings.

Neville works especially in the theoretical and evaluative modes of religious philosophy, occasionally dips into the phenomenological, historical, and comparative modes, and tends to avoid the analytical and literary modes. All of his writings are expansive, detailed, and bursting with the same signature promise for reframing our view of the world that has always made past philosophical visions objects of intense contemporary attention. That will probably be the ultimate fate of his work as well. In the meantime, if nothing else, his corpus shows that the ontotheological tradition of religious philosophy has been thoroughly renewed, even in advance of widespread recognition of this fact.

The premier instance of the ontotheological tradition renewed under the banner of being as manifestation, with this understood in phenomenological-cognitive terms, is the European phenomenological tradition springing from Edmund Husserl, as suggested above. Tellingly, this tradition runs through both the Nazi Martin Heidegger and the Jews Emmanuel Lévinas and Jacques Derrida. It flows down to a host of intellectuals captivated by the power of this tradition to conjure delicately instead of naming violently. This line of thinkers is well known for delivering a devastating critique of ontotheological pretensions in religious philosophy. But the critique actually only makes contact with the anthropomorphic and anthropocentric distortions of ontotheology.

Meanwhile, the Husserl-Heidegger-Lévinas-Derrida line powerfully renews the same tradition that it rightly criticizes, typically without saying that this is occurring. But this is precisely what happens when the Other or the Face becomes a manifestation of transcendence or the unconditioned, whether conceived of as God or as moral obligation and the foundation of ethics. All of this springs from an essentially Husserlian analysis of the human condition in terms of intentional consciousness. We constantly form the world into some sort of order that makes us comfortable by making everything cognizable and controllable. This is Kant's interpretation of understanding made tense with evolutionary theory's framing of the survival of the fittest, with anthropology's growing awareness of cultural diversity, and eventually with the visceral experience of evil within the very soul of European civilization.

The fundamental moral and religious question then became not rational evidences for the existence of God—*what could be more absurd and offensive?*—but rather whether anything can have an absolute claim on us. Friedrich Nietzsche's frank recognition that we can now only assert ourselves in a world in which nothing has an absolute claim on us produced will-to-power ethics, which was and remains terrifyingly arbitrary and is fulfilled as much by Nazi self-assertion as by Jewish and Gypsy and Gay and Disabled sacred honor.

Lévinas and Derrida both saw something more than Nietzsche did. The question remains whether they saw something that was, after all, not actually there. This question lies at the heart of theology, also, and is reason enough to call them theologians of a sort. Regardless, they laid a foundation for moral responsibility and intimated transcendence in the failures of human efforts at structuring and controlling reality. They saw the Other, and in the Other a claim on the Self that brooked no refusal and could be denied only on pain of Self-destruction. For Lévinas, the Other manifests God, especially through the founding of moral responsibility in this encounter. For Derrida, the human shapings of environment and culture are shot through with cracks in which shines that which claims us unconditionally, like a blade of grass triumphantly pressing up through a concrete sidewalk. Lévinas risks naming what Derrida will not, but they seem to speaking of the self-same reality, if it can truly be called even that. The shining through of this reality in human cognition and experience is the manifestation of Being Itself.

Note that Lévinas challenges the Husserlian intentional-consciousness approach by interpreting encounter with the Other as the primal event constituting human identity, and by criticizing as "ontological event" the opposed (to him, dangerous) view of human identity as conscious-unconscious substance preexisting the obliging encounter and objectifying the Other.[6] This is a small indication of how massively tangled and contradictory the varied deployments of the word *ontology* have become. Obviously a broader usage that includes the Lévinasian view is in use here, as well as in the conception of the ontotheological tradition itself. This broader usage reclaims the word from more idiosyncratic usages (for example, it doesn't narrowly presume that being-talk must necessarily imply a substance metaphysics, or that the tradition is exhausted by the so-called ontological argument for the existence of God) and is more consistent with the natural lexical possibilities of the word.

There are sharp contrasts between Neville's philosophy of engagement and the philosophy of Otherness in Lévinas and Derrida. One affirmation they make in common is their confidence that the beings, the otherness, and the fractures of this world bespeak something ultimately Other, with which religious philosophy is centrally concerned. And this renews the ontotheological tradition.

The Cosmotheological Tradition

The cosmotheological tradition focuses on the universal features, general conditions, and intelligibility of reality. Its fundamental intellectual instinct is that, if the primary relation of reality to ultimacy is one of dependence, then the conditions for the very possibility of a dependent reality should disclose something about the character of that on which reality is dependent.

The cosmotheological tradition is historically most strongly associated with the so-called cosmological argument for God's existence. This argument's variations proceed along several related paths—from natural causes to a first cause, from natural laws to a law giver, or from the harmony between cosmic order and human rationality to a rational Logos. Each turns fundamentally on the idea of ontological dependence, whereby the character of the cosmos reflects or participates in the character of ultimacy.

The extent to which the cosmological argument for the existence of God persuades philosophers seems tied to how compelling they find this key premise about dependence. Does a network of causes (such as the entire universe, however understood) require a logical and ontological (not temporal) first cause, as Aristotle believed? Or can such a network of causes, as a whole, be somehow self-subsistent and uncaused, as in the *pratītya-samutpāda* metaphysics of Nāgārjuna? Within Islamic religious philosophy, the Kalām thinkers perceptively addressed this point in their debates over actual infinity. Those who argued that actual infinities were impossible could clinch the cosmological argument for the existence of God in a way that their opponents could not, because they had a natural way of blocking the logical possibility of an infinite regress of causes and other sorts of dependencies.

The cosmological argument also asks us to construe the purported existent being compatibly with standard religious ideas of God. But this is deeply problematic. For instance, can a first cause, a law giver, or a Logos be said to exist or act? Can it make plans and does it possess conscious awareness of human beings and worldly affairs? To construe it in these ways appears to set up a vicious regress of questions in which we ask for an ultimate first cause behind the causal activities of this (apparently intermediate) divine being, and for an ultimate lawgiver behind its (apparently intermediate) lawmaking activities. This is the philosophical equivalent of the child's question upon hearing that God created everything: "But then who made God?" But to construe a first cause, a law giver, or a Logos in a way that really does bring the regress of questions about cosmological dependence and origins to an immediate end is decisively to distance this concept of ultimacy from the normal usage of "God" in popular theistic religious contexts.

The cosmological argument for the existence of God may be the historic centerpiece of the cosmotheological tradition of philosophical theology, but the cosmological argument is not the entire content of that tradition. Many exponents have accepted the arguments of Immanuel Kant and others that the cosmological argument cannot succeed in proving the existence of God.[7] Yet they still contend that the dependence relation allows study of the cosmos to illumine the character of its ontological ground. This is where much of the interesting work occurs in our time, along two lines of development.

On the one hand, there is conditional inference, in the following form: if the existence of a Creator God is granted for the sake of argument, then the character of the cosmos discloses something about the character of this Creator. This is most commonly seen among theologians who share the faith assumptions of their religious communities (for example, "God is Creator") and then go on to articulate the meaning of those beliefs using cosmotheological argumentative strategies. This is not a decisive form of religious knowledge, of course, because the assumption of the reality of God is not made available for interrogation. But shoring up confidence in the existence of God is not the aim of religious philosophers working in such contexts because a satisfying degree of religious knowledge is achieved within the religious community in other ways. In these cases, religious philosophy's role is merely explicative, pedagogical, and edifying, fleshing out the full implications of belief in a creator God. But it is also often creative and intellectually compelling.

On the other hand, some philosophers refuse the idea that ultimacy could be an existent being and yet argue that it is through study of the cosmos that we unearth the ontological ground of the cosmos, which is the proper object of God-talk in both theology and religious philosophy. This was the approach of Paul Tillich throughout his writings, for example. While rejecting the idea of a divine being that could be said to exist (or not exist, for that matter), Tillich believed that understanding the world's structures and processes could produce an understanding of its depths, its very ground, and its power.[8] Heidegger pursued a similar inferential approach in *Being and Time*, though his focus was more on human beings than on the world as a whole because he took the latter to be accessible only through the former.⁹

The mention of Heidegger both here and under the ontotheological tradition illustrates the sorts of overlaps that occur in the crisscrossing history of these six traditions of religious philosophy. In Heidegger's case, and in Tillich's case also, the cosmotheological work is implemented as a strategy to serve the broader ontotheological goal. That is, one way to study being is to study dependence relations evident in universal features of the world (Tillich) or of human-beings-in-the-world (Heidegger). These important overlaps are masked when traditions of religious philosophy are reduced to their famous centerpiece arguments.

This sort of reduction also makes it appear that the tradition collapses when the centerpiece argument no longer seems compelling. But the widespread acceptance of Kant's judgment that the cosmological argument for the existence of God fails actually helps the cosmotheological tradition to refocus its efforts. The failure of the centerpiece argument draws attention to the problems of anthropomorphism and reification within the tradition. These silent contributors have perpetually produced distorted conceptions of ultimacy and then strained arguments for the existence of an ultimate being answering to the distorted description. Noticing this immediately shows where the tradition went wrong and how refocusing on the fundamental theme of dependence repairs and strengthens it, even if the centerpiece argument is abandoned. I argued above that the same problems were what criticisms of the ontotheological tradition successfully impacted, not the strategy of the ontotheological tradition itself.

One of the most felicitous expressions of the cosmotheological tradition of philosophical theology is rarely explicitly associated with it. Philosopher-theologian Friedrich Schleiermacher recognized dependence at the heart of the God-world relationship so clearheadedly that he called the ultimacy on which the world depends simply the "Whence."¹⁰ No other name more perfectly captures the guiding principle of this tradition. The minimalism and formality of "Whence" reflects Schleiermacher's resistance to allowing existing ideas of God in living religious traditions prematurely to influence philosophical inquiry.

Thomas Aquinas displayed a similar resistance when formulating his so-called "Five Ways," ending each with "and this we call God" in one or another variation of phrasing.¹¹ This formula acknowledges the naming habits of living religion while refusing to allow those cognitive habits to muddy the waters of philosophical argumentation. Both Thomas and Schleiermacher were personally and professionally involved in religion, and intended no attack on its ideas of God. But they were exquisitely sensitive to the yawning gap between the ideas of God in religious traditions and the ideas of ultimacy that can be supported by rigorous philosophical argumentation. This sensitivity is too often lacking in religious philosophy, past and present, rendering it vulnerable to powerful critiques of special pleading and covert premises favoring outcomes desirable within living religious faiths.

Debate over the conventional cosmological argument still continues, particularly in the most traditional and rationalistic parts of theistic religions. Catholic philosophy continues to teach Thomas's Five Ways with great conviction. Conservative evangelical theologians lay out lists of proofs for the existence of God and pay close attention to the cosmological argument. Notably, the Kalām arguments over actual infinities have been resuscitated in the West, which is a pleasing sign of cooperation in a world that needs a lot more of the same in every dimension of cultural exchange.[12]

Much as in the case of the ontological argument, therefore, the literature continues to grow around traditional expressions of the cosmological argument. Most of this work is repetitive, in the sense of preservative. Some of it rings the changes on scholarly minutiae, which can be exciting only for the thoroughly initiated. And it continues to be deeply rooted socially, institutionally, affectively, and intellectually in living traditions of theistic belief. While I have nothing against this sort of rooting, I do object to the stubborn failure to recognize its presence and influence, to the refusal to test the same arguments in nontheistic conceptual and social frameworks, and to the perpetual insensitivity of this kind of literature to anthropomorphic habits of mind.

Many religious philosophers nowadays recognize that the cosmotheological approach does not produce results that are immediately applicable to the religious beliefs of living theistic religions. This realization marks the end of an era within this tradition of religious philosophy and the beginning of another. In the new era, which has been dawning for some time, the cosmotheological tradition is as useful for nontheistic as for theistic forms of religious philosophy. Its ideas of ultimacy are closer to Schleiermacher's Whence, with its crosscultural flexibility, than to the anthropomorphic God ideas that have dominated discussion of the cosmological argument within theistic traditions. And its natural home is within institutions willing to nurture traditions of philosophical inquiry persisting more or less independently of living religions.

In fact, this is one way secular academic institutions can acknowledge their debt to the religious institutions that founded them, and repay that debt with interest in the form of their own gift: the deliverances of inquiries nurtured within robust traditions of religious philosophy. A religious institution may or may not be consistently interested in those results. But they ought to be sufficiently soundly produced, and sufficiently attuned to world cultures, that a religious institution's outright dismissal of them would be manifestly a mere failure of nerve, a resort to special pleading. Call this gift a Greek gift, then. In my view, a safe future for our world requires religious philosophers consistently to confront the arbitrariness of religious authority as much as the world needs them to critique the absurd pretense that human beings do not ultimately depend on anything. Both are self-destructive intellectual impulses, and both are dangerous to the human future.

The literary mode of religious philosophy may have done more than the other modes to consolidate in our time the cosmotheological instinct of dependence. In one way, ordinary and extraordinary novels often achieve this as they confront the reader with the smell of death, the specter of everything suddenly going terribly wrong, the failure of a mind to make sense of its world, or the terrible arbitrariness of moral and cultural certainties. All such plots set loose self-awareness of our dependence on seen and unseen aspects of our physical and cultural environment. There is also fiction that aims not only to entertain, to provoke, or to change, but also to get indirect philosophical work done. Such works, once conceived and written, read and digested, can make a far more persuasive and insightful contribution to the cosmotheological tradition of religious philosophy than any analysis of the cosmological argument.

A classic example of this is the loose tradition of Russian novels that seem as much theological and philosophical as they are narratives. One of the most frequently cited examples is Fyodor Dostoevsky's *The Brothers Karamazov*. At one point in that book, the Grand Inquisitor is made to deliver a monologue by the silence of the supernaturally returned but now-arrested Jesus Christ. Using this device, Dostoevsky presents a perspective on the human condition and the form of political organization necessary to control and develop it. This political solution requires deception of the masses by the few burdened by the responsibilities of their powerful leadership positions. Dostoevsky also confronts that perspective with the deafening silence of Christ, whose presumed viewpoint the Grand Inquisitor himself expresses in his criticisms. The ultimate judgment—to burn Christ on the next day—turns especially on the danger to human happiness that Christ represents. Christ raises questions, magnifies options, and increases confusion—a thoughtless form of exquisite cruelty in the eyes of the Grand Inquisitor, and one that must be resisted absolutely for the sake of the people.

In relation to the cosmotheological tradition of religious philosophy, the profound question raised here is about the extent to which the fact of our dependence and our very human need for dependence align. The Grand Inquisitor violently refutes Christ's trust that they do—Christ believes that that we have nothing to lose and everything to gain by telling the truth about the Whence of dependence. The Inquisitor proposes instead to conceive of political and social arrangements as means to limit the enormous pain of the discrepancy between the human need for dependent orientation and security, and the sorts of orientation and security actually available in the cosmos. This mismatch must be managed; meddling Messiahs must be murdered.

A less well-known but equally provocative example is Nicolai Leskov's *On the Edge of the World*. A glorious short novel, the book tells the tale of a fervent evangelist-priest in the Russian Orthodox Church whose charge is to convert natives of the freezing Siberian region. The young priest survives a deadly snowstorm thanks to the wisdom and self-sacrifice of a guide who the priest does not trust until it is too late, thinking the guide an ignorant heathen. As an aged and sage church bureaucrat, he recounts the events with remorse, but also with joy and thankfulness. The intended effect of the dramatic retelling is to rein in the evangelical eagerness of his colleagues and subordinates with a story of how love and honor, loyalty and sacrifice were found where the Church refused to allow any such virtues could exist, and indeed failed to exhibit such virtues itself.

Like many novels, Leskov's story has elements of survival against odds in a hostile natural environment, which says something about human dependence. But the deeper question raised within and for the cosmotheological tradition of religious philosophy concerns how we encounter the Whence of absolute dependence and how stably it presents itself across boundaries of culture and religion. Leskov's personal experience in the region transforms his story into a compelling argument to the effect that the dependence relation between human beings and the cosmos does reliably reproduce the familiar range of moral virtues and vices, beliefs and superstitions, across cultures, times, and languages. The quieter but no less compelling argument is that religious claims of special access to the Whence of our dependence may mask the truth and distort perception of the Other as much as they facilitate understanding and achieve salvation.

In the sense in which I am elaborating the renewed cosmotheological tradition of religious philosophy, it has become an exciting, multifaceted, and existentially charged inquiry into the human condition and its dependence on a wider natural, social, and spiritual environment. It arcs across the modes of religious philosophy in complex ways. Yet the central dependence theme persists throughout, tying the various inquiries close to experience. This regulates inquiries and causes them to produce comparable results. The net effect is a cumulative tradition of inquiry, despite the diversity of active approaches.

The Physicotheological Tradition

The physicotheological tradition focuses on the detailed arrangement of the physical world. Its fundamental intellectual instinct is that, if a relation of design obtains between God and the world, then the detailed arrangements of physical reality should disclose the character of the world's designer.

Unlike the cosmotheological tradition, which focuses on basic conditions for the world as a whole, the physicotheological tradition focuses on evidence for divine design in the complex entities and processes of the natural world. The centerpiece of the physicotheological tradition is the so-called argument from design, which infers from apparent design in nature the existence of an intentional designer. This argument is also called the teleological argument because any inference to design is inevitably tangled up with purposes (*teloi*). Thomas gave this ancient argument a particularly pointed form in the last of his Five Ways. It has been the object of intense scrutiny ever since the rise of the scientific study of the natural world. It is a particularly hot topic in religious philosophy at the current time, thanks to the intellectual and political aspirations of so-called intelligent-design theorists. Their confidence in a particular form of the design argument is so strong that they believe it should be taught in high school science classes as a check on the pretensions of evolutionary theory.

We saw in the case of the ontotheological and cosmotheological traditions that their centerpiece arguments constituted only a part of their scope, and indeed a shrinking part as these traditions reform and renew themselves. In the case of the physicotheological tradition, however, the centerpiece argument remains very much in the center of debate. This is due especially to the way the natural sciences continually fuel the impression of *apparent design* in nature, which then begs for philosophical and theological interpretation. Yet the design argument has changed dramatically over the centuries, gradually becoming more differentiated in step with the natural sciences, and steadily becoming more focused as philosophical consensus forms around the argument's strengths and weaknesses. Currently, the design argument has two wings, corresponding to the relatively sharp distinction between contemporary physics and biology. I will discuss each in turn.

The cosmological wing of the design argument has an ancient heritage. Most Pre-Socratic Greek philosophy focused on detecting common natures in the observable world. This is an intellectual enterprise more within the cosmotheological than the physicotheological tradition because the focus was on dependence rather than design. But Pythagoras (Πυθαγόρας; c. 570–c. 495 BCE) pursued a different line of argument that proved to be extremely influential both in inspiring Plato and in crystallizing the physicotheological tradition of religious philosophy. The Pythagoreans detected apparent design in the detailed arrangement of the physical world and believed they could soundly infer from this the reality a principle of design behind the scenes.

For example, they noticed that there was a mathematical pattern hidden within pleasing musical harmonies. A plucked string produces a base tone, with reference to which its harmonics can be compared. When the base length is halved, the tone is an octave higher. When the base length is divided by three, the tone is a fifth higher again; if divided by four, the tone is a fourth higher still, now two octaves above the base tone. When the base length is divided by five, the tone is a major third higher than that. At this point, all of the components of the pleasant-sounding major triad are present. The Pythagoreans concluded that these mathematical ratios power musical harmony. Similarly, they detected potent and rationally provable mathematical truths lurking quietly beneath the surface of the ordinary geometric shapes of human experience—such as the theorem relating the sides of a right-angled planar triangle.

This experience of discovering mathematical patterns underlying the beauty and order of ordinary experience was extremely compelling, to the point that Pythagoras founded a monastic community devoted to uncovering and exploring these patterns. This famously crystallized the tradition of Western mathematics but it also defined one version of the cosmological form of the design argument. The design argument has typically been interpreted as aimed at proving the existence of a personal, intelligent designer being, but this was not the way it worked among the Pythagoreans. They inferred a mathematical-musical harmony beneath the surface appearances of the world, not a designer deity.

This allows us to see the way that the design argument has been profoundly influenced by the dominant form of religious imagination, much as was the case with the ontological and cosmological arguments. If we picture ultimate reality as the rational Logos of the experienced world, then apparent design in nature will lead us to a portrayal of the depth structures of reality. If we picture ultimate reality as an intelligent being, then apparent design in nature will lead us to an intelligent designer. This historic pattern also demonstrates how difficult it is to regulate the role of religious imagination in the design argument's inferences.

Some proponents of the design argument have learned this lesson, perhaps especially from the example set by Thomas Aquinas in his Fifth Way. As noted above, Thomas carefully distinguished between what the design argument can achieve and the way his religious tradition tends to conceive of ultimate reality. Contemporary intelligent design theorists attempt to duplicate this caution in their own way, saying only that apparent design in nature supports inference to an intelligent designer, not to God as theists conceive God. However, Thomas's caution was often lacking in the way the design argument was constructed during the early modern period when mathematical physics was being born. This is nowhere clearer than in the role religion played in inspiring and guiding the inquiries of the scientists struggling for an understanding of the organization of the solar system.

Untangling the strange trajectories of heavenly objects in the night sky was a prodigiously difficult task. For a long time it made sense even to the most sophisticated intellectual to attribute rational forces to the heavenly bodies, so that in Aristotelian fashion their movements were expressions of their rational natures. Of course, the common imagination pictured angels flapping wings to fly stars in circles and supernatural beings occasionally arranging things so as to block out the sun or moon and to make Mars travel backwards for a short while. Sophisticated intellectuals did not buy into such superstitions but they still believed that only the attribution of rational natures to the heavenly bodies could successfully explain their motions. When the modern era of the physical study of the night sky dawned, this sophisticated, antisuperstitious, and thoroughly Aristotelian method of untangling cosmological appearances defined the state of the art, as well as the longstanding consensus in natural philosophy.

Galileo Galilei's disagreement with this powerful consensus was essentially philosophical. He had used the Pythagorean rather than the Aristotelian approach successfully to furnish a mathematical description of motion along inclined planes. That is, he aimed at and achieved a mathematical description rather than a metaphysical explanation. Now Galileo wanted to do the same for the motions of heavenly bodies. For that project, the self-satisfied Aristotelian "motion derives from a thing's rational nature" approach was merely an inquiry stopper. So Galileo set it aside and sought for the mathematical description, which he felt sure must be lurking behind the scenes.

From the point of view of the natural philosophy of the day, Galileo was blithely ignoring the intellectual's responsibility to *explain* motions; a mere mathematical *description* could never possibly be metaphysically satisfying. Both viewpoints were worthy, of course, and the argument between them persists in a host of forms down to the present day. Metaphysical explanations of natural phenomena are needed but scientific inquiry can get bogged down prematurely if it seeks them. Galileo could not have seen in his time how strongly ramified his instincts about this would be in succeeding centuries, as physics more and more confined itself to mathematized description and prediction. His confident dismissal of his Aristotelian rivals' insights seems brash and premature as a result. But he was prescient in the sense that science became built around the principle of advancing research programs, leaving science-stopping metaphysical theories to philosophers and theologians.

Galileo's gamble also paid off in the sense that his work did in fact fund the subsequent mathematical description of the tangled night sky by Johannes Kepler and Isaac Newton. None would have been more thrilled by this achievement than Pythagoras. He must have spent a great deal of time staring at the night sky and wondering what mathematical secrets it held. With Galileo's conceptual shift of picturing planets orbiting the sun, Kepler was able to apply Tycho Brahe's incredibly precise observations to derive three mathematical laws of planetary motion. After that, Newton was able to unify those three laws with the laws of terrestrial gravity under a single inverse-square law of gravitation. This explained everything at once, in the particular sense of using an elegant mathematical theory to explain existing observations and make predictions about the future.

Of course, the Aristotelian demand for another type of explanation persisted, and still persists to this day. At this level, which these days would be located within the philosophy of physics rather than within physics itself, there are many complications. Galileo was dismissive of valid calls for explanations of planetary motions, which his theory could not provide. Brahe regarded a sun-centered planetary system merely as a convenient device for calculation, not as a true description of the system's mechanics, which he continued to conceive in Aristotelian terms as ideal circular motions. Kepler was a Neoplatonist who wanted the sun at the center of the planetary system for religious reasons. Newton could not make any sense of gravitational action at a distance and was deeply frustrated by the fact that his mathematical theory of gravitation seemed to entail it. Moreover, he realized that previous competing ways of speaking about the planetary system—with the earth at the center or with the sun at the center—were both oversimplifications because multibody systems gravitate around their center of mass, not around a favored object. At the level of metaphysical explanation, Galileo set the cat among the pigeons, and things have never since been as well organized as they were in the Aristotelian natural philosophy of his day.

Despite their varying metaphysical expectations and assumptions, all of these scientists were united in experiencing the thrill of seeing the mathematical secrets of the apparent design of the night sky yield to their prodigious efforts. Such is the power of the cosmological form of the design argument: it overcomes other metaphysical disagreements and consolidates consensus around the basic point that the planetary system is intelligently designed. As usual, these scientists pictured the intelligent designer in the terms that suited them. In the era of Galileo and Newton, it was a mathematical creator God, whose very language was mathematics and who hid within the orderly but strange motions of heavenly objects the mathematical evidence to show beyond a shadow of a doubt that it was all God's beautiful handiwork. More elaborated religious convictions merely rang the changes on this basic picture.

For example, Newton became extremely worried about the fact that he could not mathematically demonstrate the stability of even a three-body system, let alone a system as complex as the solar system. Supremely confident that his mathematical failure showed a design flaw, he proposed that the mathematical designer God must occasionally reach into the system to adjust planetary trajectories slightly to prevent devastating collisions. Nothing less than such supernatural intervention could ever do justice to Newton's ideal of divine providence. Subsequently, using a kind of perturbation theory, Gottfried Leibniz solved the mathematical puzzle that Newton had not. But not even Leibniz could rule out collisions between bodies within our complicated planetary system.

This brings us to the close of the first phase of the modern form of the cosmological design argument. We are left with a strange tension between widespread religious beliefs about God, on the one hand, and what the apparent design of the solar system can support by way of inference to an intelligent designer, on the other. Perhaps this God can't design a system to avoid planetary collisions, in which case we naturally worry about God's power. Perhaps God can design a perpetually stable solar system but simply chose not to, in which case we worry about God's providential intentions. Perhaps this is the best of all possible worlds, and God merely miraculously adjusts things from time to time in the name of merciful providence, in which case we worry whether this sort of supernatural intervention is really coherent. Or perhaps this nest of difficulties just shows that there is no design inference to be drawn, that we should content ourselves with the mathematical description and forego indulging the Aristotelian metaphysical instinct for a deeper explanation.

Meanwhile, I suspect that Pythagoras would be wondering what all the fuss is about. Can't those early modern scientists see that their ideas of God are the problem, not the design inference? Instead of trying to force the cosmos to match a preconceived notion of God, or a preconceived notion of a Godless reality, it is better to allow a minimalist form of the design argument to lead us to a morally ambiguous yet aesthetically intense vision of the mathematical depth structures of reality. That line of inference does not take us as far, but it carries us more surely and in a manner less dependent on the specifics of active religious traditions.

The next major phase in the development of the cosmological design argument began in the middle of the twentieth century with the discovery of so-called big-bang cosmology. Things have moved quickly since that time. At this stage—and this is astonishing given the longer history of the design argument—even quite intricate moves in physical cosmology that once would have been too minor to affect anything in philosophy, now have profound implications for the cosmological form of the design argument.

People have often underestimated the inferential complexities in moving from big-bang cosmology to philosophy and theology. For example, in 1951 after Edwin Hubble's observational confirmation of big-bang cosmology, Pope Pius XII issued an allocution asserting that the big bang confirmed the Catholic Church's teaching about the divine creation of the universe. Years later, in a 1978 article for the *New York Times*, astronomer Robert Jastrow wrote that scientists through their arduous labors had accidentally confirmed what religious folk had naively believed all along—namely, that God created the world from nothing.[13] Both forms of enthusiasm (delighted or frustrated, as the case may be) were premature.

The intricate changes in physical cosmology over the last three decades have impacted the prospects for the cosmological wing of the design argument several times. After the acceptance even among some astronomers of the design argument's relevance, described above, Stephen Hawking developed a slightly different and empirically equivalent account of the big bang, in which there is no mathematical singularity at $t=0$.[14] The singularity results from running the cosmological equations backwards toward $t=0$. It was the singularity that got everyone excited about signs of cosmic design, reasoned Hawking, so it is quite reasonable to expect that the elimination of the singularity should reduce everyone's excitement. Indeed, it did, and theologians who kept up with physics were forced to rely more heavily on cosmological dependence arguments (for example, where did the laws of nature come from?) than on design arguments as such.

That soon changed with the expanding awareness of the philosophical and theological significance of cosmological fine tuning. Scientists work with numerous constants in their mathematical theorizing efforts. Constants express the strength of the electromagnetic and gravitational forces, the electron-proton mass ratio, the electron charge, and so on. There are dozens of constants such as these and they appear to be independent of one another, in the sense that setting one through a hypothetical physical process does nothing to influence others. By imaginatively varying each constant within the theoretical edifice of the big bang, it was soon discovered that the suite of constants appears to be fine tuned for carbon-based life. Even quite small changes in most of the constants produce a lifeless universe—one with no stars, for example, or one with no chemistry.[15]

This impression of a universe fine-tuned for life as we know it propelled proponents of the design argument into dizzying heights of rapture. Finally, science has discovered the very fingerprints of God! The cartoon picture of a designer God in a white lab coat turning knobs on some universe-creation machine to get things just right fell far short of popular theism's portrayal of a loving, attentive, active deity. But, in an era when some religious people feared for the very continuation of belief in God, the advent of cosmological fine tuning was a great relief, no matter what sort of designer God was implicated. Our existence, at least in general terms, was foreseen and planned; we are not alone! It is not difficult even for religious skeptics and brave-new-world humanists to appreciate the existential appeal of what the design argument does with cosmological fine tuning.

Just as Hawking reframed the big-bang singularity to alter the implications for design inferences, however, it was not long before multiverse proposals in theoretical cosmology came along to dampen the fires of enthusiasm burning within the fine-tuning design camp. Hawking was fully aware of the theological implications of what he was doing, and may even have been motivated to explore his imaginary time hypothesis by his hopes for its antidesign theological fruits. By contrast, multiverse proposals in physical cosmology seem not to have been theologically motivated. Inflationary cosmology was an enhancement of big-bang cosmology designed to solve technical and observational problems in standard big-bang cosmology. Inflation proposed a new kind of antigravity force that could get the universe large in much less time than ordinary big-bang cosmology. This mathematical device did its job so well that eventually it was almost universally accepted by cosmologists and astronomers, even though it is difficult to know what to make of the idea of a gravitational repulsion force. A side effect of inflationary theory is that the process of universe expansion, which we call the big bang, should occur repeatedly—in fact, infinitely many times, within a much larger space. Certainly there was no reason to expect that the processes involved would occur only once.[16]

The resulting picture of infinitely many expanding universes was enough to send shivers down the spine of people with lingering anthropocentric beliefs about the meaning and centrality of planet Earth. But one additional hypothesis made all the difference for the design argument. Suppose the set of fundamental cosmological constants was different for each of these universes. In that case, the multiverse scenario would no longer require fine tuning. Eventually, universes with serendipitous sets of fundamental constants would spring up, and conscious, intelligent creatures within that universe would eventually start asking where they came from, just as we do. Gone was the lab-coated, knob-fiddling designer God. In its place was a master universe or multiverse with no need for any design work, at least at the level of cosmology and fundamental constants of physics.

Since the time that inflationary big-bang cosmology accidentally deflated fine-tuning enthusiasm in this way, a number of highly speculative so-called quantum cosmologies have built more sophisticated multiverse frameworks. These frameworks articulate the hypothesis that the set of fundamental constants changes from universe to universe in more compelling ways. For example, one version of string theory proposes a quantum landscape of universes complete with probabilistic quantum rules to determine the way constants in one universe relate to those in already existing universes—something like a cosmic version of radioactive decay.[17]

Are these speculative theories correct? By definition, observation of other universes is impossible. Moreover, observation in this universe of features that indirectly support multiverse hypotheses against competitor views is proving extremely tricky. But the sheer fact that there is a plausible scenario for the origin of the universe we know, which does not require cosmological fine tuning or intentional design, has had an immediate and profound effect on the design argument. It is important to keep in mind that the rapid flapping evident on the cosmological wing of the design argument probably means that things will change yet again before long.

The biological wing of the design argument has been far more controversial than the cosmological wing. It is also much more complicated logically and conceptually. The main reason for this difference in complexity is simply that we can easily picture what a designer entity might have to do to produce a fine-tuned universe (that is, twist the ontological equivalent of knobs controlling fundamental physical constants) but it is relatively difficult to conceive of what such a designer entity would have to do to make biological life. Is this a matter of supernaturally assembling key organic macromolecules, or getting existing macromolecules together at the right place and time, or making eyes and optic nerves from out of thin air? In other words, the complexity difference derives from the fact that the causal mechanics of nature are more complex and more densely articulated in the biological case than in the cosmological case. But this increased complexity in the biological case also makes the design hypothesis more difficult to falsify and thus easier to sustain in the face of scientific objections. This in turn is why intelligent design theory has a prominent political face while fine-tuning design theory does not.

As with the cosmological wing of the design argument, the biological wing is ancient. Aristotle repeatedly makes the case for design in his numerous biological writings.[18] He invokes principles such as "Nature makes the organs for the function, and not the function for the organs"[19]; "Nature never fails nor does anything in vain so far as is possible in each case"[20]; "Nature creates nothing without a purpose, but always the best possible in each kind of living creature by reference to its essential constitution"[21]; and "Nature never makes anything that is superfluous."[22] His reasoning is bizarre at times, but his observations and taxonomies are stunning, to put it mildly—so stunning that they stood with only minor modifications and elaborations for well over two thousand years. His philosophical imagination is extremely impressive, also. In *Physics*, he *states the central thesis of evolutionary theory* (random variation and natural selection) and then refutes it using an ancient version of what is now called the "design inference."[23]

Of course, Aristotle did not see a personal designer God at the root of all the apparent design in the biological world. He saw a vast teleological organism in which every part operated according to its inbuilt nature, expressed in its form. Behind it all was a prime mover, but this was more like a life principle of the entire cosmic organism than a conscious, agential designer. By contrast, William Paley's famous 1802 form of the biological design argument contended that apparent design in nature not only justifies inference to a personal, conscious, intentional, intelligent designer deity, but also guarantees God's moral goodness and providential loving kindness.[24]

This contrast between Aristotle's and Paley's designers, by itself, demonstrates that the biological wing of the design argument, if it works at all, can take the philosopher in many different theological directions. For this reason, intelligent design theorists of our day are wise to back away from overconfident stipulations about the sort of God we can infer from apparent design in nature and focus instead solely on the generic concept of an intelligent designer. We can frame this generic idea in a host of ways—from Paley's personal God (which most intelligent design theorists would prefer) to Aristotle's life principle of a cosmic organism (which many might find distasteful).

In its contemporary form, the biological design argument centers on the inference from apparent design in nature to intelligent design. This is far more modest an inference than Paley had in mind but the basic logic persists. Something looks intelligently designed when its complexity perfectly matches its distinctive function. Intelligent design theorists call this "specified complexity."[25] The existence of evolutionary theory means that the mere feeling of amazement when beholding specified complexity (such as an eye or a molecular mechanism) does not count as evidence for intelligent design, in the sense of nonevolutionary design. This feeling did count for Paley, however, who appealed to it to dismiss the possibility that chance could explain something as intricately organized as the eye. Despite protestations to the contrary, the feeling of awe in the face of specified complexity may persist as a vital factor behind the scenes in forming the guiding convictions and core hypothesis of contemporary intelligent design theorists. The Paley-style appeal to amazement surfaces rather often in literature from that domain. As the best intelligent design theorists clearly recognize, amazement is not the right criterion, and should not be relevant, for detecting intelligent design. The theory of emergent complexity working through evolution, if correct, produces these very results, and reactions of amazement along with them.

Not only must the biological design argument bracket emotional reactions such as awe and amazement; it must also accept that it is futile to attempt to identify mechanistic, causal means by which intelligent design works in biological systems. This is the domain of the biological sciences, not philosophy, and in that domain the descriptive and explanatory approaches of the sciences reign supreme. Fundamentalist "creation science" has indulged intricate speculations about the causal mechanisms whereby an active deity supposedly got things done in the world. But, if we are to speak of natural causes and events at all, science is our best tool, and indeed our only reliable tool, for isolating them, describing them, and authenticating them. In other words, either science discovers that the so-called young-earth creationists are right about the six thousand-year age of the earth, or the claim has no standing in debates about the nature of the earth.

With amazement and the investigation of causal mechanisms not available to the biological design argument—and with its inferential target contracted from Paley's grand and good God to a vaguely understood intelligent designer—it is easy to see that the argument is now more modest than ever. It is also more under pressure than ever from the natural sciences. These days, it operates not positively—with explanations of how intelligent design works—but negatively, as a philosophical explanation of scientific ignorance. Of course, scientific ignorance is transitory, which produces embarrassing situations from time to time. Several times now, intelligent design theorists have said that biology has no explanation for phenomenon X, and then within a few years (or months!) a biological explanation for X arrives on the scene. This then forces the design argument to shift ground constantly. With each shift, confidence in the strategy of explaining transitory scientific ignorance dissipates.

In effect, the biologists hold all the cards and those wanting to argue on behalf of the biological design argument just have to wait to see what is played; they have no cards of their own to play. To shift analogies, the proponent of the biological design argument in our time is akin to a person standing on a sand island in a rising tide. He or she is betting that the ocean of science won't cover the wondrous sand of specified complexity. Scientists, strictly speaking, should be indifferent to whether or not the ocean eventually covers the sand island. But they are rightly confident that their methods are the only ones pertinent to deciding the question.

To bolster their case, intelligent design theorists in our era launch arguments from probability. The probabilities are drawn from evolutionary theory, naturally, and the calculations attempt to estimate the unlikelihood that evolutionary theory can explain a particular instance of specified complexity (such as a human eye or the biomolecular machinery of the flagellum). To the extent that the probability of successful explanation on the terms of the evolutionary hypothesis is extremely small, intelligent design theorists conclude that the competing hypothesis of an intelligent designer is confirmed.

The difficulty here is obviously that the probability calculations are utterly dependent on our knowledge of biochemistry and evolutionary theory. As scientists working in these fields learn more about biochemical processes—which they do, in huge leaps, virtually every day—the probability calculations change. For example, if we don't understand the mechanisms of protein folding, we will estimate the probability of a usefully shaped protein forming by chance as "astronomically small." But, as we learn about cellular protein folding mechanisms, the same probability estimate changes to "almost inevitable." Such probability estimates are too volatile to be of much value at the present time. Moreover, the direction of change in probability estimates is not both up and down; it is monotonically increasing over time, which dramatically weighs against the intelligent design hypothesis.

This account of the cosmological and biological wings of the design argument shows that both have struggled to stabilize themselves in relation to rapidly shifting scientific data and theories. In both cases, it is possible to give up on the physicotheological strategy of drawing inferences from apparent design and simply resort to the cosmotheological strategy of drawing inference from dependence. After all, that dependence relation persists even if every instance of apparent design in nature proves useless for theological inference.

With the advent of multiverse theory, and with the rapid advance of biochemistry and evolutionary theory, the prospects for the design argument look bleak—in the sense not of hopeless but of not achieving a stabilizing breakthrough. For the immediate future, it will probably remain a much talked about but finally a philosophically unsatisfying form of religious philosophical argumentation. This suits some religious philosophers, particularly those uninterested in a theological account of ultimate reality that is remotely like a personal designer deity. I count myself among them. For us, literary accounts of the wonders of the cosmos and the biosphere are more compelling than the probability estimates of intelligent design theorists.

The Psychotheological Tradition

The psychotheological tradition focuses on human nature, and particularly on human conscious experience and altered states of consciousness. Its fundamental intellectual instinct is that human consciousness is the best tool to employ in a quest to understand ultimacy.

The first three traditions of religious philosophy are better defined than the others in the context of Western philosophy. This is mostly due to the fact that they host centerpiece arguments that establish long-lasting lines of interpretation and debate. By comparison, the psychotheological, axiotheological, and mysticotheological traditions of religious philosophy are more diffuse in the West. Yet they have appeared in many of the world's philosophical cultures with great impact. In fact, in South Asian philosophy, no tradition of religious philosophy is more definitive of the central project, or is more intricately developed, than the psychotheological tradition. Western philosophy registers most of the key questions and concepts somewhere. But they achieve the status only of fascinating eddies peripheral to its central currents.

The West's physical orientation began early with the Milesian philosopher-physicists. It accelerated powerfully through Aristotle's observation-based science, and culminated in the birth of the modern natural sciences. This spectacular trajectory yielded a predictable problem that resists solution using traditional Western concepts and tools: the mind-body problem. What exactly is the relationship of the physical world to our first-person experience of consciousness? Every now and again a Western philosopher faces the problem squarely and makes a specific proposal. René Descartes did this when he tentatively suggested that the pineal gland might be the connecting point between consciousness and the bodily nature of human beings.[26] Quite apart from the inaccuracy of Descartes' speculative suggestion, and the complexities of interpreting Descartes on this issue, his tentative proposal is not satisfactory even as a *type* of solution to the mind-body problem. But he seems to have recognized the difficulty.

These kinds of solutions have embarrassed later Western philosophers, but it is not as if many have done any better. At the turn of the twentieth and twenty-first centuries, it was common to see mainstream philosophical books with *consciousness* in the title, yet containing between the covers neither a solution to the mind-body problem nor much substantive discussion of consciousness.[27] Some have even proposed to eliminate the phenomena of consciousness altogether from the inventory of real things.[28] Denying that consciousness has any ontological standing releases them from the obligation to furnish a philosophical explanation for it. It is easy to appreciate the attractiveness of such a strategy, and there certainly are enough problems with folk-psychological interpretations of human experience to invite systematic deconstruction. But the elephant is still in the philosophers' room. As other philosophers from C.D. Broad to John Searle have pointed out, the "problem of consciousness" can't be eliminated by stipulating that consciousness is not there, and this remains so no matter how misleading folk psychology is.[29] The painfully obvious upshot of all this is that mainstream forms of Western philosophy are at a total loss to explain consciousness.[30]

To South Asian philosophers who have not surrendered wholesale to the influence of British analytical philosophy in India, this agonized writhing of Western philosophers over the problem of consciousness has a funny side. It is always psychically painful to deny obvious failure, yet there is always a chance that something might come along to produce a solution that turns failure into success, thus making the pain worthwhile. But that is not going to happen in this case. The predominant physicalist stream within Western philosophy just does not have what it takes. And that is so obvious that the refusal to accept this painful fact of philosophical life seems comically stubborn.

Not all modern Western philosophers have been so obdurate. For example, William James, Alfred North Whitehead, and Charles Hartshorne are famous representatives of a group that realized something was awry in the foundations of Western philosophical ontology. Each took consciousness seriously by pairing the mental with the physical in a dipolar ontology. True to form, however, the mainstream of Western philosophy has paid little attention to these philosophers. At this point, the comedic writhing threatens to become corruption.

Meanwhile, for at least twenty-five hundred years, with few interruptions or divergences, South Asian philosophy has approached reality from the other side of the mental-physical polar contrast. Consciousness, the great Indian philosophers contended, is the most obviously real aspect of life. As such, it is the doorway into understanding everything important, from human nature to ultimate reality. This emphasis made South Asian cultures fertile soil for the introspective study of human psychology, for elaborating an intricate phenomenology of conscious states, and for developing powerful theories of enlightenment.

The ancient Cārvāka philosophers famously dissented from this consensus. In fact, they are remembered specifically for that unwelcome dissent, as their name indicates; Cārvāka was a villain in the epic

Mahābhārata. This tells us something important about the strength of the consensus. The modern grand narratives of the history of Indian philosophy list Cārvāka among the unorthodox schools (*nāstika*) and never fail to point out that the conceptual experiment in materialism and atheism failed utterly. Their disappearance is recounted as an object lesson for those who might be tempted to replicate the materialist mistake.

The influence of British analytical philosophy on Indian philosophy during the twentieth century was another moment in which the consensus broke. But this was especially because the traditional Indian concern with consciousness seemed ill-suited for engaging the modern world of science and technology and nation-states. Indeed, in some ways, this remains so. Yet the traditional concerns persisted, both within Indian universities and beyond them in ashram-based Indian educational settings. The failure of Western philosophy to solve the hard problem of consciousness from within its physicalist framework suggests that there may be some wisdom in the South Asian approach.

The key moment in the history of South Asian philosophy's journey with consciousness was the composing of the Upaniṣads in the centuries surrounding 500 BCE. One of the many revolutionary transformations of the so-called axial age in the history of religions, the Upaniṣads won a place within Vedic literature partly by contesting it. The Vedas recount the actions of the Gods in the events of nature, in the cycle of the seasons, and in human affairs. They rejoice in the materiality and sensuality of reality and celebrate the intense extremities of human experience. They commend hymns of praise and sacrifices to appease the Gods and win salvation.

By contrast, the Upaniṣads teach the pious to seek for the one spiritual principle behind the changing appearances of worldly experience. They urge detachment from the shifting shadows of reality and from distorting emotional entanglements. They claim that this ultimate reality (Brahman) is most deeply present within the individual soul (*Ātman*) and that journeying inward through the landscape of human consciousness defines the path to salvation. In fact, they assert an identity between Brahman and *Ātman*. To know oneself is precisely to know the ultimate. The "*Ātman* is Brahman" affirmation lies at the root of subsequent South Asian philosophy. It radicalizes the prevailing view of consciousness and centralizes it as the vehicle for gaining both experiential wisdom and philosophical understanding of anything and everything.

The fifteen principal Upaniṣads are also known as Vedānta, which means the end of the Vedas—a reference to their culminating status as well as their temporal location in Vedic literature. The Vedānta school of Indian philosophy, one of the six orthodox schools (*āstika*), thus takes its name from the Upaniṣads. This school traces its origins to Bādarāyana, one of the many scholars who tried to organize and systematize the sprawling Vedas in the fifth century BCE. Bādarāyana's *Brahmasūtras* was a well-organized collection of easy-to-remember aphorisms intended to help students learn the significance of the Vedic material, which they committed to memory. Among other things, the *Brahmasūtras* gather together what the Vedas have to say about Brahman. Taking the Upaniṣadic material as their synthesizing cue, they show that the material concerning Brahman is consistent and conceptually robust; they then explain its significance for the religious end of salvation, understood as unity with Brahman. Bādarāyana's achievement was profoundly influential as a way of making sense of the Vedas and Upaniṣads.

The locus classicus for the Vedānta school is Śankara (flourished in the early ninth century), and particularly his commentaries on the Upaniṣads and his commentary on the *Brahmasūtras*. Śankara brought philosophical sophistication to Bādarāyana's regularization of the Upaniṣadic worldview, and creatively formed it into a powerful and coherent system of thought. Like Bādarāyana, Śankara's monism affirms that all is Brahman, which is deeply problematic given the differentiated and complex character of human experience in the world. Unlike Bādarāyana, however, Śankara sought to explain in some detail how the experiential world of diverse appearances can arise from the unity of Brahman.

Śankara's main conceptual device for doing this is a process of cognitive correction, by which human beings rectify and refine judgments. This process of rectification causes us to see what is familiar in a broader and richer context, which makes it newly unfamiliar while also preserving it in a reframed way. For example, Śankara holds that we can learn to see our experience of differentiation between subject and object (perceiver versus perceived) as a limited perspective on a reality that is more adequately grasped as wholly one, beyond subject-object distinctions. This idea of rectification of perception or belief allows Śankara to discriminate less from more accurate perception. This in turn allows him to establish an ontological hierarchy in which lower realities are still present, but somehow sublated, in higher realities.

Coordinating ontological sublation with epistemological rectification in this way furnishes a potent framework for religious philosophy. Śankara points the way simultaneously to Brahman, in which everything is ultimately sublated, and to enlightenment, in which human consciousness achieves this ultimate awareness. This ties philosophy and religion intimately together. To master states of human consciousness and the vagaries of perception is, in this view, to know the absolute, to be one with Brahman, and to achieve liberation from the tyranny of attachment and delusion. Brahman is conceived as having no determinate attributes (*nirguṇa* Brahman). This reflects the Upaniṣadic assertion that negation (*neti neti*) is the best way to speak of ultimate reality. Intense introspection of states of consciousness, under the guidance of a wise teacher, discloses these attachments and delusions, and propels the mind toward its own fundamental ground and true identity: Brahman. Philosophy and religion alike are matters of Brahman finding itself, again and again.

If Bādarāyana's organized presentation of the Upaniṣadic teachings on Brahman triggered endlessly fascinating debates, then Śankara's systematization set the standard for philosophic rigor in conducting those debates. Moreover, Śankara inspired responses specifically designed to correct what subsequent Vedānta thinkers regarded as errors or distortions in his system. Śankara's system became known as nondual, or *advaita* Vedānta, which reflects his emphasis on describing the whole of reality from the imagined unitary perspective of the absolute, in which all entities and relations are sublated. Among numerous alternative viewpoints within the Vedānta school, the two most well known are the dualist (*dvaita*) school (*Tattvavāda* or True Philosophy) of Madhvacharya (flourished in the late thirteenth century), and the qualified nondualism (*vishishtādvaita*) of Rāmānuja (flourished in the early twelfth century).

The dualist view (*dvaita*) asserts that the ultimate ontological inventory contains more than Brahman alone. In fact, there are ontologically basic distinctions among and between the various insentient things, the various souls, and God. The religious goal for dualists is not the advaitan's unity with Brahman but rather a loving relationship with God thought of as creator (*Īśvara*). The epistemological upshot of this is to protect the integrity of ordinary experience—without which, the dualists contend, there is no point or value in life at all. In this view, therefore, the contents of consciousness can be taken more or less at face value as indicating what is ultimately real and religiously important. We do not need to debunk the illusions of conscious experience, such as the distinction between subject and object, in order to gain a correct and spiritually transformative understanding of reality. We can achieve these goals simply by examining our conscious experience in a straightforward way.

The qualified nondualist view (*vishishtādvaita*) takes up middle ground between the extremes, conceptually, though historically Rāmānuja presented it before Madhvacharya gave the dualist view definitive expression. Rāmānuja affirmed a God with determinate characteristics and a personal nature (*saguṇa* Brahman). He also affirmed the reality of the entities and relations of perceptual experience. But he qualified these assertions by saying that the entities and relations of perceptual experience could not exist without Brahman; they were ontologically dependent on their creator. Thus, Brahman could still be one and ultimate, even while the reality of the ordinary objects and events of daily life could be taken seriously and literally. The task of philosophical introspection and religious meditation in this case is to discern this dependence. That is, phenomenological analysis of the subject-object distinction in human experience should produce not knowledge of unity beneath delusion (as in *advaita*), nor support for straightforward ontological plurality (as in *dvaita*), but rather evidence of ontological dependence. This prompts us to affirm both the conditional reality of the world of experiential distinctions and the ultimate vesting of this world in the unconditioned reality of the divine creator.

A key point of dispute among these views is the interpretation of ignorance (*avidyā*). This goes to the heart of the way the psycho-theological tradition works in the context of South Asian religious philosophy, and indeed elsewhere in the world. Overcoming *avidyā* is a shared goal, of course, but the meaning of *avidyā* varies dramatically among the various thinkers. In Śankara, ignorance virtually causes the phenomenal world. Human beings misperceive themselves as self-contained identities due to ignorance. They read similarities and distinctions out of ignorance. They judge what is important and attach themselves to ideals and goals out of ignorance. As a result, they are deeply confused about what is real and what is merely apparent. Overcoming ignorance means paying extremely close attention to patterns of perception and inference so as to discern what is real in and through the flow of appearances. Śankara was supremely confident that human experience contains within itself clues sufficient to guide the seeker out of the illusions and self-delusions of *avidyā*, and thus to see that all is Brahman. The Vedas and wise teachers play crucial stimulating roles but everything they urge is confirmed in the subtlest and truest contours of actual experience.

In the dualist and qualified nondualist views, ignorance is less creative than this. It is a problem to be overcome, to be sure, because it generates misperceptions that cause suffering and bar our path to spiritual liberation. But both Rāmānuja and Madhvacharya affirm the reality of the phenomenal world, with varying degrees of dependence on the creator Īshvara. For them, ignorance does not cause these things to have the ontologically distinct appearance they possess for the untutored mind; it merely masks the true nature of the relation between Brahman and the world of dependently real particulars. Rāmānuja and Madhvacharya agree with Śankara that the path of knowledge (*jñāna yoga*) is a valid way to overcome ignorance, and that human beings possess enough clues in their ordinary experience to lead them to the freedom of undistorted knowledge of Brahman even under the limitations of this life. But Śankara ranks the path of knowledge above the other traditional Hindu paths of devotion (*bhakti yoga*) and action (*karma yoga*). Unsurprisingly, Rāmānuja and Madhvacharya do not follow Śankara in this regard, because they do not ascribe to ignorance the powers that he does. Judgments about the powers of ignorance and the goal of overcoming it directly affect the way that philosophers implement the psychotheological tradition of religious philosophy in practice.

The disputes among these three viewpoints, and the numerous others that meditation on the Upaniṣads produced, display distinctive patterns. There is logical and linguistic analysis, much as in the West. But the authority of the Vedas and especially of the Upaniṣads was more prominent for South Asian philosophers than the authority of religious texts was for Western philosophers. The latter drew a sharper distinction between philosophy and religion than their counterparts in South Asia did—a distinction based on the more limited role of sacred scriptures in guiding reasoning. In the West, religious reasoning honors the authority of sacred scriptures but philosophy does not. Not so in India. Moreover, introspection and analysis of states of consciousness played a much larger role in South Asian philosophy than it did at every stage of the Western philosophical tradition.

The psychotheological tradition appears in Western philosophy in numerous ways, all relatively muted and scattered by comparison with the South Asian philosophy. In ancient Greece, Parmenides affirmed that all is one and that change is illusory, which is a claim befitting the much later Śankara. The Neoplatonists and especially Plotinus articulated a vision of the one and the many that is remarkably similar to Śankara's—including conceptual devices such as negation for describing the One, correction of epistemological distortions, and something akin to sublation for making sense of the ontological relation between the ultimate One and the proximate many. But these viewpoints are better thought of as contributions to the mysticotheological tradition of religious philosophy (see below) because they do not centralize human psychology and states of consciousness to the degree that Indian philosophy does.

Closer to the mark are thinkers who explicitly built psychological modes of reflection into their philosophic approach. Augustine wrote his *Confessions* in the form of a personal address to God, which involved intense spiritual and philosophical introspection. Similarly, Anselm often conducted his philosophical reflection in prayer, and sometimes wrote in the form of prayer. The peculiar form of Anselm's ontological argument in the *Proslogion* derives directly from its emphasis on states of consciousness—such as doubting and entertaining and certainty—and his belief that things can *exist* in consciousness even if they do not exist in reality. Admittedly these are relatively rare exceptions to the Western pattern. By contrast, it has been common in South Asia to combine philosophical inquiry with analytical meditation. This only makes sense, given the generic influence of the Upaniṣads on Indian philosophy. To see and to know truly is necessarily to be enlightened. But these examples do show that South Asian questions do have a presence in Western philosophy.

There was a moment when the South Asian perspective took deeper root in Western philosophy. It was the so-called "turn to the subject" of modern philosophy, associated particularly with John Locke and Immanuel Kant.[31] As the phrase rightly suggests, early modern philosophy approached questions about reality by examining the way human beings understand and experience the world. Careful introspection and analysis of states of consciousness produced a host of epistemological insights in Locke's and Kant's writings. And just as in South Asian philosophy, those epistemological insights collectively constituted a critique of the reflexive, everyday understanding of reality and thus of the speculations of philosophers who rely on such everyday understandings.

The introspective analyses of Locke and Kant do not approach the intensity of introspection in Indian philosophy. Kantian philosophers do not have to become experts in meditation in order to discern their distinctions. Even the prodigious phenomenological disciplines of Edmund Husserl and his followers do not achieve the intensity that follows from linking spiritual liberation to philosophical understanding. Yet there is impressive precision in Western introspective philosophy. It lacks the traditional Indian confidence in the validity of philosophical inferences drawn from introspective observation of states of consciousness. The resulting skepticism has sometimes paralyzed creative philosophical work, particularly in ontology and theology. But this has probably proved to be a virtue overall. Certainly the more cautious Western approach serves as a healthy contrast to the more confident South Asian approach.

One of the most interesting Western ventures in the psychotheological tradition of religious philosophy is the German idealism of contemporaries Johann Fichte (1762–1814), Georg Hegel (1770–1831), and Friedrich Schelling (1775–1854). The starting point for these thinkers was Kant. Kant's philosophy introspectively analyzes the operations of perception and cognition. This is how it both makes discoveries about, and adumbrates limitations on, the capacities of human reason, with associated critiques of psychology, ontology, and theology (corresponding to self, world, and God). But Kant does not say much about the perspective from which this analysis is made. The host of analyzed perceptions and cognitions and judgments is the very subject that inspired the phrase "turn to the subject." But what precisely is this subject? This was probably the most Indian question ever asked in Western philosophy, a sure sign that the time was ripe for a revolutionary new perspective. Fichte answered that it is the ego and the absolute idealists went on in various ways to elaborate something akin to a Western version of the Upaniṣadic affirmation that *Ātman* is Brahman—the ego is the Absolute.

The Hegelian version of this is probably best known and certainly most influential.[32] With confidence befitting Śankara and Rāmānuja, Hegel concluded that disciplined introspection disclosed something utterly extraordinary behind the ordinary appearances of life. The Absolute is not beyond or opposed to the world but it is the world—the "what" of the world as well as its "how" and "why." Its most intense expression is human rational consciousness and its richest expression is world history itself. In the world process, the Absolute strives for a kind of self-consciousness, which it achieves in human self-consciousness. This claim would not be so striking if the philosophical literature of the West took its rise from the Upaniṣads. In the Western context, however, it was and is stunning.

The philosophical and political consequences of absolute idealism were immeasurable. Some so-called right-wing Hegelians saw in Hegel's system, and particularly in his view of the incarnation of Jesus Christ, precisely the revolutionary interpretation of Christian theology for which they had been seeking. Other right-wing thinkers discerned the longed-for rationale for affirming national identity against the travails of modernity. Meanwhile, the so-called left-wing Hegelians received Hegel's diagnosis of human consciousness as a call to arms, enshrining the virtue of authenticity as they rooted out all forms of false consciousness—whether in politics or religion, society or morality.

This early modern flourishing of the psychotheological tradition in the West was intense and short-lived, quickly transmuting into a host of other projects. If its presence in South Asian philosophy is like a candle's steady flame, then in the West it was akin to a brilliant fireworks display. The Upaniṣadic qualities of absolute idealism proved unable to carve much of a foothold in the dominant forms of Western cultural and religious imagination. Similarly, the early medieval experiments with prayerful philosophic introspection did not catch on but split apart into spiritual disciplines and rational disciplines.

The Western habits of mind underlying these historic tendencies are doubtless deficient at some level. Admittedly, it is difficult to imagine the West birthing the modern natural sciences without this bias toward the material world of determinate objects and relations, which casually finesses the ego's role as host of interpretation and reason. There is virtue in this form of philosophic negligence. But the West had found it extremely difficult to give consciousness its due, and even to pay patient attention to the facts in this aspect of life. Thus, the psychotheological tradition of religious philosophy still persists mostly in eddies off to the side of the main Western currents, while it continues to define the main current of native South Asian and Buddhist philosophy.

The principal contemporary transformation in the psychotheological tradition of religious philosophy is directly related to the relative skepticism of the West and the relative optimism of South Asia about the epistemological value of states of consciousness. For many centuries prior to the Enlightenment in the West, the question of the reliability of information from states of consciousness, especially information about ultimate realities, seemed to be a matter of opinion, settled arbitrarily within tradition-guided habits of mind. This unattractive specter of intractable disagreement contrasts sharply with the South Asian high-level consensus described above. Through the nineteenth century, however, Western philosophy gradually discovered that the question of the reliability of information from states of consciousness was a partially tractable one. This occurred first through the careful introspection of Enlightenment thinkers already discussed, then through the projection theorists of religion such as David Strauss and Ludwig Feuerbach, and eventually through the birth of analytical psychology with Sigmund Freud and experimental psychology with William James. In the second half of the twentieth century, psychology joined the biological sciences in the ventures of sociobiology and evolutionary psychology, and also combined forces with the cognitive sciences and neurosciences, to produce a compelling empirical picture of the ways in which the human mind is both reliable and unreliable for producing knowledge.

The overall import of this transformation remains to be seen. It is clear that these Western perspectives on human psychology are spreading quickly throughout the world and influencing religious philosophers in every tradition. The Dalai Lama is well-known for urging the usefulness of neuropsychology for understanding the human condition, and most traditions that stress meditation have embraced functional imaging of the brain despite uncertainty about its significance. It is also clear that certain aspects of the reliability-of-consciousness problem are more tractable than others. For example, cognitive psychologists now have a sturdy understanding of the ways that the human brain is liable to make mistakes of perception and inference. This leads to a formal, scientific catalogue of the same cognitive peculiarities that magicians and charlatans have relied on for thousands of years.[33] Yet the questions of most concern to the psychotheological tradition of religious philosophy seem harder to settle.[34]

It seems likely that religious philosophers can leverage the new sciences of the brain and mind to clarify the epistemological significance for their distinctive concerns about the cognitive contents of consciousness—at least to some degree and in some ways. The complexities and uncertainties notwithstanding, therefore, this is an extremely fertile time for the psychotheological tradition of religious philosophy, even in the West.

The Axiotheological Tradition

The axiotheological tradition focuses on value. Its fundamental intellectual instinct is that moral and aesthetic valuing participates in and reflects value that has ontological standing independent of value judgments, value judges, and value contexts; and that ultimacy is best understood as the ground of this value.

If there is a single tradition of philosophy that pervades the history of Chinese thought, it is probably political philosophy. But the axiotheological tradition of religious philosophy runs a close second. The intricate network of Chinese cultural worlds has typically hesitated to speak of a single creator God, as in West Asia, and has displayed little sympathy for the impracticalities of theological speculations about the ultimate unity of the world with its ontological ground, as in South Asia. Rather, Chinese religious philosophy from the time of its classic founding documents has stressed the recognition and cultivation of value at every level of the human project, from individual spiritual quests to shared adventures in creating civilizations. Thus, even political philosophy can be construed as deeply related to the traditional axiological interests of Chinese thought. It is illuminating to sketch some of the development of this type of thinking within Chinese philosophy.

Prior to the axial-age burst of fecundity in Chinese religious philosophy around 500 BCE, a number of writings were important to sages. Of these, several were employed extensively and also supposedly edited by Confucius, thus giving rise to a canon of the *Five Classics* (*Wǔjīng* or *Wu Ching* or 五經 or 五经). The *Five Classics* have been preserved down to the present day—with the *Classic of Music* (*Yuèjīng* or *Yüeh Ching* or 樂經 or 乐经), commonly regarded as a sixth classic, substantially lost by the time of the Han Dynasty (*Hàn Cháo* or *Han Ch'ao* or 漢朝 or 汉朝; 206 BCE–220 CE). This was also the time during which the *Five Classics* achieved their canonical status. Each of the surviving five books exercised a profound impact on the development of the axiological tradition of religious philosophy in this part of the world.

The *Classic of Poetry* (*Shījīng* or *Shih Ching* or 詩經 or 诗经) is an organized collection of 305 poems. This work spurred several commentarial traditions within which the meaning of the poems is discussed and the connection to value and virtue becomes extremely clear. The dominant school of interpretation was that of the Mao (毛), and their edition includes commentarial prefaces encapsulating their reading of each poem's ethical and historical significance. The pattern is more or less the same throughout: a poem is taken to be about some virtue that is vital for sagehood and social health, and the poem is usually linked to a well-known political figure who exemplifies either the achievement or the failure to achieve the virtue in question.

The *Classic of History* (*Shūjīng* or *Shu Ching* or 書經 or 书经) gathers documents from ancient China into fifty-eight chapters, recounting the circumstances surrounding the rise and fall of dynasties and the great and not-so-great deeds of emperors. Like the *Classic of Poetry*, the *Classic of History* is laced with moral meanings and handy historical lessons. The central message is that there is a direct connection between virtue and success. In particular, political and social flourishing directly depend on the moral quality of the ruler, who must cultivate virtue and prize above all the welfare of the people. This kind of ruler also enjoys personal power, great wealth, long life, and happiness.

The *Spring and Autumn Annals* (*Chūn Qiū* or *Ch'un Ch'iu* or 春秋), also known as *Linjing* (*Línjīng* or *Lin Ching* or 麟經 or 麟经), chronicles events in Confucius's own state of Lu (now part of Shandong Province) from 722–481 BCE. There were many such chronicles in ancient times, but most have not survived. There were also many commentaries on these chronicles, elaborating on the significance of the unfolding events. As with the *Classic of History*, these commentaries routinely draw out the moral significance of the tersely described events, reinforcing the message that statecraft is intimately linked with the virtue of rulers.

The *Classic of Rites* (*Lǐ Jì* or *Li Chi* or 禮記 or 礼记) describes the rites and religious practices common during the Zhou Dynasty (*Zhōu Cháo* or *Chou Ch`ao* or 周朝; 1122–256 BCE). This dynasty is revered as the longest in Chinese history despite its scattered control of Chinese territory, and is also the period during which the philosophical and political classics developed. As received by Confucians, the *Classic of Rites* expresses the role of ritual practices in establishing the proper patterns of behavior founding political success, social harmony, and individual virtue. These linkages between ritual and character, on the one hand, and between ritual and politics, on the other, express typically Confucian instincts and pervade Chinese culture and civilization. But these are not merely practical linkages based on observation. In the *Classic of Rites*, they are given a cosmological frame, expressing the conviction that the entire universe supports and powers these linkages. That is, the axiological quality of human life reflects both cause-and-effect patterns within the world of human affairs and correlations between earthly events and the wider cosmic environment for human life.

The *Classic of Changes* (*Yìjīng* or *I Ching* or 易經 or 易经) presents a systematic analysis of the cosmic-human correlations that the *Classic of Rites* attempts to marshal and control. The practical point of the *Classic of Changes* is that circumstances always change but that meaningful patterns can be detected within the flux of events—this meaning helps anxious human beings adapt to change and inspires them to accept change as an inevitable part of life. The cosmological apparatus for the analysis of the patterns hidden within the flux of events involves the entangling of two complementary primal powers within the cosmos: in traditional terms, the receptive, dark, feminine principle of *yin* and the creative, light, masculine principle of *yang*. Setting aside for now the picture of sex differences that this inspires, the two ideas are mutually correlative and dependent. The *Classic of Changes*, in its fully developed form, presents commentaries and predictions on each of the many ways that yin and yang can combine in a six-slotted arrangement called a hexgram. Each of the six slots in a hexgram holds either a symbol for yin or a symbol for yang, making sixty-four possible combinations. Each hexgram represents a process of change with both cosmic and human significance. Various methods were used to make a selection from among the hexgrams that would be relevant to a particular person or situation or decision, and then the *Classic of Changes* was consulted for guidance. The underlying assumption of correlations between cosmic structures and human circumstances vests the axiological categories of Chinese thought, such as virtue and ritual propriety, with cosmic significance.

Confucius coordinated the diverse insights of the Chinese classics into the *Analects* (*Lúnyǔ* or *Lun yü* or 論語 or 论语), which had as profound a synthesizing and catalyzing effect in China as the Upaniṣads did in India. At the heart of the way of thinking expressed in the *Analects* is the concept of human-heartedness (*rén* or *jen* or 仁), which Confucius conceived as the highest virtue of human life—that for which each person must strive above all, thereby aspiring to be an exemplary virtuous person (*jūnzǐ* or *chun-tzu* or 君子). Confucius was practical in his outlook and recognized that people were not always predisposed to cultivate human heartedness. Thus, he stressed the role of ritual propriety (*lǐ* or *li* or 禮 or 礼) in governing human affairs. Appropriate rituals and practices guide people toward virtue by conditioning them to behave in ways that stabilize society and naturally produce human-heartedness. The Confucian stress on filial piety (*xiào* or *hsiao* or 孝) and deference to elders and rulers derives from this emphasis but its proper meaning encompasses five cardinal relationships (*wǔlún* or *wu-lun* or 五倫 or 五伦): ruler-subject, parent-child, elder brother-younger brother, husband-wife, and friend-friend. Confucius held that, when people lose track of the importance of virtue in properly executing their responsibilities, the rectification of names (*zhèngmíng* or *cheng-ming* or 正名) should be invoked, whereby (for example) the ruler is called to behave in a way that is appropriate to the name of the office of ruler. Beneath and above all of this conceptual apparatus for the management and moral orientation of human life, Confucius prized education as a way of learning to think for oneself in the light of the great wisdom of the past, and as a guide to self-cultivation.

Chinese philosophers in the subsequent three centuries inevitably read the *Five Classics* through the lens of the *Analects*. The resulting creative commentarial process of debate eventually yielded, in the terms of Zhu Xi (Zhū Xī or Chu Hsi or 朱熹; 1130–1200 CE), a distinction between orthodox Confucianism and heterodox Confucianism. Xunzi (Xún Zǐ or Hsün Tzu or 荀子; 310–237 BCE) was the inspiration for the heterodox school, which strongly influenced Hanfeizi (Hánfēizǐ or Han Fei Tzu or 韓非子 or 韩非子; 280–233 BCE) and the legalist school of Chinese political philosophy. But the axiological tradition of religious philosophy is most clearly perpetuated in the three key works that, with the Analects, constitute the orthodox school's Four Books (*Sì Shū* or *Ssu Shu* or 四書 or 四书). In what follows, I will discuss how the axiological tradition unfolds in each of these three key works.

The *Great Learning* (*Dà Xué* or *Ta-Hsüeh* or 大學 or 大学), which began its life as Chapter 42 of the *Classic of Rites*, consists of a short text attributed to Confucius and then ten sections of commentary by his disciple Zengzi (Zēngzǐ or Tsengtzu or 曾子; 505–436 BCE). It encapsulates the teachings of the *Five Classics* as Confucius received them and processed them. The fact that this text was so important in Chinese philosophy, education, and government shows the extent to which axiological themes, framed in a pervasively religious-cosmological way, penetrated deeply into the Chinese way of life. The axiological linkage between individual self-cultivation and the responsible exercise of public office is unmistakable in this text, though its religious-cosmological framing is not as evident here as it is in other Confucian works. The main text is so short that it is worth quoting in full here, in the translation of James Legge.[35]

> What the Great Learning teaches, is—to illustrate illustrious virtue; to renovate the people; and to rest in the highest excellence.
>
> The point where to rest being known, the object of pursuit is then determined; and, that being determined, a calm unperturbedness may be attained to. To that calmness there will succeed a tranquil repose. In that repose there may be careful deliberation, and that deliberation will be followed by the attainment of the desired end.
>
> Things have their root and their branches. Affairs have their end and their beginning. To know what is first and what is last will lead near to what is taught in the Great Learning.
>
> The ancients who wished to illustrate illustrious virtue throughout the kingdom, first ordered well their own States. Wishing to order well their States, they first regulated their families. Wishing to regulate their families, they first cultivated their persons. Wishing to cultivate their persons, they first rectified their hearts. Wishing to rectify their hearts, they first sought to be sincere in their thoughts. Wishing to be sincere in their thoughts, they first extended to the

utmost their knowledge. Such extension of knowledge lay in the investigation of things.

Things being investigated, knowledge became complete. Their knowledge being complete, their thoughts were sincere. Their thoughts being sincere, their hearts were then rectified. Their hearts being rectified, their persons were cultivated. Their persons being cultivated, their families were regulated. Their families being regulated, their States were rightly governed. Their States being rightly governed, the whole kingdom was made tranquil and happy.

From the Son of Heaven down to the mass of the people, all must consider the cultivation of the person the root of everything besides.

It cannot be, when the root is neglected, that what should spring from it will be well ordered.

It never has been the case that what was of great importance has been slightly cared for, and, at the same time, that what was of slight importance has been greatly cared for.

The *Doctrine of the Mean* (Zhōng Yōng or *Chung-Yung* or 中庸), originally Chapter 31 of the Classic of Rites, and traditionally attributed to Confucius's grandson Kong Ji (孔伋; later known as Zǐsī or Tzu-ssu or 子思; c. 481–402 BCE), helps to fill in some of the religious-cosmological framing of the Confucian concept of virtue. The thirty-three short chapters of the *Doctrine of the Mean* prescribe heaven's way (*dao*) by which to realize perfect virtue for everyone, from the loftiest ruler to the lowliest citizen. Like the *Great Learning*, the *Doctrine of the Mean* emphasizes the linkage from individual virtue to social effects and vice versa. But it also positions the heavenly way of virtue between two extremes—between the knowing and talented and virtuous who go beyond it and the stupid and worthless who do not come up to it (1:4)—thus, the idea of a mean. The *Doctrine of the Mean* also manifests the links between human virtue and conformation to both the character of nature and to the mandate of heaven, thereby surfacing the cosmological-religious framework supporting the moral teachings of Confucianism. Chapter 26 puts it this way:

Hence to entire sincerity there belongs ceaselessness. Not ceasing, it continues long. Continuing long, it evidences itself. Evidencing itself, it reaches far. Reaching far, it becomes large and substantial. Large and substantial, it becomes high and brilliant. Large and substantial;—this is how it contains all things. High and brilliant;—this is how it overspreads all things. Reaching far and continuing long;—this is how it perfects all things. So large and substantial, the individual possessing it is the co-equal of Earth. So high and brilliant, it makes him the co-equal of Heaven. So far-reaching and long-continuing, it makes him infinite. Such being its nature, without any display, it becomes manifested; without any movement, it produces changes; and without any effort, it accomplishes its ends. The way of Heaven and Earth may be completely declared in one sentence. They are without any doubleness, and so they produce things in a manner that is unfathomable (26:1-7).[36]

Chapter 22 employs the linkage among heaven, earth, and the fully sincere person to explain how virtue is rooted in the natural and the heavenly way of things:

It is only he who is possessed of the most complete sincerity that can exist under heaven, who can give its full development to his nature. Able to give its full development to his own nature, he can do the same to the nature of other men. Able to give its full development to the nature of other men, he can give their full development to the natures of animals and things. Able to give their full development to the natures of creatures and things, he can assist the transforming and nourishing powers of Heaven and Earth. Able to assist the transforming and nourishing powers of Heaven and Earth, he may with Heaven and Earth form a ternion.

Note that a ternion is a set of three sheets of paper folded in half to make a small booklet. The interlocking closeness of the three sheets is akin to the relations among the virtuous person, earth, and heaven. The metaphor evokes both the cosmological rooting and the social significance of virtue in human life.

The *Mencius* (*Mèngzǐ* or *Meng-Tzu* or 孟子) is named after the philosopher Mencius (probably 372–289 BCE), who is traditionally regarded as the student of Confucius's grandson. The *Mencius* is his most influential work. It is treasured especially because of its optimistic view of human beings. Book 2 Chapter 6 of the *Mencius* argues that benevolence, righteousness, propriety, and knowledge are intrinsic characteristics of human beings, and Book 3 Chapter 1 asserts that anyone cultivating these natural characteristics can achieve virtue equal to that of the revered sages of past eras. In Mencius's view of the world, the problems of achieving virtue are due not to any intrinsic defect of human nature, but rather to the deleterious effects of society on individuals. Indeed, the *Mencius* is dominated by hagiographic stories of how Mencius attempts to set right one mistake after another, and to educate diverse rulers toward greater wisdom and virtue, all conveyed by means of compact epigrams and thought-provoking nuggets of wisdom.

Mencius's optimism is more or less opposite to the view of Xunzi, who attributed the difficulty of achieving virtue to human selfishness and depravity and regarded society as a civilizing and ennobling force capable of taming innate human tendencies to violent and selfish behavior. The resulting conflict between Mencius's and Xunzi's ideas, or perhaps their complementarity, defines one of the great debates in Chinese political philosophy, with parallels in the political philosophies of other civilizations.

The goal on both sides of this debate is the same—the individual and social realization of human virtue in peace and prosperity—but the different diagnoses produce different prescriptions about how to deal with the problems we face. Where Xunzi urged authentic Confucian education as well as authoritarian state control to manage perpetually corrupt individuals by means of socially constructed and universally imposed moral systems, Mencius emphasized education to evoke the student's memory of the good self, which lies smothered beneath the distortions of social conditioning. Book 7 Chapter 1 of the Mencius makes clear the cosmic significance of such education: "Mencius said, 'He who has exhausted all his mental constitution knows his nature. Knowing his nature, he knows Heaven.' " In this way, the *Mencius* continues the Chinese emphasis on giving theological and cosmological significance to axiological categories—the hallmark of the axiotheological tradition of religious philosophy.

While these Confucian sages were developing the spiritual, social, and political aspects of the valuational features of reality in human experience, the more mystical aspects of the same Chinese classics were unfolding in Daoist thinkers. Beginning with Laozi—traditionally identified as the author of the seminal *Dao De Jing* (*Dàodéjīng* or *Tao Te Ching* or 道德經 or 道德经)—the Daoist tradition developed especially through the *Classic of Perfect Emptiness* (*Lièzǐ* or *Lieh-Tzu* or 列子), attributed to Lie Yukou (Liè Yǔ-kòu or Lieh Yü-k'ou or 列圄寇 or 列禦寇; flourished c. 400 BCE), and the *Zhuangzi*, attributed to the philosopher of that name (*Zhuāngzǐ* or *Chuang-Tzu* or 莊子 or 庄子; c. 370–c. 301 BCE). Confucianism and Daoism are sometimes treated as sharply opposed traditions of thought, but this is both historically and conceptually misleading. Though there were characteristic differences, both traditions spring from the Chinese classics, both remain aware of one another throughout their development, both have significantly overlapping interests, both share key principles, and many Chinese sages did not hesitate to draw from both. In fact, it is truer to say that the two traditions are complementary expressions of a Chinese philosophical tradition. This complementarity is seen most clearly through an axiological lens.

The *Dao De Jing* cryptically elicits the conceptual elusiveness of ultimate reality and draws our attention to the deceptiveness of our all-too-human adventures in self-cultivation. When the question is about the methods for realizing the most prized values of happiness and effective sagehood, Daoists stress one of Confucius's most important insights, namely, that spontaneity, understood in the very particular sense of *wu-wei* (*wúwéi* or 無為 or 无为, active nonaction) is superior to the strict application of even the most strongly attested guidelines for behavior. The *Dao De Jing*, and indeed the entire thrust of Daoist philosophy, resolutely centralizes the magnificent artistry of spontaneity as a necessary condition for sagehood, and sees that insistence fully present within the Chinese classics. It is not that Daoists reject the formal social organization of practices of self-cultivation, though they are often enough accused of this. Rather, they point out the futility of such social arrangements for the achievement of the highest human values if they are not powered by emotional, spiritual, and social adeptness—that is, wu-wei. Cultivating the prized value of sagehood may be assisted by many habits and practices, but it requires spontaneous spiritual genius in its heart of hearts; virtue can never be reduced to a rational or procedural formula. Confucius's appreciation for spontaneity is no less pronounced than that of the Daoists, but he continually articulates the mutuality of spontaneity and ritual propriety, whereas most Daoists express suspicion of the value of formal social arrangements.

In the West, the axiotheological tradition of religious philosophy is not as clearly defined or extensively elaborated. Its fertile influence is evident in ancient Greece, and particularly in Plato's writings. Plato sees the Good at the root of reality, and he appears to have meant this less in the moralistic sense that dominated its Jewish, Christian, and Muslim applications, and more in the sense of a coherent valuational source of goodness, truth, and beauty. Plato's Form of the Good was as much mathematical and musical as moral, and it was above all beautiful and harmonious. This axiological vision of the depths of reality determines Plato's fundamental ontological and epistemological commitments, compactly expressed in the image of the "divided line" from his *Republic*. This "line" marks a division between unchanging realities, which can be known with certainty, and ephemeral realities, which are subject to merely probable belief. Value structures such as coherence, elegance, and harmony occupy the loftiest position, above value-laden structural forms that are independent of but expressed in the world. Beneath the line is the concrete world of changing things in contexts, and below that images, conceived of as abstractions from concrete things.

Plato's positioning of valuational structures as the highest form of reality raises the question about the relation of the Form of the Good to the divided line. Subsequent Jewish and Christian thought, relying especially on Plato's speculative account of creation in the *Timaeus*, tended to associate the Form of the Good with the creative demiurge of the *Timaeus*, and saw the biblical concept of God in both ideas. But the *Republic* and other dialogues suggest that the Form of the Good is not a separate being from the world but rather the valuational structures that appear in and through the concrete objects and processes of the world. This latter reading gives a particularly prominent role to value structures, identifying them with the fecund ontological basis and the creative power of the divine depths of reality.

This immanent axiological vision of deity sharply conflicts with the Bible's concretely personal and moral portrayal of a divine being with a center of consciousness and powers to act. This conflict bequeathed first to Jewish and Christian philosophy, and later to Muslim philosophy in a different form, the so-called Athens-Jerusalem tension, which has played out in every imaginable way in the history of Western religious thought. A safe generalization here is that the axiological portrayal of the divine depths of nature has persisted on the underside of traditions of religious thought that centralize the idea of God as a being with determinate personal characteristics. Some individual philosophers, and as we will see below a few traditions of mystical philosophy, have reversed this relationship—seeing the axiological vision of the depths of nature as ontologically fundamental and the idea of a personal divine being as a symbolic expression of the existential relevance of divinity for human life. But this is relatively rare. On the whole, Western religious thought has either tried to keep the Athens and Jerusalem impulses together in a kind of inarticulate tension or else has clearly subordinated Athens to Jerusalem. This is why the axiotheological tradition of religious philosophy has always remained somewhat scattered within the West, despite its conceptually fertile presence in Plato's writings.

Within one swath of modern philosophy, an uneasy skepticism about personal deities was fertilized by nature-appreciating romantics and a burgeoning natural science, and subsequently blossomed during the nineteenth century into a pointed rebellion against the "Jerusalem" emphasis in religious philosophy. A series of thinkers from Georg Hegel and Friedrich Schelling to David Friedrich Strauss, Ludwig Feuerbach, Karl Marx, and Friedrich Nietzsche gave renewed life to the axiotheological tradition of religious philosophy. Nietzsche's powerful writings were perhaps the most important among these for giving updated content to axiological instincts. He achieved this principally by aggressively subordinating moral categories to aesthetic ones. That is, he argued in a compelling way that human judgments of "good" and "bad" reflect social and contextual interests rather than the putative morality-stabilizing personality of any divine being. Human life is best understood not as moral striving but as artistic and spiritual self-expression in a world that has no definitive moral rules but only more and less beautiful possibilities.[37]

In the contemporary period, the axiotheological tradition of religious philosophy has two impressive representatives. On the one hand, twentieth-century continental philosophy's widespread rejection of the ontotheological tradition—due especially to thinkers such as Martin Heidegger but unfolding in a variety of directions—drew attention to the valuational aspects of human life. One of the most impressive results has been a phenomenologically sensitive framework for interpreting human behavior and thought, which richly registers human embodiment and social contexts. Partly in response to this development, theologians such as Paul Tillich unfolded the ancient idea of the Ground of Being in place of personalistic ideas of deity. And historians such as Michel Foucault assembled powerful evidence for the arbitrary and constructed character of social mores, thereby disclosing the way that morality serves ideological interests to such a degree that it is properly subordinated to the aesthetics of power and creativity.

On the other hand, the tradition of American pragmatic philosophy—springing from Charles Peirce, William James, and John Dewey—brought a distinctive accent to the axiological tradition of religious philosophy.[38] Its influence is clearly evident in the axiologically potent philosophical moves made within the systems of Alfred North Whitehead, Charles Hartshorne, Frederick Ferré, and Robert

Neville.[39] For example, Whitehead interprets God not as omnipotent creator but as one expression of creativity with the particular role of sensing the world in such a way as to synthesize a history of experience that maximizes value. Ferré and Neville present entire systematic philosophies built around value, the centerpieces of which are Ferré's three-volume series on constructive postmodern philosophy (*Being and Value*, *Knowing and Value*, *Living and Value*) and Neville's three-volume *Axiology of Thinking* series mentioned above (*Reconstruction of Thinking*, *Recovery of the Measure*, and *Normative Cultures*).

These and many other intellectual exertions show that the axiotheological tradition of religious philosophy is once more alive and well within the West. Meanwhile, despite the relative lack of official interest in the Chinese classics within Communist China, the axiological emphasis of early Confucianism and Neo-Confucianism continues in contemporary thinkers such as Tu Weiming.[40] At this point, the axiotheological tradition of religious philosophy appears to possess a power to orient philosophical reflection that morality-based forms of religious philosophy have lost in the rising tide of religious and cultural pluralism.

The Mysticotheological Tradition

The mysticotheological tradition focuses on experiences of cognitive breakdown, which may or may not be associated with mystical experiences as these are usually understood. Its fundamental intellectual instinct is that ultimacy surpasses absolutely the cognitive grasp of human beings and that inquiry into ultimacy proceeds optimally when it registers awareness of its inevitable breakdown all along the way in the content and method of inquiry.

If there is one tradition of religious philosophy that is more or less evenly represented across the world's religious and philosophical traditions, it is the mysticotheological tradition. Every wisdom tradition bequeathed to its adherents at least one line of mystical experience and thinking, and every philosophical tradition generated at least one significant arc of reflection on and inquiry into mystical modes of experience and thought.

This is a fascinating and important piece of empirical evidence, which some religious philosophers have been quick to pounce on in support of their contention that it is in mysticism that we find the common core of all religious traditions, despite their manifold differences in most respects of comparison. In the contemporary period, this argument has been made most forcefully by so-called perennial philosophers such as Aldous Huxley, Frithjof Schuon, and Huston Smith.[41] Schuon was the leading theorist of this trio, and Huxley the writer with the greatest public reach. Smith has functioned as the synthesizer who brought his formidable knowledge of world religions to the task of arguing that the perennial philosophy really is the oldest and most universal stream of religious and philosophical thought worldwide. As discussed in Chapter 5, Smith's argument in *Forgotten Truth: The Primordial Tradition* overreaches by imposing a comprehensive theoretical framework on an enormous diversity of beliefs and practices without also properly acknowledging relevant differences. It is a theological tour de force in both the good and bad senses of the term. The great strength of the argument, and its empirically most stable aspect, is the positioning of a mystical ultimate beyond every manifestation of positive religious behavior, belief, and experience. Thus, we have the West Asian God beyond God, the South Asian *nirguṇa* Brahman beyond *saguṇa* Brahman, and the East Asian Dao that cannot be described beyond proximate realities that can be described more or less adequately. Smith and other perennialists are right to pick up on this structural feature of world religions and philosophies, and they register it in more or less the right way.

The core hypothesis of an ultimate reality beyond all beings, all divinities, and all conceptions is the defining mark of the mysticotheological tradition in religious philosophy. Expressions of the mysticotheological tradition of religious philosophy are relatively less appealing to many intellectuals than the more positive and constructive traditions of religious philosophy already mentioned. Presumably this is due to the curious conceptual status of an intellectual project whose aim is rigorous reflection on and inquiry into a subject matter that is acknowledged from the outset to be entirely surpassing cognitive efforts. But there are two other valid questions that rightly cause intellectuals to hesitate before committing themselves to a mystical approach to philosophical inquiry.

The first question that gives intellectuals pause as they consider committing themselves to a mystical approach to philosophical inquiry is this: does not such a path of inquiry commit the philosopher to a hierarchy of more and less adept knowers—and thus both to a kind of condescension toward ordinary religious knowing and to a kind of gnostic mystery within philosophy? Mystical traditions have often acknowledged the necessity of such social and intellectual differentiation, and there is no question that many philosophers, perhaps particularly in our era of democracy and equal rights, find all this quite distasteful. This hierarchical awareness is strongest of all within the perennial philosophy, because rising levels of knowledge and experience are correlated with both degrees of ontological intensity of religious objects (from nature to discarnate entities to personal deities to the God beyond God) and with degrees of value (from least valuable to most valuable). That is, the great chain of being is a value-loaded hierarchy that explains people's interest in sub-ultimate levels of ontology and experience in terms of lower spiritual maturity and weaker spiritual perceptiveness.[42] In the South Asian context, the implied insult is reframed and slightly softened through the doctrine of *saṃsāra*, whereby everyone can follow the path toward the highest knowledge and experience at their own pace and as they see fit. Proposing that people are at different places on a long path of many lives is certainly less insulting to slow movers than positing a definitive and permanent defect in the spiritual maturity and perceptiveness of those whose spirituality revolves around nature or discarnate entities or personal deities.

In both samsaric and nonsamsaric contexts, despite the subtle variations, the great chain of being does posit an elaborate hierarchy of spiritual advancement and does imply the need for social differentiation to distinguish adepts and also-rans. This is a genuine problem for philosophical inquiry because it redefines the key concept of "qualified experts." In most philosophical inquiries, everyone with serious knowledge of the subject matter has a stake in the outcome, as well as a role to play. But the gnostic layering of knowledge in mysticism introduces an alien type of qualification that philosophers committed to open inquiry find difficult to assimilate: all philosophers have a stake in the inquiry but only a few have significant roles to play. This is not an impossible situation to manage in practice because social differentiation tends to separate such "spiritually advanced" philosophers from others, so they don't need to cope with the friction of implied insults and resentments. And certainly the theory of inquiry elaborated here has no difficulty making sense of such social differentiation in terms of species of specialized discourse communities. But the problem remains that the mysticotheological tradition of religious philosophy may be doomed to a perpetually inefficient style of inquiry because it must limit its access to available expertise on its own, particularly narrow, terms.

It is important to note, therefore, that mystical worldviews need not embrace the great chain of being's ontology in order to venture the core hypothesis of an ultimate reality beyond cognitive grasp. This core hypothesis only requires a rather modest ontological framework, which I shall call the "Sparse Ontology." It expresses as simply and directly as possible the minimal ontological implications of the core hypothesis of inquiries in the mysticotheological tradition of religious philosophy by supposing merely the fundamental ontological contrast between ultimate reality and dependent reality. The great chain of being's ontology is an extension of the minimalist Sparse Ontology, one that elaborates hierarchical relationships among the various types and levels of dependent beings. These types and levels of being are, in the Sparse Ontology, symbolic engagements with ultimate reality emerging within dependent reality as people seek to make sense of their world. Despite this marked difference, the great chain of being remains consistent with the Sparse Ontology's commitment to all beings and relations being ontologically dependent on that which is beyond cognitive grasp, beyond being, and beyond relation.

The significance of this minimalist approach to the ontological framing of inquiries within the mysticotheological tradition of religious philosophy is both ethical and intellectual. On the ethical side, the dubious moral aspects of the great chain of being derive from its hierarchical description of degrees of intensity of being and matching spiritual personality types or levels of spiritual maturity and perceptiveness. But the moral consequences of such hierarchies, if deemed unwarranted and unwanted, do not arise in relation to the Sparse Ontology, and so cannot count against the moral viability of the mysticotheological tradition of religious philosophy as such. On the intellectual side, the Sparse Ontology offers a framework for inquiry open to anyone with relevant expertise; there is no basis *in the framework for inquiry itself* to exclude anyone from the outset. So people for whom the highest reality is a comprehensible personal deity could involve themselves in mysticotheological inquiries even though they would be excluded as unqualified from inquiries within the perennial philosophy's ontological framework.

The second question that causes intellectuals to hesitate before committing themselves to a mystical approach to philosophical inquiry is more practical: precisely how is one supposed to pursue such an inquiry? The unintelligibility of ultimate reality in the mysticotheological tradition's conception of it poses an epistemological paradox of the first order for inquiry. This paradox has stimulated extraordinary creativity within what has come to be called the apophatic tradition of mystical theology. Something similar commonly arises in theology more generally because most theologians regard ultimate reality as *difficult* to grasp, and perpetually subject to human idolatry and self-interested distortion. Theists regard this problem as resolved for practical purposes—if not by the natural powers of human reason examining the created world, then by divine self-revelation, which places reliable and comprehensible understanding at human disposal. But apophatically minded mystical theologians reject these moves as evasions of the real sharpness of the problem of religious knowledge. In Søren Kirkegaard's phrase, there is an "infinite qualitative distinction" between time and eternity, between the reach of our cognition and the ultimate reality that we seek to know. Great theologians have always seen this. In the Christian context, Karl Barth affirmed divine self-revelation as the condition for the possibility of knowledge of God but also insightfully insisted that God is revealed, even in Jesus Christ, as *unknown*. The *Dao De Jing* makes the same point for the nontheistic Chinese context in many of its chapters, recapitulating the paradox of actually speaking about that which is beyond speech.

Given the achievements of apophatic theologians and philosophers, it would be harsh indeed to treat their apparently futile linguistic exertions as signs of flabby and self-indulgent philosophic minds.[43] Yet philosophers and theologians have demonstrated significant squeamishness around mysticism, because of their dual concerns about religious enthusiasm and irrationality, to the point that attacking mysticism has sometimes been de rigour for certain schools of theology.[44] So what do apophatic thinkers have to say about how to handle the paradox at the heart of the mysticotheological tradition of religious philosophy? The answer to this question calls for (1) a distinction among techniques for managing the tension between conventional expressibility and ultimate ineffability, (2) an interpretation of knowledge as engagement rather than as propositionally expressible comprehension, and (3) an exploration of prospects for the mysticotheological tradition of religious philosophy.

First, to begin with techniques for expression of the inexpressible, any fair-minded interpreter has to grant that apophatic mystical thinkers have displayed virtually limitless inventiveness. Naturally, techniques begin with metaphor and analogy; in fact, all theological speech that regards ultimacy as difficult to grasp (whether or not impossible finally to comprehend) must make hearty use of imagination-stimulating analogies and metaphors that spring the mind free of the thing to which ultimacy is likened by implying that ultimacy is also unlike and other than that thing. But mystical philosophers have always gone well beyond metaphors and analogies. For example, Thomas Aquinas for most of his life regarded analogy as a relatively well-controlled means of knowledge of the divine, on the grounds that analogy could be regulated by the *analogia entis* (analogy of being), which proportionally links the comparison of this-worldly and divine attributes to the comparison of this-worldly and divine being. But apophasis typically rejects the idea of ultimacy as a being, as having being, or even as having any attributes whatsoever, and thus has little use for the *analogia entis* except as a way of getting a better conversation started.

To go further, apophatic thinkers typically established elaborate mechanisms of imaginative control using trajectories of images. For example, the anonymous fifth-century Neoplatonist writer Pseduo-Dionysius distinguished between the *via positiva* and the *via negativa*. These two ways of speaking have a great deal in common. Each is both a philosophical technique and a spiritual practice. Each begins with symbolic speech and ends in silence. Each establishes a trajectory of images that can propel imaginative powers toward a controlled experience of cognitive breakdown. Each expresses a more or less unanalyzed confidence that approaching ineffability along a tightly controlled trajectory makes the inevitable cognitive breakdown meaningful and informative about ultimacy.

The main differences between the *via positiva* and the *via negativa* are the different way the two trajectories are defined, and the way arcing along each trajectory produces a differently modulated silence in response to the final state of cognitive breakdown. The *via positiva* organizes symbolic representations of ultimacy from the most to the least adequate and affirms them in that order, thereby eventually claiming every possible and actual thing for ultimacy, relativizing every name, and blanketing ultimacy in a whitewashed silence of plenitude. The *via negativa* organizes symbols in the opposite order and denies their literal application to ultimacy from the least adequate to the most apt, thereby driving the mind to a silence of emptiness. The ordered trajectories of symbols are set by tradition. Following either trajectory loosens attachment to symbols while powering the imagination in a calculated direction.

Other strategies involve sentence-level techniques. For example, most instances of apophatic mystical writing involve negation. Indeed, this is one of the marks of apophatic literature. But the negations are not merely ordinary propositional negation. There is also, to use the language of John Searle's theory of speech acts, negation of illocutionary force, which is to say negation of the sense in which something is stated.[45] Overlapping to some degree with verb moods, illocutionary force is the point of a speech act, and involves stating or commanding or expressing or enacting-through-speaking. Correspondingly, illocutionary force negation involves, for example, denying that one is asserting something, whereas regular propositional negation involves asserting that one is denying something. There is ample evidence of illocutionary force negation as well as complicated combinations of types of negation in the writings of apophatic mystics. And there are other sentence-level techniques besides these.[46]

Yet other strategies operate at the level of entire systems of discourse. The active symbol systems of many religious groups involve balancing mechanisms. Every narration of characteristics of ultimacy will inevitably be one-sided and will distort understanding if interpreted artlessly. The distortions are relatively easy to detect within the discernment structures of religious communities, so multiple complementary narratives tend to be juxtaposed with one another as correctives to distortions. The expectation is that multiple complementary symbolic narrations will help to balance the picture of ultimacy that emerges in the practices and beliefs of those whose lives and imaginations are formed under the weight of those symbols. For example, all known religious traditions use both personal and nonpersonal symbols for ultimate reality and make each type of symbol prominent at various times and in ways that minimize cognitive dissonance while still provoking salutary effects. The salutary effect is a more generous understanding of ultimacy with less attachment to one type of symbol. Even though an individual believer may be able to name only one side of the balance comfortably—depending on the prevailing self-understandings in his or her religious community—the other side is also present, possibly subordinated but probably also helpfully sublimated in beliefs and practices that the person does not typically analyze. There are many techniques for expressing the inexpressible at the symbol-system level besides balancing mechanisms.[47]

It is valuable to grasp the entire range of mystical techniques for the purposes of understanding mystical writings, of course. But philosophers mounting inquiries in the mysticotheological tradition of religious philosophy may also be forced to use such techniques themselves. After all, these linguistic devices are not merely amusing diversions to help writers express with flair what it is they feel provoked to say. Rather, they are methods of expression and communication forced upon communities of inquirers by the nature of the subject matter itself. These techniques approach the sophistication and self-containment of the technical languages developed in some specialized discourse communities, as described in Chapter 6. When stabilized within a community of discussion and debate, they can be invaluable tools for philosophical inquiry (which is just as well because they are actually unavoidable).

Second, moving from techniques of ineffability to the meaning of engaging the ineffable, we must ask the following questions: What is the value of indirection in ultimacy talk? Why go to the trouble of developing elaborate techniques for indirectly expressing the ineffable? How does all this inventiveness advance inquiry? Does it have an essentially spiritual purpose? If so, how is the philosophical interest in inquiry registered?

One of the most prominent schools of Indian Buddhist philosophy (Mādhyamaka) is named for the problem of walking a middle way between the ordinary world of conventional perception and expression and the extraordinary and ineffable world of ultimate concerns toward which the quest for enlightenment ineluctably draws us. At the heart of Mādhyamaka's strategic thinking about speaking-on-the-way-to-Enlightenment, and indeed an essential component in South Asian speech about *mokṣa* generally, is a distinction between conventional and ultimate reality—and the concept of *upāya* (artful means) as a way of meditating between the two. We rely on the *mudrā*, the *mantra*, and the *mandala* (special gestures, sayings, and diagrams) to connect to ultimacy. We use song and ritual and formal discourse. We offer ourselves in *bhakti* devotion to a deity, we reach out to others in *karmic* good works, we fight for what we believe is right, we deploy spiritual yogic practices, and we strive for spiritual knowledge (*jñāna*) with all our might. All of these actions and words and symbols are instances of *upāya*. They are means by which we engage effectively that which cannot be contained affectively or grasped cognitively or expressed actively. Though we may be emotionally and habitually attached to particular *upāya* at various times in our lives, none is definitive for the ultimate attainment of enlightenment, and thus all must be shed along the way. Thus the famous Zen saying, with roots in the Mādhyamaka philosopher Bhavaviveka: "If you see the Buddha on the road, kill him." Even the Buddha is *upāya*.

To assert that *upāya* works is to assert that we can engage that which we cannot finally comprehend. This instinct defines a vital aspect of inquiries within the mysticotheological tradition—namely, that engaging the finally incomprehensible ultimacy lying behind dependent reality is feasible despite ineliminable cognitive, emotional, and practical difficulties. The mysticotheological tradition of religious philosophy rises or falls on this point. So it is important to head off a potential misunderstanding about spiritual engagement.

The apophatic tradition has sometimes treated spiritual engagement in a disembodied, otherworldly way, as if bodily human existence were the only problem interfering with the longed-for goal of achieving enlightenment or entering into the beatific vision. This was classically so in the Neoplatonic scheme because the great chain of being assigns materiality to the very lowest rung, where it is little more than a problem to be worked around. Just as the mysticotheological tradition of religious philosophy is not confined to the great chain of being, however, so it is not doomed to repeat the associated habits of valuation and disvaluation. In fact, the Sparse Ontology can be extended not only in the direction of the perennial philosophy but also in the direction of a metaphysics that affirms human bodies as essential to human nature, and indeed physicality as essential to value itself—which is to say, a kind of religious naturalism.[48] In any such scheme, the idea of engagement is not something that bodies interfere with; bodies make engagement possible, even as bodies frustrate and complicate it.

The corollary of this is a warning about how *not* to interpret engagement. Engagement is *not* a means of knowledge that somehow keeps working even when ultimacy defies the reach of our capacities for cognition, emotion, and action. It is not a partially hidden cognitive faculty that functions as an unaccountable exception to apophatic principles, despite having often functioned that way in metaphysically dualist frameworks. Within the core hypothesis of the mysticotheological tradition of religious philosophy, there is no exception to the rule that ultimacy defies finite comprehension. This is only the consistent interpretation of transcendence. But our lives are also lived within the ambit of ultimacy, which is the practical consequence of saying that everything is dependent on ultimacy, and the only consistent interpretation of immanence. Note that this does not require a theistic interpretation of dependence as that between creator and created; the Buddhist *pratītya-samutpāda* doctrine works just as well, with the exhaustive dependence of things on other things yielding a vision of ultimate emptiness (*śūnyatā*). Thus, to speak of engagement in the causal sense intended here is to locate human beings in a proximate environment that is dependent in some absolute sense on an ultimate environment—its Whence, its Abysmal Ground, its final doom and promise. This way of thinking of engagement is not an exception to apophatic principles, nor does it locate a path to knowledge unavailable in other ways. It does assert that our knowledge, emotion, and action in the ambit of ultimacy are the effects and expressions of our engagement with ultimacy.

Third, what then are the prospects for the mysticotheological tradition of religious philosophy? One often overlooked point is that the core hypothesis of the mysticotheological tradition is actually extremely plausible. It makes prima facie sense to suppose that everything we know is dependent on something so dense with value and meaning that we only ever can engage fragments of it, and also that we can and do engage it in our fragmentary ways. The plausibility of this supposition only fails when we insist on conceiving this ultimate in terms that pick up on only one aspect of reality, as occurs in anthropomorphic renderings of God or in pictures of ultimacy as the mathematical deep structures of the laws of nature. At the vague level, this core hypothesis is generally compelling—to atheist, nontheist, and theist alike. This is enough to make the mysticotheological tradition a perpetual presence within religious philosophy, even if it never yields feasible forms of inquiry.

But, in fact, I think the mystical traditions of the world show creativity commensurate with the claim that we do witness here feasible forms of inquiry. Overconfident intellectuals do deride mystical thinkers as incoherent from time to time. But the problem mystical philosophers have to face is not failure of intellectual nerve or discipline or skill, as their critics assert. Rather, the problem derives directly from the subject matter under study: the ineffability of ultimacy. And this is how it should be; the form of the inquiry should properly reflect the cognitive difficulties of the subject matter.

Given the all-surpassing quality of ultimacy, what might a religious philosopher expect to gain through an inquiry framed in the terms of the mysticotheological tradition? Is one doomed merely to repeat the rules of the game—we can't say anything; we have to rise above attachment to everything; and we strive for heaven or *mokṣa*—or can we uncover new information? Though the core hypothesis of the mysticotheological tradition does reach deeply into all inquiries conducted under its auspices, mystical thinkers of the past achieved a great deal more than the mantric repetition of the rules of the game, and so can we in our time. In particular, we can learn how to leverage pluralism of mystical visions for the sake of new insights.

Religious pluralism in general is so severe that any philosophical study guided by it is extremely arbitrary and inefficient, at least at this point. But the structural similarities within diverse mystical traditions make philosophical study far more promising.[49] In particular, whereas religious thinking diverges right from the outset in most cases, we can frame the subject matter of mystical thought in such a way that shared agreements extend a long way before we start to see divergence. And we can further suppose that the divergences we notice are caused by that which mystical traditions engage. Thus, the last words we speak before lapsing into inevitable silence may be those that limn ultimacy as the cause of disagreement within established mystical viewpoints, as that which honest engagement inevitably registers as fragments that can never be reassembled coherently.

As with the other traditions of religious philosophy discussed above, the mysticotheological tradition is displaying signs of renewal. The key to this transformation is overcoming the limitations associated with conceiving this tradition in the theologically narrow terms of the perennial philosophy—with its great chain of being, its antiphysical bias, and its morally dubious value structure. The Sparse Ontology does not exclude the great chain of being as a valid elaboration, but it also contains many other ontological possibilities, including some that are suggestive of religious naturalism. Moreover, apophasis is more consistent with the interpretation of engagement offered here than with interpretations that make spiritual engagement a kind of pure and disembodied exception to the rules of cognitive breakdown. The transformation involved in encompassing frameworks other than that furnished by the great chain of being removes barriers to appreciating how plausible and appealing is the core hypothesis of the mysticotheological tradition.

Status Report

Each of the six major traditions of religious philosophy is in a process of significant transformation. The forces driving the transformation are the encounter with multiple philosophical and religious traditions and the realization that many disciplines have something relevant to say about inquiries in religious philosophy, including especially the natural and human sciences. This transformation is still underway but it already appears to be increasing adaptability and empirical robustness within the various traditions of religious philosophy. These are signs of improving intellectual health.

Each of these six traditions of religious philosophy has a distinctive focus: being, dependence, design, consciousness, value, and cognition. These six traditions do not exhaust what there is to be said about religious philosophy. Nevertheless, the literature and arguments of the six traditions I have sketched constitute the six beating hearts of the complex body that is religious philosophy.

Interpretation of the past achievements and prospects of these six traditions of religious philosophy largely determines the fate of religious philosophy as a whole, both within the secular academy and in the minds of working philosophers. Thus, it is important to keep in mind the by-now obvious, yet oddly elusive, facts that there are at least six ancient and active traditions of religious philosophy, not just one. Each is guided by a fundamentally plausible intellectual instinct, which constitutes something like a core hypothesis for the corresponding venture in inquiry. Each is articulated in large bodies of literature reaching across all seven styles of religious philosophy, from the literary to the evaluative.

Frankly, we can assess the historic accomplishments of these traditions of religious philosophy rather differently, depending on the purpose of the assessment. For example, these achievements seem far more impressive in context than they do when abstracted from their historic and cultural settings and evaluated (anachronistically) with today's philosophical sensitivities. Indeed, I have criticized each of them from a contemporary point of view. But careful readers of the literature in these six traditions also encounter a robust challenge to the working assumptions of contemporary philosophy, and particularly to its cavalier acceptance of arguments about what is possible and what is not in philosophical inquiry. Religious philosophy bites back. These traditions persist and continually renew themselves because they encode refined philosophical wisdom, and because they actually prove themselves as worthy of allegiance to those who invest effort to master them.

We live at a time when wholesale arguments against the very possibility of these traditions of religious philosophy, or against their moral and socio-political consequences, are more often precipitous than persuasive. Each of the six traditions has been transforming itself under the impact of new developments in the natural and human sciences. Each is responding to the complexities presented by the world's philosophical and religious traditions. Old debates are being diagnosed as moribund or enslaved to hidden premises. Criticism disturbs but it also liberates. New and compelling problems are opening like flowers in the morning sunshine. Each tradition appears to be surviving the traumas of modern and postmodern philosophy and emerging more poised and penetrating than ever. From this point of view, it is an exciting time to be a religious philosopher. And it is an important time for the modern academy to claim for itself a role in nurturing and advancing these transforming and newly vital traditions of religious philosophy.

Afterword

Religious Philosophy in the Modern University

There is widespread skepticism within university religion and philosophy departments, as well as in allied disciplines, about the value or possibility of inquiries in religious philosophy. The argument of this book suggests that this skepticism is hasty and reductive in that it treats certain types of philosophical activity in relation to religion—in relation to which such skepticism may be appropriate—as representative of all such activity, whereas in fact there are important differences among operative approaches and methods. In particular, religious philosophy understood as multidisciplinary comparative inquiry has a natural and vital place in modern universities, because its secular morality of inquiry comports well with the principles of open and unbiased inquiry that, to varying degrees, guide and inspire the modern university. Accordingly, it is time to reassess the place of religious philosophy within the modern university.

Skepticism about the value of religious philosophy is palpable in some circles. I have addressed such concerns throughout this book, and specifically as they arise in very different forms within the three allied disciplinary domains of religious studies, philosophy, and theology (Chapter 1). I have presented a theory of inquiry showing how it is feasible to interpret religious philosophy as multidisciplinary comparative inquiry (Chapters 4 through 7). I have explained the diverse styles and contexts of religious philosophy (Chapter 2 and Chapter 3) and its major traditions (Chapter 8). And I have drawn sharp contrasts with other conceptions and practices of philosophical work in relation to religion, so as to make clear what religious philosophy as multidisciplinary comparative inquiry is not, as well as what it is.

Furthermore, I argued that the more controversial theoretical and evaluative styles of religious philosophy yield inquiries consistent with the values of the modern university. This is because these styles of inquiry, when pursued in the multidisciplinary comparative way definitive for religious philosophy, have six important virtues: (1a) they do not conform to the authority structures of religious communities; (1b) they do not operate within the ambit of assumptions about putatively supernaturally authorized revelatory information, which pervade confessional forms of theology; (1c) they do not serve the institutional or intellectual interests of any particular religious groups; yet (2a) they function in full awareness of these and other features of religious traditions; (2b) they incorporate every kind of naturally derived human knowledge as it bears on religious subject matters; and (2c) they strive for consistency with the less theoretically aggressive styles of religious philosophy (especially the phenomenological, comparative, historical, and analytic styles).

In this afterword, I briefly consider skepticism about the value of religious philosophy in relation to the question of its place within modern universities. This involves recapitulating the rebuttals to skepticism already mentioned (the "deconstructive" part of my case). It also involves taking account of the wider intellectual scene in a way that university administrators have to do and disciplinary specialists often do not (the "constructive" part of my case). Finally, it involves asking about the place of religious philosophy in the educational, research, and public missions of the diverse kinds of modern universities.

Summary of the Deconstructive Case in Support of Religious Philosophy

The deconstructive part of the case rebuts the prevalent skepticisms of religious philosophy. In fact, I am aware of no direct criticisms of religious philosophy in the precise sense of "religious philosophy as multidisciplinary comparative inquiry," which is the way it is articulated here. It will be interesting to see if the idea of comparative multidisciplinary inquiry operating within the purview of a secular morality of inquiry—once clearly articulated as a way of framing research in religious philosophy that includes theoretical and evaluative tasks—provokes more specific criticisms. But unquestionably there is a veritable horde of criticisms of fields allied with and overlapping the various tasks of religious philosophy.[1]

One compelling practical reason to define religious philosophy as "multidisciplinary comparative inquiry" is specifically to draw a contrast between the kinds of inquiry this phrase entails and the kinds of inquiry that appear to induce justified anxiety in some scholars and university administrators. I have argued against views, propounded by people both religious and nonreligious, that dismiss the possibility or value of religious philosophy with a wave of the hand. Defining religious philosophy in the way I do enables me to acknowledge what is sound in those criticisms while clearly distinguishing religious philosophy from intellectual activities that may well deserve such criticisms.

I have also argued against condemnations of religious philosophy as dangerous because it threatens religious piety. These religious criticisms may well be correct in what they assert, though they appear to construe piety in a rather narrow and fragile way. But concerns about the psychological and social impact of inquiry are not central to the native procedures of religious philosophy. They are, however, secondary issues for assessing the morality of inquiry and for deciding which kinds of inquiry to pursue. Thus, such concerns properly figure in the calculations of educational institutions as they consider whether supporting religious philosophy is consistent with their institutional missions. As I will point out below, such calculations produce significantly different results depending on the heritage and interests of the institution in question.

A practical motivation for staking out semantic territory using the relatively under-determined phrase "religious philosophy" is that existing controversy over associated intellectual activities has muddied the meanings of more prominent terms. Scholars and administrators within colleges and universities are sometimes deeply biased for or against activities that they name with a phrase such as such as "philosophy of religion" or "philosophical theology." They expect others to understand what they mean by these terms, even if they do not possess a clear idea of what they themselves mean by them. Merely uttering such a phrase can efficiently trigger profoundly consensual reactions, whether negative or positive. Yet the articulated reasons for these reactions can sometimes prove to be paper-thin rationalizations for biases that warrant closer scrutiny.

This has become evident to me in a number of memorable conversations about the possibility and prospects of religious philosophy, under whatever name is used in context to suggest the tasks involved. Those conversations go something like this. I say, "I have been listening carefully to you. You seem suspicious of religious philosophy. Why?"

They say something like, "Because it is anti-intellectual nonsense and covert ideology." I say, "Please be specific. What is wrong with this particular instance of religious philosophy?" and furnish an example. They say, "Well I guess there is nothing wrong with that example." I say, "Then why do you say that religious philosophy is anti-intellectual nonsense and covert ideology?"

This is where things get interesting. They say, "But the way you do it in that example is not representative of the nonsensical way it is usually done." Or they say, "I don't immediately know what is wrong with that example of religious philosophy but I know it is impossible because of Kant" (or Comte, or Ayer, or Heidegger). Or they say, "If we are to have any credibility in the secular university, we have to distance ourselves from anything that has been historically tainted with theological interests, which includes religious philosophy, because such activities tolerate unlimited speculation in place of evidence, and they suggest greater commitment to religious special interests than to impartial inquiry." Or they say, "We have to mount a political attack on religious philosophy to overcome the lamentable pattern of bias in favor of institutional religious interests. What happens to legitimate forms of religious philosophy is acceptable collateral damage." (At least that last response frankly acknowledges the possibility that an injustice is occurring.)

The root causes of the widespread bias against the tasks of religious philosophy are hinted at in these conversations. They are as follows. (1) The academy is devoted to goals, including pursuing honest inquiry wherever it may lead, that are sometimes in conflict with the institutional interests of organized religion. (2) The morality of rational inquiry in a secular academic context means refusing to honor claims of supernaturally derived information or supernatural authorization of particular religious beliefs. (3) The perpetual disagreements in metaphysics and religious thought, together with the secular academy's interest in efficient economics of inquiry, jointly suggest that academic research will be better off focusing its efforts on tractable parts of reality, even if that means a brutal departure from tradition in the form of cutting off support for anything that smacks of metaphysics or theology. And, finally, (4) the prospects of religious studies achieving credibility in the academic world crucially turn on being able to demonstrate that it is not infected by the special interests of religious institutions. Each of these four causes of suspicion taints intellectual activities even vaguely associated with religion, and philosophical work in relation to religion is affected.

Sometimes suspicion is warranted, and I too have articulated some of these criticisms. For example, there are ways of doing theology so geared into to the special interests of religious institutions, so vulnerable to special pleading, and so immune to correction from other disciplinary insights that they really do not conform to the morality of inquiry that pervades the academic world. While these kinds of activities may be legitimate forms of inquiry in their proper institutional contexts, and they may enjoy special advantages of efficiency and productiveness in such places, I believe they have no claim on a native place within the secular academy because the associated moralities of inquiry are deeply at odds.

Importantly, however, not all religiously related intellectual activity is vulnerable to charges of excess abstraction, disciplinary parochialism, and ideological bias. In particular, religious philosophy as multidisciplinary comparative inquiry can rise above the difficulties that provoke such criticisms of some other forms of religiously-related intellectual work. Moreover, I have carefully considered throughout this book the charge of intellectual futility leveled against the philosophical discussion of religious topics. And I have argued that the advent of comparative philosophy and the emergence of novel multidisciplinary approaches jointly open new possibilities for religious philosophy, so long as it operates as a form of multidisciplinary comparative inquiry. Neither the morality-of-inquiry nor the futility-of-effort arguments have much to commend them in relation to religious philosophy understood as multidisciplinary comparative inquiry.

This is not to defend as fully realizable the ideal of untainted knowledge, free of inefficiency and ideology, in religious philosophy or in any other intellectual activity. The fallibilist commitment of a pragmatic theory of inquiry makes such claims seem grossly idealistic. But it is to defend the value of striving for impartiality and efficiency of inquiry in religious philosophy by seeking correction in every possible form and by making inquiries vulnerable to every corrective resource having the power to advance them.

Summary of the Constructive Case in Support of Religious Philosophy

The constructive part of the case argues that religious philosophy properly belongs within modern universities because of its intrinsic value, its native characteristics, and its morality of inquiry. This half of the case has two sides.

One side refers to the native purpose of religious philosophy. Existentially potent questions about the meaning of life and the wellsprings of value arise constantly within intellectual work. It is preeminently the task of religious philosophy to pursue such questions as far as possible—not necessarily in service to the identity interests of any particular religious community, but drawing on insights from numerous wisdom traditions and all relevant academic disciplines, and penetrating into the very ground of nature and experience in search of the most compelling answers.

I have already mentioned the decline over the last decade or so in philosophy of religion positions in North American secular university philosophy and religion departments. Evidently leaders of the relevant departments and university administrators are not convinced about the value of philosophical work on religious themes. But a steep price is paid for this neglect. One way or another, the sorts of problems taken up in religious philosophy constantly arise in universities, both at the borders of research in other disciplines and in classrooms and passionate hallway discussions. These issues keep coming up because they are existentially vital, historically important, and intrinsically interesting. It is no wonder that they pervade the great philosophical and literary traditions of Western, South Asian, and East Asian civilizations. The standard demands for excellence require that such issues be addressed as knowledgably and intelligently as possible. Even if there are no final answers to the questions of religious philosophy, the modern university must supply experts to pursue them, as it would any other area of fundamental inquiry. The worrying question for university administrators should be whether these questions will be discussed in amateurish or expert fashion. Religious philosophers are the experts and any college or university that cares about standards needs them.

The other side of the constructive case concerns the efficiency of such inquiries. University administrators are rightly concerned to support research and education that both makes a difference and is cost effective. Now, research in religious philosophy is *relatively* cheap in the way that all humanities research is cheap, though anything involving libraries, offices, and students is not cheap in the normal sense of that word. So the question of effectiveness comes down to the tractability of such inquiries. How far can religious philosophy as multidisciplinary comparative inquiry go?

In the context of a fallibilist, hypothetical pragmatic theory of rationality, I have argued that this must remain an empirical question. At that level, circumstances suggest that religious philosophy is entering a new era of sophistication and progress. Existing multidisciplinary and comparative efforts in philosophy make contemporary inquiries in religious philosophy markedly different from traditional forms of philosophy of religion in both appearance and substance, even while remaining continuous with them. So the question of the prospects for religious philosophy is wide open in an extremely promising way. And that should be exactly what university administrators curious about supporting religious philosophy need to know.

Religious Philosophy and the Diversity of Higher Education

How does this argument about the place of religious philosophy in modern universities relate to the diversity of higher educational institutions? Obviously, each college or university needs to sort out what the place of religious philosophy is relative to its own distinctive mission. The kinds of considerations that prove relevant, will be quite different depending in particular on whether the institution in question claims a secular or a religious mission.

In the secular context, after the arguments refuting criticisms and affirming the value of religious philosophy have been processed, the question remains of where to locate research and teaching in religious philosophy. Sadly, this discussion may turn out to be more like throwing a live grenade from hand to hand than jostling for the bridal bouquet. I have argued that religious philosophy is both a form of philosophy and a form of religious studies and that it has a natural home in both departmental locations. It can also fit within divinity schools that promote academic identity alongside denominational religious identity. In all cases, however, a comfortable home only exists where the possibility and legitimacy of religious philosophy as multidisciplinary comparative inquiry is acknowledged. Such acknowledgement is not always easy or natural because of the internal disciplinary hostilities that I have discussed. At some point, however, university administrators must demand an accounting of this hostility and then subject departmental explanations of opposition to religious philosophy to thorough public scrutiny in light of a wider and less jaundiced intellectual viewpoint. It is at this point that the real paucity of objections to religious philosophy as multidisciplinary comparative inquiry will become evident—no matter how strong these objections may be when leveled against other intellectual ventures, such as parochial forms of traditional philosophy of religion or confessional theology.

It is also important to admit openly that the idea of a "secular" social location for academic work is somewhat ill-defined. The secular academy has an indeterminate heritage and lacks a completely consistent and coherent self-interpretation. In fact, there is such perplexity surrounding its basic principles that scholars are beginning to speak of the "post-secular academy" and the "return of religion."[2] These complications notwithstanding, my references to the morality of inquiry in the "secular academy" are relatively straightforward: inquiry is unbridled by religious or other ideological institutional interests, it does not indulge special pleading or favoritism, it is fully responsive to the insights of whatever disciplines have a claim in the subject matter, and it earnestly and assiduously seeks out sources of correction wherever they may be found. In this sense of "secular academy," religious philosophy properly belongs there.

The situation is quite different in universities with strong religious identities. After all, religious philosophy, which has a natural home in the secular academy, does not accept the presuppositions for intellectual work that are familiar and often demanded within many institutionally religious contexts—assumptions such as revealed sacred scriptures or authoritative sources of religious teachings. Moreover, the results of inquiry in religious philosophy may conflict with some of the vested interests of academic institutions with explicitly religious missions. Given this, representatives of religious educational institutions may choose to turn their backs on religious philosophy, opting instead to engage the relevant issues on terms better suited to their internal confessional institutional interests.

Any significant degree of engagement with religious philosophy requires academic institutions with religious missions to balance their customary concerns for maintaining corporate religious identity with the uncomfortable challenge of remaining open to learn about themselves from less familiar disciplinary perspectives. For instance, the gap between what Buddhist thinkers say about the nature of the *saṅgha* (Buddhist community) and what sociologists of religion say about it can be quite striking. In some situations, it may be neither natural nor comfortable for Buddhist faithful operating an institution of higher education to pay attention to the external perspectives of other religions and a variety of academic disciplines on Buddhist communities.

This exemplifies the challenge that experts in religious philosophy pose to academic institutions with essentially religious missions. In actual fact, many universities and colleges with explicitly religious missions are not only open toward but also eager for the kind of far-reaching inquiries pursued within the framework of religious philosophy. Indeed, it is this very impulse that gave birth to most of the private universities in the Western world: regardless of their contemporary missions, almost all have origins in religious intellectual leaders who sought the best and most impartial knowledge about every subject, including disciplines that impinge on their own religious beliefs.

Do secular and religious academic institutions have different obligations in relation to the support of religious philosophy? For example, must a public university in the United States refuse to host religious philosophy due to separation of church and state policies? Or can a private university with an explicitly religious mission refuse to host religious philosophy because it is likely to challenge its prevailing religious outlook and thus perhaps disrupt the religious faith of students whose fee-paying parents are relying on the college specifically to nurture that faith?

A private academic institution such as a Jewish or Christian or Muslim or Buddhist university has the right to make its own decision about whether to support research and teaching into topics that are important to it. More than that, the leadership of such religious educational institutions must also decide what approaches to the study of religion they can live with. For example, will they permit intellectual endeavors that conform to the traditions and expectations of the secular research university? When push comes to shove, will their scholars have academic freedom to follow inquiry wherever it leads? Will the religious institution protect its own welfare with requirements to sign statements of faith and with punishments for scholars who stray from the narrow ideological path laid out for them? To the extent that such institutions select policies that enshrine the secular morality of inquiry, religious philosophy has a natural home. If the policies venture in a more parochial direction, then it will be impossible for inquiries in religious philosophy to be pursued openly in such locations.

Public academic institutions with secular missions do not have the same ideological basis for excluding religious philosophy, and I can see no basis for exclusion apart from considerations of economic survival. In particular, church-state separation is not a relevant concern in relation to religious philosophy, even though it may be for other educational issues, such as whether to include a religious seminary as a professional school within a public university. I presume that for the foreseeable future professional religious leadership training in state universities would remain extremely rare in the United States. It is interesting to note, however, that affiliations between public universities and denominationally specific religious education have recently been more common in other nations, such as Australia, where universities are seeking every ounce of government financial support they can get—support that depends on the number of registered students in classrooms regardless of subject matter. As is so often the case in life, economic considerations trump ideological purity.

Private universities with secular missions sometimes *choose to offer* support to religious institutions for their own reasons. Many do this when they host divinity schools or seminaries, Christian theology or Bible departments. Often this honors their heritage as a religiously affiliated university, despite their explicitly secular mission in the current era. Such hosting decisions may also honor the tradition of research universities supporting professional training, particularly in the fields of medicine, law, and divinity. Sometimes university support is more or less unconditional, and offered on whatever terms an affiliated religious institution wants to set—perhaps because the religious institution in question pays the university for educating its seminary students. At other times, the college or university institution supporting the interests of a particular religious group will insist on the same academic standards and morality of inquiry that apply throughout the university. In all cases, the resulting religious-academic institutional relationships can potentially be valuable for both institutions but they can also produce misunderstanding among university faculty with little sympathy for the leadership's conception of the university's wider mission. This in turn can make life difficult for practitioners of religious philosophy, which is often tainted by association with religious institutions, despite the fact that it can produce results that those religious institutions find difficult to digest.

In all cases, I would argue that a religious institution such as a living religious denomination is *not entitled to unconditional support* for its religious interests from secular academic institutions. Rather, universities offer such support for compelling reasons, such as maintaining the intellectual integrity of the leaders of religious institutions, which are vital strands within the social fabric that a university might see itself as committed to protecting and strengthening. By contrast, religious philosophy as multidisciplinary comparative inquiry *is entitled to support* from secular academic institutions. In fact, religious philosophy in this sense is a form of inquiry whose only natural home and principal nurturing tradition is the secular academy. Religious institutions and thinkers may learn from religious philosophy and participate in it but it is essentially a secular academic intellectual project. This concreteness of social location and heritage is limiting in some respects, of course, as I have noted, particularly in the discussion of theological critiques of religious philosophy in Chapter 1; religious philosophy simply can't take on all of the inquiries that confessional theology can. But this secular social location is enabling in other respects, including freeing religious philosophy from the burdensome constraint of having to support the institutional demands and vested interests of religious institutions.

Conclusion

I draw this afterword to a close with a pointed observation. Religious philosophy as multidisciplinary comparative inquiry is a rigorous and vigorous area of research, nurtured in secular academic institutions, with which its morality of inquiry comports well. But religious philosophy also has a complex heritage and sustains affiliations with disciplines such as religious studies, which have fought for a viable academic identity partly by distancing themselves from intellectual activities that espouse a morality of inquiry at odds with that of the secular university. The leaders of disciplines represented within philosophy, religious studies, and theology departments may therefore remain wary of religious philosophy, despite the lack of any real cause for concern. In these cases, such leaders should lift their eyes beyond the parochial identity politics of their own disciplines and consider the place of religious philosophy amid the wider intellectual currents and social challenges of our troubled world. And, when disciplinary leaders have difficulty doing this, university academic leadership should demand to know why, and if necessary do it for them. Religious philosophy lies precisely as close to the beating heart of every secular university's native mission as the existentially potent subject matter of religious philosophy is vital for human life.

Notes

Notes for Preface

1. Meister and Copan, *The Routledge Companion to Philosophy of Religion* contains significant sections on philosophical issues in the world religions and draws on important religious philosophers from diverse religious cultures.
2. See Stoehr, *Philosophies of Religion, Art, and Creativity,*.
3. See the year's events at http://www.bu.edu/ipr/lecture/index.html.
4. See Wildman, "Rational Theory Building."
5. See Wildman and Neville, "How Our Approach to Comparison Relates to Others."
6. Wildman, "Comparing Religious Ideas."
7. Wildman, "The Resilience of Religion in Secular Social Environments: A Pragmatic Philosophical Analysis."
8. Wildman, "The Resilience of Religion in Secular Social Environments: A Pragmatic Philosophical Analysis Regarding Scientific and Religious Problems."
9. Neville, Comparative Religious Ideas Project: vol.1, *The Human Condition*; vol.2: *Ultimate Realities*; vol. 3: *Religious Truth*.

Notes for Chapter 1

1. Kant, *Critique of Pure Reason*, 385–86.
2. Ibid., 396.
3. Representative examples of such works, older and newer, are Brown, *The Case for Theology in the University*; Cady and Brown, *Religious Studies, Theology, and the University*; Capps, *Religious Studies*; Coulson, *Theology and the University*; Fitzgerald, *The Ideology of Religious Studies*; Frankenberry, *Radical Interpretation in Religion*; Frankenberry and Penner, *Language, Truth, and Religious Belief*; Griffin and Hough, *Theology and the University*; McCutcheon,

Manufacturing Religion; Preus, *Explaining Religion*; Runcie et al., *Theology, the University and the Modern World*; Sharpe, *Comparative Religion*; Strenski, *Thinking about Religion*; Wiebe, *The Politics of Religious Studies*.

4. This reflects historical statistics from the American Academy of Religion's job placement service. Specifically, there were only five academic positions classified as primarily in philosophy of religion in the four years 2003 through 2006. More formal survey data on this question would be welcome—including qualitative data because internal departmental stories matter as much as placement statistics in assessing the reasons for the decline of philosophy of religion positions.

5. Among many other works, Carolyn Merchant's classic *The Death of Nature* and Londa Schiebinger's *Nature's Body* document many ways in which scientific work expresses cultural bias, with awareness and correction of these biases being slow to arrive. In religious studies, specifically, see the historical studies mentioned above: Capps, *Religious Studies*; McCutcheon, *Manufacturing Religion*; Preus, *Explaining Religion*; Sharpe, *Comparative Religion*; Strenski, *Thinking about Religion*; and similar works.

6. Note that a consensus of U.S. government agencies categorizes a research doctorate in religion under the humanities rather than the social sciences. This reflects the ongoing challenge of consolidating a place for the academic study of religion as a social and historical science in the secular university context. Meanwhile, research doctorates in theology and religious education are categorized as professional degrees, a classification that accurately conveys the difficulty facing any attempt to define a home for theology in the secular academy. See Doctoral Recipients from United States Universities: Summary Report, 2002—published by the National Opinion Research Center at the University of Chicago (2003), which was jointly sponsored by the National Science Foundation, the National Institutes of Health, the U.S. Department of Education, the National Endowment for the Humanities, the U.S. Department of Agriculture, and the National Aeronautics and Space Administration.

7. See Lévinas, *Humanism of the Other*.

8. See van Huyssteen, *Alone in the World?* which offers a close (though debatable) analysis of the theological significance of ancient cave art.

9. For representative examples, see Jackson and Makransky, *Buddhist Theology*; Suh, *The Confucian-Christian Dialogue*; van Ess, *The Flowering of Muslim Theology*; and Sherwin, *Studies in Jewish Theology*.

10. See Tillich, *Systematic Theology*, vol. I

Notes for Chapter 2

1. William Alston's "Religion" entry in the *Encyclopedia of Philosophy* lists the following nine characteristics: "1.Belief in something sacred (gods or other supernatural beings). 2. A distinction between sacred and profane objects. 3. Ritual acts focused on sacred objects. 4. A moral code believed to

have a sacred or supernatural basis. 5. Characteristically religious feelings (awe, sense of mystery, sense of guilt, adoration), which tend to be aroused in the presence of sacred objects and during the practice of ritual. 6. Prayer and other forms of communication with the supernatural. 7. A world view, or a general picture of the world as a whole and the place of the individual therein. This picture contains some specification of an over-all purpose or point of the world and an indication of how the individual fits into it. 8. A more or less total organization of one's life based on the world view. 9. social group bound together by the above." (7: 141–142.)

2. Whitehead, *Process and Reality*, 3.

3. See Forman, *Mysticism, Mind, Consciousness* and Smith, *Forgotten Truth*.

4. See Katz, *Mysticism and Philosophical Analysis* and Proudfoot, *Religious Experience*.

5. See Stace, *Mysticism and Philosophy*.

6. See Forman, *Mysticism, Mind, Consciousness*, Chapter 7.

7. See James, *Essays in Radical Empiricism* and Whitehead, *Process and Reality*.

8. The most recent example from the neurosciences is Beauregard and O'Leary, *The Spiritual Brain*.

Notes for Chapter 3

1. See, for example, van Huyssteen, *The Shaping of Rationality* and Murphy, *Beyond Liberalism and Fundamentalism*.

2. For a review of this history, and of the meanings of ideology that have emerged since early modernity, see the classic review of Eagleton, *Ideology*.

3. Paglia, *Sexual Personae*.

4. Foucault, *Madness and Civilization*; Foucault, *The Archeology of Knowledge*; Foucault, *The Birth of the Clinic*; Foucault, *The History of Sexuality*; and Foucault, *Discipline and Punish*.

5. For an eminently intelligible argument that politics should remain the primary domain of application for the idea of ideology, see Freeden, *Ideology*.

6. Hegel, *Lectures on the Philosophy of World History*.

7. See Schrag, "Transversal Rationality."

8. Van Huyssteen, *The Shaping of Rationality*, 118.

Notes for Chapter 4

1. A highly respected survey is Klein, *Interdisciplinarity*, which was more or less definitive for its era. Since that time, a large number of articles and books have been published. A notable volume containing the proceedings

of a conference on current issues is Klein, *Transdisciplinarity*. Other valuable volumes of a theoretical kind (that is, excluding policy and strategy volumes and publications focusing on cooperation between particular disciplines) are Klein, *Crossing Boundaries* and Somerville and Rapport, *Transdisciplinarity*.

2. Some of these terms are defined in Augsburg, *Becoming Interdisciplinary*. Though useful for specific purposes, such definitions presuppose an overly sharp view of the methodological distinctiveness and independence of disciplines, and thus are less than ideally satisfactory, philosophically. For example, *hyperdisciplinarity* (not defined by Augsburg) is often used to indicate that a subject matter has to be studied in such a way as to allow its intrinsic profile of importance to emerge, rather than remaining enslaved to the perspectives of contributing disciplinary perspectives. But respecting the intrinsic importance of a subject matter is vital in all inquiries, so the function of "hyperdisciplinarity" is actually to catalyze attention to the problem of distortion in multidisciplinary inquiries. This can be very important in specific contexts even though the name lacks a clear conceptual basis to distinguish it from alternative names. Much the same is true of the other names: the philosophical substance of a general theory of inquiry is needed to make sense of problem-oriented research because names alone do not go deeply enough into the structure and dynamics of human inquiry.

3. For example, see Eckel, *To See the Buddha*.

4. Kant, *Critique of Pure Reason*.

5. Husserl, *The Idea of Phenomenology*.

6. James, *Principles of Psychology*.

7. See Heidegger, *Being and Time*, especially Division 1, Chapter 2; and Peirce, "The Fixation of Belief."

8. Saint Anselm, *Proslogion*, especially the Preface and Chapter 1, 82–87.

9. Ibid., Chapter 2, 87.

10. Ibid., Chapter 15, 96.

11. Ibid., Chapter 16, 96–97.

12. Ibid., Chapters 2–4, 87–89.

13. Saint Anselm, *Monologion*, 5–81, especially Chapters 1–4, 11–16, and Chapter 28, 43–45.

14. For a contemporary example of treating the question of ontological dependence at the right level and with proper sensitivities to at least several relevant domains of experience and knowledge, see Neville, *God the Creator*. Neville does not relate his argument to Anselm's *Monologion* argument but he could have. Some of the connections to other disciplines are filled out in Neville's subsequent volume, *The Cosmology of Freedom*.

15. Indeed, Huston Smith has argued this, though more as a blunt critique of the natural sciences than by relating his perennial philosophy to the natural sciences in patient detail. See Smith, *Forgotten Truth*.

16. From the theological perspective, the classic work is Barth, *Fides Quaerens Intellectum*. From the logical side, the most subtle and determined effort is Campbell, *From Belief to Understanding*. Other key works on the *Pro-*

slogion argument are Hick and McGill, *The Many-Faced Argument* and Evans, *Anselm and Talking About God*.

17. The decline of Buddhism in India is widely traced to this long period of debate, stretching from the ninth to the twelfth centuries, with the debates themselves estimated as key factors in that decline. But claims that orthodox Hindu philosophers heroically battled off the atheists, though common enough, appear strained. It may be that some Hindu philosophers and their students succeeded over many centuries in making Buddhist (and other forms of) atheism less compelling than personal theism for some Indians. But this factor was minor compared with whether the political regime in a local region was unfavorably disposed to Buddhism. And the most important factor in the sharp decline in the fortunes of Buddhism was the destruction of Buddhist temples and the massacre of Buddhist monks by invading Muslims at the end of the twelfth century, which triggered mass migration of surviving Buddhists out of India.

18. See Dravid, *Nyāyakusumāñjali of Udayanācārya*, vol. 1, which includes an English translation.

19. The formulation of the tenth argument follows the analysis of Sri Swami Sivananda, "Isvara Or The Universal Soul."

20. For example, Sri Swami Sivananda's motivation in *God Exists* involves not overcoming Buddhist atheism but building confidence in Hindu teachings for modern people in the grip of a tendency to distrust authority and intuition and direct experience, and to rely instead on reason and the senses alone for sources of knowledge, whereafter God is a deeply problematic concept. See "Philosophical Proofs For The Existence Of God."

21. Swinburne, *The Coherence of Theism*, 5–7.

22. Swinburne, *The Existence of God*, 1–3.

23. Ibid., 15.

24. Ibid., 90–93. He provides a more compact statement of the meaning of "God" on 8 and 9.

25. See the summary in Swinburne, *The Existence of God*, 8 and the original argument in *The Coherence of Theism*, Chapter 12, 215–22.

26. Specifically, Swinburne's calculation of both the prior probability and the conditional probability of his God hypothesis (h) are invalidated by his failure to take account of competitor hypotheses. Suppose k refers to the background evidence pertinent to assessing the probability of h, and e is the other evidence specific to our current consideration of it. Then the prior probability of h is denoted $P(h\S k)$—the probability of the hypothesis given background knowledge and disregarding the evidence specifically under evaluation. It is possible that another hypothesis (h*) may have $P(h^*\S k) > P(h\S k)$, or the probabilities may be the other way around: $P(h\S k) > P(h^*\S k)$. An estimate of $P(h\S k)$ depends in a context on our knowledge of $P(h^*\S k)$ for all serious competitor hypotheses h*. That is, we might be inclined to think that Swinburne's personal divine being is the only explanation for the reality we encounter, and rate $P(h\S k)$ very highly. But if someone informs us that we overlooked ten other serious competitor hypotheses for the reality we

encounter, we would have to estimate P(hSk) much more modestly. Another way of expressing the same point is to say that P(hSk) depends on whether we include in the background knowledge, k, our knowledge from other disciplines that powerful alternative hypotheses to h exist. The conditional probability of h is denoted P(hSek)—the probability of h given both background knowledge, k, and the evidence under current consideration, e. Swinburne considers six pieces of evidence and argues that P(hSke)>P(hSk) for each piece individually. He considers one piece of contrary evidence and argues that P(hSke)=P(hSk) in that one case. But none of the evidence Swinburne considers includes the existence of serious competitor hypotheses, other than the flattened out atheistic alternative, which he finds himself able to dismiss rather easily. Moreover, for the six pieces of evidence that he does consider, he neither estimates the conditional probabilities of these serious competitors nor seeks to compare them to P(hSke). Knowledge of other disciplines forces us to admit competitor hypotheses to Swinburne's personal God hypothesis. We have to take preliminary account of them either as current evidence (e) or as background knowledge (k). We have to allow for them when we estimate P(hSk). We have to allow for them when we estimate P(hSke), and when we conclude that P(hSke)>P(hSk), for any piece of evidence, e. We have to estimate P(h*Ske) as carefully as we estimate P(hSke), and worry equally over whether P(h*Ske)>P(h*Sk). And we definitely have to worry about them when we seek to compare P(hSke) with P(h*Ske). Swinburne skips all of these steps, and covers the lack by eliminating serious competitor hypotheses without argument. Such a procedure crucially depends on the interests of the community for which he writes being essentially parochial in respect of knowledge brought by other disciplines about competitor hypotheses.

27. Swinburne explicitly acknowledges his obligation to estimate likelihood of hypotheses other than his own (*The Existence of God*, 18–19) but he does not make probability estimates of any of the good competitor hypotheses and also gives no argument for eliminating these serious competitor alternatives from consideration.

28. Swinburne, *The Existence of God*, 10.

29. For example, the March/April 2001 issue of the newsstand magazine and journal *Philosophy Now* included a section devoted to philosophy and food, with engaging essays such as Jeremy Iggers' introductory meditation on the American proverb "you are what you eat" and Raymond D. Boisvert's wittily titled "Philosophy Regains Its Senses," in which he argues that philosophers' historic disdain for food has had disastrous consequences for their philosophies. The openDemocracy website—which describes itself as the leading independent website on global current affairs—contains extensive resources on food and a multi-faceted debate under the heading of "Food without Frontiers" that includes an insightful philosophical essay by Roger Scruton entitled, "Eating the World: The Philosophy of Food." The quarterly journal *Gastronomica* occasionally contains articles on the philosophy of food. Key books on the philosophy of food include Curtin and Heldke, *Cooking, Eating, Thinking*; Heldke, Mommer, and Pineo, *The Atkins Diet and Philosophy*;

Korsmeyer, *Making Sense of Taste;* Onfray, *Le Ventre des Philosophes;* Onfray, *La Raison Gourmande,* and a series of other works; and Telfer, *Food for Thought.* As for conferences, in 1999 the Society for the Advancement of American Philosophy conference in Eugene, Oregon held a session on the philosophy of food. Mississippi State University hosted a conference organized by Glenn Kuehn on "Know Thyself: Food and the Human Condition" in 2002. In 2005, Oregon State University hosted a seminar on the philosophy of food. The 2007 meeting of the American Philosophical Association's Pacific Division included a mini-conference on the philosophy of wine.

30. There are large literatures on food and religion from disciplines other than philosophy, with hundreds of books containing discussions of the topic. The following list samples books specifically on religion and food covering a wide variety of disciplinary angles—from anthropology to theology, from economics to ethics, and from history to literature. Chitrita Banerji, *The Hour of the Goddess;* Beckman, *Grace at the Table;* BeDuhn, *The Manichaean Body;* Bell, *Holy Anorexia;* Bender, *Heaven's Kitchen;* Berry, *Food for the Gods;* Bynum, *Holy Feast and Holy Fast;* Curran, *Grace Before Meals;* De Silva, *Cultural Rhapsody;* Ehrlich, *Miriam's Kitchen;* Dutney, *Food, Sex, and Death;* Eisen, *Rethinking Modern Judaism;* Gabaccia, *We Are What We Eat;* Gardella, *Domestic Religion;* Grassi, *Bumping into God in the Kitchen;* Greenspoon, Simpkins, and Shapiro, *Food and Judaism;* Griffith, *Born Again Bodies;* Heinrich, *Strange Fruit;* Heinrich, *Magic Mushrooms in Religion and Alchemy;* Hollar, *Hunger for the Word;* Hussaini, *Food and Nutrition in Islam;* Juengst, *Breaking Bread;* Jung, *Food for Life;* Lelwica, *Starving for Salvation;* Mckenna, *Food of the Gods;* Morales, *The Guinea Pig;* Riaz and Chaudry, *Halal Food Production;* Rogak, *Death Warmed Over;* Rosen, *Diet for Transcendence;* Sack, *Whitebread Protestants;* Sider, *Rich Christians in an Age of Hunger;* Sterckx, *Of Tripod and Palate;* Vandereycken and Van Deth, *From Fasting Saints to Anorexic Girls;* and Vogt, *Tortillas for the Gods.*

31. I do develop a theological-philosophical anthropology elsewhere, with a strong emphasis on embodiment, though with less stress on food than the hypothesis here expounded suggests might be possible. See Wildman, *Science and Religious Anthropology.*

32. See Wittgenstein, *Philosophical Investigations.*

33. See Phillips, *Wittgenstein and Religion.*

34. See Lindbeck, *The Nature of Doctrine.*

35. Gadamer, *Truth and Method.*

36. In linguistics, see Ferdinand de Saussure; in anthropology, see Claude Levi-Strauss; in history, see Michael Foucault; in philosophy, see Jacques Derrida; in literary criticism and social theory, see Roland Barthes; in psychoanalysis, see Jacques Lacan. All of these figures, while initially given to structuralist modes of analysis and interpretation, eventually also criticized structuralism—and so, ironically, appear also on lists of representatives of what is now loosely called "post-structuralism"; obviously, then, the contrast is overdrawn.

37. In addition to those mentioned in above, philosopher Emmanuel Lévinas played a key role in raising consciousness about the importance of

the Other as routinely effaced in abstraction and as imposing an irreducible moral obligation upon us. See Lévinas, *Totality and Infinity*.

38. See Feyerabend, *Against Method*.

39. See Kuhn, *The Structure of Scientific Revolutions*.

40. Representative works in science studies are Barnes, Bloor, and Henry, *Scientific Knowledge*; Bloor, *Knowledge and Social Imagery*; Latour, *Science in Action*. Also see Biagioli, *The Science Studies Reader*.

41. Donald Davidson made something like this argument in "On the Very Idea of a Conceptual Scheme," in *Proceedings and Addresses of the American Philosophical Association*, 47 (1974). The article is reprinted in Davidson, *Inquiries into Truth and Interpretation*.

42. See Borthers, *Friday's Footprint*, xii.

Notes for Chapter 5

1. Witness the impact of Carl Linnaeus's famous taxonomy of animals and plants. The first edition of Linnaeus's taxonomy, *Systema Naturae*, was published in 1735 and it subsequently went into many editions, growing from a slender pamphlet to a multivolume work. It is still in use today, though with many changes and expansions. This is but one example of the many taxonomies and classifications in use our age, from product catalogues to types of religion.

2. The criticisms of Linnaeus' taxonomy are legion but the deepest problems with the taxonomy arise when morphological similarity makes organisms seem related, yet genomic information suggests evolutionary distance. This clouds the very concept of a species, which is one of the most crucial comparative categories of the classification.

3. See Aristotle, *Physica*, 1252b and Aristotle, *Generation of Animals*, I 728a.

4. See Plato, *Republic*, in which Plato allows women a role in the ruling class. But in *Timaeus*, 90e, the best that women can hope for in the process of rebirth is to become a man.

5. See Brothers, *Friday's Footprint*.

6. On the importance of this point for religion, see Wildman, "Cognitive Error and Contemplative Practices: The Cultivation of Discernment in Mind and Heart." Psychologists have produced many compendiums of errors due to biological limitations on human rationality and overactive pattern recognition, including examples of the ways that unscrupulous people exploit such vulnerabilities for their own profit and amusement. See, for example, Gilovich, *How We Know What Isn't So*; Piatelli-Palmarini, *Inevitable Illusions*; Plous, *The Psychology of Judgment and Decision Making*; Randi, *Flim Flam*; Sagan, *The Demon-Haunted World*; and Shermer, *Why People Believe Weird Things*.

7. There are many useful surveys available to those seeking more comprehensive and less quarrelsome coverage. Other ways of summariz-

ing approaches to the study of religion and the comparison of religious ideas include Sharpe, *Comparative Religion*; Helmer Ringgren, "Comparative Mythology" in *Encyclopedia of Religion*; Ninian Smart, "Comparative-Historical Method," ibid.; David Tracy, "Theology: Comparative Theology," ibid.; Capps, *Religious Studies*; and Clooney, *Seeing through Texts*. Also see Smid, *Methodologies of Comparative Philosophy*.

    8. For example see Wiebe, *Religion and Truth* and Wiebe, *Beyond Legitimation*.

    9. Doniger, *Women, Androgynes, and Other Mythical Beasts* and Doniger, *Dreams, Illusion and Other Realities*.

    10. Eckel, *To See the Buddha*.

    11. Clooney, *Theology after Vedānta* and Clooney, "Comparative Theology: A Review of Recent Books (1989–1995)."

    12. Smith, *Imagining Religion* and Smith, *Map is Not Territory*.

    13. On the question of how effective it is possible for cooperative problem solving to become, see Page, *The Difference*.

    14. See among numerous others Rahner, "Christianity and the Non-Christian Religions," and Pannenberg, "Toward a Theology of the History of Religions."

    15. For example, see Huxley, *The Perennial Philosophy*; Schuon, *The Transcendent Unity of Religions*; and Smith, *Forgotten Truth*.

    16. For example, see Campbell, *The Masks of God*, 4 vols.: *Primitive Mythology, Oriental Mythology, Occidental Mythology, Creative Mythology*; Eliade, *Cosmos and History*; Eliade, *Myths, Dreams, and Mysteries*; Eliade, *Images and Symbols*; Eliade, *The Sacred and the Profane*; Eliade, *Patterns in Comparative Religion*; and Eliade, *A History of Religious Ideas*: Volume 1, *From the Stone Age to the Eleusinian Mysteries*, Volume 2, *From Gautama Buddha to the Triumph of Christianity*, Volume 3, *From Muhammed to the Age of Reforms*.

    17. For example, see Hick, *An Interpretation of Religion*.

    18. The fruits of this research effort are especially evident in Smith, *The World's Religions*, a revised and updated edition of *The Religions of Man*.

    19. Frazer, *Creation and Evolution in Primitive Cosmogonies and Other Pieces*; Frazer, *The Golden Bough*; Spencer and Harrison, *The Nature and Reality of Religion*; and Tylor, *Primitive Cultures*.

    20. Durkheim, *The Elementary Forms of the Religious Life*; Lévi-Straus, *Totemism*; Lévi-Straus, *Structural Anthropology*; Douglas, *Natural Symbols: Explorations in Cosmology*; and Douglas, *Implicit Meanings*.

    21. Weber, *The Protestant Ethic and the Spirit of Capitalism*; Weber, *From Max Weber*; Weber, *The Religion of China*; Geertz, *The Interpretation of Cultures*; Geertz, "Deep Play: Notes on the Balinese Cockfight"; Berger, *The Sacred Canopy*; Berger and Luckmann, *The Social Construction of Reality*; and Berger, *The Other Side of God*.

    22. Jaynes, *The Origin of Consciousness in the Breakdown of the Bicameral Mind*; Ashbrook, *The Human Mind and the Mind of God*; D'Aquili, Laughlin, and McManus, *The Spectrum of Ritual*; d'Aquili and Andrew B. Newberg,

"Religious and Mystical States: A Neuropsychological Model"; and d'Aquili and Newberg, "The Neuropsychological Basis of Religions, or Why God Won't Go Away."

23. Boyer, *Religion Explained*; Boyer, *The Naturalness of Religious Ideas*; Wilson, *Darwin's Cathedral*; and Atran, *In Gods We Trust*.

24. Freud, *The Future of an Illusion*; Freud, *Civilization and Its Discontents*; Erikson, *Young Man Luther*; and Rizzuto, *The Birth of the Living God*.

25. Hegel, *Lectures on the Philosophy of Religion*: Volume 1, *Introduction and the Concept of Religion*, volume 2, *Determinate Religion*, volume 3, *The Consummate Religion*. Also see Toynbee, *An Historian's Approach to Religion*.

26. This criticism is made forcefully in Smith, *Imagining Religion*.

27. For example, see van der Leeuw, *Religion in Essence and Manifestation*; Kristensen, *The Meaning of Religion*; and Jastrow, *The Study of Religion*.

28. Sharpe, *Comparative Religion*; Sharpe, *Understanding Religion*; Smart, *The Phenomenon of Religion*; Smart, "Comparative-Historical Method"; Smith, *Faith and Belief*; and Smith, *Towards a World Theology*.

29. Though less systematic than any of the examples so far mentioned, one of the most pervasive suppliers and reinforcers of comparative categories is the almost universally used classification system of the United States Library of Congress. See Runchock and Droste, *Library of Congress Classification Schedules*.

30. Otto, *The Idea of the Holy*. Also relevant here are Ricoeur, *The Symbolism of Evil* and Ricoeur, *The Conflict of Interpretations*.

31. See Watson, *The Architectonics of Meaning* and Dilworth, *Philosophy in World Perspective*.

32. Tillich, *Systematic Theology*, vol. I.

33. Husserl, *Ideas* and Husserl, *The Crisis of European Sciences and Transcendental Phenomenology*.

34. Dennett, "A Method for Phenomenology."

35. Psychologists have made numerous efforts to regularize first-person reports of experiences so as to make them useful for constraining third-person theoretical hypotheses about the experiences in question. For example, see Pekala, *Quantifying Consciousness*; Pope and Singer, *The Stream of Consciousness*; and Revonsuo, *Inner Presence*.

36. For one account of how neurophysiology might make such a contribution to the study of religious experience, see Wildman and Brothers, "A Neuropsychological-Semiotic Model of Religious Experiences." Also see Wildman, *Religious and Spiritual Experiences*, Chapter 2.

37. Under the leadership of Robert Neville, the Comparative Religious Ideas Project brought together six tradition specialists (Frank Clooney, David Eckel, Paula Fredriksen, Noman al Haq, Livia Kohn, Anthony Saldarini) and four comparative generalists (Peter Berger, John Berthrong, Robert Neville, Wesley Wildman), as well as a number of graduate students. See Neville, *Ultimate Realities*.

38. Neville, *Normative Cultures*.

39. For an account of the self-conscious dialectic method in relation to the Comparative Religious Ideas Project, see Neville, *Ultimate Realities*,

Chapter 8, and the summary in Chapter 1 of that volume. A fuller account is furnished in several parts of Neville, *The Human Condition*. For a still more detailed presentation, though lacking some of the insights accrued during the process of the project, see Neville, *Normative Cultures*.

40. See Smith, "In Comparison a Magic Dwells," in *Imagining Religion*. The paper was initially presented to the History of Judaism section of the American Academy of Religion in 1979.

41. On this matter, see the discussions in Neville, *The Human Condition*, Chapters 1 and 2, and Neville, *Normative Cultures*, 74–84.

42. Smith, *Imagining Religion*, 21.

43. Ibid., 25. Note that Smith was an advisor on the CRIP project and concluded that one of its principal contributions consists in the fact that it effectively addresses the critique of comparison made in *Imagining Religion*. See Smith's Foreword to Neville, *Religious Truth*, xi-xii.

44. See the appendices to each of the volumes of the CRIP project for my account of the CRIP process.

45. Lakatos, "Falsification and the Methodology of Scientific Research Programmes."

46. Kuhn, *The Structure of Scientific Revolutions*.

47. Feyerabend, *Against Method*.

48. See Lakatos and Feyerabend, *For and Against Method*, which includes Lakatos's lectures on scientific method and the Lakatos-Feyerabend correspondence.

49. Newman, *An Essay in Aid of a Grammar of Assent*.

50. Popper, *The Logic of Scientific Discovery*.

51. Peirce, "The Fixation of Belief" and Dewey, *Logic*.

52. Peirce, *Essays in the Philosophy of Science*.

53. For an alternative presentation of the general theory of inquiry suggested here, as well as an application of it to religion, see Wildman, "The Resilience of Religion in Secular Social Environments: A Pragmatic Analysis."

54. See Atran, *In Gods We Trust* and Boyer, *Religion Explained*.

55. Something like this is ventured in Wildman, "From Law and Chance in Nature to Ultimate Reality."

56. For a fuller discussion of this conception of natural theology, see Wildman, "Comparative Natural Theology."

Notes for Chapter 6

1. See Hartshorne and Weiss, *Collected Papers of Charles Saunders Peirce*. Convenient collections of relevant writings exist, such as Buchler, *Philosophical Writings of Peirce* and Wiener, *Charles S. Peirce*.

2. See especially James, *Pragmatism* and James, *The Meaning of Truth*.

3. See especially Dewey, *Logic*.

4. See especially Whitehead, *Adventures of Ideas* and Whitehead, *Science and the Modern World*.

5. For example, see Wieman, *Religious Inquiry*

6. See Allan, *The Patterns of the Present*; Buchler, *Metaphysics of Natural Complexes*; Cohen, *The Case for Religious Naturalism*; Corrington, *A Semiotic Theory of Theology and Philosophy*; Crosby, *A Religion of Nature*; Ferré, *Knowing and Value*; Frankenberry, *Religion and Radical Empiricism*; Hardwick, *Events of Grace*; Johnston, *Saving God*; Shook and Kurts, *The Future of Naturalism*; Murry, *Reason and Reverence*; Neville, *The Highroad Around Modernism*; Nielson, *Naturalism and Religion*; Peden, *New Essays in Religious Naturalism*; Peters, *Dancding with the Sacred*; Ritchie, *Understanding Naturalism*; Rue, *Religion Is Not About God*; Santayana, *The Essential Santayana*; and Stone, *Religious Naturalism Today*.

7. James articulates a pragmatic theory of the meaning of truth, whereas Peirce held a correspondence view of the meaning of truth. Despite this disagreement, both allowed pragmatic considerations to count as criteria for justification. I follow Peirce against James in this matter. See James, *Pragmatism*; James, *The Meaning of Truth*; and especially vol. V of Peirce, *The Collected Papers of Charles Saunders Peirce*.

8. See Rorty, *Philosophy and the Mirror of Nature*.

9. For a standard catalogue of reasoning tendencies in human beings that routinely lead to mistakes, all of which are well tested in empirical psychology, see Gilovich, *How We Know What Isn't So*. Other empirically robust accounts of biological limitations on human rationality include Piatelli-Palmarini, *Inevitable Illusions* and Plous, *The Psychology of Judgment and Decision Making*.

10. There are numerous presentations of the effects on human belief systems of people not being educated enough to overcome their reasoning liabilities. See, for example, Sagan, *The Demon-Haunted World* and Shermer, *Why People Believe Weird Things*. Examples of the way that unscrupulous people exploit biologically based rational vulnerabilities for their own profit and amusement are presented in Randi, *Flim Flam*.

11. Cooper, *The Evolution of Reason*.

12. Dewey, *Logic*.

13. Ibid., iii.

14. Ann Swidler, in many of her works, writes of culture in settled and unsettled social conditions, developing a distinction originated by Geertz in *Interpretation of Cultures*. This distinction, as Swidler uses it, corresponds to the distinction here between the entire fabric of rational and cultural activity, much of which we absorb but do not think about—and those moments, periods, and places where things seem disturbed and problematic. For example, see Swidler, "Culture in Action: Symbols and Strategies."

15. See Byrne and Whiten, *Machiavellian Intelligence*; Cheney and Seyfarth, *How Monkeys See the World*; Humphrey, *A History of the Mind*; and Leaky, *The Origin of Humankind*.

16. See Brothers, *Friday's Footprint*.

17. On art, see Lewis-Williams, *The Mind in the Cave*. On language, see Deacon, *The Symbolic Species*. On the evolution of consciousness, see Humphrey, *The Inner Eye*.

18. Gould, *The Structure of Evolutionary Theory*, 1342; italics added.
19. See Gibson, *The Perception of the Visual World* in which he introduces the idea of "affordance." He generalized the theory to other senses in *The Senses Considered as Perceptual Systems*. The most developed form of the theory is laid down in Gibson's *The Ecological Approach to Visual Perception*.
20. Harry Heft traces out the connection between pragmatism and the ecological psychology of Gibson and others in *Ecological Psychology in Context*.
21. See the comments on the limited penetration of ecological psychology categories in James M.M. Good, "The Affordances for Social Psychology of the Ecological Approach to Social Knowing."
22. The best resource for investigating the intricacies of ecological psychology is the journal *Ecological Psychology*.
23. Hubert Dreyfus makes this same argument, not against the possibility of artificial intelligence research in principle, but against its possibility in practice. He draws on Martin Heidegger's account in *Being and Time* of human beings as "thrown"—as always, already embodied and embedded in a prodigiously complex and dynamic environment. See Dreyfus, *What Computers Still Can't Do* and Dreyfus and Dreyfus, *Mind Over Machine*.
24. Kant, *Critique of Pure Reason*.
25. See Sosis, "Religious Behaviors, Badges, and Bans: Signaling Theory and the Evolution of Religion."
26. See Chomsky, *Aspects of the Theory of Syntax*.
27. See the original work in Wierzbicka, *Semantic Primitives*. The semantic primes are explained in Wierzbicka, *Semantics*, and tested in Wierzbicka and Goddard, *Semantic and Lexical Universals—Theory and Empirical Findings* and Peeters, *Semantic Primes and Universal Grammar*. The Natural Semantic Metalanguage website (http://www.une.edu.au/bcss/linguistics/nsm/9) has recent lists of semantic primes in this ongoing research program.
28. See Austin, *How to Do Things with Words* and Searle, *Speech Acts*.
29. See De Saussure, *Course in General Linguistics*. For an introduction to semiotic analysis of large-scale communicative acts, see Barthes, *Elements of Semiology*.
30. Gödel, "Über formal unentscheidbare Sätze der Principia Mathematica und verwandter Systeme, I." For an English translation, see Gödel, "Some Basic Theorems on the Foundations of Mathematics and Their Implications."
31. See Rorty, *Philosophy and the Mirror of Nature* and James, *The Meaning of Truth*.
32. See Lakatos, *The Methodology of Scientific Research Programs*. Also see Lakatos and Musgrave, *Criticism and the Growth of Knowledge*.
33. See Feyerabend, *Against Method* and Lakatos and Feyerabend, *For and Against Method*.
34. See Clayton, *Explanation from Physics to Theology* and Murphy, *Theology in the Age of Scientific Reasoning*.

Notes for Chapter 7

1. See Beauchamp and Childress, *Principles of Biomedical Ethics*; Dorff, *Matters of Life and Death*; Harris, *The Value of Life*; and Pence, *Medical Ethics*.

2. See Larson andWitham, "Scientists are Still Keeping the Faith." Also see Larson and Witham, "Leading Scientists Still Reject God." Of course, believing in a supernatural realm does not entail belief in God, nor does the affirmation of some God concepts require supernaturalism. Nonetheless, Larson and Witham's research gives some indication about belief in supernaturalism among scientists in the United States.

3. On both discoveries, see Jonathan Haidt, "The New Synthesis in Moral Psychology"; Laura Helmuth, "Moral Reasoning Relies on Emotion"; and Waldmann, "A Case for the Moral Organ?"

4. There are numerous examples of scientists reflecting on scientific boundary questions outside their formal scientific work; many public pronouncements of scientists are of this type. Particularly interesting in this regard is the Science and the Spiritual Quest Project mounted by the Center for Theology and the Natural Sciences. See Richardson and Slack, eds., *Faith in Science*; Richardson, Russell, Clayton, and Wegter-McNelly, *Science and the Spiritual Quest*; and Clayton and Schaal, *Practicing Science, Living Faith*.

5. Chadwick, *The Secularization of the European Mind in the Nineteenth Century*.

6. Berger, *The Sacred Canopy*.

7. See, for example, Smith at al., *American Evangelicalism*, in which Smith argues that it is in part the conflicts and boundary questions provoked by secular culture and scientific rationality that help some forms of evangelicalism to thrive in the United States.

8. Accurate population statistics are difficult to produce at the best of times, and this is made more difficult by the varied techniques for estimating religious populations. The figures provided here are from a December 23, 2005 BBC report, which assembled data from numerous sources. See http://news.bbc.co.uk/2/hi/europe/4385768.stm7.

9. Berger, "The Desecularization of the World: A Global Overview."

10. Ibid., 9.

11. Ibid., 10.

12. See Draper, *History of the Conflict between Religion and Science* and White, *History of the Warfare of Science with Theology in Christendom*.

13. See, for example, Brooke, *Science and Religion*; Lindberg and Westman, *Reappraisals of the Scientific Revolution*; Numbers *Galileo Goes to Jail*; and Welch, "Dispelling some Myths about the Split between Theology and Science in the Nineteenth Century."

14. See Berger, "The Desecularization of the World," 11.

15. See Hawking, *A Brief History of Time*. See an analysis of Hawking's proposal in Russell, "Finite Creation Without a Beginning."

16. See James, *The Will to Believe*.

17. This point is made in a humorous yet compelling way in the 2007 film *Flock of Dodos* by American biologist Randy Olson.

Notes for Chapter 8

1. Marion, *God Without Being*. See also his *Being Given*, which is a fine expression of the tension mentioned above within the ontotheological tradition between the causal and manifestation of approaches to understanding ultimacy through being.

2. See Kant, *Critique of Pure Reason*, Second Division (Transcendental Dialectic), Book II (The Dialectical Inferences of Pure Reason), Chapter III (The Ideal of Pure Reason), Section 4 (The Impossibility of an Ontological Proof of the Existence of God).

3. For Guanilo's reply to Anselm, see "In Behalf of the Fool," in *Anselm of Canterbury: The Major Works*. For Gottfried Leibniz's version, see Leibnitz, *New Essays Concerning Human Understanding*. For Immanuel Kant's discussion of the argument, see *Critique of Pure Reason*.

4. See Neville, *God the Creator*.

5. See Neville, *The Axiology of Thinking*. Volume 1: *Reconstruction of Thinking*. Volume 2: *Recovery of the Measure* Volume 3: *Normative Cultures*.

6. See Lévinas, *Totality and Infinity* and Lévinas, *Otherwise Than Being*.

7. See Kant, *Critique of Pure Reason*, Second Division (Transcendental Dialectic), Book II (The Dialectical Inferences of Pure Reason), Chapter III (The Ideal of Pure Reason), Section 5 (The Impossibility of a Cosmological Proof of the Existence of God).

8. See Tillich, *Systematic Theology*, vol. 1.

9. Heidegger, *Being and Time*.

10. See the Introduction to Schleiermacher, *The Christian Faith*.

11. See Thomas Aquinas, Part 1 Question 2 of *Summa Theologiae*.

12. See Craig and Smith, *Theism, Atheism, and Big Bang Cosmology* and Craig, *The Kalām Cosmological Argument*. In the latter book, especially, Craig draws on both Muslim and Jewish resources—the first of the great Muʿtazilite philosophers Isḥāq al-Kindi (c 801–c 873), the most renowned Ashʿarite philosopher, al-Ghāzāli (1058–1111), and the medieval Jewish thinker Saadia ben Joseph (882–942).

13. Robert Jastrow, "Have Astronomers Found God?" The subhead and premise of the article is, "Theologians are delighted that the astronomical evidence leads to a biblical view of Genesis—but curiously, astronomers are upset."

14. This argument is presented in an accessible form in Hawking, *A Brief History of Time*.

15. The classic reference is Barrow and Tipler, *The Anthropic Cosmological Principle*. For an updated account in astrobiological terms, see Barrow, Morris,

Freeland, and Harper, *Fitness of the Cosmos for Life*. Also see Manson, *God and Design* and Ratzsch, *Nature, Design, and Science*.

16. An excellent work surveying this territory by one of the original creators of the theory is Alexander Vilenkin, *Many Worlds in One*. Also see Linde, *Inflation and the Quantum Cosmology* and Steinhardt, *Endless Universe*.

17. See Susskind, *The Cosmic Landscape*.

18. Aristotle's biological and zoological works include *Parts of Animals* (*De partibus animalium*), *On the Gait of Animals* (*De incessu animalium*), *Generation of Animals* (*De generatione animalium*), *On the Motion of Animals* (*De motu animalium*), *History of Animals* (*Historia animalium*), and *Short Physical Treatises* (*Parva naturalia*).

19. Aristotle, *Parts of Animals*, IV.12, $694^b.13$ (this refers to book.chapter, page^{column}line of the Berlin Greek text of Aristotle's works).

20. Aristotle, *Generation of Animals*, V.8, $788^b.22$.

21. Aristotle, *Gait of Animals*, 2, $704^b.15$.

22. Aristotle, *Generation of Animals*, IV.11, $691^b.4$.

23. Aristotle's statement of evolutionary theory is in *Physics* (*Physica*) II.8, $198^b.17-32$, referring to Empedocles' "man-faced ox-progeny" as an illustration of what we now call random variation. See Empedocles, *On Nature*. Aristotle's (less convincing) refutation follows in $198^b.34-199^b.32$.

24. Paley, *Natural Theology—of Evidences of the Existence and Attributes of the Deity Collected from the Appearances of Nature*.

25. The classic references include Dembski, *The Design Inference* and Behe, *Darwin's Black Box*. A survey work covering multiple positions in the intelligent design debate is Pennock, *Intelligent Design Creationism and its Critics*. Also see Dembski and Ruse, *Debating Design* and Shermer, *Why Darwin Matters*.

26. See René Descartes, *Treatise of Man* and *The Passions of the Soul*.

27. On the issue of philosophical evasiveness, see Searle, *The Mystery of Consciousness*.

28. For example, see Churchland, "Eliminative Materialism and the Propositional Attitudes"; Churchland, *Matter and Consciousness*; Churchland, *Neurophilosophy*; Stitch, *From Folk Psychology to Cognitive Science*; and Stitch, *Deconstructing the Mind*.

29. See Broad, *The Mind and Its Place in Nature*; Searle, *The Rediscovery of Mind*; and Shear, *Explaining Consciousness*.

30. For an account of the difficulties, see Chalmers, *The Conscious Mind*.

31. See Locke, *An Essay Concerning Human Understanding* and Kant, *Critique of Pure Reason*.

32. Hegel, *The Phenomenology of Spirit*.

33. A classic catalogue of this sort is Gilovich, *How We Know What Isn't So*.

34. The significance for religious philosophy of experimental psychology's discoveries about the cognitive reliability of human perception and

reasoning is discussed in Wildman, "Cognitive Error and Contemplative Practices" and Wildman, *Science and Religious Anthropology*.

35. Legge, *The Chinese Classics*.

36. Legge, *Confucian Analects, The Great Learning, and the Doctrine of the Mean*.

37. See Nietzsche, *Beyond Good and Evil* and Nietzsche, *A Genealogy of Morals*.

38. For example, see Peirce, *Values in a Universe of Chance*; Dewey, *Reconstruction in Philosophy*; and James, *Essays in Radical Empiricism*.

39. For example, see Whitehead, *Process and Reality*; Hartshorne, *The Divine Relativity*; Ferré, *Being and Value*; Ferré, *Knowing and Value*; Ferré, *Living and Value*; and Neville, *The Axiology of Thinking*, 3 vols.

40. For example, see Tu, *Confucian Thought* and Tu, *Humanity and Self-Cultivation*.

41. Classic works include Huxley, *The Perennial Philosophy*; Schuon, *The Transcendent Unity of Religions*; and Smith, *Forgotten Truth*. Also see the Perennial Philosophy Series from World Wisdom Publishers of Bloomington, Indiana, which has published several dozen titles since 2002.

42. For variations and historical developments of this idea, see Lovejoy, *The Great Chain of Being*.

43. This appears to be the view of Kai Nielson, who regards as incoherent what I am calling the core hypothesis of the mysticotheological tradition of religious philosophy. See Nielson, *Naturalism and Religion*.

44. For example, in the Christian context, so-called Liberal Protestants such as Albrecht Ritschl and Adolf von Harnack, in harmony with their theological culture, occasionally expressed deep misgivings about mystical experience and the sorts of theology to which it gave rise. In the Jewish context, Kabala has often been regarded with suspicion. And Confucians frequently deemed their mystically minded Daoist brethren as given to excesses of irrational enthusiasm.

45. See Searle, *Speech Acts* and Searle, *Expression and Meaning*.

46. See Sells, *Mystical Languages of Unsaying* and Knepper, "How to Say What Can't Be Said: Techniques and Rules of Ineffability in the Dionysian Corpus."

47. See Wildman, "Strategic Mechanisms within Religious Symbol Systems," 273–91.

48. Just such a view is presented in Wildman, *Science and Religious Anthropology*.

49. The similarities among mystical-theological conceptual frameworks are more pronounced than the similarities among mystical writings and mystical experiences. Indeed, one of the criticisms of contextualists in the study of mystical writings and experiences is that perennialists underestimate the context-specific intricacy of accounts of mystical experience in order to buttress the perennialist conceptual framework. For standard contextualist critiques, see Steven Katz, *Mysticism and Philosophical Analysis*; Proudfoot, *Religious Experience*;

and Bagger, *Religious Experience, Justification, and History*. The concern here is with the conceptual frameworks, not with mystical writings or experiences. For a thorough analysis of this issue as well as a constructive theory of the cognitive reliability of mystical and other religious experiences, see Wildman, *Religious and Spiritual Experiences*.

Notes for Afterword

1. Scholars have made many criticisms and defenses of the possibility and value of tasks related to religious philosophy in passing, and as such they are almost immune from evaluation. Only a few criticisms and defenses have received extended treatment in scholarly writings. For a short list of book-length discussions of the relevant issues from numerous points of view in the last few decades, see Antes, Geertz, and Warne, *New Approaches to the Study of Religion*, 2 vols., especially vol. 1, sec. 2 on "Critical Approaches"—as well as other volumes in de Gruyter's Religion and Reason series; Coulson, *Theology and the University*, especially Chapters 1 and 8–11; Griffin and Hough, *Theology and the University*, especially Chapters 1–8; Jakelić and Pearson, *The Future of the Study of Religion*; McCutcheon, *Critics Not Caretakers*, as well as other volumes in the SUNY series Issues in the Study of Religion; Penner, *Impasse and Resolution*, as well as other volumes in Pater Lang's Toronto Studies in Religion series; Wiebe, *Religion and Truth*, as well as other volumes in Mouton's series in Method and Theory in the Study and Interpretation of Religion; Wiebe, *Beyond Legitimation*; and Wiebe, *The Politics of Religious Studies*.

2. See Mahoney and Schmalzbauer, "Religion and Knowledge in the Post-Secular Academy."

Bibliography

Allan, George. *The Patterns of the Present: Interpreting the Authority of Form.* Albany, NY: State University of New York Press, 2001.

Alston, William P. "Religion." In *The Encyclopedia of Philosoophy*, Paul Edwards, Editor in Chief, vol. 7, 140-145. New York: Macmillan Publishing Co. and The Free Press, 1967.

Anselm, Saint. *Anselm of Canterbury: The Major Works*, edited by Brian Davies and G.R. Evans. Oxford and New York: Oxford University Press, 1998.

———. *Monologion.* In *Anselm of Canterbury: The Major Works*, edited by Brian Davies and G.R. Evans. Oxford and New York: Oxford University Press, 1998.

———. *Proslogion.* In *Anselm of Canterbury: The Major Works*, edited by Brian Davies and G.R. Evans. Oxford and New York: Oxford University Press, 1998.

Antes, Peter, Atmin W. Geertz, and Randi R. Warne, eds. *New Approaches to the Study of Religion*, 2 vols. Berlin and New York: Walter de Gruyter, 2004.

Aristotle. *Generation of Animals (De generatione animalium).* Loeb Classical Library (Aristotle, vol. XIII), translated by A. L. Peck. Cambridge, MA: Harvard University Press.

———. *History of Animals (Historia animalium).* Loeb Classical Library (Aristotle, vols. IX, X, XI), translated by A. L. Peck (vols. IX, X), D. M. Balme (vol. XI). Cambridge, MA: Harvard University Press.

———. *Parts of Animals (De partibus animalium), Movement of Animals (De motu animalium), Progression of Animals (De incessu animalium).* Loeb Classical Library (Aristotle, vol. XII), translated by A. L. Peck and E. S. Forster. Cambridge, MA: Harvard University Press.

———. *Physics (Physica).* Loeb Classical Library (Aristotle, vols. IV, V), translated by P. H. Wicksteed and F. M. Cornford. Cambridge, MA: Harvard University Press.

———. *Short Physical Treatises (Parva naturalia)*. Loeb Classical Library (Aristotle, vol. VIII), translated by W. S. Hett. Cambridge, MA: Harvard University Press.

Ashbrook, James B. *The Human Mind and the Mind of God: Theological Promise in Brain Research*. Lanham, MD: University Press of America, 1984.

Atran, Scott. *In Gods We Trust: The Evolutionary Landscape of Religion*. Evolution and Cognition Series. Oxford and New York: Oxford University Press, 2002.

Augsburg, Tanya. *Becoming Interdisciplinary: An Introduction to Interdisciplinary Studies*, 2nd ed. Dubuque, IA: Kendall/Hunt Publishing Company, 2006.

Austin, John L. *How to Do Things with Words*, 2nd ed. Cambridge, MA: Harvard University Press, 1975.

Bagger, Matthew C. *Religious Experience, Justification, and History*. Cambridge, UK: Cambridge University Press, 1999.

Banerji, Chitrita. *The Hour of the Goddess: Memories of Women, Food, and Ritual in Bengal*, 2nd ed. London: Penguin Global, 2007.

Barnes, S. Barry, David Bloor, and John Henry. *Scientific Knowledge: A Sociological Analysis*. Chicago: University of Chicago Press, 1996.

Barrow, John D. and Frank J. Tipler. *The Anthropic Cosmological Principle*. With a foreword by John A. Wheeler. Oxford: Clarendon Press, 1986.

Barrow, John D., Simon Conway Morris, Stephen J. Freeland, and Charles L. Harper, Jr., eds. *Fitness of the Cosmos for Life: Biochemistry and Fine-Tuning*. Cambridge Astrobiology Series, no. 2. Cambridge, UK: Cambridge University Press, 2008.

Barth, Karl. *Fides Quaerens Intellectum: Anselm's Proof of the Existence of God in the Context of His Theological Scheme*. Translated by I. Robertson. London: SCM, 1960.

Barthes, Roland. *Elements of Semiology*. Translated by Annette Lavers and Colin Smith. London: Jonathan Cape, 1967.

Beauchamp, Tom L. and James F. Childress. *Principles of Biomedical Ethics*, 6th ed. Oxford and New York: Oxford University Press, 2008.

Beauregard, Mario and Denise O'Leary. *The Spiritual Brain: A Neuroscientist's Case for the Existence of the Soul*. New York: HarperOne, 2007.

Beckman, David. *Grace at the Table: Ending Hunger in God's World*. Mahwah, NJ: Paulist Press, 1999.

BeDuhn, Jason David. *The Manichaean Body: In Discipline and Ritual*. Baltimore, MD: The Johns Hopkins University Press, 2000.

Behe, Michael J. *Darwin's Black Box: The Biochemical Challenge to Evolution*. New York: Free Press, 1996.

Bell, Rudolph M. *Holy Anorexia*. Chicago: University of Chicago Press, 1985.

Bender, Courtney. *Heaven's Kitchen: Living Religion at God's Love We Deliver*. Chicago: University of Chicago Press, 2003.

Berger, Peter L. "The Desecularization of the World: A Global Overview." In *The Desecularization of the World: Resurgent Religion and World Politics*,

edited by Peter L. Berger, 1–19. Grand Rapids, MI: The Ethics and Public Policy Center and William B. Eerdmans Publishing Company, 1999.
———, ed. *The Other Side of God: A Polarity in World Religions*. Garden City, NY: Doubleday & Co., 1981.
———. *The Sacred Canopy: Elements of a Sociological Theory of Religion*. Garden City, NY: Doubleday & Co., 1967.
Berger, Peter L. and Thomas Luckmann. *The Social Construction of Reality: A Treatise in the Sociology of Knowledge*. Garden City, NY: Doubleday & Co., 1966.
Berry, Rynn. *Food for the Gods: Vegetarianism and the World's Religions*. New York: Pythagorean Books, 1998.
Biagioli, Mario, ed. *The Science Studies Reader*. New York: Routledge, 1999.
Bloor, David. *Knowledge and Social Imagery*, 2nd ed. Chicago: University of Chicago Press, 1991.
Boyer, Pascal. *Religion Explained: The Human Instincts that Fashion Gods, Spirits, and Ancestors*. London: Heinemann and New York: Basic Books, 2001.
———. *The Naturalness of Religious Ideas: A Cognitive Theory of Religion*. Berkeley, CA: University of California Press, 1994.
Broad, C. D. *The Mind and Its Place in Nature*. London: Routledge & Kegan, 1925.
Brooke, John Hedley. *Science and Religion: Some Historical Perspectives*. New York and Cambridge, UK: Cambridge University Press, 1991.
Brothers, Leslie A. *Friday's Footprint: How Society Shapes the Human Mind*. New York: Oxford University Press, 1997.
Brown, W. A. *The Case for Theology in the University*. Chicago: The University of Chicago Press, 1938.
Buchler, Justus. *Metaphysics of Natural Complexes*. Albany, NY: State University of New York Press, 2008
Bynum, Caroline Walker. *Holy Feast and Holy Fast: The Religious Significance of Food to Medieval Women*. Berkeley and Los Angeles, CA: University of California Press, 1987.
Byrne, Richard and Andrew Whiten. *Machiavellian Intelligence: Social Expertise and the Evolution of Intellect in Monkeys, Apes, and Humans*. Oxford: Clarendon Press, 1988.
Cady, L. E. and D. Brown. *Religious Studies, Theology, and the University: Conflicting Maps, Changing Terrain*. Albany, NY: State University of New York Press, 2002.
Campbell, Joseph. *The Masks of God*, 4 vols.: *Primitive Mythology, Oriental Mythology, Occidental Mythology*, and *Creative Mythology*. New York: Viking Press, 1959–1968.
Campbell, Richard. *From Belief to Understanding*. Canberra, Australia: Australian National University, 1976.
Capps, Walter H. *Religious Studies: The Making of a Discipline*. Minneapolis, MN: Fortress Press, 1993.

Chadwick, Owen. *The Secularization of the European Mind in the Nineteenth Century: The Gifford Lectures in the University of Edinburgh for 1973-4.* Cambridge. UK and New York: Cambridge University Press, 1975.

Chalmers, David J. *The Conscious Mind: In Search of a Theory of Conscious Experience.* New York: Oxford University Press, 1996.

Cheney, Dorothy L. and Robert M. Seyfarth. *How Monkeys See the World.* Chicago: University of Chicago Press, 1990.

Chomsky, Noam. *Aspects of the Theory of Syntax.* Cambridge, MA: The MIT Press, 1965.

Churchland, Patricia S. *Neurophilosophy: Toward a Unified Science of the Mind/Brain.* Cambridge, MA: The MIT Press, 1986.

Churchland, Paul M. "Eliminative Materialism and the Propositional Attitudes." *Journal of Philosophy* 78 (1981): 67–90.

———. *Matter and Consciousness*, rev. ed. Cambridge, MA: The MIT Press, 1988.

Clayton, Philip. *Explanation from Physics to Theology: An Essay in Rationality and Religion.* New Haven, CT: Yale University Press, 1989.

Clayton, Philip and Jim Schaal, eds. *Practicing Science, Living Faith: Interviews with Twelve Leading Scientists.* New York: Columbia University Press, 2007.

Clooney, Frank. "Comparative Theology: A Review of Recent Books (1989–1995)." *Theological Studies* 56 (1995): 521–50.

———. *Seeing Through Texts: Doing Theology among the Srivaisnavas of South India.* Albany, NY: State University of New York Press, 1996.

———. *Theology After Vedānta: An Experiment in Comparative Theology.* Albany, NY: State University of New York Press, 1993.

Cohen, Jack Joseph. *The Case for Religious Naturalism: A Philosophy for the Modern Jew.* Jenkintown, PA: Reconstructionist Press, 1958.

Cooper, William S. *The Evolution of Reason: Logic as a Branch of Biology*, Cambridge Studies in Philosophy and Biology. Cambridge, UK and New York: Cambridge University Press, 2001.

Corrington, Robert S. *A Semiotic Theory of Theology and Philosophy.* Cambridge, UK and New York: Cambridge University Press, 2000.

Coulson, John, ed. *Theology and the University: An Ecumenical Investigation.* Baltimore, MD: Helicon Press and London: Darton, Longman & Todd, 1964.

Craig, William Lane. *The Kalām Cosmological Argument.* Eugene, OR: Wipf and Stock Publishers, 1979.

Craig, William Lane and Quentin Smith. *Theism, Atheism, and Big Bang Cosmology.* Oxford: Clarendon Press, 1993.

Crosby, Don. *A Religion of Nature.* Albany, NY: State University of New York Press, 2002.

Curran, Patricia. *Grace before Meals: Food Ritual, and Body Discipline in Convent Culture.* Champaign, IL: University of Illinois Press, 1989.

Curtin, Deane and Lisa M. Heldke, eds. *Cooking, Eating, Thinking: Transformative Philosophies of Food.* Bloomington, IN: Indiana University Press, 1992.

d'Aquili, Eugene and Andrew B. Newberg. "Religious and Mystical States: A Neuropsychological Model." *Zygon* 28/2 (1993): 177–99.

———. "The Neuropsychological Basis of Religions, or Why God Won't Go Away." *Zygon* 33/2 (1998): 190–91.

d'Aquili, Eugene, Charles D. Laughlin, and J. McManus. *The Spectrum of Ritual: A Biogenetic Structural Analysis*. New York: Columbia University Press, 1979.

Davidson, Donald. "On the Very Idea of a Conceptual Scheme." In *Inquiries into Truth and Interpretation*, 2nd ed, 183–198. Oxford: Clarendon Press, 2001.

de Saussure, Ferdinand. *Course in General Linguistics*. Translated by W. Baskin. Glasgow, UK: Fontana/Collins, 1977.

De Silva, Vinodini. *Cultural Rhapsody: Ceremonial Food and Rituals of Sri Lanka*. Colombo, Sri Lanka: Unilever Cultural Conservation Trust of Sri Lanka, 2000.

Deacon, Terrence. *The Symbolic Species: The Coevolution of Language and the Brain*. New York: W.W. Norton & Company, 1998.

Dembski, William A. and Michael Ruse. *Debating Design: From Darwin to DNA*. Cambridge, UK and New York: Cambridge University Press, 2004.

Dembski, William J. *The Design Inference: Eliminating Chance through Small Probabilities*. Cambridge, UK: Cambridge University Press, 1998.

Dennett, Daniel C. "A Method for Phenomenology." In *Consciousness Explained*, 66–98. Boston: Little, Brown and Company, 1991.

Descartes, René. *The Passions of the Soul*. In *The Philosophical Writings of Descartes*, 2 vols., edited by J. Cottingham, R. Stoothoff, and D. Murdoch. Cambridge, UK: Cambridge University Press, 1984.

———. *Treatise of Man*. In *The Philosophical Writings of Descartes*, 2 vols., eds., J. Cottingham, R. Stoothoff, and D. Murdoch. Cambridge, UK: Cambridge University Press, 1984.

Dewey, John. *Logic: The Theory of Inquiry*. New York: Henry Holt, 1938.

———. *Reconstruction in Philosophy*. New York: Henry Holt and Co., 1920.

Dilworth, David A. *Philosophy in World Perspective: A Comparative Hermeneutic of the Major Theories*. New Haven, CT: Yale University Press, 1989.

Doniger, Wendy. *Dreams, Illusion and Other Realities*. Chicago: University of Chicago Press, 1984.

———. *Women, Androgynes, and Other Mythical Beasts*. Chicago: University of Chicago Press, 1980.

Dorff, Elliot N. *Matters of Life and Death: A Jewish Approach to Modern Medical Ethics*. Philadelphia, PA: Jewish Publication Society, 1998.

Douglas, Mary. *Implicit Meanings: Essays in Anthropology*. New York: Methuen, 1978.

———. *Natural Symbols: Explorations in Cosmology*. New York: Random House, 1972.

Draper, John William. *History of the Conflict between Religion and Science*. New York: D. Appleton and Company, 1875.

Dravid, N.S. *Nyāyakusumāñjali of Udayanācārya*, vol. 1. New Delhi, India: Indian Council of Philosophical Research, 1996.
Dreyfus, Hubert L. *What Computers Still Can't Do: A Critique of Artificial Reason*, 3rd ed. Cambridge, MA: The MIT Press, 1992.
Dreyfus, Hubert L and Stuart E. Dreyfus. *Mind Over Machine: The Power of Human Intuition and Expertise in the Era of the Computer*. New York: Free Press, 1986.
Durkheim, Emile. *The Elementary Forms of the Religious Life*. Translated by Joseph Ward Swain. New York: The Free Press and London: Collier Macmillan Publishers, 1915.
Dutney, Andrew. *Food, Sex, and Death: A Personal Account of Christianity*. Melbourne, Australia: Uniting Church Press, 1993.
Eagleton, Terry. *Ideology: An Introduction*. London and New York: Verso, 1991.
Eckel, Malcolm David. *To See the Buddha: A Philosopher's Quest for the Meaning of Emptiness*. San Francisco, CA: Harper and Row, 1992.
Ehrlich, Elizabeth. *Miriam's Kitchen: A Memoir*. New York: Penguin, 1998.
Eisen, Arnold M. *Rethinking Modern Judaism: Ritual, Commandment, Community*. Chicago: Chicago University Press, 1998.
Eliade, Mircea. *Cosmos and History: The Myth of the Eternal Return*. New York: Harper, 1954.
———. *A History of Religious Ideas*, vol. 1, *From the Stone Age to the Eleusinian Mysteries*. Translated by Willard R. Trask. Chicago: University of Chicago Press, 1978.
———. *A History of Religious Ideas*, vol. 2, *From Gautama Buddha to the Triumph of Christianity*. Translated by Willard R. Trask. Chicago: University of Chicago Press, 1982.
———. *A History of Religious Ideas*, vol. 3, *From Muhammed to the Age of Reforms*. Translated by Alf Hiltebeitel and Diane Apostolos-Cappadona. Chicago: University of Chicago Press, 1985.
———. *Images and Symbols*. New York: Sheed & Ward, 1961.
———. *Myths, Dreams, and Mysteries*. New York: Harper, 1960.
———. *Patterns in Comparative Religion: A Study of the Element of the Sacred in the History of Religious Phenomena*. Translated by Rosemary Sheed. New York: Sheed and Ward, 1958.
———. *The Sacred and the Profane: The Nature of Religion*. Translated by Willard R. Trask. New York: Harcourt, Brace, 1959.
Empedocles. *On Nature*. In *The Presocratic Philosophers*, 2nd ed., edited by G. S. Kirk, J. E. Raven, and M. Schofield. Cambridge, UK: Cambridge University Press, 1983.
Erikson, Erik H. *Young Man Luther: A Study in Psychoanalysis and History*. New York: W.W. Norton, 1958.
Evans, G.R. *Anselm and Talking About God*. Oxford: Oxford University Press, 1978.
Ferré, Frederick. *Being and Value: Toward a Constructive Postmodern Metaphysics*. Albany, N.Y.: State University of New York Press, 1996.

———. *Knowing and Value: Toward a Constructive Postmodern Epistemology.* Albany, NY: State University of New York Press, 1998.

———. *Living and Value: Toward a Constructive Postmodern Ethics.* Albany, NY: State University of New York Press, 2001.

Feyerabend, Paul K. *Against Method: Outline of an Anarchist Theory of Knowledge,* 3rd ed. London and New York: Verso, 1993.

Fitzgerald, T. *The Ideology of Religious Studies.* New York: Oxford University Press, 2000.

Forman, Robert K. C. *Mysticism, Mind, Consciousness.* Albany, NY: State University of New York Press, 1999.

Foucault, Michel. *The Archeology of Knowledge.* Translated by A.M. Sheridan Smith. New York: Pantheon Books, 1972.

———. *The Birth of the Clinic: An Archeology of Medical Perception.* Translated by A.M. Sheridan Smith. New York: Pantheon Books, 1973.

———. *Discipline and Punish: The Birth of the Prison.* Translated by Alan Sheridan. New York: Vintage Books, 1977.

———. *The History of Sexuality.* Translated by Robert Hurley. New York: Pantheon Books, 1978.

———. *Madness and Civilization: A History of Insanity in the Age of Reason.* Translated by Richard Howard. New York: Pantheon Books, 1965.

Frankenberry, Nancy. *Radical Interpretation in Religion.* Cambridge, UK: Cambridge University Press, 2002.

———. *Religion and Radical Empiricism.* Albany, NY: State University of New York Press, 1987.

Frankenberry, Nancy, and H. H. Penner. *Language, Truth, and Religious Belief: Studies in Twentieth-Century Theory and Method in Religion.* Atlanta, GA: Scholars Press, 1999.

Frazer, James. *Creation and Evolution in Primitive Cosmogonies and Other Pieces.* New York: Ayer, 1935.

———. *The Golden Bough.* New York: Macmillan, 1985.

Freeden, Michael. *Ideology: A Very Short Introduction.* Oxford: Oxford University Press, 2003.

Freud, Sigmund. *Civilization and Its Discontents.* New York: W.W. Norton, 1984.

———. *The Future of an Illusion.* New York: W.W. Norton, 1975.

Gabaccia, Donna R. *We Are What We Eat: Ethnic Food and the Making of Americans,* 2nd ed. Cambridge, MA.: Harvard University Press, 2000.

Gadamer, Hans-Georg. *Truth and Method.* New York: Crossroad, 1989.

Gardella, Peter. *Domestic Religion: Work, Food, Sex, and Other Commitments.* Cleveland, OH: Pilgrim Press, 1998.

Geertz, Clifford. "Deep Play: Notes on the Balinese Cockfight." In *Interpretive Social Science: A Second Look,* edited by by Paul Rabinow and William M. Sullivan, 195-240. Berkeley, CA: University of California Press, 1988.

———. *Interpretation of Cultures: Selected Essays.* New York: Basic Books, 1973.

Gibson, James J. *The Ecological Approach to Visual Perception.* Boston: Houghton Mifflin, 1979.

———. *The Perception of the Visual World*. Boston: Houghton Mifflin, 1950.
———. *The Senses Considered as Perceptual Systems*. Boston: Houghton Mifflin, 1966.
Gilovich, Thomas. *How We Know What Isn't So: The Fallibility of Human Reason in Everyday Life*. New York: The Free Press, 1991.
Gödel, Kurt. "Some Basic Theorems on the Foundations of Mathematics and Their Implications." In *Collected Works*, vol. 3, edited by Solomon Feferman, 304–23. Oxford and New York: Oxford University Press, 1951.
———. "Über formal unentscheidbare Sätze der Principia Mathematica und verwandter Systeme, I," *Monatshefte für Mathematik und Physik* 38 (1931): 173–98.
Good, James M.M. "The Affordances for Social Psychology of the Ecological Approach to Social Knowing." *Theory and Psychology* 17/2 (2007): 265–95.
Gould, Stephen J. *The Structure of Evolutionary Theory*. Cambridge, MA: Harvard University Press, 2002.
Grassi, Dominic. *Bumping into God in the Kitchen: Savory Stories of Food, Family, and Faith*. Chicago: Loyola Press, 2007.
Greenspoon, Leonard J., Ronald A. Simpkins, and Gerald Shapiro, eds. *Food and Judaism*. Omaha, NE: Creighton University Press, 2006.
Griffin, David Ray, and Joseph C. Hough, Jr., eds. *Theology and the University: Essays in Honor of John B. Cobb, Jr*. Albany, NY: State University of New York Press, 1991.
Griffith, R. Marie *Born Again Bodies: Flesh and Spirit in American Christianity*. Berkeley and Los Angeles, CA: University of California Press, 2004.
Haidt, Jonathan. "The New Synthesis in Moral Psychology." *Science* 316 (May 18, 2007): 990–1002.
Hardwick, Charley D. *Events of Grace: Naturalism, Existentialism, and Theology*. Cambridge, UK: Cambridge University Press, 1996.
Harris, John. *The Value of Life: An Introduction to Medical Ethics*. London and New York: Routledge, 1985.
Hartshorne, Charles. *The Divine Relativity*. New Haven, CT: Yale University Press, 1948.
Hawking, Stephen W. *A Brief History of Time*, updated and expanded tenth anniversary ed. New York: Bantam Books, 1998.
Heft, Harry. *Ecological Psychology in Context: James Gibson, Roger Barker, and the Legacy of William James' Radical Empiricism*. Mahwah, NJ: Erlbaum, 2001.
Hegel, Georg Wilhelm Friedrich. *Lectures on the Philosophy of Religion*, 3 vols. Edited by Peter C. Hodgson. Berkeley, CA: University of California Press, 1984–1987.
———. *Lectures on the Philosophy of World History*. Translated by Hugh Barr Nisbet. Cambridge, UK and New York: Cambridge University Press, 1975.
———. *The Phenomenology of Spirit*. Translated by A. V. Miller. Oxford: Oxford University Press, 1977.

Heidegger, Martin. *Being and Time.* Translated by John Macquarrie and Edward Robinson. New York: Harper & Row, 1962.
Heinrich, Clark. *Magic Mushrooms in Religion and Alchemy.* Montpelier, VT: Park Street Press, 2002.
———. *Strange Fruit: Alchemy, Religion and Magical Foods: A Speculative History.* London: Bloomsbury Publishing, 1995.
Heldke, Lisa, Kerri Mommer, and Cynthia Pineo, eds. *The Atkins Diet and Philosophy.* Chicago: Open Court, 2005.
Helmuth, Laura. "Moral Reasoning Relies on Emotion." *Science* 293 (September 14, 2001): 1971–72.
Hick, John H. *An Interpretation of Religion: Human Responses to the Transcendent.* New Haven, CT: Yale University Press, 1989.
Hick, John H. and A.C. McGill, eds. *The Many-Faced Argument* New York: Macmillan, 1967.
Hollar, Larry. *Hunger for the Word: Lectionary Reflections on Food and Justice.* Collegeville, MN: Liturgical Press, 2004.
Humphrey, Nicholas K. *A History of the Mind.* New York: HarperCollins, 1993.
———. *The Inner Eye.* London: Faber & Faber, 1986.
Hussaini, Muhammad Muzhar. *Food and Nutrition in Islam.* New Delhi, India: Kitab Bhavan, 1995.
Husserl, Edmund. *The Crisis of European Sciences and Transcendental Phenomenology: An Introduction to Phenomenological Philosophy.* Translated by David Carr from the edition of Walter Biemel. Evanston, IL: Northwestern University Press, 1970.
———. *The Idea of Phenomenology.* Translated by Lee Hardy. Dordrecht, The Netherlands and Boston: Kluwer Academic, 1999.
———. *Ideas: A General Introduction to Pure Phenomenology.* Translated by W.R. Boyce Gibson. New York: Collier Books, 1962.
Huxley, Aldous. *The Perennial Philosophy.* New York: Harper Brothers, 1945.
Jackson, Roger R. and John J. Makransky, eds. *Buddhist Theology: Critical Reflections by Contemporary Buddhist Scholars.* Richmond, England: Curzon Press, 2000.
Jakelić, Salvica and Lori Pearson, eds. *The Future of the Study of Religion: Proceedings of Congress 2000.* Leiden, The Netherlands and Boston: Brill, 2004.
James, William. *Essays in Radical Empiricism.* New York, 1904.
———. *Pragmatism: A New Name for Some Old Ways of Thinking, and The Meaning of Truth: A Sequel to Pragmatism.* Cambridge, MA and London: Harvard University Press, 1975.
———. *Principles of Psychology.* New York: H. Holt, 1890.
———. *The Meaning of Truth: A Sequel to Pragmatism.* New York: Longmans, Green, and Co., 1909.
———. *The Will to Believe: and Other Essays in Popular Philosophy.* New York: Longmans, Green and Co., 1896.

Jastrow, Morris. *The Study of Religion*. Atlanta, GA: Scholars Press, 1981.
Jastrow, Robert. "Have Astronomers Found God?" *New York Times Magazine*, June 25, 1978, SM5.
Jaynes, Julian. *The Origin of Consciousness in the Breakdown of the Bicameral Mind*. Boston: Houghton Mifflin Company, 1976.
Johnston, Mark. *Saving God: Religion After Idolatry*. Princeton, NJ: Princeton University Press, 2009.
Juengst, Sara Covin. *Breaking Bread: The Spiritual Significance of Death*. Philadelphia, PA: Westminster John Knox Press, 1992.
Jung, L. Shannon. *Food for Life: The Spirituality and Ethics of Eating*. Minneapolis, MN: Augsburg Fortress Publishers, 2004.
Kant, Immanuel. *Critique of Pure Reason*. Translated by Norman Kemp Smith. London: Macmillan and New York: St. Martin's Press, 1929.
Katz, Steven T., ed. *Mysticism and Philosophical Analysis*. New York and Oxford: Oxford University Press, 1978.
Klein, Julie Thompson. *Crossing Boundaries: Knowledge, Disciplinarities, and Interdisciplinarities*. Charlottesville, VA: University Press of Virginia, 1996.
———. *Interdisciplinarity: History, Theory, and Practice*. Detroit, MI: Wayne State University, 1990.
———, ed. *Transdisciplinarity: Joint Problem Solving among Science, Technology, and Society—An Effective Way for Managing Complexity*. Basel, Switzerland and Boston: Birkhäuser Verlag, 2001.
Knepper, Timothy D. "How to Say What Can't Be Said: Techniques and Rules of Ineffability in the Dionysian Corpus." Ph.D. diss., Boston University, 2005.
Korsmeyer, Carolyn. *Making Sense of Taste: Food and Philosophy*. Ithaca, NY: Cornell University Press, 2002.
Kristensen, W. Bede. *The Meaning of Religion: Lectures on the Phenomenology of Religion*. Translated by John B. Carman. The Hague, The Netherlands: Martinus Nijhoff, 1968.
Kuhn, Thomas S. *The Structure of Scientific Revolutions*, 3rd ed. Chicago: University of Chicago Press, 1996.
Lacan, Jacques. *Ecrits: The First Complete Edition in English*. New York: W.W. Norton & Company, 2005.
Lakatos, Imre. "Falsification and the Methodology of Scientific Research Programmes." In *Criticism and the Growth of Knowledge*, edited by Imre Lakatos and Alan Musgrave, 91–196.
———. *The Methodology of Scientific Research Programs*. Edited by John Worrall and Gregory Currie. Cambridge and New York: Cambridge University Press, 1978.
Lakatos, Imre and Alan Musgrave, eds. *Criticism and the Growth of Knowledge*. Cambridge and New York: Cambridge University Press, 1970
Lakatos, Imre and Paul Feyerabend. *For and Against Method*. Edited by Matteo Motterlini. Chicago: Chicago University Press, 1999.
Larson, Edward J. and Larry Witham. "Leading Scientists Still Reject God." *Nature* 394 (1998): 313.

———. "Scientists are Still Keeping the Faith." *Nature* 386 (1997): 435–36.
Latour, Bruno. *Science in Action: How to Follow Scientists and Engineers through Society*. Cambridge, MA: Harvard University Press, 1987.
Leaky, Richard. *The Origin of Humankind*. New York: Basic Books, 1994.
Legge, James. *The Chinese Classics: With a Translation, Critical and Exegetical Notes, Prolegomena, and Copious Indexes*, 5 vols. London: Trubner, 1861–1872.
———, ed. and trans. *Confucian Analects, The Great Learning, and the Doctrine of the Mean*. New York: Dover Books, 1971.
Leibniz, Gottfried. *New Essays Concerning Human Understanding* [1709]. Translated by Peter Remnant and Jonathan Bennett. Cambridge, UK: Cambridge University Press, 1996.
Lelwica, Michelle Mary. *Starving for Salvation: The Spiritual Dimensions of Eating Problems among American Girls and Women*. New York: Oxford University Press, 1999.
Lévinas, Emmanuel. *Humanism of the Other*. Translated by Nidra Porter. Urbana, IL: University of Illinois Press, 2003.
———. *Otherwise Than Being: Or Beyond Essence*. Martinus Nijhoff Philosophy Texts. The Hague, The Netherlands and Boston: Martinus Nijhoff, 1981.
———. *Totality and Infinity: An Essay on Exteriority*. Translated by Alphonso Lingis. Pittsburgh, PA: Duquesne University Press, 1969.
Lévi-Straus, Claude. *Structural Anthropology*. Chicago: University of Chicago Press, 1976.
———. *Totemism*. Translated by Rodney Needham. Boston: Beacon Press, 1963.
Lewis-Williams, David. *The Mind in the Cave: Consciousness and the Origins of Art*. London: Thames and Hudson, 2002.
Linnaeus, Carl. *Systema Naturae, 1735* [Selections]. With an introduction and a first English translation of the "Observationes" by M.S.J. Engel-Ledeboer and H. Engel. Nieuwkoop, The Netherlands: B. de Graaf, 1964.
Lindbeck, George A. *The Nature of Doctrine: Religion and Theology in a Postliberal Age*. Philadelphia, PA: Westminster Press, 1984.
Lindberg, David C. and Robert S. Westman, eds. *Reappraisals of the Scientific Revolution*. New York and Cambridge, UK: Cambridge University Press, 1990.
Linde, Andre D. *Inflation and the Quantum Cosmology*. Boston: Academic Press, 1990.
Locke, John. *An Essay Concerning Human Understanding*. Edited by Peter H. Nidditch. New York: Oxford University Press, 1975.
Lovejoy, Arthur O. *The Great Chain of Being: A Study of the History of an Idea*. Cambridge, MA: Harvard University Press, 1936.
Mahoney, Kathleen and John Schmalzbauer. "Religion and Knowledge in the Post–Secular Academy." Working Paper circulated prior to "Are We Living in a Post-Secular World? A Working Meeting on Social Science and the 'Return of Religion.'" Sponsored by the Social Science Research Council, New York, June 2007.

Manson, Neil A. *God and Design: The Teleological Argument and Modern Science.* London and New York: Routledge, 2003.
Marion, Jean-Luc. *Being Given: A Phenomenology of Givenness.* Translated by Jeffrey L. Kosky. Palo Alto, CA: Stanford University Press, 2002.
———. *God without Being.* Translated by Thomas A. Carlson. Foreword by Thomas Tracy. Chicago: University of Chicago Press, 1991.
McCutcheon, Russell T. *Critics Not Caretakers: Redescribing the Public Study of Religion.* Albany, NY: State University of New York Press, 2001.
———. *Manufacturing Religion: The Discourse on Sui Generis Religion and the Politics of Nostalgia.* New York: Oxford University Press, 1997.
Mckenna, Terrence. *Food of the Gods: The Search for the Original Tree of Knowledge: A Radical History of Plants, Drugs, and Human Evolution.* New York: Bantam, 1992.
Meister, Chad and Paul Copan, eds. *The Routledge Companion to Philosophy of Religion.* London and New York: Routledge, 2007.
Merchant, Carolyn. *The Death of Nature: Women Ecology and the Scientific Revolution.* New York: Harper Collins, 1980.
Morales, Edmundo. *The Guinea Pig: Healing, Food, and Ritual in the Andes.* Tucson, AZ: University of Arizona Press, 1995.
Murphy, Nancey. *Beyond Liberalism and Fundamentalism: How Modern and Postmodern Philosophy Set the Theological Agenda.* Harrisburg, PA: Trinity Press International, 1996.
———. *Theology in the Age of Scientific Reasoning.* Ithaca, NY: Cornell University Press, 1990.
Murry, William R. *Reason and Reverence: Religious Humanism for the 21st Century.* Boston: Skinner House Books, 2006.
National Opinion Research Center at the University of Chicago. *Doctoral Recipients from United States Universities: Summary Report, 2002.* http://www.norc.org/nr/rdonlyres/0aa0b47b-8f62-434b-9956-4223b1354c0d/0/sed2002.pdf.
Neville, Robert Cummings. *The Cosmology of Freedom.* New Haven, CT: Yale University Press, 1974.
———. *God the Creator: On the Transcendence and Presence of God.* Chicago: University of Chicago Press, 1968.
———. *The Highroad Around Modernism.* Albany, NY: State University of New York Press, 1992.
———. *Normative Cultures.* The Axiology of Thinking, vol. 3. Albany, NY: State University of New York Press, 1995.
———. *Reconstruction of Thinking.* The Axiology of Thinking, vol. 1. Albany, NY: State University of New York Press, 1981.
———. *Recovery of the Measure.* The Axiology of Thinking, vol. 2. Albany, NY: State University of New York Press, 1989.
———, ed. *The Human Condition.* A Volume in the Comparative Religious Ideas Project, vol. 1. Albany, NY: State University of New York Press, 2001.

———, ed. *Religious Truth*. A Volume in the Comparative Religious Ideas Project, vol. 3. Albany, NY: State University of New York Press, 2001.
———, ed. *Ultimate Realities*. A Volume in the Comparative Religious Ideas Project, vol. 2. Albany, NY: State University of New York Press, 2001.
Newman, John Henry. *An Essay in Aid of a Grammar of Assent*. Notre Dame, IN: Notre Dame Press, 1979.
Nielson, Kai. *Naturalism and Religion*. Amherst, NY: Prometheus Books, 2001.
Nietzsche, Friedrich. *Beyond Good and Evil: Prelude to a Philosophy of the Future*. Authorized translation by Helen Zimmern. Edinburgh and London: T.N. Foulis, 1907.
———. *A Genealogy of Morals*. Translated by William A. Haussmann. New York: Macmillan, 1897.
Numbers, Ron L., ed. *Galileo Goes to Jail: And Other Myths about Science and Religion*. Cambridge, MA: Harvard University Press, 2009.
Onfray, Michel. *La Raison Gourmande: Philosophie du Goût*. Paris: B. Grasset, 1995.
———. *Le Ventre des Philosophes: Critique de la Raison Diététique*. Paris: B. Grasset, 1989.
Otto, Rudolf. *The Idea of the Holy: An Inquiry into the Non-Rational Factor in the Idea of the Divine and its Relation to the Rational*, 3rd ed. Translated from the 9th German ed. by John W. Harvey. London: Oxford University Press, 1925.
Page, Scott. E. *The Difference: How the Power of Diversity Creates Better Groups, Firms, Schools, and Societies*. Princeton, NJ: Princeton University Press, 2007.
Paglia, Camille. *Sexual Personae: Art and Decadence from Nefertiti to Emily Dickenson*. New Haven, CT and London: Yale University Press, 1990.
Paley, William. *Natural Theology—of Evidences of the Existence and Attributes of the Deity Collected from the Appearances of Nature*, 2nd ed. Oxford: J. Vincent, 1828. First published by J. Vincent in 1802.
Pannenberg, Wolfhart. "Toward a Theology of the History of Religions." In *Basic Questions in Theology*, vol. 2, translated by George H. Kehm, 65–118. Philadelphia, PA: Westminster, 1971.
Peden, W. Creighton, ed. *New Essays in Religious Naturalism*. Macon, GA: Mercer University Press, 1994.
Peeters, Bert, ed. *Semantic Primes and Universal Grammar: Empirical Evidence from the Romance Languages*. Amsterdam, The Netherlands: John Benjamins, 2006.
Peirce, Charles Saunders. *Charles S. Peirce: Selected Writings*. Edited by Philip P. Wiener. New York: Dover Publications, Inc., 1958.
———. *Collected Papers of Charles Saunders Peirce*, 8 vols. Edited by Charles Hartshorne and Paul Weiss (vols. I–VI) and Arthur W. Burks (vols. VII–VIII). Cambridge, MA: Harvard University Press, 1931–1935, 1958.
———. *Essays in the Philosophy of Science*. Edited by Vincent Tomas. Indianapolis, IN: Bobbs-Merrill, 1957.

———. "The Fixation of Belief." In *Charles S. Peirce: Selected Writings*, edited by Philip P. Wiener, 91–112. New York: Dover Publications, 1958.
———. *Philosophical Writings of Peirce*. Edited by Justus Buchler. New York: Dover Publications, Inc., 1955.
———. *Values in a Universe of Chance: Selected Writings*. New York: Doubleday Anchor, 1958.
Pekala, Ronald J. *Quantifying Consciousness: An Empirical Approach*. New York and London: Plenum Press, 1991.
Pence, Gregory. *Medical Ethics: Accounts of the Cases that Shaped and Define Medical Ethics*. New York: McGraw-Hill, 2007.
Penner, Hans H. *Impasse and Resolution: A Critique of the Study of Religion*. New York and Bern, Switzerland: Peter Lang, 1989.
Pennock, Robert T., Jr., ed. *Intelligent Design Creationism and its Critics: Philosophical, Theological, and Scientific Perspectives*. Cambridge, MA: The MIT Press, 2001.
Peters, Karl E. *Dancing with the Sacred: Evolution, Ecology, and God*. Valley Forge, PA: Trinity Press International, 2002.
Phillips, D.Z. *Wittgenstein and Religion*. London: Macmillan and St. Martin's Press, 1993.
Piatelli-Palmarini, Massimo. *Inevitable Illusions: How Mistakes of Reason Rule Our Minds*. New York: John Wiley and Sons, 1996.
Plato. *Republic*. Loeb Classical Library (Plato, vols. V, VI), translated by Paul Shorey. Cambridge, MA: Harvard University Press.
———. *Timaeus*. Loeb Classical Library (Plato, vols. IX), translated by R. G. Bury. Cambridge, MA: Harvard University Press.
Plous, Scott. *The Psychology of Judgment and Decision Making*. New York: McGraw-Hill, 1993.
Pope, Kenneth S. and Jerome L. Singer, eds. *The Stream of Consciousness: Scientific Investigations into the Flow of Human Experience*. New York and London: Plenum Press, 1978.
Popper, Karl. *The Logic of Scientific Discovery*, 3rd ed. New York: Basic Books, 1968.
Preus, J. S. *Explaining Religion: Criticism and Theory from Bodin to Freud*. New Haven, CT: Yale University Press, 1987.
Proudfoot, Wayne. *Religious Experience*. Berkeley, CA: University of California Press, 1985.
Quine, W. V. O. "Two Dogmas of Empiricism." http://www.ditext.com/quine/quine.html.
Rahner, Karl. "Christianity and the Non-Christian Religions." In *Theological Investigations*, 5: 115–34. Baltimore, MD: Helicon Press, 1966.
Randi, James. *Flim Flam: Psychics, ESP, Unicorns and other Delusions*. Amherst, NY: Prometheus Books, 1982.
Ratzsch, Delvin Lee. *Nature, Design, and Science: The Status of Design in Natural Science*. SUNY Series in Philosophy and Biology. Albany, NY: State University of New York Press, 2001.

Revonsuo, Antti. *Inner Presence: Consciousness as a Biological Phenomenon.* Cambridge, MA: The MIT Press, 2006.
Riaz, Mian N. and Muhammad M. Chaudry. *Halal Food Production.* Boca Raton, FL: CRC Press, 2003.
Richardson, W. Mark, Robert John Russell, Philip Clayton, and Kirk Wegter-McNelly, eds. *Science and the Spiritual Quest: New Essays by Leading Scientists.* New York: Routledge, 2001.
Richardson, W. Mark and Gordy Slack, eds. *Faith in Science.* New York: Routledge, 2001.
Ricoeur, Paul. *The Conflict of Interpretations: Essays in Hermeneutics.* Edited by Don Ihde. Evanston, IL: Northwestern University Press, 1974.
———. *The Symbolism of Evil.* Translated by Emerson Buchanan. Boston: Beacon Press, 1969.
Ringgren, Helmer. "Comparative Mythology." In *Encyclopedia of Religion*, edited by Mircea Eliade. New York: Macmillan, 1987.
Ritchie, Jack. *Understanding Naturalism.* Durham, UK: Acumen Publishing, 2009.
Rizzuto, Ana-Maria. *The Birth of the Living God: A Psychoanalytic Study.* Chicago: University of Chicago Press, 1979.
Rogak, Lisa. *Death Warmed Over: Funeral Food, Rituals, and Customs from Around the World.* Berkeley, CA: Ten Speed Press, 2004.
Rorty, Richard. *Philosophy and the Mirror of Nature.* Princeton, NJ: Princeton University Press, 1979.
Rosen, Stephen. *Diet for Transcendence: Vegetarianism and the World Religions*, 2nd ed. Badger, CA: Torchlight Publishing, 1997.
Rue, Loyal D. *Religion Is Not About God: How Spiritual Traditions Nurture our Biological Nature and What to Expect When They Fail.* Piscataway, NJ: Rutgers University Press, 2004.
Runchock, Rita and Kathleen Droste, eds. *Library of Congress Classification Schedules: Class B, Subclasses BL, BM, BP, BQ. Religion: Religions, Hinduism, Judaism, Islam, Buddhism.* Washington, DC: Library of Congress, Processing Services, Subject Cataloguing Division, 1992.
Runcie, R. A. K. et al. *Theology, the University and the Modern World.* London: L. Crook Academic Publishers, 1988.
Russell, Robert John. "Finite Creation without a Beginning: The Doctrine of Creation in Relation to Big Bang and Quantum Cosmologies." In *Quantum Cosmology and the Laws of Nature: Scientific Perspectives on Divine Action*, edited by Robert John Russell, Nancey Murphy, and C. J. Isham, 291–325. Vatican City State: Vatican Observatory and Berkeley, CA: The Center for Theology and the Natural Sciences, 1993.
Sack, Daniel. *Whitebread Protestants: Food and Religion in American Culture.* New York: Palgrave Macmillan, 2005.
Sagan, Carl. *The Demon-Haunted World: Science as a Candle in the Dark.* New York: Random House, 1996.

Santayana, George. *The Essential Santayana; Selected Writings*, edited by Martin Coleman. Bloomington, IN: Indiana University Press, 2009.

Schiebinger, Londa. *Nature's Body: Gender in the Making of Modern Science*. Boston: Beacon Press, 1993.

Schleiermacher, Friedrich D.E. *The Christian Faith*. Translated from the 2nd German edition of 1830 by H.R. Mackintosh and J.S. Stewart. Edinburgh, UK: T. & T. Clark, 1928.

Schrag, Calvin O. "Transversal Rationality." In *The Question of Hermeneutics: Essays in Honor of Joseph J. Kockelmans*, edited by Timothy J. Stapleton. Dordrecht, The Netherlands and Boston: Kluwer Academic Publishers, 1994.

Schuon, Frithjof. *The Transcendent Unity of Religions*. Translated by Peter Townsend. Introduction by Huston Smith. Wheaton, IL: The Theosophical Publishing House, 1984.

Scruton, Roger. "Eating the World: The Philosophy of Food." *openDemocracy*, May 14, 2003. http://www.opendemocracy.net/globalization-foodwithoutfrontiers/article_1224.jsp.

Searle, John R. *Expression and Meaning: Studies in the Theory of Speech Acts*. Cambridge, UK and New York: Cambridge University Press, 1979.

———. *The Mystery of Consciousness*. New York: New York Review Books, 1990.

———. *The Rediscovery of Mind*. Cambridge, MA: The MIT Press, 1992.

———. *Speech Acts: An Essay in the Philosophy of Language*. Cambridge, UK and New York: Cambridge University Press, 1969.

Sells, Michael A. *Mystical Languages of Unsaying*. Chicago: University of Chicago Press, 1994.

Sharpe, Eric J. *Comparative Religion: A History*, 2nd ed. La Salle, IN: Open Court, 1986.

———. *Understanding Religion*. New York: St. Martin's Press, 1984.

Shear, Jonathan. *Explaining Consciousness: The Hard Problem*. Cambridge, MA: The MIT Press, 1997.

Shermer, Michael. *Why Darwin Matters: The Case Against Intelligent Design*. New York: Times Books, 2006.

———. *Why People Believe Weird Things: Pseudoscience, Superstition, and Other Confusions of Our Time*. New York: W.H. Freeman and Company, 1997.

Sherwin, Byron L. *Studies in Jewish Theology: Reflections in the Mirror of Tradition*. London and Portland, OR: Vallentine Mitchell, 2007.

Shook, John R.; Kurts, Paul; eds. *The Future of Naturalism*. Amherst, NY: Humanity Books, 2009.

Sider, Ronald J. *Rich Christians in an Age of Hunger: Moving from Affluence to Generosity*, 20th Anniversary Edition. Nashville, TN: Word Publishing, 1997.

Sivananda, Sri Swami. *God Exists*. Tehri-Garhwal, Uttar Pradesh: The Divine Life Society, World Wide Web edition, 1998. http://www.sivanan-

dadlshq.org/download/god_exists.htm. First published by The Divine Life Society in 1958.
———. "Isvara or The Universal Soul." In *God Exists*.
———. "Philosophical Proofs For The Existence Of God." In *God Exists*.
Smart, Ninian. "Comparative-Historical Method." In *Encyclopedia of Religion*, edited by Mircea Eliade. New York: Macmillan, 1987.
Smart, Ninian. *The Phenomenon of Religion*. London: Macmillan, 1973.
Smid, Robert. *Methodologies of Comparative Philosophy: The Pragmatist and Process Traditions*. SUNY Series in Chinese Philosophy and Culture. Albany, NY: State University of New York Press, 2009.
Smith, Christian, et al. *American Evangelicalism: Embattled and Thriving*. Chicago: University of Chicago Press, 1998.
Smith, Huston. *Forgotten Truth: The Common Vision of the World's Religions*, 2nd ed. San Francisco, CA: HarperSanFrancisco, 1992.
———. *The World's Religions*, revised and updated edition of *The Religions of Man* [New York: Harper, 1958]. San Francisco, CA: HarperSanFrancisco, 1991.
Smith, Jonathan Z. *Imagining Religion: From Babylon to Jonestown*. Chicago: University of Chicago Press, 1982.
———. *Map is Not Territory*. Chicago: University of Chicago Press, 1978.
Smith, Wilfrid Cantwell. *Faith and Belief*. Princeton, NJ: Princeton University Press, 1979.
———. *Towards a World Theology: Faith and the Comparative History of Religion*. Philadelphia PA: Westminster, 1981 and Maryknoll, NY: Orbis, 1989.
Somerville, Margaret A. and David J. Rapport, eds. *Transdisciplinarity: Recreating Integrated Knowledge*. McGill-Queen's University Press, 2003. First published Oxford: Encyclopedia of Life Support Systems Publishers, 2000.
Sosis, Richard. "Religious Behaviors, Badges, and Bans: Signaling Theory and the Evolution of Religion." In *Where God and Science Meet: How Brain and Evolutionary Studies Alter Our Understanding of Religion*, vol. 1, *Evolution, Genes, and the Religious Brain*, edited by Patrick McNamara, 61–86. Westport, CT and London: Praeger, 2006.
Spencer, Herbert, and Frederic Harrison. *The Nature and Reality of Religion: A Controversy between Frederick Harrison and Herbert Spencer*. New York: D. Appleton, 1885.
Stace, W. T. *Mysticism and Philosophy*. Philadelphia, PA: Lippincott, 1960.
Steinhardt, Paul J. *Endless Universe: Beyond the Big Bang*. New York: Doubleday, 2007.
Sterckx, Roel. *Of Tripod and Palate: Food, Politics, and Religion in Traditional China*. New York: Palgrave Macmillan, 2005.
Stitch, Stephen. *Deconstructing the Mind*. New York and Oxford: Oxford University Press, 1996.
———. *From Folk Psychology to Cognitive Science: The Case Against Belief*. Cambridge, MA: The MIT Press, 1983.

Stoehr, Kevin, ed. *Philosophies of Religion, Art, and Creativity.* The Proceedings of the Twentieth World Congress of Philosophy, vol. 4. Bowling Green, OH: Philosophy Documentation Center, 1999.

Stone, Jerome A. *Religious Naturalism Today: The Rebirth of a Forgotten Alternative.* Albany, NY: State University of New York Press, 2008.

Strenski, I. *Thinking about Religion: An Historical Introduction to Theories of Religion.* Malden, MA and Oxford: Blackwell Publishers, 2006.

Suh, Ignatius. *The Confucian-Christian Dialogue: A Comparative Theology from the Yi Dynasty in Korea.* South Bend, IN: Cloverdale Books, 2007.

Susskind, Leonard. *The Cosmic Landscape: String Theory and the Illusion of Intelligent Design.* New York: Little, Brown, and Co., 2006.

Swidler, Ann. "Culture in Action: Symbols and Strategies." *American Sociology Review* 51 (April 1986): 273–86.

Swinburne, Richard. *The Coherence of Theism.* Oxford and New York: Oxford University Press, 1977.

———. *The Existence of God.* Oxford and New York: Oxford University Press, 1979.

Telfer, Elizabeth. *Food for Thought: Philosophy and Food.* Abingdon, UK: Routledge, 2005.

Thomas Aquinas. *Summa Theologiae.* Cambridge, UK and New York: Cambridge University Press, 2006.

Tillich, Paul. *Systematic Theology*, vol. 1. Chicago: University of Chicago Press, 1951.

Toynbee, Arnold. *An Historian's Approach to Religion*, 2nd ed. Oxford and New York: Oxford University Press, 1979.

Tu Weiming. *Confucian Thought: Selfhood as Creative Transformation.* Albany, NY: State University of New York, 1985.

———. *Humanity and Self-Cultivation: Essays in Confucian Thought.* Freemont, CA: Asian Humanities Press, 1979.

Tylor, Edward Burnett. *Primitive Cultures: Researches into the Development of Mythology, Philosophy, Religion, Art, and Custom*, 2 vols. London: Murray, 1873–1874.

Tracy, David. "Theology: Comparative Theology." In *Encyclopedia of Religion*, edited by Mircea Eliade. New York: Macmillan, 1987.

van der Leeuw, Gerardus. *Religion in Essence and Manifestation*, 2nd ed. Foreword by Ninian Smart. Translated from the 2nd German ed. by Hans H. Penner. Princeton, NJ: Princeton University Press, 1964.

van Ess, Joseph. *The Flowering of Muslim Theology.* Translated by Jane Marie Todd. Cambridge, MA: Harvard University Press, 2006.

van Huyssteen, J. Wentzel. *Alone in the World? Human Uniqueness in Science and Theology.* Grand Rapids, MI: William B. Eerdmans Publishing Company, 2006.

———. *The Shaping of Rationality: Toward Interdisciplinarity in Theology and Science.* Grand Rapids, MI: William B. Eerdmans Publishing Company, 1999.

Vandereycken, Walter and Ron Van Deth. *From Fasting Saints to Anorexic Girls: The History of Self-Starvation.* New York: New York University Press, 1994.

Vilenkin, Alexander. *Many Worlds in One: The Search for Other Universes.* New York: Hill and Wang, 2006.
Vogt, Evon Zartman. *Tortillas for the Gods: A Symbolic Analysis of Zinacanteco Rituals.* Cambridge, MA: Harvard University Press, 1976.
Waldmann, Michael R. "A Case for the Moral Organ?" *Science* 314 (October 6, 2006): 57–58.
Watson, Walter. *The Architectonics of Meaning: Foundations of the New Pluralism.* Albany, NY: State University of New York Press, 1985.
Weber, Max. *From Max Weber: Essays in Sociology.* Edited and translated by H. H. Gerth and C. Wright Mills. New York: Oxford University Press, 1946.
———. *The Protestant Ethic and the Spirit of Capitalism*, 2nd ed. Translated by Talcott Parsons. New York: Charles Scribner's Sons, 1958.
———. *The Religion of China.* Edited and translated by Hans H. Gerth. New York: Free Press, 1951.
Welch, Claude. "Dispelling some Myths about the Split between Theology and Science in the Nineteenth Century," 29–40. In *Religion and Science: History, Method, Dialogue*, edited by W. Mark Richardson and Wesley J. Wildman. New York: Routledge, 1996.
White, Andrew Dickson. *History of the Warfare of Science with Theology in Christendom.* New York: D. Appleton and Company, 1898.
Whitehead, Alfred North. *Adventures of Ideas.* New York: Macmillan, 1933.
———. *Process and Reality: An Essay in Cosmology*, corrected edition. Edited by David Ray Griffin and Donald W. Sherburne. New York: The Free Press, 1978.
———. *Science and the Modern World.* New York: Macmillan, 1926.
Wiebe, Donald. *Beyond Legitimation: Essays on the Problem of Religious Knowledge.* New York: St. Martin's Press, 1994.
———. *The Politics of Religious Studies: The Continuing Conflict with Theology in the Academy.* New York: St. Martin's Press and Basingstoke, UK: Macmillan, 1999.
———. *Religion and Truth: Towards an Alternative Paradigm for the Study of Religion.* The Hague, The Netherlands and New York: Mouton Publishers, 1981.
Wieman, Henry Nelson. *Religious Inquiry: Some Explorations.* Boston: Beacon Press, 1968.
Wierzbicka, Anna. *Semantic Primitives.* Frankfurt, Germany: Athenäum, 1972.
———. *Semantics: Primes and Universals.* Oxford and New York: Oxford University Press, 1996.
Wierzbicka, Anna and Cliff Goddard, eds. *Semantic and Lexical Universals— Theory and Empirical Findings*, 2 vols. Amsterdam, The Netherlands: John Benjamins, 1994.
Wildman, Wesley J. "Cognitive Error and Contemplative Practices: The Cultivation of Discernment in Mind and Heart." *Buddhist-Christian Studies* 29 (2009): 59–79.
———. "Comparative Natural Theology." *American Journal of Theology and Philosophy* 27/2&3 (May/September 2006): 173–90.

———. "Comparing Religious Ideas: There's Method in the Mob's Madness." In *Comparing Religions: Possibilities and Perils?*, edited by Thomas Athanasius Indinopulos, Brian C. Wilson, and James Constantine Hanges, 77–113. Leiden, The Netherlands: Brill Academic Publishers, 2006.

———. "From Law and Chance in Nature to Ultimate Reality." In *Creation, Law, and Probability*, edited by Fraser Watts, 155–179. Aldershot, UK: Ashgate Publishing, 2007.

———. "Rational Theory Building: Beyond Modern Enthusiasm and Postmodern Refusal (A Pragmatist Philosophical Offering)." In *The Evolution of Rationality: Interdisciplinary Essays in Honor of J. Wentzel van Huyssteen*, edited by F. LeRon Shults, 30–46. Grand Rapids, MI: Wm. B. Eerdmanns Publishing Company, 2006.

———. "Strategic Mechanisms within Religious Symbol Systems." In *Metaphor and God-talk*, edited by Lieven Boeve and Kurt Feyaerts, 273–91, Religions and Discourse series, James Francis, gen. ed., vol. 2. Bern, Switzerland: Peter Lang, 1999.

———. "The Resilience of Religion in Secular Social Environments: A Pragmatic Philosophical Analysis." In *Scientific Explanation and Religious Belief: Science and Religion in Philosophical and Public Discourse*, edited by Thomas M. Schmidt and Michael G. Parker, 58–80. Frankfurt, Germany: Mohr-Sieback, 2005.

———. "The Resilience of Religion in Secular Social Environments: A Pragmatic Philosophical Analysis Regarding Scientific and Religious Problems" (in Chinese). *Studies in Dialectics of Nature* 20/12 (December 2004): 79–84.

———. *Religious and Spiritual Experiences: A Spiritually Evocative Naturalist Interpretation*. Cambridge, UK; Cambridge University Press, 2010.

———. *Science and Religious Anthropology: A Religious Naturalist Interpretation of the Human Condition*. Aldershot, UK: Ashgate, 2009.

Wildman, Wesley J. and Leslie A. Brothers. "A Neuropsychological-Semiotic Model of Religious Experiences." In *Neuroscience and the Person: Scientific Perspectives on Divine Action*, edited by Robert John Russell, Nancey Murphy, Theo Meyering, and Michael Arbib, 347–416. Vatican City State: Vatican Observatory and Berkeley, CA: Center for Theology and the Natural Sciences, 2000.

Wildman, Wesley J. and Robert Cummings Neville. "How Our Approach to Comparison Relates to Others." In *Ultimate Realities*, edited by Robert Cummings Neville, 211–36. Albany, NY: State University of New York, 2001.

Wilson, David Sloan. *Darwin's Cathedral: Evolution, Religion, and the Nature of Society*. Chicago: University of Chicago Press, 2002.

Wittgenstein, Ludwig. *Philosophical Investigations*, 50th Anniversary Commemorative Edition. Translated and revised by G.E.M. Anscombe. London: Blackwell Publishing, 2001.

Index

abstraction, 14, 57, 72, 75, 75, 85–99, 105, 114–17, 122–24, 175–79, 196–97, 230, 249, 292, 311, 326
abysmal ground, 83, 302
  see also ultimate reality
Advaita Vedānta, 33, 230, 275–78
  see also Ātman; Brahman; monism; Śaṅkara; Vedānta
aesthetic(s), 2–4, 7, 39, 42, 51, 75, 90, 219, 221, 225–30, 242, 266, 283, 293
  criteria, 75, 221, 226–29, 242
  see also beautiful, the; big-question philosophy; judgment
agriculture, 109, 112–13
alienation, 111–13, 223
Allah, 114, 152
  see also God(s); Islam; ultimate reality
Allen, George, 170, 337
Alston, William, x, 320–21, 337
American Academy of Religion (AAR), 19–20, 320, 329
Analects (Lún Yǔ or Lun yü or 論語 or 论语), 286–87, 335, 347
  see also Confucius; Chinese Classics
anātman/anattā (no substantival self), 54, 101, 133
Anselm, Saint, 31, 96–99, 102, 105, 123, 251, 280, 322–23, 337
  and Augustine, 96, 102
  Monologion, 96–98, 102, 251, 322, 337
  ontological argument, 96–99
  Platonism of, 97
  Proslogion, 31, 96–99, 251, 280, 322, 337
  see also ontotheological tradition
anthropology, 17, 22–23, 75, 94, 105–6, 116–17, 132–33, 144, 150, 219, 234, 253, 325, 327, 335, 341, 347, 356
apophasis, 79–83, 297–304
  see also via negativa
archetype, 142–44
Aristotle (Ἀριστοτέλης), 9–10, 33, 87, 130–31, 171, 174, 213, 242, 249, 255, 263–66, 269–70, 273, 326, 334, 337
Ātman (Soul), 23–24, 275, 277–78, 281
Augustine, Saint, 9–10, 31, 96, 104, 249, 250, 280
  Confessions, 31, 280
  Neoplatonism of, 249
Austin, John, 195, 331, 338
authority, 30–34, 43–44, 47, 53, 57–61, 63–65, 101–2, 147, 180, 190, 198, 202, 209, 213, 219, 232–33, 236, 238, 243, 259, 310, 314, 323

authority *(continued)*
  of religious institutions, 33–34, 232–33, 308
  of sacred texts, 32–34, 101–2, 190, 279
  sociology of, 44
  of traditions, 30–33, 213, 232–33, 308
avidyā (ignorance), 169, 278
axiology, 284–87, 290–94, 333, 335, 348
axiotheological tradition, xiv, 273, 283–94
  see also aesthetic(s); axiology; Chinese Classics, Daoist; Dewey, John; Chinese Classics, *Five Classics*; Chinese Classics, *Four Books*; Confucianism; Ferré, Frederick; Feuerbach, Ludwig; James, William; Hartshorne, Charles; Heidegger, Martin; Hegel, Georg Wilhelm Friedrich; good, the; Marx, Karl; morality; Neo-Confucianism; Neville, Robert Cummings; Nietzsche, Friedrich; Peirce, Charles Saunders; philosophy, Chinese; Plato; pragmatism; pragmatic-naturalist tradition; religious philosophy; Schelling, Friedrich; Strauss, David Friedrich; Tu Weiming; ultimacy; Whitehead, Alfred North
Ayer, A.J., 8, 11, 76, 310

Bhagavad-gītā, 27, 41
beautiful, the, 3, 27, 42, 68, 82, 90, 120, 143, 147, 185, 211, 222, 226, 228, 248, 262, 265, 291–93
  see also aesthetics; big-question philosophy; good, the; truth
being, 208, 248–56, 293
  see also ontology; ontotheological tradition

belief(s), xv, 16, 18, 24, 27–28, 33, 36–37, 43, 51, 65, 77, 79, 81, 93, 100, 120, 132, 142, 145, 150, 156, 159, 163–65, 168–70, 173, 177, 181–83, 190, 197–98, 210, 232, 234, 237–39, 241–44, 256, 258, 260, 265, 267–68, 276, 280, 292, 295, 300, 310, 315
  folk, 161, 163, 274, 334, 353
  physics, 163
  psychology, 163, 274, 334, 353
  see also ideas; interpretation, theory of; practice(s), religious; superstition; worldview
Berger, Peter, xx, 220, 238–40, 327, 328, 332, 338–39
bhakti (devotion), 100, 301
bhakti yoga, 279
bias, xi, xvi, 13, 16–18, 22–23, 25–26, 29, 31, 40, 56, 69, 74, 76, 92, 105, 132, 135–38, 146, 214, 304, 307, 309–11, 320
  objection to comparison, 135–39
  problem of, 13, 16–18, 22–23, 146
  selection, 171
Bible, 19, 41, 292
  Christian, 19, 41, 292, 316
  Hebrew, 161
  see also text, sacred
big-question philosophy, 1–13, 22, 44, 46–47
  see also epistemology; ethics; metaphysics; philosophy; religious philosophy; theology
biology, 8, 18, 27, 63, 65, 69, 75, 91, 108, 111, 114–17, 121, 124–25, 136, 170–79, 181, 186, 189, 196–98, 233, 262, 269–72, 282, 326, 330, 333, 334
Boston University, xx
  Institute for Philosophy and Religion, xiii
  Science, Philosophy, and Religion doctoral program, xx
  see also science and religion
Brahmasūtras, 276

see also Upaniṣads; Vedānta; Vedas, the
Brahman, 2, 23, 54, 133, 142, 144, 152, 160, 275–79, 281, 295
  nirguṇa, 142, 160, 277, 295
  saguṇa, 142, 160, 278, 295
  see also Ātman; God(s); Godhead; Hinduism; Īśvara; philosophy, Indian, Hindu; ultimate reality
brain, 50, 121, 144, 168, 170, 171, 176–77, 181, 188, 204, 283, 321, 338, 340, 341, 353
Brothers, Leslie, 121, 326, 328, 330, 339
Buchler, Justus, 170, 329, 330, 339
Buddhism, xiii, 26, 28, 32, 33, 54, 89–90, 97, 100–2, 104, 133, 136, 140, 144, 169, 171, 193, 208, 243, 249, 255, 282, 301, 302, 314, 315, 320, 323, 345, 351, 355
  Mahāyāna, 140–41
    see also Mādhyamaka; Nāgārjuna; Yogācāra
  Theravāda, 133, 140–41
  Tibetan, 171, 283
  Zen, 171, 301
  see also anātman/anattā (no substantival self); Buddha; consciousness; *Dhammapada*; karma; liberation; meditation; nirvāṇa; *pratītya-samutpāda* (dependent co-arising); reincarnation; religious philosophy; *saṃsāra* (cycle of lives); saṅgha; *śūnyatā* (ultimate emptiness); theology; *vijñāna* (consciousness)
Buddha, 39, 90, 301, 322, 327, 342

Cārvāka, 32, 100, 101, 102, 274, 275
causation, 2, 38, 62, 100, 139, 144–45, 161, 188, 189, 199, 217–18, 231–32, 236, 247, 249, 252, 255–56, 269, 271, 302, 333
certainty, 4–5, 9, 11, 57–60, 62–63, 70, 177–78, 197–98, 280, 292

Chadwick, Owen, 238, 332, 339
  see also secularism
Chicago School of religious naturalism, 170
  see also pragmatic-naturalist tradition; naturalism, religious
Chinese Classics, 33, 41, 286–91, 294, 335, 347
  Classic of Music (Yuèjīng or Yüeh Ching or 樂經 or 乐经), 284
    see also Confucianism
  Daoist, 290–91
    see also *Dao De Jing* (*Dàodéjīng* or *Tao Te Ching* or 道德經 or 道德经); *Classic of Perfect Emptiness* (*Lièzǐ* or *Lieh-Tzu* or 列子); Daoism; *Zhuangzi* (*Zhuāngzǐ* or *Chuang-Tzu* or 莊子 or 庄子)
  Five Classics (*Wǔjīng* or *Wu Ching* or 五經 or 五经), 284–86
    see also Classic of Changes (*Yì Jīng* or *I Ching* or 易經 or 易经); *Classic of History* (*Shūjīng* or *Shu Ching* or 書經 or 书经); *Classic of Poetry* (*Shījīng* or *Shih Ching* or 詩經 or 诗经); *Classic of Rites* (*Lǐ Jì* or *Li Chi* or 禮記 or 礼记); Confucianism; *Spring and Autumn Annals* (*Chūn Qiū* or *Ch'un Ch'iu* or 春秋; *Linjing* or *Línjīng* or *Lin Ching* or 麟經 or 麟经)
  Four Books (*Sì Shū* or *Ssu Shu* or 四書 or 四书), 286–90
    see also Analects (*Lún Yǔ* or *Lun yü* or 論語 or 论语); Confucianism; *Doctrine of the Mean* (*Zhōng Yōng* or *Chung-Yung* or 中庸); *Great Learning* (*Dà Xué* or *Ta-Hsüeh* or 大學 or 大学); *Mencius* (*Mèngzǐ* or *Meng-Tzu* or 孟子)

Chomsky, Noam, 194, 331, 340
  see also language
Christianity, 16–17, 18–19, 20, 22, 28, 53, 132, 190, 208, 258, 266
  Catholic, 28, 53, 258, 266
  Orthodox, 259–60
  Protestant, 53, 335
  see also Anselm, Saint; Augustine, Saint; Bible, Christian; church(es); Dostoevsky, Fyodor; Eucharist; faith; God(s); Godhead; Jesus Christ; Leskov, Nicolai; Newman, John Henry; philosophy, Christian; philosophy, of religion; Plantinga, Alvin; practice(s), religious; religious philosophy; revelation; ritual; Schleiermacher, Friedrich; Society of Christian Philosophers; spirituality; theism; theology; Thomas Aquinas; Tillich, Paul; ultimacy; ultimate concern; ultimate reality
church(es), 58, 60, 190, 208, 243, 260, 266, 315
Church of Jesus Christ of Latter-day Saints (Mormonism), 190
Classic of Changes (*Yì Jīng* or *I Ching* or 易經 or 易经), 285–86
Classic of History (*Shūjīng* or *Shu Ching* or 書經 or 书经), 284–85
Classic of Perfect Emptiness (*Lièzǐ* or *Lieh-Tzu* or 列子), 290–91
Classic of Poetry (*Shījīng* or *Shih Ching* or 詩經 or 诗经), 284
Classic of Rites (*Lǐ Jì* or *Li Chi* or 禮記 or 礼记), 285, 287, 288
Clooney, Frank, xx, 327, 328, 340
cognition, 12, 21, 39, 44, 48, 49, 65, 69, 73, 78, 89–90, 93, 96, 105–7, 114–15, 116, 120, 126, 127, 129, 131, 138–41, 144, 161, 162–64, 167, 168, 170, 176, 179, 184, 186, 187–89, 197, 207–8, 210, 224, 228, 231, 242, 247, 249, 250–54, 258, 276, 281–83, 294–304, 326, 334, 335, 336
  see also neurology; pattern recognition; psychology; science, cognitive
Cohen, Jack Joseph, 170, 330, 340
colonialism, 70–71, 72
communication, 42, 67, 86, 91, 114–16, 119–24, 136, 148–49, 171, 181, 195, 220, 300, 321, 331
  see also language
community, religious, xii, xiii, xv, 21, 25–26, 43, 208–9, 232, 234, 242, 256, 300, 308, 312
  see also church(es); *saṅgha*
comparative philosophy *see* philosophy, comparative
comparative religion *see* religious studies, comparative
Comparative Religious Ideas Project (CRIP), xviii, xx, 150, 319, 328, 348–49
comparative theology *see* theology, comparative
comparison, 125–65
  and commensurability, 135–37, 148–49, 157
  comparative category, 126–34, 136, 138–40, 142–48, 150–62, 165, 326, 328
    subordinate, 129
    vague, 127–29, 136
  comparative judgment, 128, 131–32, 136–37, 149–51, 154–55, 157, 164
  dialectic of abstraction and particularity, 124
  dialectic of data and categories, 147–52
  explicit, 125–26, 134–41
  implicit, 119, 125, 138–41
  as impossible, 135–38
  justification of categories, 135, 141–47
  objections to, 136–38

bias, 136–37
incommensurability, 85–95, 136
morality, 137
respect of comparison, 127–30
role of theories of religion, 141–45
similarity, 145–47
successful, 135, 137, 139
vagueness in, 126–29, 131
defined 36
see also fallibilism; inquiry; stability
complexity, 42, 86, 88–93, 99, 139–40, 153, 158, 164, 175, 181, 207, 218, 269–72
Comte, Auguste, 76, 310
Confucianism, 28, 55, 87, 169, 283–91, 294
see also axiology; axiotheological tradition; Confucius (Kong Fu Zi or K'ung-fu-tzu or 孔夫子); Chinese Classics, *Classic of Music* (*Yuèjīng* or *Yüeh Ching* or 樂經 or 乐经), Five Classics (*Wǔjīng* or *Wu Ching* or 五經 or 五经), Four Books (*Sì Shū* or *Ssu Shu* or 四書 or 四书); *Dao* (*Dào* or *Tao* or 道; ultimate way); Kong Ji (孔伋; later, *Zǐsī* or Tzu-ssu or 子思); Mencius; Mencius (*Mèngzǐ* or *Meng-Tzu* or 孟子); Neo-Confucianism; *qi* (*ch'i* or 氣 or 气; life force); religious philosophy; ritual; *Tian* (*Tiān* or *T'ien* or 天; heaven); Tu Weiming; ultimacy; virtue; Xunzi (*Xúnzǐ* or Hsün Tzu or 荀子 or荀子); Zengzi (Zēngzǐ or Tsengtzu or 曾子); Zhuangzi; *Zhuangzi* (*Zhuāngzǐ* or *Chuang-Tzu* or 莊子 or 庄子); Zhu Xi (Zhū Xī or Chu His or 朱熹)
Confucius (Kong Fu Zi or K'ung-fu-tzu or 孔夫子), 86, 213, 284, 286–89, 291

consciousness, 2, 12, 49–50, 52, 55, 68, 83, 90–91, 111, 120–21, 176, 253–54, 273–83
problem(s) of, 12, 273–74
consensus, ix–xi, 14, 58, 75, 77–79, 170, 180–85, 188, 200–4, 222, 225–27, 229, 236, 240–42, 249–50, 262–63, 265, 274–75, 282
of qualified experts, 77, 203, 225–27, 236, 240
and timing, 196–97, 203
infinite long run (Peirce), 203
see also pragmatic theory of inquiry
conservativism, 54–55, 62, 71, 124, 158, 204, 244, 258
context, 35, 40, 45–50, 59–61, 64–65, 78, 89, 95, 102, 116–17, 120, 151, 173, 175, 184, 200, 214, 226, 293
cooperation, 53, 60, 88, 107, 110, 121, 140–41, 167–68, 170–71, 177, 179–81, 186, 191, 214, 258
sharing, 107–8, 155
correction *see* fallibilism; feedback potential; inquiry; pragmatic theory of inquiry; reality
Corrington, Robert, 170, 330, 340
cosmology, 33, 98, 102, 242, 266–68
big-bang, 242, 266–68
philosophical, 33, 98, 102
cosmotheological tradition, xiv, 255–61, 262, 277
see also Aristotle; causation; cosmology; creation, divine; God(s); Dostoevsky, Fyodor; ground of being; logos; Kalām; Leskov, Nicolai; philosophy, Islamic; *pratītya-samutpāda* (dependent co-arising); religious philosophy; Schleiermacher, Friedrich; Thomas Aquinas; Tillich, Paul; ultimacy
crafts, practical/professional, 35, 215, 225, 228–31, 243, 315
law, 35
medicine, 35

crafts, practical/professional (*continued*)
  politics, 35
  religious leadership, 25, 225, 315
  social work, 225, 243
creation, 2, 58, 219, 235, 242, 244, 266–67, 271, 292
  creationism, 219, 244
  divine, 2, 58, 235, 242, 266–67, 292
  science 271
creativity, xiii, 2, 53, 88, 117, 121, 136, 201, 293–94, 297, 303
critical theory, 70, 196–99, 203, 220, 221
Crosby, Donald, 170, 330, 340

Dao (*Dào* or *Tao* or 道; ultimate way), 2, 27, 83, 152, 295
  dao (way), 288
Dao De Jing (*Dàodéjīng* or *Tao Te Ching* or 道德經 or 道德经), 27, 290–91, 298
  see also Laozi (*Lǎozǐ* or Lao Tzu or 老子)
Daoism, 26–28, 55, 169, 243, 290–91
  see also Chinese Classics, Daoist; *Classic of Perfect Emptiness* (*Lièzǐ* or *Lieh-Tzu* or 列子); Dao (*Dào* or *Tao* or 道; ultimate way); Dao De Jing (*Dàodéjīng* or *Tao Te Ching* or 道德經 or 道德经); Laozi (*Lǎozǐ* or Lao Tzu or 老子); qi (*ch'i* or 氣 or 气; life force); yang (*yáng* or 陽 or 阳; lighter masculine element); yin (*yīn* or 陰 or 阴; darker feminine element); Zhuangzi; Zhuangzi (*Zhuāngzǐ* or *Chuang-Tzu* or 莊子 or 庄子)
de Saussure, Ferdinand, 195, 325, 331, 341
  semiotics, 195
death, 37, 38, 65, 81, 108, 113, 133, 235, 259
deconstruction, 5–8, 73, 81, 125, 274

demarcation, xi, 79, 176, 214–37
  disciplinary, 79, 217–37
  problem, 215–17
Dennett, Daniel, 149, 328, 341
dependence, 10, 32–33, 47, 66, 77, 79, 93, 95–99, 101–2, 106, 113–14, 130–31, 134, 145, 164, 235, 255–58, 259–62, 267, 272, 278, 302, 304
Derrida, Jacques, 66–67, 76, 81, 83, 213, 253–54, 325
Descartes, René, 59–60, 64, 204, 273, 334, 341
  see also epistemology; foundationalism; philosophy, modern
Dewey, John, 11, 63, 158, 169, 178, 205, 252, 293, 329, 330, 335, 341
  see also pragmatism
Dhammapada, 41
Dilworth, David, 147, 328, 341
discarnate beings, 142, 164, 296
discipline, academic, ix–xiii, xv, xix, 1–34, 87, 91–93, 214–37, 312, 314
  defined, 217
discourse, 52, 65–70, 74–76, 85–86, 117, 124, 135, 174, 189–96, 199–202, 227, 231–33, 296, 300–1
  specialized, 52, 86, 174, 189–96, 199, 201–2, 227, 231–33, 296, 300–1
  community, 86, 174, 189–96, 199, 201–2, 231–33, 296, 300–1
  see also language
diversity, ix–xi, xv, xvii, 53, 112, 125, 176–77, 207, 214, 224, 243–44, 253, 261, 295
  in higher education, 313–17
Doctrine of the Mean (*Zhōng Yōng* or *Chung-Yung* or 中庸), 288, 335, 347
  see also Kong Ji (孔伋; later, *Zǐsī* or *Tzu-ssu* or 子思)
Dostoevsky, Fyodor, 259
dualism, 54–55, 215, 277–78, 302
  mind-body, 54–55

Durkheim, Emile, 19, 220, 327, 342
Dvaita Vedānta (Tattvavāda), 230,
    277–78
  see also Ātman; Brahman; Īśvara;
    Madhvacharya; Vedānta

Eckel, Malcolm David, xiii, xx, 322,
    327, 328, 342
ecology, 70, 105, 113–14, 186–89
education, xvi, xix–xx, 14, 20–21, 25,
    60, 69, 87–88, 132, 171, 179, 239,
    275, 286–87, 290, 308–9, 312,
    313–17
empirical fidelity, 57, 77–79
empiricism, 11, 21, 55, 57, 73–74,
    77–79, 90, 96, 118, 124, 130–31,
    136–37, 142, 153, 162–63, 168,
    170–71, 174, 184, 186–87,
    194–97, 199, 201, 215, 219–21,
    224, 227, 230, 242, 250, 267, 282,
    294–95, 304, 312
energy, 54–55, 75, 108, 110, 112–13,
    124, 212, 241
engagement, 21, 31, 249, 252, 254,
    297–98, 301–4, 314
  see also language; Neville, Robert
    Cummings; ritual; symbolism
enlightenment, 140, 199, 220, 231,
    274, 276, 301–2
Enlightenment, the, 9, 19, 52, 58,
    237, 238, 282
environment, xx, 26, 48, 50, 60–61,
    89, 91, 108–13, 117, 125, 173–74,
    181, 197, 200, 223, 237, 241, 244,
    254, 259–61, 285, 302
  social 50, 60–61, 241, 244
epidemiology of representation, 44
epistemology, xvii, 1–4, 8–12, 32,
    46, 48, 52, 57–61, 70–79, 80, 119,
    148, 167, 169, 177, 196–205, 242,
    249, 276–80, 282–83, 292, 297
  see also empiricism;
    foundationalism; inquiry;
    knowledge; philosophy;
    pragmatic theory of inquiry;
    rationalism; rationality, theory
    of
ethics, philosophical, 1–3, 7, 12, 35,
    224, 253–54, 284, 297
  see also morality
evangelicalism, 81, 96, 101–3, 258,
    260
evolution, 12, 21, 36, 53–54, 63,
    69, 75, 82, 105, 107–8, 111–12,
    115, 117, 125, 144, 162–63, 170,
    177–78, 180–81, 185, 219, 233,
    240, 242, 244, 253, 261, 269–72,
    275, 282
  adaptation, 111, 175–77
experience, mystical, 38, 48–50,
    96–97, 294–304
experience, religious, 30, 48–49
explanatory principle, 2–3
exploitation, 71, 81–82

faith, 26, 96–97, 100–2, 205, 232, 236,
    242–43, 256, 315
fallibilism, xvi, 4–13, 46–47, 51, 57,
    72, 74–77, 80, 170, 177–78, 198,
    203, 311–12
  and correction, 3–6, 26, 47, 51–52,
    63, 69, 72, 74–77, 80, 130–32,
    135, 137–38, 140, 143, 145, 148,
    151–53, 158, 170, 173–74, 177,
    182–83, 188–89, 192–93, 198–99,
    203, 214, 216–23, 233, 236, 241,
    276, 279, 311, 314
  see also comparison; feedback
    potential; hypothesis; inquiry;
    pragmatic theory of inquiry
feedback-potential, 78–79, 170,
    182–86, 189, 191–92, 198, 201–5,
    214–22, 227, 233–34, 241–45
  see also reality; truth
Ferré, Frederick, 170, 293–94, 330,
    335, 342
  see also axiology
Feuerbach, Ludwig, 282, 293
Feyerabend, Paul, 118, 157, 205, 326,
    329, 331, 343

fine arts, 28, 39, 181, 191, 225–30
food, religious aspects of, 39, 85, 93, 95, 105–14, 325
Forman, Robert, 49–50, 321, 343
   see also perennial philosophy
Foucault, Michel, 66, 76, 293, 321, 325, 343
foundationalism, 1, 9, 11–13, 46–47, 51, 54, 57–64, 70, 72–73, 75–77, 80, 149, 177–78, 198
   antifoundationalism, 62, 198
   nonfoundationalism, 11–13, 47, 51, 57, 62–64, 70, 73, 75–76, 177
   postfoundationalism, 47, 57–58, 61–63, 75
   see also epistemology; modernism; philosophy, modern; postmodernism
Frankenberry, Nancy, 170, 319, 330, 343
Frankfurt School, 197–98, 220
   see also critical theory
Freud, Sigmund, 67, 188, 220, 282, 328, 343
fundamentalism, religious, 239, 271

Gadamer, Hans-Georg, 66–67, 116–17, 325, 343
Galilei, Galileo, 87, 192–93, 216, 240, 263–65
game theory, 107–8
Gaṇeśa, 133
gathering, 107–9
generality, 57, 71–77, 80, 120, 158
   critique, 73–75
genius, religious, 44–45, 291
Gibson, James, 185–89, 331, 343, 344
   affordance, 185–86, 188, 189, 331
   theory of perception, 185, 187–88
God(s), 2–3, 12, 25, 27, 29–31, 36, 54, 56, 59, 81, 83, 85, 94–105, 123, 133, 142–43, 147, 152, 160–61, 163–64, 236, 248–58, 261, 263, 265–68, 270–71, 275, 277–78, 280–81, 283, 292, 294–96, 298, 303

existence, arguments for, 12, 59, 85, 94, 95–105, 123, 164, 253–58
   Thomas Aquinas, Five Ways, 257–58, 261
   see also creation, divine; Godhead; religious philosophy, traditions of
   see also Allah; Brahman; creation, divine; discarnate beings; Gaṇeśa; Godhead; ground of being; Īśvara; Jesus Christ; Shang Di (Shàng Dì or Shang Ti or 上帝; ultimate emperor or supreme God); Śiva; Tian (Tiān or T'ien or 天; heaven); theism; ultimate reality; Viṣṇu
Gödel, Kurt, 196, 331, 344
Godhead, 142–43
   see also Brahman, nirguṇa; God(s); ultimate reality
good, the, 3, 291–92, 295
Gould, Stephen Jay, 185, 331, 344
great chain of being, 142, 296–97, 302, 304, 335, 347
Great Learning (Dà Xué or Ta-Hsüeh or 大學 or 大学), 287–88, 335, 347
   see also Zengzi (Zēngzǐ or Tsengtzu or 曾子)
ground of being, 208, 293
   see also God(s); ultimate reality

Habermas, Jürgen, 67, 198
Hajj, 243
hallucination, 111
Hardwick, Charley, 170, 330, 344
Hartshorne, Charles, 274, 293, 329, 335, 344
Hawking, Stephen, 242, 267–68, 332, 333, 344
Hegel, Georg Wilhelm Friedrich, xii, 19, 73, 281, 293, 321, 328, 334, 344
   see also history, consciousness of; philosophy, modern

Heidegger, Martin, 91, 168, 250, 253, 256–57, 293, 310, 322, 328, 334, 344
hermeneutics, xvii, 23, 33, 91, 116–17, 152, 156, 203
 see also interpretation, theory of
Hinduism, 17, 26, 28, 33, 95, 99–100, 102, 114, 133, 144, 161–62, 169, 193, 230, 243, 249, 275–79, 323
 see also Advaita Vedānta; Ātman; avidyā (ignorance); Bhagavad-gītā; bhakti (devotion); bhakti yoga; Brahman; Brahmasūtras; Dvaita Vedānta; Gaṇeśa; Īśvara; jīva (soul); jñāna (knowledge); jñāna yoga; karma; karma yoga; Madhvacharya; Mahābhārata; Mīmāṃsā; mokṣa; Navya-Nyāya (New Nyāya school); Nyāya; puja; Rāmānuja; reincarnation; religious philosophy; saṃsāra (cycle of lives); Śaṅkara; Śiva; theology; Udayana; Upaniṣads; Vaiśeṣika; Vedānta; Vedas, the; vijñāna (consciousness); Viśiṣṭādvaita Vedānta; Viṣṇu; Yoga
history, 4, 15, 17, 18–19, 21–23, 25, 39–40, 44, 67, 73, 94, 144, 150, 164, 168, 193, 251, 257, 275, 281, 284–85, 294
 consciousness of, 64–66, 117
history of religion(s) see religious studies, history of religion(s)
Hubble, Edwin, 193, 266
human condition, the, 68, 82, 106, 114, 139, 143, 159, 253, 259, 261, 283
humanities, 221–24
Hume, David, 36, 103
hunting, 107–9, 171–72
Husserl, Edmund, 40, 90, 126, 149, 253–54, 280, 322, 328, 345
 see also phenomenology
Huxley, Aldous, 295, 327, 335, 345

hypothesis, xvii, 4–8, 10–11, 13, 30, 33, 41, 45, 50–51, 55–56, 63, 72, 75–79, 94, 103–6, 117, 122, 131, 138, 140, 151–53, 155–58, 160, 163–64, 168–70, 173–74, 178, 181–85, 189–95, 198–205, 209–11, 214–20, 222–24, 226–28, 230–34, 237, 240–41, 247, 268–72, 295–97, 302–5
 see also fallibilism; inquiry; pragmatic theory of inquiry; problem(s); problem-oriented research; science

idea(s), religious, 3, 15–16, 19, 21, 28, 40, 64, 94, 125, 131, 134–35, 137–38, 140–42, 144, 150–51, 155, 159–62, 211, 214, 255, 319, 326–28
 see also Comparative Religious Ideas Project (CRIP)
idealism, 281–82
 see also epistemology; Fichte, Johann; Hegel, Georg Wilhelm Friedrich; Kant, Immanuel; philosophy, modern; Schelling, Friedrich
identity, x–xi, xv, 15, 18–22, 24, 26, 28, 32, 43, 49–50, 65–66, 70, 72–73, 88, 94, 108, 132, 136, 181–82, 185, 190–92, 202, 213, 217–18, 220–21, 225, 242, 254, 275, 277, 281, 312–14, 317
 politics, 94, 317
ideology, 63–80, 198, 310–11
imagination, 10, 38, 52–53, 65, 68, 94, 118, 122–24, 135–36, 153, 163, 173, 186, 244, 263, 267–70, 282, 298–300
immortality, 35, 54
incommensurability, 53, 85–86, 114–24, 135–37, 148–49, 157,
 thesis, 115–19, 122
 see also comparison; discourse; inquiry
indeterminacy, 116–17, 176, 313–14

inference-to-best-explanation
    argument(s), 12–13, 162–65, 173
inquiry, 1–34, 35–56, 167–245,
    307–17
  adaptiveness of, 177–78
  audaciousness of, 43–45
  community of, 155
  dynamic sociality of, 120–25, 138
  efficiency of, xi–xii, 6, 10–11, 33,
    46, 52–53, 69, 124, 157, 173,
    180–85, 204, 221–22, 230, 296,
    303, 309–10
  order, first-, xvii, 6, 16, 21, 24,
    156, 211, 229–32, 234–35
  order, second-, 211, 229–32, 234–
    35
  passivity in, 43–45
  styles of, xiv–xv, xvii, 5–7, 14–16,
    22, 25, 35–45
    analytical, 38
    comparative, 38
    evaluative, 39
    historical, 38
    literary, 38
    phenomenological, 38
    theoretical, 39
  theory of, 76–79, 85, 88, 114–15,
    158, 167–205, 207, 209, 214–15,
    218, 220–28, 237, 241, 244, 296,
    307, 311
  see also comparison; fallibilism;
    pragmatic theory of inquiry;
    problem-oriented research
instrumentation, theories of, 153,
    156–59, 193, 241
intelligent-design, 261–72
interestedness, 67, 69, 128, 175
interpretation, theory of, xvi, 5–8,
    51, 63, 67, 69–73, 81, 91–92, 95,
    116–17, 130, 136–37, 148, 150–
    53, 159, 167–205, 220
  see also hermeneutics
interreligious dialogue, 137, 141
intuition, 64–65, 153, 157–58, 197
Islam, 26, 28, 32–33, 114, 161, 228,
    239, 243, 249, 255, 291–92, 315

  see also Allah; causation; creation;
    faith; God(s); Godhead; Hajj;
    Kalām; monotheism; Mullā
    Sadrā; philosophy, Islamic;
    practice(s), religious; Qur'an
    (Qur'ān or Koran or Al-Qur'ān
    or القرآن); religious philosophy;
    revelation; theism; theology;
    text, sacred; ultimacy; ultimate
    reality
Īśvara, 100–2, 227–28
  see also Brahman, saguṇa; God(s);
    Hinduism

James, William, xiv, xx, 19, 48, 49,
    55, 69, 90, 169–70, 185–86, 200–
    1, 242, 282, 293, 321, 322, 329,
    331, 332, 335, 345
  see also naturalism; pragmatism;
    pragmatic-naturalist tradition;
    psychology
Jesus Christ, 190–91, 243, 259–60,
    281, 298
jīva (soul), 2, 54, 101, 133, 193
jñāna (knowledge), 301
jñāna yoga, 279
Johnson, Mark, 170, 347
Judaism, 20, 26, 28, 32, 33, 81, 114,
    136, 161, 237, 239, 243, 253–54,
    291, 292, 315
  see also Bible, Hebrew; faith;
    God(s); monotheism; Moses;
    philosophy, Jewish; practice(s),
    religious; religious philosophy;
    revelation; ritual; Talmud;
    text, sacred; theism; theology;
    ultimacy
judgment, 16, 40–43, 51, 58–61, 63,
    91, 122, 128, 131, 136–37, 149–
    51, 157, 181, 183, 192, 196–97,
    202–3, 210–12, 215, 224, 226,
    257, 259, 276, 279, 281, 283, 293
  see also aesthetics; beautiful, the;
    bias; comparison; good, the;
    inquiry; morality; truth
Jung, Carl, 142, 220

justice, xvii, 23, 66–67, 69, 72–73, 172, 221, 225, 228, 310
justification, 6, 36, 135, 140–62, 330, 335–36
  qualified expert approval, 4, 14–15, 18, 58, 77–78, 135, 146, 151, 202–3, 226–28, 236, 296
  qualified adherent approval, 14–15, 137

Kalām, 255, 258, 333, 340
Kant, Immanuel, 8–13, 49, 76, 90, 97, 103, 171, 188–89, 197, 215–16, 251, 253, 256–57, 280–81, 310, 319, 322, 331, 333, 334, 346
  see also epistemology; noumena(l); phenomena; philosophy, modern
karma, 101
karma yoga, 279
Katz, Steven, xx, 49–50, 321, 346
Kepler, Johannes, 264–65
Knepper, Timothy D., xx, 335, 346
knowledge, 11–12, 32, 41, 44, 46, 49–51, 57–63, 66, 69, 71, 82, 86–88, 96–99, 101–6, 109–10, 117, 123, 131, 138, 148, 168–70, 180, 188, 194, 197, 199, 213, 215–16, 227, 236–38, 241, 249, 252, 256, 272, 278–79, 282, 288–89, 295–96, 298, 301–2, 308, 311, 315
  see also epistemology
Kong Ji (孔伋; later, Zǐsī or Tzu-ssu or 子思), 288
Kuhn, Thomas, 118, 156, 326, 329, 346
Kurts, Paul, 170, 330, 352

Lakatos, Imre, 156–58, 205, 329, 331, 346
Laozi (Lǎozǐ or Lao Tzu or 老子), 213, 290
language, 3, 5, 10, 51–52, 123, 193–96, 309
  formal, 123, 193, 196, 301
    logic, 123, 196
    mathematics, 123

grammar, 194–95
  physiological aspects, 194–95
  pragmatics, 195
  semantics, 3, 5, 10, 193–96, 309
  technical, 123, 194–95
    specialized terminology, 51–52, 123, 192–96
  see also discourse; linguistics; speech act theory
Leibniz, Gottfried, 251, 265, 333, 347
Leskov, Nicolai, 260
Lévinas, Emmanuel, 24, 213, 249, 253–54, 320, 325–26, 333, 347
liberalism, 62, 71, 321, 348
liberation, 27, 37, 44–45, 143, 277–78, 280
Lindbeck, George, 116, 325, 347
linguistics, 42, 117, 194, 234, 325, 331
literary criticism, 81, 116–17, 223–24, 229, 325
literature, ix, xv, 8, 19–21, 28, 31, 32, 35, 38–41, 44–45, 48–49, 51, 55, 68, 81, 94, 102, 116–17, 158, 212, 223–24, 229, 233–35, 253, 259, 272, 305, 312, 325
  (auto)biography, 48, 224
  dialogue, 48
  fiction, 48
  poetry, 201, 284
Locke, John, 64, 171, 197, 215, 280, 334, 347
  see also empiricism; epistemology; philosophy, modern
logic, 5, 123, 174, 177–79, 196, 205, 251
logical positivism, 12, 197
logocentrism, 138
logos, 58, 78, 255–56, 263

Madhvacharya (Madhva), 171, 277–79
  see also Dvaita Vedanta
Mādhyamaka, 33, 171, 255, 301
  see also Buddhism, Mahāyāna, Tibetan, Zen; Nāgārjuna; *upāya*

Mahābhārata, 41, 274–75
  see also *Bhagavad-gītā*
Mahāyāna see Buddhism, Mahāyāna
Marion, Jean-Luc, x, 250, 333, 348
Marx, Karl, 55, 68, 113, 293
Mecca, 243
medicine, 35, 54, 60, 82, 109, 124, 225, 316
meditation, 25, 44, 48, 52, 59, 78, 89–90, 278–80, 283
memory, 53, 106, 114, 163, 176–77, 185, 276, 290
Mencius, 289–90
Mencius (*Mèngzĭ* or *Meng-Tzu* or 孟子), 289–90
metaphor, 138–39, 249, 252, 289, 298
metaphysics, 1, 6–7, 9, 11–13, 29–30, 33, 35, 52, 59–60, 78–79, 142–44, 158, 162, 164, 176, 183, 186, 205, 215–19, 230–33, 235–36, 242, 249, 254–55, 264–66, 302, 310
methodological self-awareness, 25–26, 132, 198, 237
microbial world, 111–12
Mīmāṃsā, 100–2
mimesis theory, 44
modernism, 61–62, 79
modernity, xvii–xviii, 55, 57–83, 239–40, 249, 281, 321
mokṣa, 144, 301, 303
monism, 50, 276
monotheism, 161–62
  see also God(s); theism
morality, 11, 72, 76–77, 106, 137, 143, 167, 214, 281, 293–94, 307–17
  see also ethics, philosophical
Moses, 27, 29
Mullā Sadrā, 249
Müller, Max, 19
multidisciplinarity, 30–31, 85–124
multidisciplinary comparative inquiry, ix, xi, xiii, xx, 1–56, 85–124, 167–245, 307–17
  see also comparison; inquiry; multidisciplinarity; problem-oriented research; religious philosophy
multiple religious and personal identity, 136
Murphy, Nancey, 62–63, 72, 75, 79, 321, 331, 348
Murry, William, 170, 330, 348
mystical theology see theology, mystical
mysticism, 27, 38, 41, 48–50, 80–83, 96–97, 142–44, 290, 294–304
  see also experience, mystical
mysticotheological tradition, xiv, 279, 294–304
  see also apophasis; Brahman; engagement; experience, mystical; God(s); great chain of being; Huxley, Aldous; language; Mādhyamaka; mysticism; naturalism, religious; perennial philosophy; Pseudo-Dionysius; religious philosophy; Schuon, Frithjof; Smith, Huston; spirituality; symbolism; ultimacy; *via negativa*; *via positiva*; wisdom

Nāgārjuna, 33, 213, 255
  see also Mādhyamaka
nirguṇa Brahman see Brahman, *nirguṇa*
narrative, 37, 66–70, 73, 114, 138–39, 170, 208–9, 259–60, 275, 300
natural theology see theology, natural
naturalism, 79, 104, 169–70, 217–19, 302, 304
  functional, 79, 217–19
  religious, 104, 302, 304
    Chicago School, 169–70
Navya Nyāya (New Nyāya school), 100
  see also Udayana
Neo-Confucianism, 294
Neoplatonism, 230, 249, 279, 299, 302

see also Aristotle; great chain of being; One, the; Plato; Platonism; Plotinus; Pseudo-Dionysius
nirvāṇa, 133, 169, 236
neurology, 42, 50, 131, 171, 174, 186–87
neuroscience, 50, 54–55, 144, 224, 228, 282
Neville, Robert Cummings, x, xx, 126, 149–50, 170, 252–53, 319, 322, 328, 329, 330, 333, 335, 348, 356
  Axiology of Thinking, 294
  and axiotheological tradition, 293–94
  Comparative Religious Ideas Project, xviii, 149–50
  and engagement, 254
  God the Creator, 252
  and pragmatism, 252–53
Newman, John Henry, 157, 329, 349
Newton, Isaac, 60, 264–65
Nielson, Kai, 170, 330, 335, 349
Nietzsche, Friedrich, 253–54, 293, 335, 349
nihilism, 97
noumena(l), 10, 216
Nyāya, 100–1

objectivity, 13–14, 16–18, 21–26, 38, 40, 62, 118, 137, 152, 203, 212
One, the, 83, 279
  see also God(s); Neoplatonism; Plotinus; ultimate reality
ontological argument, 96–97, 251–52, 254, 258, 280
  see also Anselm, Saint; Descartes, René; Leibniz, Gottfried; Kant, Immanuel; ontotheological tradition
ontology, 2–4, 7, 52, 54, 55, 79, 96–99, 101–2, 119–20, 142–44, 160–64, 169–70, 177–78, 184, 189, 199, 208, 210, 219, 235, 237, 250–56, 258, 263, 269, 274, 276–81, 292, 296–97, 302, 304
  sparse, 296–97, 302, 304
  see also being; great chain of being; metaphysics; ontological argument; ontotheological tradition
ontotheological tradition, xiv, 123, 248–54, 257, 261, 293, 333
  see also Anselm, Saint; Aristotle; Augustine, Saint; being; Buddhism; consciousness; Derrida, Jacques; engagement; great chain of being; Heidegger, Martin; Husserl, Edmund; Kant, Immanuel; Leibniz, Gottfried; Lévinas, Emmanuel; Marion, Jean-Luc; metaphysics; Mullā Sadrā; Neoplatonism; Neville, Robert Cummings; Nietzsche, Friedrich; ontological argument; ontology; other, the; Plato; Platonism; Plotinus; religious philosophy; Thomas Aquinas; ultimacy; Vedānta
Other, the, 24, 71, 249, 253–54, 260
Otto, Rudolf, 146, 328, 349

Paley, William, 270–71, 334, 349
Parmenides, 169, 279
parochialism, ix–xii, xvi, 5, 21, 56, 96, 98–99, 102–3, 121, 244, 311, 313, 315, 317, 324
pattern recognition, 73, 129, 131, 163, 171, 173, 326
  see also cognition; perception
Peden, Creighton, 170, 330, 349
Peirce, Charles Saunders, xx, 11, 63, 91, 158, 169–70, 195, 200, 203, 205, 252, 293, 322, 329, 330, 335, 349–50
perception, 69, 90, 126–34, 174–89, 228, 260, 276–78, 280
  and comparison, 126–34
  see also cognition; pattern recognition

perennial philosophy, 49, 142–43, 152–53, 295–97, 302, 304, 322, 335, 345
  see also Forman, Robert; Smith, Huston
Peters, Karl, 170, 330, 350
phenomena, 5, 10, 14, 24, 38–39, 54, 64, 77, 92, 134, 136, 146–47, 175, 192, 211, 216, 230, 234, 264, 273–74, 278
  religious, xv, 14, 18, 93–94, 139, 146–47, 156–57, 162, 213
  breadth, 35–37
  criteria, 37
phenomenology, 17, 23, 35, 38–40, 43–45, 48–50, 52, 55, 89, 93–94, 145–46, 149, 153, 162, 212, 227–28, 233, 249, 252–53, 274, 278, 280, 293, 308
Phillips, D.Z., x, 116, 325, 350
philosophical theology see theology, philosophical
philosophy, 1–165, 207–317
  analytic, 11–12, 14, 35, 38–45, 55, 94, 178, 212, 233, 253, 274–75, 282, 308
  Chinese, 55, 97, 284–91
    Confucian, 55, 169, 284–90
      see also Confucianism
    Daoist, 55, 290–91
      see also Daoism
  Christian, xii, 292
    see also Christianity
  comparative, xv, xviii, 1, 9, 12–13, 126, 134–35, 213, 247, 311
  contemporary, 6, 55, 99, 102, 115, 179, 252, 305
  continental, 12, 55, 80, 293
  Indian, 14, 55, 100, 274–76, 279–80
    Hindu, 99–100
      see also Hinduism
    Buddhist, 33, 89–90, 100–1, 169, 171, 282, 301
      see also Buddhism
  Islamic, 249, 292
    see also Islam; Kalām

  Jewish see Judaism
  medieval, 58, 61, 251
  of mind, 55
  modern, 22, 57–79, 90, 177, 280, 293–94, 305
    see also modernism
  pragmatic see pragmatism; pragmatic-naturalist tradition
  postmodern see postmodernism
  of religion, ix–xvi, 13, 16–18, 21, 26, 93, 95, 99, 105, 114, 142, 156, 162, 213–14, 236, 309, 312–13
  of science, 4, 60–61, 117–18, 156–59, 215
  systematic, 7, 252, 294
    see also big-question philosophy; epistemology; ethics, philosophical; logic; metaphysics; pragmatism; religious philosophy
physicalism, 50, 54, 274–75
physicotheological tradition, xiv, 261–72
  see also Aristotle; biology; cosmology; creation, divine; creation, science; evolution; fundamentalism; Galileo Galilei; God(s); Hawking, Stephen; intelligent-design; Kepler, Johannes; Leibniz, Gottfried; Newton, Isaac; Paley, William; physics; Pythagoras; religious philosophy; reality; Thomas Aquinas; ultimacy
physics, 2, 18, 59, 78–79, 163–64, 192, 205, 215–19, 241, 262–64, 267–69
piety, 133, 249, 250, 286, 309
Plato (Πλάτων), 33, 86, 130, 213, 262, 291–92, 326, 350
  divided line, 292
  Form of the Good, 291–92
  Republic, 169, 292, 326, 350
  Timaeus, 292, 326, 350
  see also axiology; Platonism

Platonism, 97, 177, 249–50
  Middle Platonism, 230
  see also Anselm, Saint; Augustine, Saint; axiotheological tradition; great chain of being; Neoplatonism; perennial philosophy; Plato; Plotinus
plausibility, 5, 65, 141–42, 178, 232, 237, 243–44
Plotinus (Πλωτῖνος), 33, 230, 249, 279
  see also Neoplatonism; One, the; Platonism
pluralism, ontological, 97, 278
pluralism, religious, xii, 19, 72–73, 144–45, 274, 303
poetry see literature, poetry
politics, 15, 27, 35, 59–62, 64–72, 74–75, 80, 88, 91, 94, 115, 124, 136, 151, 161, 172, 180, 182, 190, 203, 209, 225, 228, 239, 243, 259–61, 269, 281, 283–91, 310, 317
polytheism, as comparative category, 133
Popper, Karl, 157, 329, 350
postmodernism, ix–xix, 12, 54–56, 57–83, 90, 120, 167, 294, 305
  criticism of, 72–83
  critiques of modernism, 63–72
poststructuralism, 117, 125, 195, 203, 213, 325
practice(s), religious, 14, 24, 36, 40, 48, 126, 133, 136, 142–43, 150, 183, 250, 285
pragmatic theory of inquiry, xvi, 76–79, 167–205, 207–45, 311–12
  antifoundationalism of, 198
  attention to experience, 170–71, 197–98, 204
  biological and social basis of, 198–99
  and critical theory, 198
  as epistemological framework, 9–11, 167
  emphases of, 170
  figures utilizing, 169–70
  and realism, 199–200

and relativism, 199
truth as word-world correspondence, 201–2
see also fallibilism; foundationalism, antifoundationalism; inquiry; multidisciplinarity; pragmatism
pragmatism, xx, 11–12, 63, 74–79, 167–205, 207–45, 293, 311–12
  see also Dewey, John; James, William; Neville, Robert Cummings; Peirce, Charles Saunders; pragmatic theory of inquiry; pragmatic-naturalist tradition
pragmaticism (Peirce), 200–1
pragmatic-naturalist tradition, 169–70
  see also Dewey, John; James, William; naturalism, religious; Peirce, Charles Saunders; philosophy, pragmatic; Whitehead, Alfred North; Wieman, Henry Nelson
pratītya-samutpāda (dependent co-arising), 2, 97, 101, 249, 255, 302
praxis, 74, 137
prayer, 31, 96–97, 114, 280, 282, 321
prestige, social, 60, 107, 109, 118
priesthood, 39, 68, 77, 150, 260
primate, 65, 180–81
problem(s), 88–105, 115, 117, 120–21, 168–79
  abstraction, 91, 95–105, 117
  emergence, 88–93, 95, 115, 120–21, 175–77, 179
  solving, 168–74
problem-oriented research, 87–88, 322
  see also inquiry
Proudfoot, Wayne, x, 49, 321, 335–36, 350
Pseudo-Dionysius, 299
psychology, 9, 21, 36–37, 42, 44, 48, 50, 59, 69, 75, 77, 90, 94, 99, 105, 112, 117, 121, 131, 144,

psychology (continued)
163–64, 171, 181, 184, 186–88,
198, 219–21, 224, 274, 279–83,
309
  developmental, 44
  ecological, 186–87, 331
  evolutionary, 36, 75, 105, 117, 163,
  282
psychosis, 111
psychotheological tradition, xiv,
273–83
  see also Advaita Vedānta; Anselm,
  Saint; Ātman; Augustine, Saint;
  avidyā (ignorance); Brahman;
  cognition; consciousness;
  Descartes, René; Dvaita Vedānta;
  epistemology; experience;
  Fichte, Johann; Hegel,
  George Wilhelm; Husserl,
  Edmund; idealism; Īśvara;
  Kant, Immanuel; Locke, John;
  Madhvacharya; Neoplatonism;
  philosophy, Indian; philosophy,
  modern; Plotinus; psychology;
  Rāmānuja; religious philosophy;
  Śaṅkara; Schelling, Friedrich;
  science, cognitive; ultimacy;
  Vedānta; Viśiṣṭādvaita Vedānta
puja, 114
purity, 68, 143
Pythagoras (Πυθαγόρας), 78, 262–64,
266

qi (ch'i or 氣 or 气; life force), 2
Quine, W.V.O., 11, 350
Qur'an (Qur'ān or Koran or Al-
Qur'ān or القرآن), 41

Rāmānuja, 171, 277–79, 281
  see also Ātman; Brahman;
  Viśiṣṭādvaita Vedānta
rationalism, 203–4, 258
rationality, 8, 58–63, 69, 71–79, 82,
118, 120, 167–205, 237, 239–41,
255
  theory of, ix–xi, xv–xvi, 167–205,
  312–13
reality, 2–5, 12, 37, 40, 57–59, 65,
72–79, 81, 83, 97, 101, 104, 119,
128, 131, 147, 162–64, 168–71,
174, 181–85, 193, 195, 203–4,
208, 217–18, 220, 228, 230, 235,
243, 248, 254, 255–61, 263, 266,
274–80, 290–92, 297, 301, 303,
310
  depth structures of, 263, 266
reductionism, 115, 168, 170–71,
217–18, 223, 257
reincarnation, 54, 101, 133
relativism, 3, 58, 62, 71, 119–20,
199–200
religion(s), characterized, 35–37
religious naturalism see naturalism,
religious
religious philosophy, ix–xx, 1–165,
207–317
  and comparison see comparison;
  philosophy, comparative;
  religious studies, comparative;
  theology, comparative
  contexts of, 45–50
  and inquiry see inquiry; pragmatic
  theory of inquiry
  and modernity, 57–83
  in the modern university, 307–17
  and multidisciplinarity, 85–124
  as multidisciplinary comparative
  inquiry see comparison;
  inquiry; multidisciplinarity;
  multidisciplinary comparative
  inquiry
  and postmodernity, 57–83
  as philosophy, 1–13
    see also big-question philosophy;
    theology, philosophical;
    philosophy; philosophy of
    religion
  as religious studies, 13–26
    see also religious studies
  styles of, xiv–xv, xvii, 37–45

tasks of, 35–45
  as theology, 26–34
  traditions of, xiv, 50–56, 247–305
    see also axiotheological tradition; cosmotheological tradition; mysticotheological tradition; ontotheological tradition; physicotheological tradition; psychotheological tradition
religious studies, ix–xx, 13–26, 35–83, 85–124, 214–45, 307–17
  comparative (comparative religion), 39–40, 48, 126, 134, 148–50, 156, 159, 162
  goal of, 14–16
  history of religion(s), 32, 39–40, 162, 191, 212, 275
  department(s) of, 16–17, 20–22, 312
  virtues of/in, 14–15
  see also university, modern
reproduction, 107, 130–31, 207
revelation, 30–32, 43, 51, 58–59, 61, 143, 191, 232, 249, 252, 298, 308
Ricoeur, Paul, 66, 328, 351
Ritchie, Jack, 170, 330, 351
ritual, 37, 39, 100–1, 105, 107, 111, 114, 143, 150, 208–9, 229, 243, 285–86, 291, 301, 320–21
romanticism, 82, 293
Routledge Companion to Philosophy of Religion, xii, 319, 348
Rue, Loyal, 170, 330, 351

sacred text *see* text, sacred
sacrifice, 108, 260, 275
saguṇa Brahman *see* Brahman, saguṇa
salvation, 25, 44–45, 260, 275–76
saṃsāra (cycle of lives), 2, 132–33, 144, 169, 236, 296
saṅgha (Buddhist community), 314
Śaṅkara, 33, 171, 213, 230
  see also *Advaita Vedānta*
Santayana, George, 170, 330, 351
Schelling, Friedrich, 281, 293

Schleiermacher, Friedrich, xii, 19, 257–58, 333, 351
Schuon, Frithjof, 295, 327, 335, 352
science, cognitive, 12, 21, 44, 89, 99, 144, 162, 170, 282
science, human, xv, 18, 19, 21, 53, 90, 94, 153–55, 168, 184, 211, 215, 219–23, 228–29, 234–35, 304–5
science, natural, xv, 2, 11–12, 18, 35, 42, 53, 60, 62, 69, 98–99, 102, 136–37, 153–55, 156–59, 164, 168, 171, 183–84, 192–93, 205, 215, 217–19, 221–23, 229, 233–35, 261–62, 271, 273, 282, 293, 304–5
science, philosophy of *see* philosophy, of science
science, social, 1, 18, 21–23, 35, 42, 144, 148, 171, 205, 211, 214, 221, 320
science and religion, xvii, 183, 241
  multidisciplinary academic field of, 213
  see also Boston University, Science, Philosophy, and Religion doctoral program
scientism, 12
scripture *see* text, sacred
Searle, John, xx, 195, 274, 299, 331, 334, 335, 352
secularism, 25, 237–45
  secularization theory, 237–41
self-awareness, 26, 69, 109–11, 132, 198, 237, 259
semiotics, 195, 328, 330, 331, 340, 356
  see also de Saussure, Ferdinand; Peirce, Charles Saunders
sensuality, 109–11, 275
sexuality, 66, 110, 321, 343, 349
shamanism, 111
shame, 22, 63–65, 68, 70–77
Shook, John, 170, 330, 352
Śiva, 133

skepticism, 8, 76, 77, 80, 103, 118, 125, 199, 250, 267, 280, 282, 293, 307–11
  see also Cārvāka
Smith, Huston, xx, 49, 142, 295, 321, 322, 327, 335, 353
  see also perennial philosophy
Smith, J.Z., 153–54, 327, 328, 329, 353
social engineering, 47, 52, 136, 155
sociality, 120–24, 169–70, 173–74, 179–83
Society for the Scientific Study of Religion (SSSR), 20
Society of Biblical Literature, 20
Society of Christian Philosophers, xii
sociology, 14, 17–18, 22–23, 44, 105, 144, 174, 179–83, 207, 214, 219–21, 234, 237–40, 244, 314
speech act theory, 41, 195, 299–300
  see also Austin, John; Searle, John
spirituality, 27–29, 31, 37, 111, 114, 231, 239, 242, 261, 275, 277–78, 280, 282–83, 290–91, 293, 296–97, 299, 301, 304
Spring and Autumn Annals (*Chūn Qiū* or *Ch'un Ch'iu* or 春秋; *Linjing* or *Línjīng* or *Lin Ching* or 麟經 or 麟经), 284–85
stability, 6, 9, 15, 30, 37, 39, 43, 51–52, 65, 77, 88, 94, 102, 125, 140, 153, 155, 159, 161, 173, 182, 192–93, 204, 208–9, 227, 241, 265, 272, 286, 293, 300
  see also comparison; discourse; inquiry
Stace, W.T., 49, 321, 353
Stone, Jerome, 170, 330, 353
Strauss, David Friedrich, 282, 293
structuralism, 117, 125–26, 195–96, 203, 213, 325
śūnyatā (ultimate emptiness), 2, 208, 302
  see also ultimacy; ultimate reality
superstition, 17, 100, 144, 163, 173, 244, 260, 263

Swinburne, Richard, 102–5, 164, 323–24, 354
syllogism, 5, 174
  see also Aristotle; logic
symbolism, 94, 114, 116, 160–62, 181, 189, 292, 297, 299–300
  see also apophasis; discourse; engagement; language; text, sacred

Talmud, 81
technology, 64, 70, 82, 118, 172–74, 275
text, sacred, 19, 23–25, 32–33, 41, 102, 275–81, 286
  see also revelation
theism, 17, 28, 30, 56, 81, 100–4, 132–33, 161–64, 250, 255–56, 258, 263, 267, 297–98, 302–3, 323
  ground of being, 208, 293
  personal, 164, 293, 323
  see also God(s); monotheism; polytheism; ultimate reality
theology, ix–xx, 26–34, 35–56, 77–83, 96–114, 125–65, 205–8, 213–17, 230–33, 247–305, 307–17
  apologetic, 96–102
  comparative, 155, 213, 327
  confessional, 27–34, 308, 313–14, 317
    and religious institutions, 20, 232–33, 308, 314
    and religious philosophy, 31–34
  mystical, 80–81, 83, 297–98, 335–36
    see also apophasis; mystico-theological tradition
  natural, 82, 162–65, 232, 329
    comparative, 164, 329
  philosophical, xiv, 28–33, 42–43, 208, 213, 247–305, 309
    see also Kalām; metaphysics; religious philosophy; philosophy, of religion; ultimacy
theopoetics, 6–7
Theravāda *see* Buddhism, Theravāda

Thomas Aquinas, 19, 104, 249, 257–58, 261, 263, 298, 333, 354
Tian (*Tiān* or *T'ien* or 天; heaven) 3
Tibetan Buddhism *see* Buddhism, Tibetan
Tillich, Paul, 31–32, 147, 152, 208, 256–57, 293, 320, 328, 333, 354
  theological circle, 31–32
translation, xix, 23, 114, 116, 118–19, 125, 148, 150, 212
truth, 3, 17, 143, 159, 200–2, 236, 238
  see also big-question philosophy; feedback potential; inquiry; judgment; pragmatic theory of inquiry; reality
Tu Weiming, 294, 354

Udayana, 100–2, 105
  see also Navya Nyāya (New Nyāya school)
ultimacy, 16, 26–30, 32, 45, 53, 162, 211, 234, 248, 250, 255–58, 273, 283, 294, 298–303, 333
  see also ultimate concern; ultimate reality
ultimate concern, 31, 208, 211, 231, 234, 301
  see also Tillich, Paul; ultimacy
ultimate reality, 16, 26, 43, 133, 151–52, 208, 231–32, 263, 272, 274–75, 277, 291, 295–98, 300–1
  see also Allah; Brahman; *Dao*; God(s); Godhead; ground of being; One, the; ultimacy
Union of Concerned Scientists, 218
universality, 57, 62, 69, 72, 74–75, 144, 203
university, modern, xii, xvi, xviii, 17, 20–25, 51–53, 87–88, 123, 307–17
Upaniṣads, 23, 33, 275–77, 279–82, 286
upāya (artful means), 301
  see also Mādhyamaka

vague category *see* comparison, category, vague

vagueness *see* comparison, vagueness in
Vaiśeṣika, 100
value, aesthetic, 225–30
  see also axiology; axiotheological tradition
van Huyssteen, Wentzel, xvii, 62–63, 72, 74–76, 79, 320, 354, 356
Vedānta, 33, 230, 249, 275–79
  see also Advaita Vedānta; Ātman; Brahman; *Brahmasūtras*; Dvaita Vedānta; Hinduism; Madhvacharya; Rāmānuja; Śaṅkara; Upaniṣads; Viśiṣṭādvaita Vedānta
Vedas, the, 32–33, 100–2, 275–76, 278
via negative, 299
  see also apophasis; mysticism; Pseudo-Dionysius
via positive, 299
vijñāna (consciousness), 2
Viśiṣṭādvaita Vedānta, 171, 277–79, 281
  see also Ātman; Brahman; Īśvara; Rāmānuja; Vedānta
Viṣṇu, 133

Weber, Max, 19, 152, 220, 327, 355
Whitehead, Alfred North, 12, 42, 55, 169–70, 252, 274, 293–94, 321, 329, 335, 355
Wieman, Henry Nelson, 170, 330, 355
Wildman, Wesley J., 319, 325, 326, 328, 329, 335, 336, 355, 356
worldview(s), 9–10, 50, 71, 132–33, 147, 209, 214, 219, 231, 234–35, 244, 276, 296
  secular scientific, 219, 244

Xunzi (Xúnzǐ or Hsün Tzu or 荀子 or荀子), 169, 286, 290

yang (*yáng* or 陽 or 阳; lighter masculine element), 21, 285
yin (*yīn* or 陰 or 阴; darker feminine element), 2, 285

Yogācāra, 171

Zen *see* Buddhism, Zen

Zengzi (Zēngzǐ or Tsengtzu or 曾子), 287

Zhuangzi, 169, 291

Zhuangzi (*Zhuāngzǐ* or *Chuang-Tzu* or 莊子 or 庄子), 290–91

Zhu Xi (Zhū Xǐ or Chu His or 朱熹), 286
see also Neo-Confucianism

www.ingramcontent.com/pod-product-compliance
Lightning Source LLC
Chambersburg PA
CBHW030125240426
43672CB00005B/29